'SAVIOURS OF THE NATION'

CW00549602

To Tito

JASNA DRAGOVIĆ-SOSO

'Saviours of the Nation'

Serbia's Intellectual Opposition and
the Revival of Nationalism

HURST & COMPANY, LONDON

First published in the United Kingdom by
C. Hurst & Co. (Publishers) Ltd,
38 King Street, London WC2E 8JZ
© Jasna Dragović-Soso, 2002
All rights reserved.
Printed in Scotland by Bell & Bain Ltd

The right of Jasna Dragović-Soso to be identified as the
author of this book is asserted in accordance with the
Copyright, designs and Patents Act, 1988.

A Cataloguing in Publication data record for
this book is available from the British Library.

ISBNs
1-85065-577-4 *casebound*
1-85065-457-3 *paperback*

ACKNOWLEDGEMENTS

Many people were very helpful to me as my project on Serbia's intellectual opposition turned first into a Master's thesis, then a Ph.D. dissertation and finally into this book, and I am deeply grateful to them. First of all I thank André Liebich and Philippe Burrin at the Graduate Institute of International Studies in Geneva for their unfailing guidance and support over the years. Jacques Rupnik at the Institute of Political Studies in Paris provided important insights that shaped my thinking in the initial stages of this work. My thanks also go to Wendy Bracewell, Dušan Puvačić and Dejan Djokić at the School of Slavonic and East European Studies (SSEES) in London, as well as to Dejan Jović at the London School of Economics, who not only stimulated my thinking and commented on my work, but also provided me with a scholarly community that made this project much more enjoyable than it would have been otherwise. The staff of SSEES library have been extremely friendly and helpful, while Dušan Puvačić's extensive personal collection was only matched by his encyclopedic knowledge of both the individuals and events covered in this book. I also thank Pedja Marković, Mile Bjelajac, Nebojša Popov, Drago Roksandić and Dušan Djordjevich for providing me with important source material. Sneža Zlatanović in Belgrade was a wonderful 'research assistant' in a field which had nothing to do with her own specialisation in the natural sciences.

A number of Belgrade intellectuals very kindly agreed to be interviewed for this project and I take this occasion to thank them (they are credited in the bibliography). I hope I will have made some contribution to their own debates on the question of intellectual responsibility in the rise of contemporary nationalism. I am also grateful to Sima Ćirković for his comments on Chapter 2 and to Nebojša Popov for his critique of an earlier version of the introduction.

Among those who commented on my work over the course of its evolution I thank, most of all, Stevan K. Pavlowitch, Desimir Tošić and Aleksa Djilas. I have been extremely privileged in being able to benefit from their deep knowledge and their generosity (as well as their amazing willingness to read 'yet another version' of my work). Their insights, criticisms and corrections have been invaluable to me, although they naturally bear no responsibility for any of the book's faults. My friend and long-time intellectual 'sparring partner', Bice Maiguashca, helped out in crucial moments with her habitual critical acuity and her unparallelled ability to dissect an argument.

My thanks also go to my parents Jelica and Svetislav Dragović and my aunt Vera Vučelić, who have been an inestimable source of encouragement and support to me over the years and who have helped me in so many ways. Finally, my husband Tito Marzio Soso has been the best imaginable partner on this journey and it is to him that this book is dedicated.

London, March 2002   J. D.-S.

CONTENTS

Acknowledgements   *page* v

Introduction   1

1. The Forging of Serbia's Intellectual Opposition   13
   The forerunners: Djilas and Mihajlov, 1952–66   17
   The critique of the Titoist system in the 1960s: the
      'Black Wave' and the 'New Left'   22
   The emergence of 'nationalists' and 'liberals', 1967–71   28
   The defence of civil rights, 1975–86   47

2. The 'Outburst of History' and the New Serbian
   Nationalism   64
   The crisis of the 1980s and the breakdown of official
      historiography   65
   'De-Titoisation' and the revision of history in Serbia:
      Yugoslavia reconsidered   77
   The theme of genocide: the Second World War revisited   100

3. The Watershed: Intellectuals and Kosovo, 1985–8   115
   Defining the 'Kosovo question', 1981–5   116
   Defending the Kosovo Serbs, 1985–7   132
   Seeking solidarity: Kosovo and Yugoslavia, 1986–8   145

4. Serbs and Slovenes: 'National Interests' in Conflict,
   1980–8   162

   Marching together, moving apart, 1981–6   163

   *Repositories of the new nationalism: the draft
   'Memorandum' of the Serbian Academy and
   'Contributions for a Slovenian National Programme'*   177

   *The constitutional debate and the scramble for national
   programmes, 1987–8*   195

5. The Victory of 'National Homogenisation', 1988–91   206

   *Serbia's intellectual opposition and Slobodan
   Milošević, 1988–9*   207

   *Disintegration, multipartism and the end of the
   Belgrade critical intelligentsia, 1989–91*   227

Conclusion   254

Bibliography   261

Index   287

INTRODUCTION

As Eastern Europe emerged from communist rule at the end of the 1980s, Serbia too went through its 'happening of the people'.[1] However, Serbia's 'revolution' did not end with the overturn of the old order but with the consolidation of the existing regime and its leader, Slobodan Milošević. Milošević's photographs adorned shop windows and buses, poets and songwriters composed verses to his glory, people lit candles and chanted prayers for his health, crowds came together and dispersed at his bidding. Not since the late President Tito had a political figure in the country been revered in such a way. Serbia's leader was loved not only by the masses, but also seduced the vast majority of what had once been the main opposition force to single party rule in the country—the large umbrella grouping of dissident intellectuals known as the 'Belgrade critical intelligentsia'.

This was a surprising turn of events, considering that after Tito's death in 1980 Serbia's intellectual opposition forged a united front around the defence of human and civil rights and mounted a growing challenge to the communist system. Milošević was not only a part of the establishment that the dissidents criticised, but had been at the forefront of some of the main witch-hunts against them in the first part of the post-Tito decade. Furthermore, Milošević's solution to the national question soon exposed itself as essentially undemocratic and repressive, which clearly went against the critical intelligentsia's proclaimed democratic orientation. In 1989 he returned Kosovo to

---

[1]The term 'the happening of the people' (*dogadjanje naroda*) was coined by the poet Milovan Vitezović in 1988 (Slavoljub Djukić, *Kako se dogodio vodja*, Belgrade, 1992, p. 271).

1

Serbia's control without heeding the protests of the province's majority Albanian population and militarily suppressed mass demonstrations against the reduction of Kosovo's autonomy. In addition, following his installation of new leaderships in Serbia's autonomous provinces of Vojvodina and Kosovo, as well as in the Republic of Montenegro, Milošević manipulated the voting system in the federal presidency, giving him disproportionate influence in decisionmaking. Despite the fact that such actions led towards confrontation rather than compromise between Serbs and other Yugoslavs, the vast majority of the Belgrade intellectual opposition tacitly or overtly endorsed Milošević and his national policy. Longstanding opponents of the regime now hailed Serbia's leader as one of their nation's greatest historical figures because he had so deliberately and so forcefully returned to the Serbs their 'national dignity'.

By tracing the trajectory of Serbia's intellectual opposition since the 1960s, this book will seek to explain why nationalist concerns came to overshadow all other aspects of its political agenda, leading many former dissidents to betray the humanist principles that were initially at the core of their activism. The Belgrade critical intelligentsia's choice of 'nation' over 'democracy' and its endorsement of Milošević represent a classic case of what French intellectual Julien Benda famously defined as 'the treason of the clerks': it shows how individuals whose self-defined social role is based on their defence of universal principles can be seduced by particularist—in this case, nationalist— ideology.[2] In Serbia this 'treason' was significant in that it removed at a crucial moment the presence of a democratic alternative to Milošević's policy, helping the regime overcome its legitimacy crisis and contributing to Yugoslavia's descent into war. Even after they resumed their opposition activity and their criticism of the regime, former dissidents tended to focus mainly on the continuing restrictions on party pluralism and the free development of civil society in Serbia; only a handful of them openly protested against the repressive measures used against the Albanian population in Kosovo and Milošević's encouragement of armed rebellion of the Serbs in Croatia and later in Bosnia-Hercegovina.

Scholars of nationalism have long espoused that intellectuals are to national movements what 'poppy-growers in Pakistan are to heroin addicts—the suppliers of the essential raw material for the market'.[3]

[2]Julien Benda, _La trahison des clercs_, Paris, 1927.
[3]E.J. Hobsbawm, 'Ethnicity and Nationalism in Europe Today', _Anthropology Today_,

As Anthony Smith notes, 'More than a style and a doctrine of politics, nationalism is a *form of culture*—an ideology, a language, mythology, symbolism and consciousness—that has achieved a global resonance, and the nation is a type of identity whose meaning and priority is presupposed by this form of culture.'[4] It therefore comes as no surprise that when dealing with intellectuals, theories of nationalism have focused mainly on their *role* in the rise of national movements—as the elaborators of the images, myths and symbols of the new collective identity known as the 'nation', which came to replace the traditional conceptions of the universal religious community and the dynastic realm in the late 18th and early 19th centuries.[5] There has been relatively less interest in the question of why intellectuals become nationalist, probably because—as Anthony Smith correctly points out—'there is insufficient evidence to formulate a general proposition about the motives of nationalist intellectuals' and individual case studies need to be examined in their historical context.[6] The two existing types of explanations have tended to be of a functionalist nature: they focus either on the intellectuals' use of nationalism to resolve their own 'identity crisis' in contexts of change and uncertainty or on more prosaic self-serving motives (Ernest Gellner rather pointedly refers to 'jobs, and very good jobs').[7] Finally, when it comes to the revival of nationalism at the end of the 20th century, the literature places considerably less emphasis on intellectuals. Although debates persist on whether contemporary nationalism is fundamentally an elite-led or a grassroots phenomenon, analysis tends to be focused on the role of the state, its governing capacity and policies, its identification with a specific ethnic constituency, its international environment, as well as the reactions to it by minorities and nondominant ethnic groups.

Studies of the disintegration of Yugoslavia have by and large

---

VIII/1, Feb. 1992, p. 1. Hobsbawm's image actually refers to historians, but may be extended to all intellectuals engaged in the '(re-)invention of tradition'.

[4]Anthony D. Smith, *National Identity*, London, 1991, pp. 91–2 (Smith's emphasis). A similar point is made by Ernest Gellner, *Nations and Nationalism*, Oxford, 1983, p. 57.

[5]See particularly, Benedict Anderson, *Imagined Communities*, London (revised edn), 1991, Anthony D. Smith, *The Ethnic Revival in the Modern World*, Cambridge, 1981, and Miroslav Hroch, *Social Preconditions of National Revival in Europe*, Cambridge, 1985.

[6]Smith, *National Identity*, op. cit., p. 95.

[7]Smith, ibid., p. 96 and Gellner, quoted in Jeremy Jennings and Anthony Kemp-Welch, 'The Century of the intellectual: from the Dreyfus Affair to Salman Rushdie' in Jennings and Kemp-Welch (eds), *Intellectuals in Politics*, London, 1997, p. 56.

conformed to this trend in the scholarship. They have tended to focus either on the role played by political elites (particularly the Serbian, Croatian and Slovenian) in bringing the country to disintegration and war, or on structural factors, whether internal ('ancient hatreds', historically conditioned national incompatibilities, Titoist policies and the evolution of Yugoslav federalism, the failure of modernisation) or external (the changing international context, the role of international financial institutions). Intellectuals, when they are mentioned, are treated only as a contributing factor—in aiding and abetting the articulation of nationalist discourse, which is used by political elites for ethnic mobilisation. Only a small group of scholars has made intellectuals and their national ideas the object of their analyses, and they examine principally the evolving visions of 'Yugoslavism', the various understandings of 'Serbism' and the complementarity and tensions between these two identitities.[8] Scholars from former Yugoslavia have, understandably, emphasised questions of intellectual responsibility for the rising nationalist momentum and deconstructed the 'discourse of hatred' in the period of state disintegration and war.[9] Although the question why Serbian intellectuals turned to nationalism is not always the focus of this diverse body of literature, it is nevertheless possible to discern three types of explanations.

The first, instrumentalist explanation, which prevails among anti-nationalist Yugoslav intellectuals, echoes Gellner's argument about opportunism. The proponents of this view argue that the 'nationalists' within Serbia's intellectual opposition were not genuine dissidents like the 'neo-Marxists' or the 'liberals', but 'strange allies' of the regime

[8]This is the focus of Andrew Wachtel's study of the evolution of the 'Yugoslav idea' since the early 19th century, *Making a Nation: Breaking a Nation. Literature and Cultural Politics in Yugoslavia*, Stanford, 1998. For contemporary visions of 'Serbism', see notably Aleksandar Pavković, 'The Serb National Idea: A Revival, 1986–92', *Slavonic and East European Review*, LXXII/ 3, 1994, pp. 440–55 and 'From Yugoslavism to Serbism: the Serb National Idea, 1986–1996', *Nations and Nationalism*, IV/4, 1998, pp. 511–28. Audrey Helfant Budding examines the causes of the shift from 'Yugoslavism' to 'Serbism' in 'Yugoslavs into Serbs: Serbian National Identity, 1961–1971', *Nationalities Papers*, XXV/3, 1997, pp. 407–26, and her PhD dissertation 'Serb Intellectuals and the National Question', Harvard University, 1998.

[9]This has been the emphasis particularly of a group of independent, anti-nationalist Serbian intellectuals known as 'the Belgrade Circle'. See their *Druga Srbija*, Belgrade, 1992 and the analyses of Olivera Milosavljević, Nebojša Popov, Drinka Gojković and Mirko Djordjević in Nebojša Popov (ed.), *Srpska strana rata*, Belgrade, 1996. This also implicitly informs the approach of a number of Croatian and Slovenian scholars, who focus on the ideological continuity of Serbian nationalism (see below).

since the 1970s, who were tolerated and allowed to organise and who were, in turn, ready to offer their services and provide a political programme when needed.[10] The nationalist intellectuals' convergence with Milošević at the end of the 1980s merely made this arrangement more explicit at a time when both sides needed it:

The intellectuals—frustrated writers of bad books, disappointed scholars who had formerly glorified communism and bitter priests who in their cells nourished hatred against everything secular—were presented with the opportunity they had been waiting for, to fulfil their dream of becoming 'engineers of the human spirit'; for its part, the old regime was able to re-legitimise and preserve its power.[11]

In this interpretation, the nationalist intellectuals' main motivation was the desire for social and political power, which—compounded by their lack of a genuine democratic orientation—made them natural bedfellows for a regime that simply switched focus from one illiberal, collectivist ideology (communism) to another (nationalism).

Although instrumentalists highlight the opportunism involved in some individual decisions to join Milošević's government, party and the regime-dominated media, they cannot explain the vast and all-encompassing nationalist momentum that grabbed the Serbian intelligentsia well-before Milošević's rise to power, as well as the genuine conviction that underlay many intellectuals' endorsement of his policy. Social and political ambition and 'jobs, good jobs' probably account more for the motives of younger communist 'cadres' or establishment intellectuals afraid for their positions than of longstanding opponents of the regime. Furthermore, the argument that 'nationalists' within the intellectual opposition were subject to greater leniency than dissidents of the 'New Left' or 'liberal' orientations also does not stand up to fact. Yugoslavia was indeed much less repressive towards critical intellectuals than other communist states, but 'nationalists' within the former intellectual opposition were not treated

---

[10]Nenad Dimitrijević, 'Words and Death: Serbian Nationalist Intellectuals' in A. Bozoki (ed.), *Intellectuals and Politics in Central Europe*, Budapest, 1999, p. 127.

[11]Ibid., p. 134. For similar views see Slavenka Drakulić, 'Intellectuals as Bad Guys', *East European Politics and Societies*, XIII/2, 1999, pp. 271–7; Svetlana Slapšak, *Ogledi o bezbrižnosti*, Belgrade, 1994; Slobodan Blagojević, *Tri čiste obične pameti*, Belgrade, 1996; and the texts by Pero Mužijević and Mirko Djordjević in *Republika*, 147, 1–15 Oct. 1996, pp. 24–5 and 179–80; 1–31 Jan. 1998, pp. 17–22 and 187; 16–30 Apr. 1998, pp. 13–18 respectively, as well as Djordjević's interview in *Naša Borba*, 31 Jan-1 Feb. 1998, p. xv.

fundamentally differently from other dissidents. Until the late 1980s intellectuals still had more to lose than to gain by raising the 'Serbian question' and could even face imprisonment if they did so in a way that challenged the basic premises of the 'Titoist' system.[12]

A second interpretation focuses on the ideological immutability of Serbian nationalism since the early 19th century. As the historian Ivo Banac put it, in order to understand the Yugoslav conflict 'one must begin with the continuity of individual South Slavic national elites and states (where they existed) with special emphasis on national and political ideologies, not with modernisation studies and research of social structures'.[13] The advocates of this approach tend to characterise Serbian national ideology as traditionally assimilatory, expansionist and hegemonic, using centralist conceptions of the state to subdue and eradicate the national consciousness of other South Slavs and deny them equality. The focus on ideology inevitably raises the question of intellectuals as its principal articulators and this approach blames the practice of 'ethnic cleansing' in the wars of Yugoslav succession on intellectuals' elaboration of a long-term Serbian programme—dating from the early 19th century and the work of linguist Vuk Karadžić to the contemporary authors of the draft 'Memorandum' of the Serbian Academy of Sciences and Arts.[14] This body of scholarship also tends to present other Yugoslav nationalisms—as well as Croatia's and Slovenia's drive for independence—as merely a 'defence mechanism' reacting to the Serbian 'onslaught'.[15]

The ideological continuity argument highlights the facts that traditional Serbian nationalism sometimes subsumed non-Serbs into its definitions of the Serbian 'nation' and that it did not necessarily consider the national strivings of other peoples sharing the same territories. Whether a constant desire for Serbian hegemony represents

[12]See Chapter 1.

[13]Ivo Banac, 'The Fearful Asymmetry of War: The Causes and Consequences of Yugoslavia's Demise', *Daedalus*, spring 1992, CXXI/2, p. 143.

[14]Mirko Grmek, Marc Gjidara and Neven Simac (eds), *Le nettoyage ethnique*, Paris, 1993, pp. 16–19. See also Bože Čović (ed.), *Izvori velikosrpske agresije*, Zagreb, 1991, Branimir Anžulović, *Heavenly Serbia*, London, 1999, and Philip J. Cohen, 'The Complicity of Serbian Intellectuals in Genocide in the 1990s' in T. Cushman and St. G. Mestrovic (eds), *This Time We Knew: Western Responses to Genocide in Bosnia*, New York, 1996, pp. 39–64.

[15]'Separating History From Myth: An Interview with Ivo Banac' in A. Rabia and L. Lifschultz (eds), *Why Bosnia?*, p. 161. See also Mojmir Križan, 'New Serbian Nationalism and the Third Balkan War', *Studies in East European Thought*, 46, 1994, pp. 47–68.

the primary motivation behind such national ideas remains, however, open to debate. Certainly, it seems appropriate to place these ideas into their particular historical context and to examine their origins in their specific political, social and intellectual climate. It also appears indispensable to examine the concurrent ideological and national currents among the Serbs' neighbours and to assess to what extent various national ideologies represented a reaction to each other— clearly this is true for Serbian nationalism as well as for the Slovenian or Croatian. The focus on ideological continuity also fails to account for the alternatives that did exist historically in approaches to the Serbian national question. Although in the region ethnic forms of national identity tended to predominate over civic ones and Serbian nationalism, like other nationalisms, traditionally posited that the national unit and the political unit (i.e. the state) should be congruent,[16] there were different ways in which both the nation and the state could be defined and a variety of means by which national goals could be pursued. Andrew Wachtel's book on the rise and fall of the Yugoslav idea, as well as the work of the historians Ljubinka Trgovčević and Wolfgang Behschnitt, show the diversity of approaches to the national question that historically existed among Serbian thinkers, while the categories provided by Aleksandar Pavković in his articles on the subject illustrate some of the contemporary options: 'federalist Yugoslavism', 'integralist Yugoslavism', 'broad Serbism' and 'narrow Serbism'.[17] Finally, explanations focused on ideological continuity do not help us understand why essentially non-nationalist intellectuals came to embrace nationalism at a given time, nor why they accepted a particular policy to achieve national goals (they also do not explain why some intellectuals never became nationalist). Only a close examination of the specific historical context in which they acted and elaborated their ideas can provide a more complete answer.

This is precisely what the third—structural-contextual—approach does, by focusing on the specific political, ideological, social and economic circumstances in which contemporary Serbian intellectuals acted in order to explain their transformations and choices. As the sociologist Veljko Vujačić argues in his comparative study of Russian and Serbian nationalism:

[16]Gellner, op. cit., p. 1.
[17]Wachtel, op. cit., Ljubinka Trgovčević, *Naučnici Srbije i stvaranje Jugoslavije, 1914– 1920*, Belgrade, 1986; Wolfgang Behschnitt, 'Nationalismus bei Serben und Kroaten', PhD thesis, University of Cologne, 1976; Aleksandar Pavković, op. cit.

National self-identifications, political experiences, historical memories and institutional legacies create the long-term social-structural and political preconditions for different types of nationalist mobilisation. Individual instances of nationalist mobilisation, however, can only be explained with reference to contextual factors that favour the 'selective reactivation' of these historical and political-cultural legacies on the part of elites and leaders.[18]

Specifically, this approach to the rise of contemporary Serbian nationalism focuses on the evolution of the Yugoslav federal system towards a more 'confederate' structure since the 1960s, which highlighted the particular position of the Serbs as the largest and most dispersed nation in Yugoslavia and as the only nation whose republic contained two autonomous provinces. Audrey Helfant Budding thus argues that Serbs tended to see the immediate post-war ideology of 'socialist Yugoslavism' as an attractive option, but that the adoption of the new, decentralising course, which was accompanied by the official condemnation of 'centralism' and 'unitarism'—identified with the 'Greater Serbian hegemony' of the first Yugoslav state—led to the 'withdrawal of the Yugoslav choice' and the search for alternative and specifically Serbian programmes to fill the vacuum.[19] Andrew Wachtel also looks to the post-1963 abandonment of official attempts at cultural nation-building and the rejection of synthetic supranational sentiment and modernist world-views as the preconditions leading to the Serbian 'backlash'.[20] Nicholas J. Miller traces the nationalism of two important Serbian intellectuals, the writer Dobrica Ćosić and artist Mića Popović, to their disappointment with the communist project, which had failed in its basic universalistic and humanitarian promises and which, in their view, had given in to the nationalist demands of non-Serbs in Yugoslavia.[21]

Like this last group of scholars, I trace the revival of the Serbian 'question' to the evolution of the Titoist system in the 1960s and 70s, with its new emphasis on the federal units and specific national

---

[18]Veljko Vujačić, 'Historical legacies, nationalist mobilization, and political outcomes in Russia and Serbia: A Weberian view', *Theory and Society*, 25, 1996, p. 783. See also his 'Serbian Nationalism, Slobodan Milošević and the Origins of the Yugoslav War', *Harriman Review*, 12, 1995, pp. 25–34, and his PhD dissertation 'Communism and Nationalism in Russia and Serbia', University of California at Berkeley, 1995.

[19]Budding, 'Yugoslavs into Serbs ...', op. cit.

[20]Wachtel, op. cit., pp. 197–8.

[21]Nicholas J. Miller, 'The Nonconformists: Dobrica Ćosić and Mića Popović Envision Serbia', *Slavic Review*, LVIII/ 3, 1999, pp. 515–36.

cultures, as opposed to the Yugoslav state as a whole and a notion of Yugoslav unity. Although Serbs were not the only Yugoslav nation to be dispersed throughout the country, the way in which the borders between the federal units had been drawn left over three million Serbs outside 'inner' Serbia (the republic minus the autonomous provinces of Vojvodina and Kosovo), amounting to 40 per cent of the total Serbian population in Yugoslavia.[22] This meant, for example, that there were approximately twice as many Serbs outside 'inner' Serbia than there were Slovenes in Slovenia or Albanians in Kosovo.[23] In this sense the raising of the autonomous provinces to republican status in all but name and the concurrent 'confederalisation' of Yugoslavia since the 1970s were bound to affect Serbs more than other Yugoslav nations. Nevertheless, this structural factor does not in and of itself preordain the kind of answer that could be given to the Serbian 'question' nor the acceptance of Milošević's undemocratic means to resolve it.

This book therefore builds on the 'structural-contextual' interpretation by exploring the tension between democracy and nationalism in the ideas and visions expounded by Serbia's intellectual opposition, arguing, firstly, that the convergence with the regime was conditioned primarily by the specific type of nationalism that came to predominate within the intelligentsia in the course of the post-Tito period. This nationalism was inherently incompatible with the intelligentsia's declared commitment to democracy because its proposed solutions were founded upon double standards and because its discourse was based on an extreme notion of victimisation, the concept of 'genocide' and conspiracy theories, all of which preclude negotiation and compromise essential to any democratic process. Moreover, such nationalism inherently made the search for a saviour figure more likely

[22]According to the 1981 census, the total number of Serbs was 8,140,000 or 36.3% of the population of Yugoslavia. Of them 4,865,000 were located in 'inner' Serbia (59.7%). The remaining 3,275,000 (41.3%) were spread out in the following way: 1,107,000 in the Autonomous Province of Vojvodina, 209,000 in the Autonomous Province of Kosovo, 1,321,000 in the Republic of Bosnia-Hercegovina, 532,000 in the Republic of Croatia, 44,000 in the Republic of Macedonia, 42,000 in the Republic of Slovenia and 19,000 in the Republic of Montenegro. The second most dispersed nation were the Croats, of whom 954,000 or 21.5% lived outside Croatia, predominantly in Bosnia-Hercegovina (758,000). (An overview of these statistics can be found in Tim Judah, *The Serbs*, New Haven, 1997, pp. 313–15)

[23]According to the 1981 census, there were 1,712,445 Slovenes in Slovenia (of the 1,754,000 Slovenes in Yugoslavia), 1,227,000 Albanians in Kosovo (of the 1,730,000 Albanians in Yugoslavia).

and provides some insight into the adulation of Milošević in the early period of his rule. It also made the disintegration of Yugoslavia and the use of violence more acceptable to its proponents, although they probably did not desire either outcome at the outset.

Secondly, I argue that it is in the post-Tito 1980s—and not before—that the undemocratic nature of the Belgrade intellectual opposition's nationalism crystallised. Although the question of the Serbs' position in Yugoslavia had been raised by a group of intellectual 'trend-setters' a decade earlier, at the outset of the 1980s the vast majority of the Belgrade intelligentsia was still committed to Yugoslavia and focused on notions of democratic systemic change and human rights. Only a minority of intellectuals at this point had a clearly nationalist orientation and even their positions progressively became radicalised in the course of the decade. However, in the second part of the 1980s their ideas became ubiquitous in the intelligentsia and the forms of political activism that had been developed to defend civil rights—petitions, committees, protest manifestations, public debates and publications—became the principal vectors of nationalist mobilisation. This evolution highlights the importance of contingency, which adds to existing structural factors, in explaining historical processes: the emphasis here is on analysing how the particular conditions and events of the post-Tito period contributed to turning the ideas of a minority into the dominant world-view of a majority.

After examining the emergence of Serbia's intellectual opposition in the 1970s and early 1980s in Chapter 1, I focus on three interrelated factors specific to the post-Tito decade, which, I believe, need to be highlighted as the key to understanding both the radicalisation of Serbian nationalism and its concurrent spread in the critical intelligentsia. The first of these, discussed in Chapter 2, was the general systemic crisis and the exacerbation of the centrifugal tendencies within the communist leadership after Tito's death, which put into question the very survival of Yugoslavia as a state by the mid-1980s. The sponsorship by the leaderships of the federal units of new cultures and histories legitimising their various 'proto-states' led by the early 1980s to the veritable disintegration of the common cultural space and eroded any notion of Yugoslav unity. The ideological vacuum left by the combined effect of systemic crisis and the disintegration of the common vision of the past spurred an all-encompassing reconsideration of Yugoslavia's historical experience in the intelligentsia and led to the breaking of an ever larger number of taboos. Rummaging through the past to explain the crisis-ridden present, Serbian intellectuals came to examine the break-up of the first Yugoslav state in 1941, the traumatic historical experience of mass extermination of Serbs in the Independent State of Croatia during the Second World War and the communist resolution of Yugoslavia's national question. The fact that these subjects were raised at a time when centrifugal tendencies were predominating in the country and Yugoslavia appeared to be failing for the second time contributed to the development of a radical set of explanations—based on notions of a communist 'stab in the back', betrayal by other Yugoslav nations, 'genocide' and a 'destiny' of victimisation—and placed the new historical vision at the centre of the emerging national one.

The second factor, analysed in Chapter 3, was the emergence of the 'Kosovo question' following the mass Albanian demonstrations for a 'Kosovo Republic' in 1981. The liberalisation of the press that occurred at that time heightened public awareness, on the one hand, of the extent of the Albanians' dissatisfaction with their official status in Yugoslavia and, on the other, of the pressures exerted against the minority Serbs that lived in the province, acting along with economic duress as a powerful incentive on them to emigrate. The beginnings of mobilisation of Kosovo Serbs in the mid-1980s and their adoption of a strategy of coming to Belgrade to voice their grievances directly compelled the intellectual opposition to take up their cause, while the authorities minimised the problem in public and appeared to be doing nothing. Most of the Belgrade critical intelligentsia saw Kosovo as both a perfect vehicle for contesting the regime and a good test of other Yugoslavs' solidarity with the Serbs. In the process of focusing its activism on the 'Kosovo question', however, Serbia's intellectual opposition showed itself incapable of overcoming the 'statist' legacy of Titoism, which defined national rights in territorial terms: instead of using the Kosovo question to widen the struggle for human and civil rights and promote the establishment of democracy as a system of peaceful regulation of ethnic differences, the critical intelligentsia's defence of the Kosovo Serbs turned into an assertion of Serbia's 'state right' over the province and became the main vehicle for propagating extreme nationalist visions and symbols.

The third factor, which provides the focus of Chapter 4, is the relationship Serbian critical intellectuals had with their Slovenian counterparts—the other main opposition force in the country. While relations with Croatian dissidents had been fundamentally conflictual since the outburst of Croatian nationalism in 1967–71, it was the deteriorating relationship with the Slovenes that provided the motor of nationalist mobilisation in the post-Tito period. Like the Serbian, the Slovenian intelligentsia contained a group of nationalist 'trend-setters', whose advocacy of democratic change combined with independent national statehood (possibly with loose 'confederate' links to the rest of Yugoslavia) progressively became dominant in the republic in the 1980s. In the same way that the Serbs' emphasis on re-centralisation and national unity in Yugoslavia strengthened Slovenian fears of loss of sovereignty, the Slovenes' rejection of any commitment to the Yugoslav state, their attitude on the issue of Kosovo and their standpoints in the debates on reforming federal institutions in turn fuelled Serbian perceptions of Slovenian 'betrayal'. The dialectical relationship between Slovenian and Serbian nationalism in the 1980s, characterised by a radicalisation of the intellectual oppositions' respective demands, produced a spiral that eventually led to their adoption of irreconcilable national programmes which would suit their—uncompromisingly defined—national interests.

While in the latter part of the 1980s the Serbian intellectual oppo-sition's rising nationalism was progressively eclipsing the democratic content of its activism, it was the rise of Slobodan Milošević and his adoption of new extra-institutional methods to deal with the national question that represented the true test of the critical intelligentsia's commitment to democracy. Chapter 5 therefore specifically focuses on this relationship between the intellectual opposition and the Milošević regime. I argue that, although part of the explanation for the surprising convergence between the two lies in Milošević's un-precedented liberalisation of the cultural sphere in the republic, it was above all his wooing of some of the most prominent dissidents, his adoption of the critical intelligentsia's national programme, along with his commitment to rectifying what most of the intelligentsia saw as 'obvious injustices' regarding Serbia's constitutional position that provide the key. Furthermore, in the context of the radicalisation of other particularist nationalisms and the increasing likelihood of Yugoslavia's disintegration, a wide range of intellectuals responded to Milošević's call for 'national homogenisation' and rallied together with the 'nation under siege'. The situation demanded that the in-tellectual opposition distance itself from both the 'masses' and the regime and articulate a principled rejection of all constitutional changes made by undemocratic, repressive means. That it did not do so—in the short-sighted illusion that democracy could wait until after the national question had been resolved—proved to be a fateful mistake that helped consolidate Serbia's new form of nationalist authoritari-anism and plunge Yugoslavia into war.

1

THE FORGING OF SERBIA'S
INTELLECTUAL OPPOSITION

Western literature on dissent in communist countries has rarely included exhaustive discussions of Yugoslavia. Since the 1948 break with the Soviet Union and the adoption of a more liberal course in 1952, Yugoslav citizens acquired greater freedoms than other East Europeans, as well as a controlled but broad possibility of expression in the non-political sphere. In addition, the favourable press Yugoslavia received in the West for its independent stance vis-à-vis the Soviet Union tended to focus analysis away from the more unsavoury aspects of the Yugoslav regime.[1] The assessment of the Yugoslav case also depends on how the concept of dissent is defined. As Aleksa Djilas put it, if one adopted a wide definition of dissent which included 'anyone politically at variance with official ideology', then Yugoslavia would be 'a serious candidate for world champion in dissent'.[2] Sociologist Sharon Zukin, on the other hand, argued that Yugoslavia represented essentially 'a case in nondissent', because it 'inspired few statements of principle that are recognised as dissent and even fewer social groups that claim the status of dissidents'.[3]

In her 1983 article on Yugoslavia, Zukin defined three necessary

---

[1]This is particularly true of the persecution of 'Cominformists' in the Yugoslav Communist Party, who sided with the Soviet Union or were suspected of pro-Soviet sympathies. See Ivo Banac, *With Stalin against Tito*, Cornell University Press, 1988, pp. x–xi. On the lack of Western support for Yugoslav 'dissidents' see Mihajlo Mihajlov, *Naša Borba*, 3–4 May, 1997, p. xv.

[2]Aleksa Djilas, 'Dissent and Human Rights in Post-Tito Yugoslavia', *Review of the Study Centre for Jugoslav Affairs*, II/5, 1980, pp. 497–8.

[3]Sharon Zukin, 'Sources of Dissent and Nondissent in Yugoslavia' in J. Leftwich Curry (ed.), *Dissent in Eastern Europe*, New York, 1983, p. 117.

conditions for dissent: public action, a critique of existing conditions combined with a refusal to conform, and an 'administrative context' which represses minority opinions.[4] In the Yugoslav case, it is the third criterion, the political and administrative context, that represents the main stumbling block in analysing dissent. Engaging in 'dissident' activity involves the voluntary transgression of the boundaries of what is socially acceptable and, clearly, Yugoslavia—where such limits were more flexible and transgressors were generally treated more leniently—was not like other communist states, as the example of Borislav Mihajlović-Mihiz, a prominent Serbian literary critic and well-known intellectual nonconformist, illustrates:

> I was thrown out of the Youth Working Action in 1946 and arrested as an enemy, but I was also able to become the literary commentator of *NIN* [the best-known Yugoslav weekly] and the director of a library, and get employment with *Avala Film* and *Atelje 212* [a leading film production company and avant-garde theatre] ... I did sometimes lose my job and there were years when I could not publish anything, but often I had more rights and opportunities than I deserved.[5]

In addition, the possibility to travel and work abroad as, for example, several of the *Praxis* professors did after they were purged from Belgrade University in 1975 (and while they were still receiving a part of their salaries in Yugoslavia despite their suspension),[6] clearly rendered the Yugoslav system very different from the rest of Eastern Europe.

Furthermore, the decentralisation of Yugoslavia since the 1960s led to different levels of repression in different parts of the country. Bosnia-Hercegovina was known as 'the dark kingdom' for its more dogmatic line and harsher treatment of critical intellectuals—joined by Croatia after the suppression of the 1971 'spring'—whereas the Serbian and Slovenian leaderships generally tended to be more lenient. Writings or literary and artistic productions prohibited in one federal unit could thus find an outlet in a more permissive one and intellectuals who came into conflict with the authorities often moved (mainly from Bosnia to either Serbia or Croatia). These regional disparities,

---

[4]Ibid., pp. 118-19.

[5]Borislav Mihajlović-Mihiz, *Kazivanja i ukazivanja*, Belgrade, 1994, p. 271. See also Mihajlo Mihajlov's statements in *Naša Borba*, 3–4 May, 1997, p. xv, and *Republika*, 181, 1–15 Feb. 1998, pp. vii–ix.

[6]This fact has provoked the claim that the Praxists were 'on the borderline of dissidence but were not real dissidents' (Mihajlo Mihajlov, *Republika*, 187, 16–30 Apr. 1998, pp. 21–4).

along with the constant efforts of the Party leadership to prevent any countrywide opposition from emerging, make it more accurate to speak of Serbian, Croatian or Slovenian dissent than of an all-Yugoslav phenomenon.

Another factor adding to the complexity of analysing dissent in Yugoslavia is that many of the most prominent critical intellectuals had long-standing links with members of the bureaucracy, the political leadership and the army, forged either during the wartime Partisan struggle or while they were still members of the communist establishment, and initially their critiques often represented the views of a particular Party faction. Many of these friendships and private contacts continued even after the regime critics parted ways with the Party, resulting in a certain amount of protectionism.[7] Some of the best known critical intellectuals thus did not go to jail or even face censorship of their texts, unless these were of a clearly political nature. These personal connections and the lack of a systematic and organised approach toward censorship[8] gave a dimension of arbitrariness to the treatment of intellectuals. Intellectual prestige and interventions from abroad also acted to dissuade the authorities' application of repressive measures.

Despite the ambiguous and complex nature of dissent in Yugoslavia, the restricted personal autonomy and limited civic freedoms of the country's intellectuals were still more akin to the situation of East European dissidents than to that of intellectuals in Western liberal democracies. As the historian Predrag Marković put it, although from the early 1950s the Yugoslav system acquired a 'Westernised' facade and trimmings—a degree of pluralism within the state and the Party, private initiative in the economy and openness of the social and cultural spheres—it nevertheless remained an essentially 'Eastern' construction whose foundation, pillars and beams were made of total political and economic power in the hands of one party, a dominant communist ideology and a 'charismatic' leader.[9] Criticism was allowed only insofar

---

[7]See Predrag J. Marković, *Beograd izmedju Istoka i Zapada 1948-1965*, Belgrade, 1996, pp. 245–6 and 510–11.

[8]Manuscripts were not examined by a state representative before publication. Rather, control over their content was the responsibility of specialist reading committees designated by the publisher to judge the suitability of a book for publication. When a book was banned, it was thus often the publisher and reading committee members who came under attack, along with the author.

[9]P.J. Marković, op. cit., p. 513. See also Zagorka Golubović, 'Društveni i kulturni milje: Jugoslavija od 1980. do 1990-ih godina' in Golubović *et al.*, *Društveni karakter i društvene promene u svetlu nacionalnih sukoba*, Belgrade, 1995, p. 22.

as it did not infringe upon this basic premise and did not represent a threat to the Party's monopoly of power.

Since the vast majority of intellectuals depended on the state for both employment and access to the public sphere, the regime could effectively use threats of dismissal from work and censorship to silence criticism. Such measures were generally accompanied by police harassment, social isolation and campaigns of abuse in the press which accused the targeted individuals of being in the service of hostile foreign powers as part of a 'special war' against socialist Yugoslavia.[10] Depending on the political climate of the time and on the nature of an intellectual's transgression, trial and imprisonment could result, usually under Article 133 of the Yugoslav Criminal Code known as 'hostile propaganda', or—more commonly—as 'verbal crime':

Whoever, by means of an article, leaflet, drawing, speech or in some other way, advocates or incites the overthrow of the rule of the working class and the working people, the unconstitutional alteration of the socialist system or self-management, the disruption of the brotherhood, unity and equality of the nations and nationalities, the overthrow of the bodies of self-management and government or their executive agencies, resistance to the decisions of competent government and self-management bodies which are significant for the protection and defence of the country, or whoever maliciously and untruthfully portrays socio-political conditions in the country shall be punished by imprisonment for from one to ten years ...[11]

As Yugoslav civil rights lawyer Rajko Danilović has noted, even the singing of songs or a private conversation between two individuals came under the notion of 'hostile propaganda', and the range of subjects that could be seen as 'inciting' the overthrow of the Yugoslav system or 'untruthfully portraying' conditions in the country were limitless.[12] Other forms of political crime were 'counterrevolution' (Article 114), 'terrorism' (Article 125) and 'conspiracy to enemy activity' (Article 137), which resulted in generally harsher treatment and longer prison sentences.[13]

---

[10]See, for example, Dušan Vilić and Milan Atejević, *Specijalni rat*, Belgrade, 1983.

[11]English translation in *Amnesty International Report on Yugoslavia 1985*, pp. 21–2.

[12]Rajko Danilović, *Upotreba neprijatelja*, Valjevo, 1993, pp. 39–44. Danilović provides a comprehensive overview of the repressive methods used in Yugoslavia and of the most important political trials.

[13]Ibid., pp. 34–8 and 45–8. When sentences were commuted following appeals to higher courts, it was usually done by applying Article 133 instead of Articles 114, 125 or 137.

Yugoslavia's combined carrot and stick approach to intellectual criticism—more extensive freedoms, on the one hand, and the threat of repression, on the other—effectively thwarted the consolidation of any organised political opposition to the regime.[14] It was only the return of a more repressive climate in the 1970s, after two decades of progressive liberalisation, that sparked new forms of political activism akin to those of East European dissidents: petitions, a 'flying university' and attempts at *samizdat* publication, followed by the creation of independent committees for the defence of human and civil rights. In Serbia, Tito's death in 1980 and the loosening of restrictions during the subsequent decade enabled this budding political challenge to come to full bloom, bringing together all the various groups of critical intellectuals around the demand for systemic change and democratisation.

The forerunners: Djilas and Mihajlov, 1952–66

After having gone through an initial phase of revolutionary extremism, marked by forced collectivisation and eradication of real or imagined political opponents (first from the 'bourgeois' right and then, after 1948, from the 'Cominformist' left), in 1952 Yugoslavia embarked on a new course aimed at defining a different and 'democratic' form of communism, superior to that existing in the Soviet Union and its satellites. The leading figure and main architect of this new policy was Milovan Djilas, head of the Agitation and Propaganda ('Agitprop') Section and a member of Tito's closest entourage. In the spirit of the Resolution of the 1952 Sixth Party Congress, which proclaimed the Party's new role as that of 'the political and ideological educator of the masses' and not as 'the direct operative manager and commander in the economy, state or social life,'[15] Djilas continued to press for a greater democratisation of Yugoslavia's system, pushing out the boundaries of public discourse and, finally, directly challenging the legitimacy of the regime to which he himself belonged.

In a series of articles published in 1953 Djilas relentlessly advo-

---

[14]George Schöpflin's distinction between 'dissent' and 'opposition' is useful here: whereas dissent is restricted to individual acts of defiance or disagreement, opposition implies a readiness to play a public role, the establishment of organisations which reject the leading role of the Party and advocacy of change in the political sphere. (George Schöpflin, *Politics in Eastern Europe, 1945–1992*, Oxford, 1993, pp. 179–80)

[15]Quoted in Dennison Rusinow, *The Yugoslav Experiment, 1948-1974*, London, 1977, p. 75.

cated reform of the Party (now renamed the League of Communists) and warned of its 'bureaucratic degeneration'. In December 1953 he went so far as to argue that communism was an overly abstract and distant goal that diverted attention from the real ills within Yugoslav society, which were Party privileges, the arbitrariness of the legal system and 'bureaucratism'.[16] A month later he called for the renunciation of the Leninist form of state and Party in favour of 'a more democratic, free and decentralised form of political life and struggle'.[17] When Djilas directly attacked the highest Party elite in his literary piece 'Anatomy of a Moral', where he denounced the luxury, privileges and intrigues of the new elite and the corrosion of 'all the ethical values behind which the secluded circles were sheltered and by which they swore',[18] he had clearly and knowingly overstepped the limits. The Third Plenum in January 1954 divested Djilas of all his functions and expelled him from the Central Committee. In the course of the proceedings, transmitted by radio countrywide, he was slandered and accused of being a traitor in the service of hostile Western forces. He attempted half-heartedly to defend himself, but finally succumbed to the pressure and repented, voting for his own exclusion from the Central Committee.

Djilas was subjected to harassment and ostracism, but his definitive break with the Party came at his own initiative. Following his excommunication, he wrote his first all-encompassing critique of the existing communist systems, entitled *The New Class*. In it, he argued that contemporary communism was a 'type of totalitarianism' which consisted of a monopoly of political power, ownership and ideology by one political party controlled by the 'new class'.[19] In his view 'the heroic era of communism' had passed, having given way to an 'epoch of practical men' without any genuine ideology or conviction: 'Authority is the basic aim and means of communism and of every true communist. The thirst for power is insatiable and irresistible... Careerism, extravagance and love of power are inevitable, and so is corruption.'[20] As a result, he argued, communism had become 'national', in the sense that ruling oligarchies had adapted to existing national conditions to compensate for the decline of ideology and the increasing sclerosis of social and economic life. To him Yugoslavia's system merely

---

[16]Milovan Djilas, 'Is There a Goal?' in *Anatomy of a Moral*, New York, 1959, p. 77.
[17]'League or Party' in ibid., p. 141.
[18]'Anatomy of a Moral' in ibid., p. 172.
[19]*The New Class*, New York, 1957, p. 166.
[20]Ibid., pp. 54, 81, 164 passim.

represented the first manifestation of this phenomenon and was, in essence, not fundamentally different from other existing communist systems.

In December 1954 Djilas gave an interview to an American journalist, calling for the creation of a second, 'democratic socialist' party in Yugoslavia.[21] At this point, his critique had gone so far as to directly challenge the ruling Party's monopoly of power and he was tried for 'hostile propaganda', receiving a suspended sentence of eighteen months in prison. At the end of 1956 he faced a new trial and a three-year sentence for condemning the Yugoslav stand towards the Soviet invasion of Hungary in the American press. The publication in the United States of *The New Class*—which saw ten editions in its first year of publication and was subsequently translated into over forty—led to the prolongation of his sentence for another seven years, but also established Djilas as one of the foremost dissidents of the communist world.[22] His next book, *Conversations With Stalin*, led to his second imprisonment, so that by the time of his final release at the end of 1966, he had been tried four times and spent a total of nine years in prison. By virtue of his writings and his extensive critique of communism in Eastern Europe, he achieved much fame in the West and became an inspiration to other dissidents in the Soviet bloc.

One of the more puzzling questions is why Djilas, Yugoslavia's most famous dissident, had such a negligible impact on the evolution of the intellectual opposition in his own country and was so absent from the post-communist political scene. A first explanation lies in the fact that association with Djilas until the second half of the 1980s could lead to all sorts of problems. After Djilas' fall from power in 1954, a few nonconformist intellectuals did begin to associate with him, notably Borislav Mihajlović-Mihiz and his friends, artist Mića Popović and publicist Živorad Stojković. However, the increased repression against Djilas after 1956 put an end to such visits. As Mihajlović-Mihiz told Djilas after losing his job with the weekly *NIN*: 'You they write about in the Western press, but I can be liquidated over the telephone'.[23] Although on Djilas's release from prison in

[21]*New York Times*, 25 Dec. 1954, pp. 1, 3.

[22]In 1995, *The New Class* was included among the one hundred books which have influenced Western public discourse since the Second World War by a group of experts at St Antony's College, Oxford. See Timothy Garton Ash (ed.), *Freedom for Publishing. Publishing for Freedom*, Budapest, 1995, p. 198.

[23]Milovan Djilas, *Rise and Fall*, San Diego/New York, 1985, p. 371. See also Borislav Mihajlović-Mihiz, *Autobiografija—o drugima*, II, Belgrade, 1994, pp. 176–89.

1966 these links were re-established and new ones were forged (notably with poet Matija Bećković, who became his closest friend), associating with him continued to be dangerous. Djilas was constantly under threat of renewed imprisonment and subject to vilification in the press, and any attempts to publish his texts, even of purely literary nature, sparked immediate repression.[24] Even the 'flying university', which was generally tolerated by the authorities, saw its only raid by the Belgrade police when Djilas was giving a talk in 1984.[25]

While the exceptionally harsh treatment of Djilas goes a long way to explain the reluctance of other intellectuals to include him in their activities, it does not account for the continued suspicion with which he was regarded in the Belgrade intelligentsia even when repression subsided. The main reason for this unwillingness to associate with Djilas was his communist past and his role as one of the architects of the Yugoslav system before 1954. As the communist regime was increasingly blamed for all the ills that beset the Serbs, Djilas's participation in the drafting of inter-republican borders, the establishment of a Montenegrin nation and republic, as well as his critical stance towards the growing nationalist momentum in post-Tito Yugoslavia, all contributed to his ostracism. In addition, his actions as a Partisan commander during the Second World War—greatly magnified by rumour and hearsay in the atmosphere of disclosure in the 1980s—and his alleged role in the repression of the 'Cominformists' were seen as unforgivable sins. The efforts of some of his contemporaries to dispel such perceptions and Djilas's own unmitigated confrontation with his revolutionary and communist past in his writings had little effect.[26] Although after 1989 he was allowed to publish in Yugoslavia and was interviewed in the press, he was never rehabilitated.[27] Even

[24]Notably, literary historian Predrag Palavestra's attempt to publish a short story by Djilas in 1971 or Momčilo Selić's and Dragoljub Ignjatović's attempt to launch a *samizdat* literary journal with Djilas in 1979. Palavestra lost his job as editor of the journal *Savremenik*, while Ignjatović and Selić were tried, with Ignjatović serving a thirty-day prison sentence. (Interview with Palavestra, 12 Aug. 1997. On Selić and Ignjatović see below.)

[25]Resulting in the trial of the 'Belgrade Six' discussed below.

[26]See notably Momčilo Djorgović, *Djilas vernik i jeretik*, Belgrade, 1989; Matija Bećković et al., *Milovan Djilas (1911–1995)*, Belgrade, 1996, and Momčilo Cemović, *Djilasovi odgovori*, Belgrade, 1997, as well as Djilas' autobiographies, *Wartime*, New York/ London, 1977, and *Rise and Fall*, op. cit.

[27]The one initiative by a group of former Partisan generals to have Djilas' military honours returned to him in 1992 bore no fruit. See Cemović, op. cit., pp. 98-103.

the proposal for a minute of silence in the Yugoslav Parliament on the news of his death in 1995 was rejected.

Even at the time, Djilas's rebellion had scant repercussions, although it appears that before his fall from power in 1954 his ideas had received a favourable echo both in certain Party circles and among younger communists.[28] His subsequent advocacy of a second, social-democratic party was certainly far more radical than even the most liberal communists were willing to consider. It only resurfaced in 1966, once again its advocate being an isolated figure without a larger following: a young Yugoslav scholar of Russian origin, Mihajlo Mihajlov.

Mihajlov's first trial and imprisonment took place in 1965, when he criticised Lenin and the Russian Revolution in an article on his travels in the Soviet Union.[29] Although the Yugoslav communists had broken with Stalin, they still regarded the Leninist heritage as a holy cow and Tito personally called for Mihajlov's punishment. Mihajlov thus received a suspended five-year prison sentence and lost his job as assistant at the University of Zadar. In 1966 he publicly criticised Djilas's imprisonment and wrote an open letter to Tito, where he characterised the Yugoslav communists' monopoly of power as a 'kind of Stalinism' and announced the creation of an independent journal as a core for a new political party.[30] He managed to gather a few intellectuals from Serbia and Croatia to endorse his project,[31] but before it could come to fruition he was put on trial and sentenced to four and a half years in prison. He was released in 1970, only to be arrested for 'hostile propaganda' once again in 1974, this time receiving a seven-year sentence. In 1977 he was released as part of a

---

[28]Only twenty-three Party members were excluded following Djilas's fall in 1954: thirteen in Serbia, three in Croatia, four in Montenegro and one each in the remaining republics (P.J. Marković, op. cit., p. 62). For approval of Djilas' ideas see ibid., loc. cit., the texts by Lazar Koliševski, Svetozar Vukmanović-Tempo, Mijalko Todorović and Mirko Tepavac in *Milovan Djilas (1911–1995)*, op. cit., pp. 21–58 passim. For Djilas's decision not to organise any Party faction or group see *Rise and Fall*, op. cit., p. 339.

[29]Mihajlo Mihajlov, 'Leto moskovsko 1964', *Delo*, Feb. 1965.

[30]Danilović, op. cit., p. 179.

[31]Among them were Zagreb scholars Danijel Ivin and Franjo Zenko, who were to reappear on the Croatian political scene in 1989 as cofounders of the Croatian Social-Liberal Party; Belgrade lawyer Jovan Barović, defence council in many political trials until his death in 1979 under mysterious circumstances; artist Mladen Srbinović, who would later join the Committee for the Defence of Freedom of Thought and Expression; and Slobodan Mašić who became a well-known independent publisher of dissident writings in the 1980s.

general amnesty for political prisoners in the wake of the Belgrade conference of the CSCE (now OSCE). Following his release, Mihajlov still did not cease his political activities; closely co-operating with Djilas, he organised contacts between Serbian and Croatian dissidents. When he left the country to visit family in the United States in 1978, another warrant for his arrest was issued and eventually his passport was withdrawn, forcing him to stay abroad. Mihajlov continued his political activities in the United States, creating a Committee to Aid Democratic Dissidents in Yugoslavia (CADDY), but remained in exile during the 1980s.[32]

Mihajlov's years of imprisonment followed by exile, as well as his more radical liberal ideas made him—like Djilas—a relatively marginal figure on the Yugoslav dissident scene. His consistent criticism of the rising nationalism in Yugoslavia in the 1980s also put him at odds with the currents that came to predominate in the post-Tito period. Yugoslavia's internationally best-known dissidents and the two precursors of the subsequent liberal-oriented activism of the 1980s thus had practically no impact on the intellectual opposition's evolution. The protagonists of this story are rather to be found elsewhere, rooted for the most part in the intellectual criticisms of the system that came to predominate in the late 1960s and early 1970s.

The critique of the Titoist system in the 1960s: the 'Black Wave' and the 'New Left'

The decade of the 1960s considerably extended intellectual freedom in Yugoslavia and represents a kind of 'golden age' in literature and the visual arts and in philosophy—the areas of intellectual activity that most seriously challenged the Titoist system. The philosophical exploration of the human condition based on a rereading of early Marx and the influence of international left-wing intellectual currents, the examination of life in contemporary Yugoslavia and the nature of its communist system, along with the experimentation with literary and artistic form, led to the development of a multifaceted critique of the unrealised promises of the Yugoslav revolution. This period of cultural experimentation and search for an alternative within the existing ideology reached a highpoint in the years 1968-71. In Serbia

---

[32]CADDY continued to function throughout the 1980s, mainly lobbying for Yugoslav dissidents and prisoners of conscience abroad and producing a newsletter informing of their activities.

two main strands of critical culture developed during this period: the 'black wave' in literature and cinema, which presented an examination of the Yugoslav reality and broke established taboos, and the 'new left', which consisted of philosophers connected to the journal *Praxis* and their students at Belgrade University calling for a return to the original 'humanist' values of the Yugoslav revolution.

Both the 'black wave' and the 'new left' represented a reaction to the evolution of the Titoist system since the adoption of self-management in 1952. In many ways they took up the Party's own condemnation of Stalinism and 'bureaucratic degeneration', except that they turned it into a critique of the shortcomings of Yugoslavia's own development. Neither of these critiques challenged the underlying premises of the Yugoslav revolution, the system of self-management, or Tito's leadership. Instead they pointed to some of the shortcomings of the system in practice and some of the seedier sides of Yugoslav life. Although both the philosophical and the artistic and literary endeavours had a political message, neither went so far as to promote the notion of a multiparty system. In fact, the 'new left' philosophers distinctly argued against such a system, preferring some form of socialist 'non-party democracy', a kind of direct self-rule of the people through their various self-managing organisations. Finally, neither of these approaches had any kind of a specifically Serbian agenda; the Praxists in particular were openly opposed to any manifestations of nationalism in all parts of Yugoslavia.

The 'black wave', characterised by an inherent pessimism and a stark portrayal of the life of the 'new socialist man' in Yugoslavia, represented a challenge to the officially promoted vision of progress brought by the communist revolution. The trend was inaugurated in 1968 by Slobodan Selenić's novel *Memoari Pere bogalja* (Memoirs of Pera the Cripple) and Dragoslav Mihailović's novella *Kad su cvetale tikve* (When Pumpkins Blossomed). Selenić's novel told the story of Pera, the son of a highly ranked former Partisan and member of the secret police, and explicitly depicted the decadent and permissive *nouveau riche* atmosphere of the peasant communist revolutionaries who settled in the houses of the old Belgrade bourgeoisie. The novel also broached several taboo subjects: notably, the official falsification of the history of the Partisan war and the civil strife that accompanied it, and the purge and imprisonment of Cominformists after 1948.[33]

---

[33]Slobodan Selenić, *Memoari Pere Bogalja* (1968), Belgrade, 1991, pp. 60, 70–4 and 143–5 respectively.

It was, therefore, bitterly attacked by regime ideologues, but nevertheless went on to receive Belgrade's prestigious 'October' literary prize. Selenić's next novel, which went further in terms of addressing the subject of the Goli Otok prison camp for Cominformists, was, however, withdrawn from publication and destroyed in 1970.[34]

Dragoslav Mihailović's novella also received much critical and popular acclaim and was reworked into a play, which was, however, banned after a few performances. Mihailović's depiction of the violent and crime-ridden milieu of the Belgrade suburbs focuses on the story of young hooligan Ljuba Šampion, a promising boxing champion, whose his life is thoroughly shaken up by the imprisonment of his father and brother as Cominformists. The family's tragedy unfolds as Ljuba's brother is sent to the Goli Otok, his father returns home a broken and ruined man, his sister is raped and commits suicide and his mother dies of grief. Ljuba's own career prospects wane as a consequence of his father's and brother's 'transgressions', and he ends up as a murderer and a fugitive from justice.[35] Mihailović's own horrifying experience as a Goli Otok inmate, where he spent fifteen months in his early twenties, and his subsequent years of unemployment, poverty and ostracism, all contributed to the extreme realism of his story. Although both the novella and the play only alluded to Goli Otok, the mere fact of placing the fate of a Cominformist family at their centre was already a suspect enterprise. The final straw that led to the banning of the play was one line, in which Ljuba's father tells his son: 'They are worse than the Germans'. This comparison between Yugoslav communists and the Nazi occupier provoked a personal intervention from Tito himself.[36]

Nowhere was the dark vision of Yugoslavia's socialist reality so vividly expressed as in film, achieving great recognition in both domestic and international festivals, and nowhere was the authorities' repression so extensive and far-reaching.[37] Some of the 'black wave's' most important representatives were literally banished from the Yugoslav cultural scene, losing their jobs and either going into exile or simply having to discontinue their work. Dušan Makavejev's 1970 film *WR: Mysteries of the Organism* is perhaps the best known example

---

[34]The only copy of the manuscript that survived was reworked by Selenić and published in 1982 under the title Heads/Tails (Pismo/Glava). See Chapter 2.

[35]Dragoslav Mihailović, *Kad su cvetale tikve* (1968), Belgrade, 1992.

[36]Milo Gligorijević, *Slučajna istorija*, Belgrade, 1988, pp. 191–8 passim.

[37]See Daniel J. Goulding, *Liberated Cinema*, Bloomington, 1985.

of the trend, winning much international acclaim and receiving the Buñuel Prize at the 1971 Cannes Festival before being banned. In *WR*, Makavejev interspersed documentary footage about Wilhelm Reich, the Austrian-born psychoanalyst who considered sexual repression as the source of oppression and fascism, with the fictional love story of Milena, a Yugoslav adherent of Reich's anarchist notions of total liberation, and Vladimir Ilyich, a young Russian Stalinist. Implicitly criticising all forms of dogmatism, from McCarthyism in the United States to Leninism and even Milena's 'Reichism', Makavejev also poked fun at the untouchable Yugoslav revolution and the People's Army, thus breaking a number of taboos and invoking the wrath of the powerful veterans' organisations. The film was immediately withdrawn from distribution and in 1973 Makavejev went into exile.

Whereas the 'black wave' broke taboos and focused on the un-blemished portrayal of Yugoslav 'socialist reality', the 'new left' that emerged in philosophy in the course of the 1960s examined the ideo-logical premises of Yugoslavia's form of communism. At the 1960 Conference of the Yugoslav Association for Philosophy and Soci-ology, a group of Marxist scholars came into open conflict with party ideologues, when they criticised 'dialectical materialism' and argued in favour of a 'creative Marxism' concerned with alienation and humanism. In 1963 the summer schools on the island of Korčula began, acting as a forum for humanist Marxists from all over the world, and in 1964 the journal *Praxis* was launched. Although its editorship was in the hands of a group of Zagreb professors, its advisory coun-cil created in 1966 included philosophers from the University of Belgrade.[38]

The best-known Belgrade members of *Praxis*, Mihailo Marković, Svetozar Stojanović, Ljubomir Tadić, Dragoljub Mićunović, Miladin Životić and Zagorka Golubović, who were between the ages of sev-enteen and twenty-five in 1948—were deeply marked by the official condemnation of Soviet Stalinism. In the words of Svetozar Stojanović, 'our Marxist-humanist intellectuals, including the writer of these lines, a young university assistant, were also impressed by the [Party's] anti-dogmatic declarations and visionary message'.[39] They positively

---

[38]For an overview of *Praxis* philosophy, see notably Gerson S. Sher, *Praxis*, Bloomington, 1977, and Robert S. Cohen and Mihailo Marković, *Yugoslavia: The Rise and Fall of Socialist Humanism*, Nottingham, 1975.

[39]Svetozar Stojanović, *Propast komunizma i razbijanje Jugoslavije*, Belgrade, 1995, pp. 32–3.

assessed Djilas' critical articles that led to his political liquidation and welcomed the liberal Party programme of 1958.[40] From the early 1960s the influence of the Frankfurt School of political philosophy also provided an inspiration for the 'criticism of all that exists', which became the maxim of the Yugoslav Praxists. They saw their own role as '*engagé* intellectuals, whose task it was to uncover and speak the truth and thus to abet the creation of progressive forces to continue the revolution, which had begun to wane'.[41] They primarily criticised the authoritarian tendencies that survived in Yugoslav society from the pre-revolution period, the Party's own 'Bolshevik' heritage, as well as the market-oriented economic reform introduced in the 1960s, which they considered to be a step back from the original idea of workers' self-management.[42] Throughout the 1960s and 1970s the Praxists were also fervent critics of nationalism, which they saw as the consequence of combined effects of the growth of the market economy and the still incomplete de-bureaucratisation of Yugoslav political life.[43]

The fact that the Praxists stopped short of advocating party pluralism (although they were proponents of extensive pluralism within the Party) and that the journal *Praxis*, despite its open criticism of the failings of the Yugoslav system, was financed by the state until 1974, has led some of the Praxists' critics to call their conflict with the regime a 'family squabble' and to accuse them of actually slowing down the process of democracy in Yugoslavia.[44] The Praxists have responded by arguing that they did represent 'an important factor in de-legitimising Tito's despotism' and that they 'demystified the ruling class, identified new forms of alienation, proved that the workers' and society's self-management in Yugoslavia was an ideological myth, criticised the privileges and lack of morality of communist functionaries, argued that the structural monopoly of the League of Communists over the state was the main obstacle to democratisation, supported the right to strike, the organisation of independent trade

---

[40]P.J. Marković, op. cit., p. 62. Unlike Djilas, however, they remained committed Marxists until the 1980s.

[41]Mihailo Marković in *Duga*, 6–20 Nov. 1993, p. 20.

[42]Nebojša Popov, *Contra Fatum*, Belgrade, 1989, p. 11.

[43]Sher, op. cit., p. 180.

[44]Miroslav Prokopijević, *Duga*, 1–14 March, 1992, p. 17. Similar accusations were levelled at the Croatian Praxists, along with criticism that they did not defend persecuted Croatian intellectuals following the crackdown on the 1971 'mass movement' (see *Danas*, 28 March 1989, pp. 35–7).

unions and peaceful demonstrations, and some even criticised Tito personally'.[45] A mote in Tito's eye from the beginning, the Belgrade Praxists nevertheless only came to be seen as a real threat with the 1968 student revolt.

These demonstrations of June 1968 were inspired by left-wing ideas of the Praxists, as well as by the wave of student unrest in the United States and Europe; although Ljubljana, Zagreb and Sarajevo were also affected, the events in Belgrade were considerably larger and more important.[46] What began as a protest against the police crackdown on student demonstrations turned over the course of a week into a veritable revolt, calling for greater social equality, a solution to the unemployment problem and 'true democracy' in all spheres of life, 'in order to guarantee quicker and more grounded establishment of self-management'.[47] Calling their university the 'Red University Karl Marx', the students protested against the introduction of 'capitalist' market mechanisms in the economy and the exodus of Yugoslav workers to Western Europe to work for 'world capital'. They also expressed their disappointment at the attempts by 'bureaucratic interests' to 'break the brotherhood and unity of our peoples' and called for the fulfilment of the proclaimed goals of the Yugoslav revolution.[48] Not only did the students have no other programme than that of the Party, but a number of their leaders joined the League of Communists at that time because 'it was a widespread desire and conviction of our generation that by entering the LCY we could try to effect change in our society'.[49] The student movement also in no way contested Tito as the leader of both the country and the revolution; in fact, the revolt ended after Tito made a speech on state television on 9 June 1968, in which he recognised the legitimacy of student demands. In this sense, although the 1968 student revolt stood out as the first challenge to the system in the form of street demonstrations and strikes, it did not represent an ideological alternative to it.

Nevertheless, as Nebojša Popov—a younger Praxist and a research assistant at Belgrade University in 1968—has noted, the lasting impact

[45]Miladin Životić in *NIN*, 21 February, 1992, p. 27, and Stojanović, op. cit., p. 223.
[46]Popov, *Contra Fatum*, op. cit., p. 15.
[47]Mirko Arsić and Dragan R. Marković, '*68. Studentski bunt i društvo*, Belgrade, 1988, p. 107.
[48]Ibid., pp. 107–13.
[49]Danilo Udovički, *Republika*, 190, 1–15 June 1998, p. 13.

of the student revolt was contained not in its left-wing ideas as much as in its inherent demand for freedom of expression, association and demonstration.[50] The practice of free thought, press and political action implied a moving away from Party control and thus represented a direct contestation of the Party as the only legitimate social force.[51] An additional aspect of the student revolt was that for the first time it brought together the different strands of Belgrade's critical intelligentsia. Other than the Praxists and professors from the Law, Philology and Dramatic Arts Faculties—the most politicised parts of Belgrade University—letters and telegrams of support came from a number of research institutes and the Writers' Association of Serbia.[52] 'Black wave' film directors Dušan Makavejev and Želimir Žilnik filmed the student demonstrations and meetings, while a number of writers, directors and actors actively took part in them.[53] It is probably this joining of different forces that brought Tito to see the student movement as a threat, despite his apparently conciliatory attitude. Already in 1969 the Serbian authorities began to designate those responsible for '1968', both within the student community and among professors of Belgrade University. The first to be targeted were the editors of the weekly *Student* and the monthly *Vidici* (Perspectives) and in November 1969, their editorial boards were purged.[54] But the main repression of the 'black wave' and the 'new left' took place only after these critiques became accompanied by the rise of new forces of contestation: nationalism and liberalism.

The emergence of 'nationalists' and 'liberals', 1967–71

Along with increasing liberalisation of the cultural sphere, the 1960s were marked by a change in national policy by Tito and the Yugoslav leadership. The communists had taken power in 1945 on the premise that social revolution went hand-in-hand with the resolution of the national question. Their 'Partisan Yugoslavism' was thus based on the legitimising myth of 'brotherhood and unity' of the Partisan struggle

---

[50]*Danas*, 21 June 1988, p. 72.

[51]Nebojša Popov, 'Univerzitet u ideološkom omotaču', in *Srpska strana rata*, op. cit., pp. 349–50.

[52]See Nebojša Popov, *Društveni sukobi—izazov sociologiji*, Belgrade, 1983, p. 59 and Živojin Pavlović, *Ispljuvak pun krvi*, Belgrade, 1984, pp. 67–76 passim.

[53]Gligorijević, op. cit., pp. 138–41.

[54]See Arsić and Marković, op. cit., pp. 159–63, and Ilija Moljković, 'Slučaj' *Student*', *Republika*, 183–5, March 1998.

and embodied by the creation of a federation of equal nations. In practice, however, the federation of six republics and their five constituent nations (the Serbs, the Croats, the Slovenes, the Macedonians and the Montenegrins) remained an essentially unitary state, where territorial autonomy was limited and political power was held by the ethnically mixed, but centralised, Communist Party. Following the break with the Soviet Union and the adoption of a 'new road' to socialism by the Yugoslav League of Communists in the 1950s, the notion of 'Partisan Yugoslavism' was progressively replaced by a supranational 'socialist Yugoslavism', which defined Yugoslavia's legitimacy as a state by its unique system of self-managing socialism. Although this new concept defined Yugoslavism as a form of internationalism, it was—like its predecessor, 'Partisan Yugoslavism'—an attempt to forge a new sense of community that would overcome traditional ethno-national differences and the wartime interethnic conflict.[55]

Both of these essentially unifying notions were effectively abandoned in the course of the 1960s, in favour of the affirmation of Yugoslavia's national diversity and the call for economic decentralisation. This decentralisation was motivated largely by economic interests that surfaced as Yugoslavia's growth began to slow down, with disputes erupting over the redistribution of funds to the less developed regions, the introduction of market mechanisms, banking reform and the retention of foreign currency reserves in the republics.[56] The greatest proponents of decentralisation and the introduction of market mechanisms into the economy were to be found in the wealthier republics of Slovenia and Croatia. Their economic arguments were often accompanied by a widespread rejection of Yugoslavism, which they saw as merely a mask for Serbian hegemony.[57] Allegations that

[55]For an overview of the development of Yugoslav idea see Lenard J. Cohen, *Broken Bonds*, Boulder, CO, 1993; Wachtel, op. cit.; and Dejan Jović, 'The Breakdown of Elite Ideological Consensus: The Prelude to the Disintegration of Yugoslavia', PhD dissertation, London School of Economics, 2000.

[56]John R. Lampe, *Yugoslavia as History*, Cambridge, 1996, pp. 271–8. See also Paul Shoup, *Communism and the Yugoslav National Question*, New York, 1968, and Rusinow, op. cit.

[57]Although Serbs were proportionally over-represented in the rank and file of the Party, the Belgrade-based federal government, the secret police and the army officer corps, all the upper echelons of the main institutions and the military were carefully balanced according to the 'national key'. In the words of Paul Shoup, 'to talk of Serbian hegemony in Yugoslavia, or to draw other parallels to the situation that existed before World War II, would be quite misleading' (Shoup, op. cit., p. 122).

Croatia and Slovenia were being exploited by Serbia's great trading and re-export firms and the centralised banking system were progressively compounded by accusations that Serbs were even 'penetrating' the Croatian tourist industry and draining its resources.[58]

Economic decentralisation was accompanied by a trend towards political decentralisation, whose main architect was Slovenian communist and the Party's ideologue, Edvard Kardelj. Already in the preface to the 1957 edition of his book *The Development of the Slovene National Question*, he warned of 'Great-State Centralism' based on the illusory vision of a Yugoslav 'nation'—a bourgeois concept like the 'integral Yugoslavism' of the interwar state. Instead, he argued in a speech to the Federal Parliament in 1962, Yugoslavia was 'a community of free, equal and independent nations and working people', unified by their common interests of building socialism and independence in an imperialist world. It was, therefore, necessary to redefine Yugoslavia as a federation of sovereign states.[59] In light of this new approach, a series of constitutional reforms were initiated and the Constitution of 1963 reintroduced the nations' rights to self-determination and secession.[60] A year later the statute adopted at the Eighth Congress of the Yugoslav League of Communists provided that the republic Party congresses convene prior to the general Party congress, enabling the republics to determine their policies before debating them on the federal level.[61]

The main opposition to this new orientation came from Aleksandar Ranković, Yugoslavia's Vice-President and head of the state security forces. Ranković, who was also Serbia's leading communist, resisted the economic reform and did what he could to undermine it in his own republic.[62] His political conservatism and his centralist tendencies concurred to create a wide coalition against him among Party liberals of various republics, including those in Serbia. Whereas his centralism was perceived in Croatia and Slovenia as an example of an underlying 'Greater Serbian' orientation aimed at the suppression of Yugoslavia's multinational character, his Serbian opponents saw him as an obstacle to their desires for market-oriented economic reform. Things came

---

[58]The main proponents of this view were Croatian economists and leading intellectuals of the 1971 'mass movement', Marko Veselica and Šime Djodan.

[59]D. Jović, op. cit., pp. 62–4.

[60]*The Constitution of the Socialist Federal Republic of Yugoslavia: Constitutional Amendments*, Belgrade, 1969, p. 6.

[61]Shoup, op. cit., p. 189.

[62]Lampe, op. cit., p. 284.

to a head in summer 1966, when the military intelligence claimed to have discovered evidence that Ranković had been spying on the other Party leaders, including Tito himself. The Fourth Plenum that was summoned at Tito's residence on Brioni thus led to Ranković's political liquidation, opening the door to both further decentralisation and liberalisation. In the aftermath of Ranković's fall, a new series of constitutional amendments were passed, giving greater power to the republics at the expense of the federation.[63] At the same time the official condemnation of 'centralism' and 'unitarism', associated with Ranković, provided the context for the public expression of national grievances, which found its first manifestation in the 1967 'language debate'.

Ranković's political liquidation was euphorically greeted in Croatia 'as primarily a victory for Croatian interests' and it gave rise to a new orientation that was both liberal and national.[64] In order to bolster support for its policy the Croatian party leadership encouraged a wide public debate on Croatian national interests, which eventually led to the 1971 'Croatian Spring', whose principal aim was the creation of a Croatian state within what was essentially to be a confederate Yugoslavia.[65] The inauguration of this movement, in March 1967, took place with a 'Declaration Concerning the Name and Position of the Croatian Literary Language', signed by one hundred and forty intellectuals representing nineteen important Croatian cultural institutions. This Declaration affirmed 'the right of each of our nations to protect the attributes of its national identity and to fully develop not only its economy but also its culture'.[66] Arguing that 'the national designation of the language spoken by the Croatian nation is of paramount importance', the signatories protested the 'etatism, unitarism and hegemony', symbolised by the use of 'Serbian' as the state language and Belgrade radio and television acting as the main federal media

---

[63]These amendments notably gave the right to the republics to appoint and dismiss their deputies to the Federal Parliament, as well as all higher and middle-rank functionaries, and to be co-responsible for the public order—as part of the purge of the state security previously controlled by Ranković (Constitutional Amendments I–VI, April 1967, in *The Constitution of the Socialist Federal Republic of Yugoslavia: Constitutional Amendments,* op. cit., pp. 169–74).

[64]Rusinow, op. cit., p. 194.

[65]According to Marko Veselica, one of the leaders of the 1971 Croatian national revival (*Danas,* 3 Dec. 1991, pp. 32–3).

[66]'Deklaracija o nazivu i položaju hrvatskog književnog jezika', *Hrvatska revija,* XVII/1–2, 1967, p. 16.

source.[67] They advocated constitutional changes which would elevate Croatian to the status of one of four literary languages of Yugoslavia (along with Slovenian, Macedonian and Serbian) and would guarantee its use in Croatian schools, media and public and political fora. Considering that more than half the signatories were Party members and that the institutions involved were the official bastions of Croatian culture, it was generally assumed in Yugoslavia that the Croatian Party leaders and even Tito himself had approved the Declaration, or had least known about it.[68]

In Yugoslavia language was always intimately connected to a larger political agenda. In the 19th and early 20th centuries it provided one of the bases of Yugoslav strivings for unification, but it also represented one of the greatest areas of dispute accompanying the assertion of individual South Slav national identities. The 1850 Vienna Agreement between Croatian and Serbian cultural leaders established the foundation for a common language with two variants (Croatian in the west and Serbian in the east) and two alphabets (Latin and Cyrillic respectively). This linguistic unity was supposed to be the first step towards cultural and eventually political unification, which was eventually achieved in 1918.[69] When the Kingdom of Yugoslavia fell apart in 1941 and the Independent State of Croatia was set up, one of the first projects of the Ustasha regime was to establish a new orthography stressing the peculiarities of the Croatian variant and separating it from the Serbian. Following the communist victory and reunification of the country, this process was reversed. As part of the policy of promoting 'socialist Yugoslavism', a new agreement was signed in 1954 in Novi Sad between the two main cultural institutions, Matica Hrvatska and Matica Srpska, reaffirming the notion of one Serbo-Croat language with two variants. The Croatian Declaration of 1967, which repudiated the Vienna and Novi Sad agreements and renewed the call for a separation of Croatian from Serbian, was thus seen as a political statement of Croatia's drive for greater independence.

[67]Ibid., loc. cit.

[68]Christopher Spalatin, 'Serbo-Croatian or Serbian and Croatian? Considerations on the Croatian Declaration and the Serbian Proposal of March 1967', *Journal of Croatian Studies*, VII-VIII, 1966–7, p. 10.

[69]The Croatian 19th-century intellectuals' adoption of the 'štokavian' dialect over the 'čakavian' and 'kajkavian' paved the way for the unity of Serbo-Croatian language (Banac, *The National Question in Yugoslavia*, Ithaca, NY, 1984, pp. 46–8 and 76–80).

The reply to the Croatian Declaration came swiftly, in March 1967, in the form of a 'Proposal for Consideration' endorsed by forty-two members of the Writers' Association of Serbia.[70] Although most were also Party members, it appears that their Proposal was drafted without the consent of their leadership.[71] The signatories agreed that 'it is a legitimate and inalienable right of each nation to make decisions regarding the name and the position of its own language' and acknowledged that the institutions which had signed the Declaration were 'the most competent in matters pertaining to the Croatian literary language'.[72] They endorsed the Croatian demand that their two languages should 'henceforth develop in full independence and equality' and called upon the Federal Parliament to remove the names 'Croato-Serbian and Serbo-Croatian' from the Constitution.[73] At the same time, they warned:

[All Serbs in Croatia and Croats in Serbia should be guaranteed] the right to a scholastic [sic] education in their own languages and alphabets according to their own national programmes, the right to use their national languages and alphabets in dealing with all authorities, the right to found their cultural societies, local museums, publishing houses and newspapers, in short the right to cultivate unobstructedly and freely all aspects of their national culture.[74]

In other words, if the Croats were announcing their desire for cultural or, implicitly, any other kind of autonomy from Yugoslavia, then they would have to grant exactly the same right to Serbs in their republic. The Serbian writers' political agenda, which underlay the issue of language, concerned the question of national unity; as the linguist Pavle Ivić later put it, 'the Declaration, which solemnly referred to

---

[70]The Writers' Association of Serbia, along with its counterparts in the other republics, was created in 1945, as part of the wider Yugoslav Writers' Union, based on the Soviet model. In practice, however, the Yugoslav Writers' Union never had nearly as much power as its Soviet counterpart, either financially or in setting literary guidelines. With the decentralisation of the Yugoslav system, in 1965 the statutes of the organisation were changed, increasing the independence of the republican organisations. See Ratko Peković, *Ni rat ni mir*, Belgrade, 1986, pp. 20–1, and Sveta Lukić, *Contemporary Yugoslav Literature*, Urbana, 1972, pp. 130–7.

[71]The President of the Writers' Association of Serbia, Dušan Matić, showed the text to his friend Stevan Doronjski, a high-ranking member of the republican Central Committee, only to be told that it was unacceptable. (See Petar Džadžić, 'Strele, jezuiti, simetrije', *Stvarnost*, I/1, 1997, p. 5.)

[72]'Proposal for Consideration' quoted in Spalatin, op. cit., p. 10.

[73]Ibid., loc. cit.

[74]Ibid., p. 11.

'the inalienable right of each people' to use its own name for its language, imposed on the Serbs of Croatia another people's name and praxis for their language and with it the linguistic *separation from their own nation*.[75]

In this way the Croatian and Serbian intellectuals implicitly linked the question of language to the problem of statehood. For Croatian intellectuals 'Yugoslavism' and the common language represented a threat to Croatian identity and sovereignty, while for their Serbian counterparts, any assertion of Croatian independence was a threat to Serbian unity, reversing the traditional 19th-century goal of 'liberation and unification' of Serbs into one state. They saw Croatian demands for sovereignty as inherently unprincipled: the Croats' call for decentralisation only applied to Yugoslavia, but not to their own republic. Croatian intellectuals, in turn, saw any demand in favour of the republic's Serbs as an attempt to keep Croatia hostage to its Serbian minority and under the 'Greater Serbian' thumb. In the end, the fact that the difference between the Croatian and the Serbian languages is about as great as that between English and American was of no concern.

The reaction of the authorities to this manifestation of nationalism was as instantaneous as it was short-lived. In Croatia, nine of the Declaration's signatories were expelled from the Party and thirteen received 'final warnings'. Despite this initial setback, however, the Croatian national revival continued unabated. In Serbia, pressure was brought to bear on the Writers' Association, whose president, Dušan Matić, resigned on the eve of the debate on the Proposal.[76] As a result, many of the forty-two signatories of the Proposal publicly 'withdrew' their signatures, receiving Party 'warnings'. The author of the Proposal, Borislav Mihajlović-Mihiz, and several other nonconforming intellectuals were dismissed from their jobs.[77] In January 1968 the association's journal *Književne novine* came under attack for transmitting the debate on the Proposal and for arguing that nationalism was being sponsored by republican leaderships, which led to the dismissal of its

[75]Pavle Ivić, 'Jezik i problemi oko njega' in Aleksa Djilas (ed.), *Srpsko pitanje*, Belgrade, 1991, p. 156 (emphasis added).

[76]For the debate in the Writers' Association see *Književne novine*, 297, 1 Apr. 1967, pp. 10–11, and 298, 15 Apr. 1967, pp. 11, 14.

[77]Mihajlović-Mihiz had to resign from his job at the publishing house Prosveta, while poet Matija Bećković and satirists Brana Crnčević and Dušan Radović were dismissed from their positions with Belgrade radio-television.

editorial board and the exclusion of its editor-in-chief, poet Tanasije Mladenović, from the Party.[78]

Several of the Serbian protagonists of the 'language debate' made up the core of the future 'nationalist' coalition in the Belgrade intelligentsia of the 1980s.[79] The most important among them were the Proposal's two instigators, Borislav Mihajlović-Mihiz and Antonije Isaković. Despite their different political orientations (Mihajlović-Mihiz was a known nonconformist and a political liberal, whereas Isaković was a former Partisan, member of the Serbian Central Committee and a declared 'child of the revolution'),[80] they had been friends for a long time and belonged to an intellectual circle known as the 'Simina 9a group', named after the address of Mihajlović's lodgings during their student days. In Mihajlović's words:

We young people of Simina 9a had many different convictions—from communism adopted through life-threatening situations and wartime heroism, to compromise and fellow-travelling, spontaneous youthful anarchism, liberal democracy, sceptical and precocious conservatism, and open and cynical reactionary ideas—but we knew that the changes that had taken place [after the war] were extensive and long-term. All of us, without exception, knew that 'this' had come to stay and that we were condemned to spend our lives in the spiritual claustrophobia of Bolshevism. With this clear understanding ... we struggled to maintain our tentative courage, our weak but already vital core of personal integrity and our budding though resolute conviction that we would not give in to the dictates and *Gleichschaltung* of the epoch.[81]

Although they do not strictly qualify as dissidents, they did represent a group of free thinkers who met on a regular basis to discuss issues ranging from the practical problems of everyday life to matters of

[78]Gligorijević, op. cit., pp. 100–6, and Ljubiša Manojlović, *Čitajte izmedju redova.* Kragujevac, 1991.

[79]Notably Borislav Mihajlović-Mihiz, Antonije Isaković, Matija Bećković, Brana Crnčević, Tanasije Mladenović, Momo Kapor, Ljubomir Simović, Petar Džadžić, Stevan Raičković, Zoran Gluščević, Aleksandar Petrov, Pavle Ivić and Milorad Pavić. The term 'nationalist', which was generally used by the authorities to discredit intellectuals, had a distinctly negative connotation in Yugoslavia and was not accepted by most of those designated by it. Here it is used to define individuals whose primary preoccupation in the course of their political activism has been the idea of Serbian national unity and statehood.

[80]Antonije Isaković, 'Revolucija je otvoren žrtvenik' (1971) in *Govori i razgovori,* Gornji Milanovac, 1991, pp. 56–64.

[81]Borislav Mihajlović-Mihiz, *Autobiografija—o drugima,* I, Belgrade, 1992, p. 142.

theory and ideology. Most of them went on to achieve considerable recognition and assume an important role in the cultural life of post-war Serbia, as university professors, writers, literary critics or artists. Several became members of the Serbian Academy of Sciences and Arts, the republic's most prestigious cultural institution.

What united these intellectuals, apart from their friendship, was their self-conscious belonging to a particular generation, imbibed with traditional national values and a particular vision of the Serbian national question, forged by their experience of the Second World War. Most of them were born around 1920 and were aged between seventeen and twenty-five in 1941, when war spread to Yugoslavia and the first common state disintegrated.[82] They witnessed not only the Axis occupation of their country, but also the civil war that pitted communist Partisans against royalist Chetniks and a ruthless campaign of mass extermination of Serbs, Jews and Gypsies in the Independent State of Croatia.[83] As writer Dobrica Ćosić, who also belonged to the group, put it, 'The generation to which I historically and fatally belong was forged by the war and our divisions during it ... Then, in that war and revolution are the origins of everything we have created since then and everything we are today.'[84]

Some, like Ćosić and Isaković, had volunteered for the Partisans and fought for communism and a 'new' Yugoslavia. For them, the Partisan struggle and communist ideology represented a way of overcoming destructive national antagonisms through the fusion of class and nation into what they perceived as a fundamentally different and progressive identity. In Isaković's words:

In that chaos [of the Second World War], when Yugoslavia was cut into pieces, ... our differences of religion and national tradition were being played up, and genocide was rampant in our regions, this is when our movement had the strength and the capability to create a Yugoslavism ... [that] was historically different. But at one moment we lost it, we somehow got lost ... We put the accent on the differences between nations.[85]

---

[82]On the notion of 'intellectual generations' and the 'formative event' see Jean-François Sirinelli, 'Générations intellectuelles. Effets d'âge et phénomènes de génération dans le milieu intellectuel français', *Cahiers de l'Institut d'Histoire du Temps Présent*, 6, 1987.

[83]Some, like art historian Dejan Medaković, who was a Serb from Croatia, did so in a very direct way (see Dejan Medaković, *Efemeris*, I-III, Belgrade, 1990–2).

[84]Dobrica Ćosić, 'Na kraju 'srećne budućnosti', *Književne novine*, 749/750, 1988, p. 5.

[85]Interview in *Zum-reporter*, 1982, reprinted in Isaković, op. cit., p. 140.

To them, 'Partisan Yugoslavism' was a fundamental ingredient of their own identity and justification for their wartime struggle. In this sense the regime's 'capitulation' to particularist nationalist aspirations represented the negation of everything they had fought for.[86]

Even those who did not fight with the Partisans had 'a curious feeling of early fatherhood' when Yugoslavia was reborn in 1945.[87] Educated in the period of King Alexander's 'integral Yugoslavism', they were taught to link traditional Serbian identity with the notion of a single Yugoslav nation. As Borislav Mihajlović-Mihiz noted in his reflections on his secondary school: 'Along with its defined and emphasised [Serbian] traditionalism—it is paradoxical but true— we were persistently and successfully impregnated with a sense of Yugoslavism and we genuinely believed that Slovenes, Croats and Serbs were one people'.[88] Along with their initial leftist leanings, this fusion of Serbian national identity and sense of Yugoslav belonging conditioned them to see in the new system a way of bridging the national differences that had produced such bloodshed and suffering during the war. With the effective abandoning of 'socialist Yugoslavism' in the 1960s, however, they could fall back on their traditional Serbian identity.

If one intellectual were to be singled out for his importance in the national revival of the 1980s, it would most certainly be Dobrica Ćosić. It is his vision of the Serbian national destiny in the 20th century, elaborated in the course of the 1970s, that became predominant in the post-Tito era. Although this vision was not fundamentally different from the ideas of the other protagonists of the 'national' critique of Yugoslavia's evolution from the end of the 1960s, Ćosić's prolific literary and public work, his reconsideration of the Yugoslav 'answer' to the Serbian 'question' and the themes he developed to explain the Serbian national experience most vividly captured the imagination of his

---

[86]This they shared with some of the Praxists of the same generation. As Mihailo Marković put it, 'Many Serbs (at least in my generation) understood the idea of internationalism literally and were ready to sacrifice their own Serbian national identity... and accept Yugoslavism as a national belonging. It is difficult today [in 1989] to understand how this was possible. Certainly for us, 'young idealists' there was no 'unitarist' calculation involved, but a sincere feeling.' (Interview in *Delo*, 13 May 1989, reprinted in Nadežda Gaće, *Jugoslavija. Suočavanje sa sudbinom*, Belgrade, 1989, p. 134.)

[87]Borislav Mihajlović-Mihiz, 'Naša generacija' in *Književni razgovori*, Belgrade, 1971, p. 5.

[88]Mihajlović-Mihiz, *Autobiografija—o drugima*, I, op. cit., pp. 71–2.

reading public.[89] As the title of a book of interviews with him aptly put it, he was indeed 'the man of his time'[90] and his early evolution from Yugoslav into Serb was paradigmatic for the subsequent transformation of many of his contemporaries. Described by his friends as a man of 'incredible communicative power of attracting people',[91] he was also at the centre of most activities of the Belgrade intelligentsia since the early 1970s and gathered around him a variety of individuals who otherwise had little in common. It is difficult to overstate both the prestige that Ćosić enjoyed in Serbia until the late 1980s and the vehemence of the criticism and blame that he has had to face since then.[92]

One of the elements that built Ćosić's reputation in the Belgrade intelligentsia was the fact that he was the first to raise the 'Kosovo question' and that he did so in a way which was later seen as premonitory. Before his famous 1968 speech on Kosovo, which led to his break with the Party, Ćosić was not only one of Yugoslavia's most prominent writers but a member of the highest elite, hand-picked by Tito to accompany him on a sea voyage around Africa in 1961. Politically active, he was a member of both the Serbian and federal parliaments and of the Central Committee of the Serbian Party. Ćosić was also an ardent advocate of 'socialist Yugoslavism', as was shown in his 1961 debate with Slovenian intellectual Dušan Pirjevec. In this exchange, Ćosić argued that Yugoslavism was a form of 'internationalism' that was 'constitutionally and historically overcoming the limits of nation and national belonging', whereas Pirjevec saw the republics as 'clearly formed national organisms' whose 'national self-determination' was a logical consequence of socialist development.[93]

In May 1968 Ćosić came into open conflict with the Party at the

---

[89]See Chapter 2.

[90]Slavoljub Djukić, *Čovek u svom vremenu*, Belgrade, 1989.

[91]Mihajlović-Mihiz, *Autobiografija—o drugima*, I, op. cit., p. 153.

[92]Ćosić has been accused of 'offering [the Serbs] an irredentist war of conquest', of having been a 'false dissident' and of being 'uneducated, *kitschig*, forgetful and always self-commiserating'. In 1997 he even appeared as a negative figure in two novels. For some of these accusations, see *Vreme*, 4 Nov. 1991, p. 20, and 31 Jan. 1998, pp. 40–1, and Slapšak, op. cit., p. 161. The two books are *Loony Tunes* by Svetislav Basara and *Mrak* by David Albahari.

[93]For Ćosić's vision of the debate see Djukić, *Čovek u svom vremenu*, op. cit., pp. 121–37. A more comprehensive analysis can be found in Budding, 'Yugoslavs into Serbs' op. cit., p. 409, Peković, op. cit., pp. 302–3, and Jelena Milojković-Djurić, 'Approaches to National Identities: Ćosić's and Pirjevec's Debate on Ideological and Literary Issues', *East European Quarterly*, XXX/1, 1996 pp. 63–73.

Fourteenth Plenum of the Central Committee of the League of Communists of Serbia, devoted to the proposal of a new set of decentralising constitutional amendments.[94] The Plenum took place in the context of a growing national movement among the Albanians in the autonomous province of Kosovo. Under Ranković, the instruments of power in the province had been held by the Serbs, and the Albanians (67% of Kosovo's population at the time) were subjected to years of harassment and strict surveillance by Ranković's secret police; after 1966 the situation changed in favour of the Albanians. Now the Serbs were pushed out of jobs as the province administration and levers of power were being 'Albanianised'.[95] Compounded by a history of rival claims over the province and periods of ethnic strife (particularly after 1912, when Serbia brutally 'reconquered' Kosovo, and in 1941–5, when Kosovo formed a part of the pro-Axis 'Greater Albania', resulting in the massive persecution and expulsion of Serbs), this new transfer of power gave rise to sporadic eruptions of violence in the course of 1967, which turned by 1968 into full-scale anti-Serbian demonstrations in several towns.[96]

During the Party Plenum Ćosić started out by denouncing the use of self-management as a cover for particularist, bureaucratic nationalism and the concurrent labelling of any opposition to it as 'unitarism' and 'hegemonism'. He said that he could not give lip-service to the decentralisation of the country, which was leading to rising anti-Serbian feelings in Croatia and Slovenia and was in turn stimulating the revival of an 'anachronic, retrograde, primitive Serbianism'.[97] He stated that the efforts to solve the national question had clearly not succeeded and that the best evidence for this could be found in Kosovo:

We cannot pretend not to see the widespread sense in Serbia of worsening relations with Albanians, the dread felt by Serbs and Montenegrins, the pressures to emigrate, the systematic removal of Serbs and Montenegrins from leading positions, the desires of the intelligentsia to leave Kosovo and Metohija, the lack of equality before the law and the non-respect of the law...

[94]Amendments XVIII and XIX in *The Constitution of the Socialist Federal Republic of Yugoslavia. Constitutional Amendments*, op. cit., pp. 191–5.

[95]By 1980, Albanians constituted 92% of those employed in the social sector, compared to only 5% of Serbs. (Sabrina Petra Ramet, *Nationalism and Federalism in Yugoslavia 1962–1991*, Bloomington, IN, 1992, p. 193.)

[96]Ibid., p. 190.

[97]Dobrica Ćosić, 'Kritika vladajuće ideološke koncepcije u nacionalnoj politici', *Stvarno i moguće*. Ljubljana/ Zagreb, 1982, p. 29.

The chauvinist mood and nationalist psychosis among Albanians is not seen in its real dimension; the irredentist and separatist mood and desires in parts of the Albanian population are unjustifiably being underestimated.[98]

He warned that 'if in Yugoslavia the traditional, nationalist–statist policies and particularistic orientations win out, if the democratic forces of socialism do not claim the final victory over the bureaucratic and petit-bourgeois forces, it might revive among Serbs the old historical goal and national ideal—unity of Serbian people in one state'.[99]

Ćosić's speech had the effect of a bombshell; it was the first open denunciation by such a high ranking communist intellectual of the new course that Yugoslavia had taken since the liquidation of Ranković and a breach of the commonly accepted practice to single out 'centralism' and 'hegemonism' for criticism. His speech was vehemently condemned along with that of historian Jovan Marjanović, who criticised the proclamation of a Muslim nation as one of Yugoslavia's constituent nations.[100] However, Ćosić, refused to recant and two months later he left the Party. Interestingly, some of his critics later acknowledged that Ćosić had 'perceived the [Kosovo] problem better and earlier than many others':

Above all he was right to point to the depth of both the Serbian and Albanian national question in Kosovo and Metohija, when he argued that—under the surface, calmed by ideological national discourse and Party resolutions— lay deeper and more durable differences that could easily escalate into conflict if they remained unresolved and neglected.[101]

In November 1968, a few months after the Plenum at which Ćosić had warned of rising Albanian nationalism, there was an explosion of unrest, as thousands of Albanian demonstrators called for an independent Albanian-language university, the status of a republic and even union with Albania.[102]

[98]Ibid., p. 31.

[99]Ibid., pp. 34–5. This last statement indicates that Ćosić had not yet moved from a position of 'socialist Yugoslavism' to his subsequent endorsement of Serbian 'spiritual and cultural' unity.

[100]For the various criticisms of Ćosić and Marjanović, see *14. Sednica CK SK Srbije, Maj 1968*, Belgrade, 1968. They are also covered in D. Jović, op. cit., pp. 119–26.

[101]Mirko Tepavac, a member of the Serbian 'liberal' leadership and Yugoslav Foreign Minister from 1969 to 1972, in: Aleksandar Nenadović, *Mirko Tepavac—sećanja i komentari*, Belgrade, 1998, pp. 111–12.

[102]Branko Horvat, *Kosovsko pitanje*, Zagreb, 1989, pp. 139–41.

The most significant long-term result of the Plenum was that the final defeat of Ćosić's preferred option of 'socialist Yugoslavism' and the dismissal of his warnings about the implications of decentralisation for Serbs outside what was to be called 'inner' Serbia resulted in the creation of an alternative political platform whose main figure Ćosić was to become. In 1969 he took over the presidency of the Serbian Literary Cooperative (Srpska književna zadruga), an important traditional institution set up in 1892 to promote the consolidation and spread of Serbian culture. Gathering around him an eclectic group of intellectuals including both fellow-writers and linguists, literary critics, artists, jurists, economists, philosophers and historians, Ćosić effectively created a budding coalition behind his new national platform of Serbian 'cultural and spiritual' unity, 'regardless of the existing republic or state borders'.[103] This coalition represented a precursor of the wider national movement in the intelligentsia in the 1980s.[104]

In his speech to the annual assembly of the Serbian Literary Co-operative in May 1971, held at the time of a new public debate on yet another set of constitutional amendments, Ćosić's position was stated explicitly:

The new orientation of Yugoslavia—as shown by its ideological motivations and aspirations—raises the problem of the socio-political principles that govern the culture of the Serbian nation as a whole. The legal right to the expression of the spiritual unity of the Serbian people, the historical and comprehensive unity of the Serbian culture, the unity that has existed as long as Serbian national consciousness is now seriously being brought into question. This intrinsic and historical unity of Serbian national culture, which exists regardless of state borders ... has been contested in the past only by Austria-Hungary and the Third Reich.[105]

Thus Ćosić outlined not only the theme of national unity as the primary focus of intellectual and cultural activity, but also for the

---

[103]Ćosić in Djukić, *Čovek u svom vremenu*, op. cit., p. 209.

[104]The members of the board of the Serbian Literary Cooperative during Ćosić's presidency included members of the Simina 9a group: the art historian Vojislav Djurić, the writer Borislav Mihajlović-Mihiz, the artist Mića Popović, the linguist Pavle Ivić and the jurist Mihailo Djurić—as well as the Praxist Mihailo Marković, the economist Kosta Mihailović and the historian Radovan Samardžić, who, along with Ivić, were to collaborate on the 1986 draft 'Memorandum' of the Serbian Academy. The board also included the writers Milorad Pavić, Ljubomir Simović, Slobodan Rakitić and Slobodan Selenić, as well as Dimitrije Bogdanović, the future author of the influential 1985 *Book About Kosovo*. (For a complete list see Ljubinka Trgovčević, *Istorija Srpske književne zadruge*, Belgrade, 1992, p. 139.)

[105]Dobrica Ćosić, 'Porazi i ciljevi', in *Stvarno i moguće*, op. cit., p. 87.

first time openly created a parallel between the Yugoslav communist leadership and the former 'enemies' of the Serbs—a theme that was to represent a central tenet of Serbian nationalism in the post-Tito period.

This preoccupation with Serbian unity in the face of state decentralisation surfaced also in the debate on the constitutional changes held at the Belgrade Law Faculty in March 1971. Once again it is important to keep in mind the context in which the discussion took place: the highpoint of the nationalist 'mass movement' in Croatia, which rallied around the goal of Croatian statehood.[106] As a striking harbinger of the events of 1990, the Matica Hrvatska, which regrouped the most radical strand of this movement, proposed a new Croatian constitution, which defined the Republic of Croatia as 'the unique national state of the Croatian nation' in which 'national sovereignty' was 'one, indivisible, inalienable and imperishable' and held solely by 'the Croatian nation'.[107] The proposal also emphasised the voluntary nature of Croatia's association with Yugoslavia, confirming the right to self-determination including secession, designated 'Croatian' as its official language and the traditional Croatian song 'Our beautiful homeland' as the state's national anthem—regardless of the fact that it had also been used during the Independent State of Croatia and was bound to recall unpleasant memories for the republic's Serbs.[108] By the autumn of 1971 the intellectuals had joined forces with the student movement, demanding together the creation of independent Croatian territorial forces, a separate foreign policy and Croatian representation in the United Nations and the revision of Croatia's borders at the expense of Hercegovina and Montenegro.[109] In response to the demands for Croatian statehood, the Serbs in Croatia mobilised around their own cultural association, Prosvjeta, and advocated federalisation of the Republic of Croatia, with separate representation for their national group in the republican parliament and extensive political, cultural and national rights.[110] The hapless Croatian leadership found that it had clearly lost control of the nationalist momentum.[111]

---

[106]Steven Burg, *Conflict and Cohesion in Socialist Yugoslavia*, Princeton, NJ, 1983, p. 126; George Schöpflin, 'The Ideology of Croatian Nationalism', *Survey*, XIX/1, 1973, pp. 123–46; and Jill A. Irvine, *The Croat Question*, Boulder, CO, 1993, pp. 258–72.

[107]Quoted in Ramet, *Nationalism and Federalism*, op. cit., p. 114.

[108]Ibid., loc. cit.

[109]Rusinow, op. cit., p. 305.

[110]Schöpflin, op. cit., p. 141. See also Irvine, op. cit., pp. 266–8.

[111]See Miko Tripalo's *Hrvatsko proljeće*, Zagreb, 1991.

In Belgrade the dramatic developments taking place in Croatia led many intellectuals to conclude that Yugoslavia was in crisis. Several speakers at the 1971 Law Faculty debate saw the Croatian 'mass movement' as not only the logical outcome of the process of decentralisation, but as dictating the further constitutional changes that were being proposed.[112] While for Croatian intellectuals the constitutional amendments fell short of what they advocated, for most Serbian intellectuals the devolution they embodied was going too far. Many asked what would be the implications of the decentralisation on Yugoslavia as a state: would it be a federation, a confederation or something else? The areas of federal competence were being reduced and the introduction of decisionmaking by consensus between the federal units was bound to cripple the federal system. They also argued that this devolution of power to the republics represented a threat to Yugoslavia's security and common market.

In addition to the critiques concerned with Yugoslavia's statehood, many participants focused on the implications of these amendments for Serbia as a republic. Professor Andrija Gams argued that Serbia had found itself in a situation in which it was unfairly being accused of centralist pretensions and hegemony and was being forced to accept a policy that was contrary to its interests.[113] Several speakers argued that by virtue of elevating the autonomous provinces to the status of constitutive elements of the federation, with powers that were the same as those of the republics, Serbia's position was not equal to that of the other republics. As Pavle Ristić explained, any general principle governing the granting of territorial autonomy would have necessarily implied equal application of autonomy throughout Yugoslavia. Why, for example, were Albanians given autonomy in the Republic of Serbia but not in Macedonia or Montenegro?[114] Why was Vojvodina, where the majority population were Serbs, given autonomy at all?[115] Why were Serbs in Croatia not given one?[116] Ristić noted that this lack of coherence in the application of autonomy was bound to have its 'most significant consequence in the strengthening of nationalist feelings of Serbs, based on a sense of subordination and unequal treatment of their native republic'.[117]

[112]See particularly Andrija Gams and Dragoslav Janković, in *Anali Pravnog Fakulteta u Beogradu*, XIX/3, 1971, pp. 234–5 and 257–60.

[113]Ibid., pp. 235–6.

[114]Ibid., p. 219, and Mihailo Djurić, p. 233.

[115]Živomir S. Djordjević, ibid., p. 251.

[116]B.T. Blagojević, ibid., p. 277.

[117]Ibid., pp. 219–20. See also Radoslav Stojanović, p. 266.

Most participants in the discussion agreed with his assessment and a few even went so far as to argue that 'in the foreseeable future it would be reasonable to expect the creation of six or eight independent states in this region'.[118] Although this was not a desirable outcome, it did mean that nobody had the right to neglect Serbia's interest.

Professor Mihailo Djurić, who was a member of both the *Praxis* and the Simina 9a groups, made the most explicit and far-reaching statement of this kind:

> We need to be clear on the point that Yugoslavia today is almost only a geographical notion, considering that on its soil, or better, on its ruins— and that under the mask of the development of equality between its peoples— several sovereign, independent and even mutually opposed nation-states are being created ... There is something insulting and demeaning in the fact that today we are all caught in the web of nationalism and are forced to deal with things that are not our greatest, let alone our only preoccupation ... The burden of nationalism that was thrust upon our shoulders by others, however, ... means that we must be aware of our historical responsibility towards the nation we belong to, and we must know that at this moment the question of identity and integrity, and the *legal and political unification* of the Serbian nation is of the greatest importance.[119]

Djurić argued that Serbs were unfairly being accused of 'centralism' and 'unitarism', whereas, in fact, centralism had been implemented after the war 'in order to prevent the raising of the question of *national* responsibilities for the genocide that had been carried out against the Serbs during the Second World War'.[120] Implying that the Croats as a nation were guilty of the genocide and that the creation of socialist Yugoslavia was merely a way of covering up that crime, Djurić's statement presaged one of the main themes of the Serbian national revival of the post-Tito period: that of the communist 'stab-in-the-back'.

Djurić concluded that the proposed constitutional change was 'aimed at the deepest existential interests' of the Serbian nation. Arguing that 'the Serbian nation has always been much more interested in Yugoslavia than any other nation, unfortunately, most often to its own detriment', he called for its 'sobering from the illusions of the past'.[121]

---

[118]Ž. Djordjević, ibid., p. 252. See also Gams, ibid., p. 240.
[119]Ibid., p. 231–2 (emphasis added.)
[120]Ibid., p. 232 (emphasis added.)
[121]Ibid., loc. cit.

It had to be recognised that Serbia's borders were neither national nor historical. The Serbian nation now had to turn to the struggle for its own existence, its threatened national identity and its unity and—instead of discussing the proposed constitutional amendments—had to strive for 'other, more serious, more responsible, historically founded solutions'.[122] By explicitly advocating the abandonment of Yugoslavism and the defence of Serbian political unity (presumably in a sovereign state with revised borders), Djurić went further than other participants in the debate. His presentation foreshadowed the discourse that would come to predominate in the mid-1980s.

Concurrently with the 'national' condemnation of the amendments, another, politically liberal, strand of intellectual critique of the system was appearing. The clearest expression of this tendency was the statement made by a lecturer, Kosta Čavoški, who criticised the way in which these amendments were being adopted (undemocratically, behind closed doors) and argued that main problem in Yugoslavia was not the proposed constitutional reform, but the lack of constitutionality itself. Citing John Locke's idea of limited government, he noted that the role of the legal order in a state was primarily to 'limit and control the state government and its representatives', but noted that, in Yugoslavia, constitutional provisions served 'some individual or group to secure the greatest and most permanent possible power, even to the end of their lives'.[123] He thus saw the proposal to make Tito Yugoslavia's president for life and the introduction of the veto into the federal and republican decisionmaking bodies as merely further manifestations of the desire to maintain this profoundly undemocratic status quo.[124]

Other participants in the debate effectively endorsed Čavoški's critique of the system. Stevan Djordjević also argued that 'for many years a large focusing of functions and power has been concentrated in one personality', which had provided for a level of arbitrariness and secrecy in decisionmaking, and called for 'normal democratic change' of Yugoslavia's leaders.[125] Stevan Vračar and Danilo Basta criticised the 'ossified and petrified personal structure' of Yugoslavia's

[122]Ibid., pp. 232–3 passim.
[123]Ibid., pp. 221–2.
[124]Ibid., p. 224.
[125]Ibid., p. 342.

leadership, characterising the amendments as the result of impenetrable deals between 'bureaucratic oligarchies' belonging to a 'vertically based, unchangeable and closed Party and state structure'.[126] Vojin Dimitrijević and Branislava Jojić emphasised that the devolution of power from the federation to the republics and provinces did not necessarily mean democratisation of the decisionmaking process and saw the decentralisation as simply giving in to irrational nationalist impulses.[127]

Finally, facing these 'nationalist' and 'liberal' critics was a small group of defenders of the Serbian regime's orientation, which favoured decentralisation.[128] They noted that communist Yugoslavia had been founded on the principle of both national and social liberation and was a community of diverse and fully formed nations. It, therefore, could not be maintained as a centralised state; in fact, they argued, resisting the other nations' desire for greater sovereignty would only strengthen separatism. Decentralisation also meant greater emancipation for Serbia, which could carry out its economic reform unhindered by federal control. Serbia had no more nor less of a stake in the existence of the federation than other republics and had to abandon the 'étatist' tradition in favour of a more modern approach. Integration in Yugoslavia could only be carried out through the economy, with the successful application of self-management. Rather than focusing on Serbian statehood, it was, therefore, more useful to promote economic integration through a relatively free and unhindered market. Only in this way would borders between the republics become meaningless.[129] The Law Faculty debate thus illustrated not only the emergence of the new nationalist platform among Serbian scholars, but the variety of approaches that existed among the intelligentsia both in assessments of the constitutional changes and of the national question. Soon such debates were forced 'underground', however, as a new wave of repression prepared, inaugurated by Tito's suppression of the Croatian 'spring' in December 1971.

[126]Ibid., pp. 335 and 356–8 respectively. See also Aleksandar Ivić, pp. 290–1, and Pavle Nikolić, p. 225.

[127]Ibid., pp. 246 and 269 respectively.

[128]For the Serbian 'liberal' regime's approval of decentralisation, see Slavoljub Djukić, *Slom srpskih liberala*, Belgrade, 1990, Latinka Perović, *Zatvaranje kruga*, Sarajevo, 1991, and D. Jović, op. cit., pp. 89–128.

[129]Miroslav Pečujlić, Vojislav Bakić, Aleksandar Vacić and Vera Petrić, in ibid., pp. 303–9, 309–11, 319–28 and 337–40 respectively.

The defence of civil rights, 1975–86

The massive purge of Croatia's Party and cultural institutions and the imprisonment of the 'mass movement's' student leaders and intellectuals gave rise in the republic to a wide sense of disillusionment with Yugoslavia and a gaining conviction that democratic change and sovereign statehood could only be achieved by secession from the common state. Because of continued repression, Croatian 'nationalists' gave little recognition to the fact that many of their initial demands for greater sovereignty were actually met by the constitutional changes that were taking place. For Yugoslavia the most important legacy of the Croatian 'mass movement' was that, for the first time since 1945, 'national homogenisation' had taken place in one republic—bringing together the Party leadership, intellectuals and wider segments of society—around the goal of creating a national state. The Croatian experience thus set a precedent for what was to take place in Serbia and Slovenia in the latter part of the 1980s.

With the crackdown on the Croatian 'spring', pressure mounted also on the Serbian 'liberal' leadership to suppress the challenges to the regime that were being launched by intellectuals and students. 1971 and 1972 witnessed a wave of interdictions of 'black wave' films and books by nonconformist intellectuals, including the Praxists, Dobrica Ćosić and members of the Serbian Literary Cooperative. These interdictions were accompanied by a number of political trials, first of several leaders of the 1968 student movement.[130] In July 1972 Professor Mihailo Djurić was sentenced to two years in prison for his presentation at the Law Faculty debate on constitutional change.[131] The *Annals of the Law Faculty*, which published the debate, was banned, along with the issue of *Student* that carried excerpts of the concurrent debate in Belgrade student union.[132] In October 1972, as the Serbian leadership faced its own political liquidation, Ćosić was forced to step down as president of the Cooperative; his resignation was accompanied by that of the entire board.

---

[130]These were Vladimir Mijanović (in 1970), Milan Nikolić, Jelka Kljajić and Pavluško Imširović (in 1972). Mijanović, Nikolić and Imširović would be tried again in the case of the 'Belgrade Six' in 1984. Božidar Jakšić, assistant at the Sarajevo Faculty of Philosophy, was also tried in 1973 (Danilović, op. cit., pp. 186–90).

[131]Danilović, op. cit., pp. 182–4. Djurić spent a total of nine months in prison.

[132]See 'Pokret studenata, profesora i književnika—protiv jednopartijske diktature', *Naša reč*, supplement XIV, 1971, p. 25.

The fall of the 'liberal' Party leadership in Serbia spelled out even harsher repression. In 1973 the young filmmaker Lazar Stojanović, former editor of both *Student* and *Vidici*, was sentenced to a year and a half in prison for his graduation project, a film called *The Plastic Jesus* (*Plastični Isus*), in which he used documentary newsreels of Hitler, Stalin and Tito in a way that allegedly 'equated the values of fascism with those of socialism'.[133] As Stojanović went to prison, his professors at the Belgrade Film Academy lost their jobs.[134] In 1974 the artist Mića Popović, who had also made several 'black wave' films, saw the closure of his exhibit at the Belgrade Cultural Centre because of his painting of Tito and his wife in full 'regal' paraphernalia next to a portrait of a Yugoslav worker on a train for Germany.[135] The 'black wave' was universally condemned by the new Serbian leaders as 'a false presentation of reality' and as an abuse of the principles of self-management.[136] Justifying this wave of repression, a series of articles appeared in Serbia's main news weekly *NIN* entitled 'From Djilas to Liberalism', linking all the facets of intellectual criticism into one large conspiracy.

Belgrade University was one of the main targets of repression. Designated by Tito himself as the primary instigators of the student movement, who had to be prevented from 'corrupting the youth', the Belgrade Praxists—Mihailo Marković, Ljubomir Tadić, Svetozar Stojanović, Zagorka Golubović, Miladin Životić, Dragoljub Mićunović and the younger lecturers Nebojša Popov and Trivo Indjić—now found themselves on the top of the Party's blacklist.[137] In 1973 the criterion of 'moral-political suitability' was introduced as a norm for employment, effectively legalising the discrimination against critical intellectuals and regime opponents.[138] In addition, a new provision was made for communist '*aktivs*' to be created in all cultural organisations. These small groups of Party members were supposed to monitor

---

[133]Quoted in Danilović, op. cit., p. 188. *The Plastic Jesus* was finally released in December 1990 and received the International Jury Critics' Award at the Montreal Film Festival in 1991. (On the case and the film see Lazar Stojanović, 'Ko behu disidenti', *Republika*, 182, 16–28 Feb. 1998, pp. vi–x, and Bogdan Tirnanić, *NIN*, 28 Dec. 1990, pp. 30–5.)

[134]Professors and 'black wave' filmmakers Aleksandar Petrović and Živojin Pavlović.

[135]For Popović's artistic and intellectual development see N. Miller, op. cit., pp. 524–33.

[136]*Politika*, 12 Jan. 1974.

[137]Tito's speech of 26 June, 1968 quoted in Sher, op. cit., p. 213.

[138]Popov, *Contra Fatum*, op. cit., p. 106.

the activities of their organisations and to exercise a kind of 'internal censorship'. In view of the considerable resistance in Belgrade University to the suspension of the Praxists, not only from students and faculty, but also from Party organisations, the law governing state-university relations was changed in 1975, allowing the state's direct interference in university affairs.[139] The suspension of the Belgrade professors was accompanied by the discontinuation of the Korčula summer school and *Praxis*, as well as *Filosofija*, the journal of the Philosophical Society of Serbia.[140] The political 'liberals' at the Law Faculty, many of whom had participated in the 1971 debate on constitutional change were also expelled from the Party and removed from their teaching jobs.[141] As the former student leader Lazar Stojanović put it on his release from prison in 1975, the atmosphere in the country resembled the late 1950s more than the relatively liberal period that had preceded his arrest.[142]

The main long-term consequence of the repression of the 1970s was that it dashed any remaining hopes that the Yugoslav system was reformable from within. For both students and professors, writers and filmmakers, the crackdown represented 'the moment of truth' which showed the face of autocratic rule for what it was and the impossibility of implementing truly liberal reforms.[143] It implied that any continuation of activism had to take place outside the existing structures and the Party, giving rise to new 'extra-systemic' forms of political protest akin to those employed by East European dissidents. By the time of Tito's death in 1980, three initial forms of intellectual activism developed: first, the drafting of open letters and petitions in

---

[139]Ibid., p. 181. The Dean of the Belgrade Philosophy Faculty, the historian Sima Ćirković, resigned his post when the 'suspension' of the Praxis professors was forced through by the law.

[140]Although these repressive measures affected the Croatian Praxists as well, none of them lost their jobs. This difference in treatment resided in the fact that the primary target of repression in Croatia after 1971 was Croatian nationalism rather than the 'new left'.

[141]Kosta Čavoški received a (suspended) five-month prison sentence for an article criticising the constitutional changes in the journal *Gledišta* and was subsequently dismissed from his teaching post, Stevan Vračar and Danilo Basta were expelled from the Party and prevented from teaching for seven years, Branislava Jojić received a Party 'reprimand' and moved to Mostar to continue teaching. Andrija Gams was sent into early retirement. Assistant Vojislav Koštunica, another liberal intellectual who had not participated in the debate, was excluded from the university and prevented from defending his PhD (Djukić, *Slom srpskih liberala*, op. cit., pp. 144–6).

[142]L. Stojanović, op. cit., p. ix.

[143]Svetozar Stojanović in Popov, *Contra Fatum*, op. cit., pp. 401–2.

the defence of civil rights, along lines inspired by the 'third basket' of the Helsinki Final Act of 1975; second, the launching of a 'flying university', denoting regular discussion groups held by proscribed intellectuals in private homes; and third, attempts at creating *samizdat* publications and journals, outside the control of the regime authorities. These activities were initiated by two groups of critical intellectuals, the 'new leftists' and the 'liberals', in collaboration with Dobrica Ćosić. From 1980, many of the prominent 'nationalists' also joined.

The 'petitionist' activity began in December 1976, with an open letter protesting the confiscation of passports from Yugoslav citizens, written by lawyer Srdja Popović, who had acted as defence counsel in many political trials, and signed by jurist Mihailo Djurić, seven of the Praxists purged in 1975[144] and several former student activists, who were all victims of this policy. The petition, which was presented as a general defence of freedom of movement eventually received a total of sixty signatures, mainly of assistants and university students of the Belgrade Philosophy Faculty.[145] Further petitions followed, demanding the abolition of the 'moral-political suitability' criterion as a requirement for employment (1978) and the establishment of freedom of the press (1979), as well as open letters supporting the founding of Charter 77 in Czechoslovakia (1977) and expressing 'solidarity with Solidarity' in Poland (1981).[146] In June 1980, one month after the death of Tito, thirty-six Belgrade intellectuals sent a petition to the new collective presidency of Yugoslavia demanding an amnesty for all political prisoners indicted for 'hostile propaganda'.[147] By December the same year this petition had turned into a more general demand to delete 'hostile propaganda' from the Yugoslav Criminal Code and had gathered 102 signatures, mainly in Belgrade but also in Zagreb and Ljubljana.[148] All these petitions were circulated through personal contacts and then sent to the state presidency and other political institutions by registered mail; copies were also sent to the main media and foreign correspondents.[149]

The second form of intellectual activity was the launching in 1976

---

[144]One of the purged *Praxists*, Trivo Indjić, accepted state employment following his ouster from Belgrade University and did not participate in the activities of the Belgrade critical intelligentsia.

[145]The text of the petition can be found in *Naša reč*, 283, 1977, pp. 3–5.

[146]See *Naša reč*: 295, May 1978, pp. 3–4; 303, March 1979, pp. 4–5; 284, Apr. 1977, pp. 3–4; and 332, Feb. 1982, p. 3.

[147]In *Human Rights in Yugoslavia*, op. cit., pp. 561–3.

[148]In ibid., pp. 567–80.

[149]Lazar Stojanović, author's interview, 28 Feb. 1998.

of the so-called 'flying university', a series of lectures and debates held in private people's homes modelled on similar actions in Czechoslovakia and Poland. From 1977 these informal gatherings multiplied and became regular occasions for critical intellectuals to meet and present their work covering topical and academic subjects, such as the concept of a just society, workers' participation in industrial democracies, the legal system under 'real' socialism, modern art, the humanist idea, the rise of Solidarity in Poland, the crisis of Marxism and the work of Leszek Kołakowski.[150] These meetings lasted until 1984 and were generally tolerated by the authorities, bringing together several hundred individuals, including visiting intellectuals from Zagreb, Ljubljana and other Yugoslav cities.

The final form of intellectual activity, attempted with less success in 1979 and 1980, was the creation of *samizdat* journals to expand the possibilities of free expression. The first of these attempts was made in 1979, when Milovan Djilas, Mihajlo Mihajlov and writers Dragoljub Ignjatović and Momčilo Selić launched a literary journal called *Časovnik* (*The Clock*). It was immediately banned and destroyed and its creators punished: Ignjatović was sentenced to one month in prison, Selić put on probation and Djilas fined. A warrant was issued for Mihajlov's arrest, forcing him to remain in the United States where he was lecturing at the time.[151] A second attempt, no more successful, was made by Dobrica Ćosić and Praxist Ljubomir Tadić in 1980. This journal, named *Javnost* (*The Public*), was launched to stimulate the free exchange of opinions between intellectuals from all parts of Yugoslavia and received considerable support in intellectual circles.[152] Once again, the Serbian authorities prohibited the journal and its two editors were subjected to a defamation campaign in the media.

One of the principal fears of the Yugoslav regime was that a transrepublican cooperation between critical intellectuals could come into being, providing the core for a countrywide political opposition.[153]

[150]See petition of 30 May 1984 in Branka Magaš, *The Destruction of Yugoslavia*, London, 1993, pp. 91–3.

[151]See *Radio Free Europe Research Report* 227, 17 Oct. 1979, pp. 3–4, and 235, 25 Oct. 1979, pp. 1–4, and *Naša reč*, 310, Dec. 1979, p. 13.

[152]According to Ćosić and Tadić, they sent out letters to over four hundred scholars and intellectuals throughout Yugoslavia announcing their intention to found the journal; by December 1980 they had received one hundred and twenty positive and only four negative responses ('Open Letter to the Supporters of *Javnost*', 6 Dec. 1980 in *Naša reč*, 321, Jan. 1981, p. 4).

[153]Aleksa Djilas, 'From Dissent to Struggle for Human Rights', in *Human Rights in Yugoslavia*, op. cit., pp. 400–1.

While some contacts between critical intellectuals in Serbia, Slovenia and Croatia did exist, they were mainly of a personal kind and through small groups. The difficulty of setting up inter-republican activities was partly due to the authorities' surveillance of communications between blacklisted intellectuals in the different republics; one of the main problems was the tapping of telephones, leading to an almost exclusive reliance on individuals travelling from one city to another.[154] In addition, persecution of nonconformist intellectuals in Croatia was considerably harsher than in Serbia and Slovenia, making a coordination of activities with the former more perilous.[155] Obstacles to inter-republican co-operation were not only the result of repression, however. In Croatia, most dissidents saw the central task as the achievement of national sovereignty, while the issue of one-party rule was less important, and they conditioned cooperation with Belgrade on the acceptance of Croatia's right to secede—a goal that was hardly conducive to unite dissidents across republican borders.[156]

The activities of Belgrade's critical intellectuals in the late 1970s remained marginal and without a wider public influence. Administrative obstacles were placed in the way of dissident actions, while the criterion of 'moral-political suitability' for employment squeezed out nonconformists from jobs that brought them into contact with the wider public and prevented them from disseminating their ideas. In addition, as Dobrica Ćosić put it,

In Yugoslavia's relatively happy, consumerist, hedonist, megalomaniac ecstasy the public word was powerless. In that noise of ovations to Tito, our critical whisper was not heard. Politics boycotted and attacked us, and the press followed the political mainstream. That is why we had a small influence and represented a sect without any larger impact.[157]

The very condition of their being 'intellectuals' also restricted their audience: the lofty theoretical level of their published work and the

[154]Petar Ladjević, author's interview, 28 Feb. 1998.

[155]Statistics on indictments for 'hostile propaganda' in the 1980s show that out of a total of 836 individuals indicted between 1981 and 1988, 505 were Albanians, followed by 172 Croats, 81 Serbs, 33 Muslims, 19 Slovenes, 7 Macedonians, 6 Montenegrins, 2 Hungarians and 5 'others' (*Borba*, 21 Oct. 1988).

[156]Matthew M. Mestrovic, 'Nationalism and Pluralism in Yugoslavia' in *Human Rights in Yugoslavia*, op. cit., p. 221. See also Marko Veselica's 1980 interview in Boris Katich (ed.), *So Speak Croatian Dissidents*, Toronto, 1983, p. 105. See also Mihajlo Mihajlov, in *Republika*, 1–15 Feb. 1998, p. viii.

[157]Quoted in Djukić, *Čovek u svom vremenu*, op. cit., p. 266.

relatively restricted orientation of their activities were not conducive to attracting a wider popular following.[158] This situation changed in the course of the 'post-Titoist' 1980s, with the progressive liberalisation of the cultural sphere and the onset of a deepening systemic crisis.

Tito's death in May 1980 removed the main pillar of authority of the Yugoslav regime and inaugurated a period of uncertainty, in which republican leaderships tried to establish a degree of legitimacy in their respective communities. In Serbia, as in Slovenia, Tito's death progressively gave rise to a new period of liberalisation. Ivan Stambolić's election to the presidency of the Belgrade City Committee in 1982 marked the beginning of a loosening of censorship and a less repressive approach towards critical intellectuals; as journalist Slavoljub Djukić put it, at the time 'it seemed that we were on the threshold of democratic rebirth'.[159] Although the Central Committee of the League of Communists of Serbia continued to hold sessions devoted to 'ideological waywardness' in culture and the media still participated in public 'witchhunts' of critical intellectuals, the sphere of public criticism and contestation of the system was, like in the 1960s, greatly extended. In contrast to the 1960s, however, liberalisation was this time taking place in a very different Yugoslavia—one that was ridden by economic problems, a crisis of legitimacy and worsening centrifugal tendencies. The rise of younger communists also inaugurated a new power struggle within Serbia's leadership, which lasted until 1987, when Slobodan Milošević managed to consolidate his power.[160]

This situation of flux and greater openness created the space for the forging of a wide, though informal, opposition umbrella movement within the intelligentsia, which was initially focused on the defence of civil rights. In addition to the already established activities—'petitionism', the 'flying university' and attempts at *samizdat*—the budding intellectual opposition revived the public debate of controversial subjects and adopted new forms of organisation and protest. The organisation of autonomous human rights committees and the holding of 'protest evenings' at the Writers' Association of Serbia were the most important of these, and their success in attracting wider public attention and large numbers of participants indicated the creation of an incipient 'civil society'.[161] Two key events that took place

---

[158]Sher, op. cit., pp. 264–5.
[159]Slavoljub Djukić, *Kako se dogodio vodja,* op. cit., p. 68.
[160]See Djukić, *Kako se dogodio vodja,* op. cit.
[161]Svetozar Stojanović, 'Ko je srušio komunizam?', *Intervju,* 28 March 1997, p. 61,

in the first half of the 1980s consolidated the Belgrade's intellectual opposition around the defence of civil rights: the sentencing of the poet Gojko Djogo for a book of poems in 1982 and the trial of several participants of the 'flying university' in 1984.

In June 1981 Djogo was arrested for 'hostile propaganda' and his just published collection of poems, *Vunena vremena* (Woollen times), was banned and destroyed. Six poems in the collection metaphorically alluded to Tito's rule as one of tyranny, indolence and ignorance and even implicitly referred to Yugoslavia's deceased leader as 'the old rat from Dedinje'.[162] Djogo's arrest and two-year prison sentence, pronounced in September 1981, took place concurrently with a wave of trials of Albanian demonstrators in Kosovo and of several well-known 'nationalist' intellectuals in Croatia, including future president Franjo Tudjman.[163] As Djogo himself noted ten years later, his case probably resulted from the necessity to 'balance' the crackdowns in Kosovo and Croatia with a show trial in Belgrade, proving to critics in the other republics that the Serbian leadership was not 'soft' on 'counterrevolutionary' manifestations in its own midst.[164]

The 'Djogo case' was the first time that 'poetry was being tried' in Yugoslavia and the veiled nature of the criticism contained in the poems made it possible to argue, as Djogo himself did, that poetry was an activity removed from politics.[165] Support for Djogo thus became a defence of the principle of freedom of literary and artistic creation, rather than a defence of freedom of expression regardless of any potentially subversive political content. This subtle but crucial

---

and Robert F. Miller, 'The Dilemmas of Civil Society in Yugoslavia: the Burden of Nationalism' in Robert F. Miller (ed.), *The Developments of Civil Society in Communist Systems*, Sydney, 1992, p. 93. 'Civil society' denotes a realm of autonomous, critical, but self-limiting public activity separate from the formal structures of the state.

[162]Gojko Djogo, *Vunena vremena* (1981), Belgrade, 1992; citation, p. 82. Djogo, a Bosnian Serb, later joined the Democratic Party. In 1991 he founded and presided the Belgrade-based Society of Serbs from Bosnia-Hercegovina, which aided the war effort of the Bosnian Serbs.

[163]In Kosovo, two hundred and forty-five sentences were pronounced between May and September of 1981, the average being eight years in prison (*South Slav Journal*, IV/3, 1981, p. 1). In Croatia, Franjo Tudjman was sentenced to three years in prison, Vlado Gotovac to two years, Dobroslav Paraga to three years, and Marko Veselica to eleven years. (On the trials of Croatian intellectuals see Danilović, op. cit., pp. 142–54.)

[164]*Politika*, 25 Feb., 1992, p. 26.

[165]Gojko Djogo, 'In My Defense', *PEN American Center Newsletter*, 52, Sept. 1983, pp. 1, 4–8 and *Naša reč*, 338, Oct. 1982, pp. 4–6.

difference made it possible for the first massive upsurge of public protest in the intelligentsia, which did not have to face the more threatening implications of defending somebody who was explicitly criticising the regime. This lowering of the stakes of activism in the Djogo case thus made it possible to forge a much wider coalition than the limited number of dissidents that had been engaged in public criticism of the regime so far. The practice of defending Djogo also enabled the crystallisation of a coalition between all the regime critics in the intelligentsia, regardless of their differing political orientations. The demands for the poet's acquittal thus not only swelled the ranks of the intellectual opposition, but brought together the 'nationalists', the 'new leftists' and the 'liberals'.[166]

Most importantly, this affair led to the establishment of the first institutional base of intellectual activism since the crackdowns of the early 1970s. The Writers' Association of Serbia, which until then mainly concerned itself with the organisation of literary debates and with the material problems of its members, became the centre of opposition activity. In May 1982, following the rejection of Djogo's appeal by the High Court of Serbia, a group of writers interrupted the assembly of the Writers' Association with the request to put the issue of freedom of creation on the top of the agenda and to take a more active stance in the defence of the poet. Dragoslav Mihailović, author of the banned 1968 play *When Pumpkins Blossomed*, criticised the way the Association's presidency had handled the case and proposed instead the creation of an independent committee within the institution, specifically charged with monitoring breaches of freedom of creation. The assembly adopted the proposal by a vast majority of votes, establishing the Committee for the Defence of Freedom of Creation.[167]

This debate marked the first public instance of the cleavage that was emerging within the Association between those who favoured 'cooperation' with the authorities and those who adopted a stance of 'no compromise'. The presidency represented the former, while the Committee for the Defence of Freedom of Creation and the

---

[166]For a complete list of signatories see *Naša reč*, 328, Oct. 1981, pp. 3–5 and 330, Dec. 1981, pp. 3–4.

[167]See *Književne novine*, 648, 27 May 1982. The proposal to create the Committee received forty-seven votes in favour and only five against (*Politika*, 20 May 1982). Its first members were Borislav Mihailović-Mihiz, Raša Livada, Milovan Danojlić, Stevan Raičković, Desanka Maksimović, Predrag Palavestra and Biljana Jovanović. (For the statutes of the Committee see *Književne novine*, 655, 30 Sept. 1982.)

Association journal, *Književne novine*, rallied together the latter.[168] From March 1982 *Književne novine* was edited by the poet Milutin Petrović, a non-Party 'liberal' intellectual, becoming increasingly politicised. It published favourable reviews of controversial books, petitions of the Committee for the Defence of Freedom of Creation, controversial articles and interviews and polemics between non-conformist intellectuals and their critics from the establishment. Critically reporting on the activities of the Association presidency, Petrović and his team increasingly came under pressure to change their 'editorial concept'. When *Književne novine* published as a separate pamphlet a new collection of 'unacceptable' poems,[169] the publishing council—a supervisory body made up of regime intellectuals—resigned, making it impossible for the journal to appear for over a year.

Things came to a head at the end of March 1983 when Djogo was finally taken to serve his sentence, after all his appeals had been rejected. His imprisonment sparked the organisation of a series of 'protest evenings' in the Writers' Association, which rallied together not only the activists from within the Association, but also the Praxists, the 'liberals' and the 'nationalists', leading the authorities to speak of 'a united opposition'.[170] The ten evenings that were held were a huge success, frequented by over three hundred people. Djogo's early release (on health grounds) was not followed by a renewed attempt to imprison him, which was perceived within the ranks of the intelligentsia as a victory. By May 1983 the increasingly free press was comparing the intelligentsia's activism to the Dreyfus case and the Writers' Association was becoming publicly perceived as the sanctuary of democratic values.[171] For Djogo—despite the fact that he was never officially pardoned—his case represented the first instance of the 'unstoppable demolition of the [communist] citadel' in Yugoslavia.[172]

The second case that contributed to the forging of Serbia's intel-

---

[168]Begun in 1948 as the weekly organ of the Yugoslav Writer's Union, *Književne novine*'s original mission was to propagate the dominant conception of literature and orient literary creation in Yugoslavia. In 1954 it became the organ of the Writers' Association of Serbia and, from 1957, it also included essays in philosophy, sociology and other disciplines.

[169]Ljubomir Simović, *Istočnice* in *Književne novine*, Apr. 1983 (see Chapter 2, pp. 109–10).

[170]*Politika*, 4 June 1983.

[171]*NIN*, 15 May 1983, and Drinka Gojković, 'Trauma bez Katarze' in *Srpska strana rata*, op. cit., pp. 366–7.

[172]*Pogledi*, 15 June 1990, p. 57.

lectual opposition took place in April 1984, following the police raid on an apartment in Belgrade where a group of the 'flying university' was listening to a presentation by Milovan Djilas.[173] The twenty-eight participants were arrested, and during the interrogations several of them were subjected to physical abuse; one attempted suicide in his cell and another was found dead a few days later under mysterious circumstances.[174] Although Djilas was released, he was immediately subjected a new campaign of abuse in the press.[175] The police investigation led to the indictment of four former 'sixty-eighters', who had been tried before (Vladimir Mijanović, Milan Nikolić, Pavluško Imširović and Dragomir Olujić), along with a journalist, Miodrag Milić, and an art history student, Gordan Jovanović. The trial of the 'Belgrade Six' was accompanied by that of the Bosnian Serb sociologist Vojislav Šešelj in Sarajevo.

The treatment of Šešelj testified to the different levels of repression that existed between Serbia and Bosnia-Hercegovina. Šešelj had first got into trouble with the local authorities when, as a young university assistant at the University of Sarajevo, he accused the a highly placed Bosnian functionary of plagiarism. His subsequent attacks on Bosnian Party intellectuals, whom he accused of Islamic fundamentalism, led to his exclusion from the League of Communists and his dismissal from the university.[176] In 1984 he sent an article to the Party organ *Komunist*, in which he argued that the League of Communists was incapable of reform and called for its 'disempowerment' and the reorganisation of the federation. Denying the specificity of the Muslim and Montenegrin nations, he advocated the abolition of the autonomous provinces and Serbia's unification with Montenegro, as well as the partition of Bosnia-Hercegovina between Serbia and Croatia.[177] Long a thorn in the side of the Bosnian regime, Šešelj's participation in the 'flying university' appeared to be a good occasion to finally put an end to his activities. In July 1984 he

[173]L. Stojanović, op. cit., p. x.
[174]The official cause of death was put down to suicide by poisoning, but the investigation was bungled and several pieces of evidence pointed to the improbability that this thirty-three-year-old man had taken his own life.
[175]See *NIN*, May–June 1984.
[176]Šešelj's articles were published in the literary journal of the Serbian youth organisation, *Književna reč*, 175, 25 Oct. 1981, p. 5; 177, 25 Nov. 1981, p. 3; and 179, 25 Dec. 1981, pp. 6–7.
[177]For Šešelj's article (in instalments) see *Naša reč*, 360, Dec. 1984, pp. 3–6; 361, Jan. 1985, pp. 3–5; 362, Feb. 1985, pp. 2–3; and 363, March 1985, pp. 2–3.

was sentenced to eight years in prison for 'counterrevolutionary activity'.[178]

In contrast to Šešelj's draconian sentence, the trial of the 'Belgrade Six' turned out to be a complete fiasco for the regime. The prosecution was able to get only one of their witnesses to actually testify against the defendants, while all the others spoke in their favour. Contrarily to the regime's intention, the trial turned into a tribunal against the system and its repression of free speech. Failing to prove 'counterrevolutionary organisation aimed at the overthrow of the constitutional order', the prosecution was forced to change its accusation to 'hostile propaganda', which represented a lesser crime. One of the six was acquitted, two saw their trials indefinitely postponed, while only three received sentences ranging from one to two years. Only one of the defendants actually ended up spending any time in prison.[179]

The trials of Šešelj and the 'Belgrade Six' sparked a near total mobilisation of the Belgrade intelligentsia and were accompanied by protests in Ljubljana and Zagreb. Compared to the earlier defence of poetry, the wording of many petitions of 1984 testifies to a radicalisation of the intellectual opposition. For example, an open letter signed by nineteen well-known Serbian intellectuals went so far as to call upon the Federal Minister of the Interior, Stane Dolanc, to 'take the consequences' of this unacceptable repression and resign.[180] Petitions, signed

---

[178]In November 1984, the High Court of Bosnia-Hercegovina changed the charge to 'hostile propaganda' and reduced Šešelj's sentence to four years. In July 1985 the Federal High Court reduced it to twenty-two months. Šešelj was released in March 1986 and moved to Belgrade. In 1989 he was proclaimed a Chetnik '*vojvoda*' by Momčilo Djujić, the only living holder of that title, exiled in the United States. During the 1990s his Chetnik movement, later renamed Serbian Radical Party, was the most extreme right-wing organisation in Serbia and its paramilitary wing directly intervened in the wars in Croatia and Bosnia; his party was then an on-and-off coalition partner for Milošević's Socialist Party.

[179]Imširović was acquitted, and Mijanović and Jovanović were temporarily discharged. In July 1985, Serbia's High Court acquitted Olujić as well and reduced Milić's and Nikolić's sentences. Milić only began serving his term in July 1986. (Danilović, op. cit., pp. 201–3)

[180]In *Naša reč*, 356, June 1984, p. 2. Nine of the signatories (Dobrica Ćosić, Borislav Mihajlović-Mihiz, Mića Popović, Dragoslav Mihailović, Mihailo Marković, Matija Bećković, Gojko Nikoliš, Kosta Čavoški and Zagorka Golubović) soon created the Committee for the Defence of Freedom of Thought and Expression. Other signatories included Antonije Isaković and Zoran Gavrilović, members of the Philosophy Society of Serbia and Vladimir Mijanović.

by unprecedented numbers of people, bombarded Serbian and Bosnian judges and political leaders for over a year; one such petition contained over two hundred names, including around forty from Croatia and Slovenia.[181] Domestic protest was accompanied by international pressure on the Yugoslav authorities to release the defendants.[182]

The cases of Šešelj and the 'Belgrade Six' also gave rise to the creation of new dissident committees, which now began to defend the freedom of expression even of those individuals who were openly opposed to the regime. The most important of these was the Committee for the Defence of Freedom of Thought and Expression created by Dobrica Ćosić in 1984. Already one of its first open letters, the 'Proposal for the Abolition of Unjustified Limitations to the Freedom of Thought and Expression' of March 1985, showed that a step had been taken beyond the simple demand for the abolition of 'hostile propaganda' clause. It questioned the Party's legitimacy in determining what constitutes 'false representation of socio-political conditions in the country' (for which critical intellectuals were tried) and called for the respect of 'the citizens' right to criticise the state leadership', thus directly undermining the Party's role as ideological vanguard. It concluded that in a democratic society, laws were based on the consensus of citizens, who express their will through a representative lawmaking body.[183] In this way the Committee put into question the very legitimacy of the Yugoslav regime, not only by rejecting its monopoly over questions of truth and falsehood, but also by contesting its claim of representing the popular will.

During the remainder of the decade, the Committee defended individuals throughout Yugoslavia whose right to free speech had been violated, including both Kosovo Serb activists and Albanians, Muslim intellectuals tried for Islamic Fundamentalism (including future president of Bosnia-Hercegovina, Alija Izetbegović) and Catholic and Orthodox clergymen, Croatian 'nationalists' (including Franjo Tudjman, the future president of Croatia, and several future leaders of Croatian political parties) and Slovenian activists (future members of the Slovenian government and opposition). Its 'Proposal for the Establishment of Rule of Law' of October 1986 demanded the abolition of the one-party system and the Party's monopoly over all

---

[181]In *Naša reč*, 357, Aug.-Sept. 1984, pp. 3–4.

[182]For all these interventions, see Danilović, op. cit., pp. 202–3.

[183]Committee for the Defence of Freedom of Thought and Expression, *Dokumenti i saopštenja 1984–1986*, Belgrade, 1986, pp. 23–4.

social spheres, and called for free elections, the right to free political association, a free press and the establishment of an independent judiciary.[184]

The Committee was made up of nineteen politically heterogeneous intellectuals, covering several generations and the whole spectrum of opinion in the Belgrade intelligentsia. Ranging in age from thirty-eight to seventy-four, its members included representatives of the 'new left' (Mihailo Marković and Ljubomir Tadić), the 'liberal' opposition (Kosta Čavoški, Nikola Milošević and Ivan Janković), the former 'black wave' (Dragoslav Mihailović and Mića Popović) and protagonists of the 'nationalist' critique of the Yugoslav system (Borislav Mihajlović-Mihiz, Matija Bećković, Tanasije Mladenović and Andrija Gams). Several had been on the board of the Serbian Literary Cooperative at the time of Ćosić's presidency (the historians Radovan Samardžić and Dimitrije Bogdanović, along with Mihajlović-Mihiz, Popović and Marković). One (the artist Mladen Srbinović) had been associated with Mihajlo Mihajlov's effort to create an independent political party in 1966. Four were also involved in the Committee for the Defence of Freedom of Creation of the Writers' Association of Serbia (Predrag Palavestra, a literary historian and president of the PEN Club of Serbia, along with Mihailović, Mihajlović-Mihiz, and Nikola Milošević). Three members had not been involved in 'dissident' activities before, which signalled a widening of intellectual discontent with the regime. The most significant of these was Gojko Nikoliš, whose impeccable communist pedigree (he was a veteran of the Spanish Civil War, a former Partisan General, a National Hero and a onetime diplomat) showed how badly the regime's legitimacy had been eroded.[185] Later the Committee was enlarged to include Praxist Zagorka Golubović, liberal intellectuals Vojislav Koštunica and Vesna Pešić and, finally, just before its demise in 1989, composer Enriko Josif.

Aside from the obvious effort to bring together a wide coalition of regime opponents, the other prominent marker of this group was that the majority of its members belonged to the Serbian Academy of Sciences and Arts.[186] Created in 1886 as the Royal Serbian Academy

---

[184]Ibid., p. 84.

[185]The other two were the archaeologist and Serbian academician Dragoslav Srejović and the sociologist Neca Jovanov.

[186]With Josif there were fourteen academicians. The other thirteen were Ćosić, Bećković, Bogdanović, Marković, Mihailović, Milošević, Nikolić, Palavestra, Popović, Samardžić, Srbinović, Srejović and Tadić.

and revived in 1946 under its new name, Serbia's most important cultural institution was brought into compliance by the communist regime in the aftermath of the war, symbolised by the election of both Tito and Edvard Kardelj as honorary members. Since the 1970s, however, it gained a reputation of harbouring nonconformist intellectuals.[187] Although most of the approximately one hundred and forty academicians generally remained apolitical, the Academy provided a second important institutional basis (along with the Writers' Association) for the activism of critical intellectuals. In May 1984 Dobrica Ćosić made an impassioned speech at its annual assembly, stating that the historical moment was 'fateful for the future of the people and the culture which we serve' and that the Academy had to break out of its 'conformist inertia' and become involved in the search for solutions to the country's deep crisis.[188] The participation of thirteen academicians in his Committee was one clear sign that the Academy was experiencing a political awakening; the other was the unanimous decision at the 1985 assembly to create a committee which would draft a 'Memorandum' to the Serbian and Yugoslav authorities accounting for the causes of the crisis and proposing new directions for policy.[189]

Belgrade's importance as the centre of opposition activity in Yugoslavia was confirmed when, in 1984, the ideologically conservative Croatian Party leadership put together a document 'on certain ideological and political tendencies in artistic creation, literary, theatre and film criticism, and on public statements of a number of cultural creators which contain politically unacceptable messages', more commonly known as the 'White Book'.[190] This document, which provided the basis for a public seminar held in the Zagreb Party headquarters, was created 'mainly to help the struggle of the League of Communists of Serbia against such occurrences', since the Serbian

[187]Notably Ćosić himself, along with Mića Popović, Dragoslav Mihailović, Matija Bećković, Mihailo Marković, Nikola Milošević, Predrag Palavestra and Ljubomir Tadić, who all became members in the 1970s or early 1980s. Ćosić explicitly admitted that he used to speak of the Academy with condescension while he was in the communist establishment and that it became a shelter for him after his fall (see Djukić, *Čovek u svom vremenu*, op. cit., pp. 235–6). Ćosić's speech to Academy of 1977 was one of the first important statements of the new Serbian nationalism (see Chapter 2).

[188]In *Naša reč*, 358, Oct. 1984, pp. 2–3.

[189]On the Memorandum see Chapter 4.

[190]The full text of this document was not published until 1989, when it appeared as a special issue of the weekly *Intervju* (special edition, 11, 10 May 1989).

leadership was being 'soft' on the 'widespread ideological counter-revolution' taking place in its republic.[191] Serbian intellectuals made up by far the greatest number of the over two hundred blacklisted individuals, and even the criticised Croatian and Slovenian intellectuals were attacked mainly for their publications in Serbia.[192] The reaction to this new offensive showed how far intellectual opposition had evolved from its tentative beginnings a few years back. Undaunted, the proscribed intellectuals branded the 'White Book' a 'police dossier' and a 'neo-Stalinist manifesto', while Belgrade-based Croatian literary critic Igor Mandić, himself blacklisted, compiled an 'index autorum prohibitorum' to 'aid' the witchhunt.[193] It was ironically remarked at the time that to be left off this list, which included the most prominent names of Serbian culture, was the greatest possible blow to an intellectual's prestige. The 'White Book' confirmed what was already common knowledge by the middle of the post-Titoist decade: that Belgrade had become the centre of the intellectual opposition in Yugoslavia and that, aside from a massive crackdown like in the early 1970s, there was very little that could be done to stop this momentum.

In the second half of the 1980s a myriad of new independent organisations mushroomed, testifying to the reluctance of the regime to stage such a crackdown.[194] The atmosphere was also becoming increasingly liberal in the rest of Yugoslavia, as developments particularly in Slovenia indicated.[195] This change of climate led in 1986 to the emergence of the first independent all-Yugoslav organisation, the

[191]Branko Puharić a member of the Central Committee of the League of Communists of Croatia, and Stipe Šuvar, the Party's main ideologue, in *NIN*, 3 June, 1984, pp. 29 and 31 respectively. (For the motives behind the initiative and the Serbian leadership's reaction see D. Jović op. cit., pp. 218–23.)

[192]See Slovene intellectual Dimitrij Rupel's statement in *Književna reč*, 238–40, 1984, p. 6. Of the listed intellectuals 170 were Serbs.

[193]For the petitions see *Naša reč*, 357, Aug.-Sept. 1984, p. 2, and for Mandić's citation, *Književna reč*, 238–40, Summer 1984, p. 5.

[194]Notably, the Yugoslav chapter of the International Helsinki Federation in October 1987 and the Yugoslav Forum for Human Rights in 1988. In Serbia, a further Committee for the Defence of Human Rights was created in 1987, along with two other committees (for the defence of the environment and for the defence of human rights) in the Writers' Association. (For all their petitions, see *Naša reč*, 1987–90. For the Yugoslav Forum for Human Rights see also *Danas*, 14 June 1988, pp. 17–18, and the interview with its president, Vojin Dimitrijević, in ibid., 7 July 1989, pp. 17–19.)

[195]See Chapter 4.

'Solidarity Fund', which was created to provide financial and material aid to 'all those whose existence is threatened because of their critical views and social activism'.[196] The Fund arose spontaneously by a group of journalists to help their colleague Dušan Bogavac, who had lost his job with the newspaper *Komunist* following the arrest of Vojislav Šešelj.[197] Very soon, it gained over two hundred adherents, which included virtually all the 'new left' activists and 'liberals' in Yugoslavia, along with a large number of journalists, students and even some workers.[198] The Solidarity Fund represented the last glimmer of hope that a pan-Yugoslav opposition could come together. It was soon suppressed by the authorities and its founding assembly scheduled for March 1987 had to be indefinitely postponed. Although it continued to issue petitions against breaches of the freedom of the press and provide financial aid to individuals who had come into conflict with the regime, the Fund never materialised into the inter-republican political opposition its initiators had had in mind.[199] Instead, by the end of 1988, when opposition parties began to be organised, Yugoslavia's various particularist nationalisms had won the day. In Serbia the nationalist revival began with the 'outburst of history' after Tito's death.

[196]The Fund's statutes, in *Naša reč*, 385, May 1987, pp. 8–9. An earlier initiative by Dobrica Ćosić to create an all-Yugoslav committee fell flat (see Chapter 4).

[197]Šešelj had sent Bogavac an uncommissioned article for his column 'What is to be Done?', which led to Šešelj's arrest. Although Bogavac denied ever receiving it, he was still dismissed.

[198]'Saopštenje br. 8', 26 Dec. 1986, in Dušan Bogavac, *Kako iz beznadja*, Belgrade, 1989, pp. 366–8. See also *Danas*, 3 March 1987, pp. 16–18, and the petitions in *Naša reč*, 1987–9.

[199]For the intentions and the developments associated with the Fund, see the documentation in Bogavac, op. cit., pp. 351–87.

2

THE 'OUTBURST OF HISTORY' AND
THE NEW SERBIAN NATIONALISM

Tito's death in May 1980 changed very little for Yugoslavia on the surface. The transition of power to the collective presidency was smooth, the agreed strategy of the leadership was continuity 'along Tito's path' and the lavish state funeral of Yugoslavia's late leader symbolised the commitment of his successors to maintaining the status quo. Appearances hid underlying tensions, however. As the journalist Slavoljub Djukić put it, 'Everything was as before—the political leadership, the army, police, censored press. But nothing was really as before.'[1] The collective presidency, dubbed during Tito's lifetime 'Tito and the eight dwarfs',[2] lacked both vision and unity of purpose to deal with the challenges of the 1980s, while the country descended into economic and political crisis. By 1986 Yugoslavia's very existence seemed to be at stake. As one Western scholar put it at the time, 'it might not be long before the country simply disintegrated—peacefully, if true 'confederation' were achieved, or violently, if nationalist programmes were to escalate'.[3]

This context of deepening crisis and the increasingly public differences within the leadership created the space for the propagation of an all-encompassing critique of Yugoslavia's system and for the articulation of new ideas to replace the old. As the official version of Yugoslavia's history was progressively abandoned in favour of new

[1]Djukić, *Kako se dogodio vodja*, op. cit., p. 15.
[2]Cited in Stevan K. Pavlowitch, *Tito: Yugoslavia's Great Dictator*, London, 1992, p. 87.
[3]Steven Burg, 'Elite Conflict in Post-Tito Yugoslavia', *Soviet Studies*, XXXVIII/2, 1986, p. 189.

legitimising myths of the individual federal units, in Serbia too a new nationalist vision came to fill the emerging vacuum. It centred around notions of permanent victimisation and a communist 'stab in the back' and a portrayal of the common Yugoslav state as the vehicle of the Serbs' destruction as a nation. Originated within the 'nationalist' strand of the intellectual opposition in the 1970s and articulated primarily by writers, philosophers and jurists, rather than professional historians, by the middle of the post-Titoist decade this vision had radicalised, spread and come to predominate throughout all strands of the intelligentsia.

The crisis of the 1980s and the breakdown of official historiography

Tito's death coincided with the onset of a grave economic crisis.[4] By 1980 Yugoslavia had depleted its foreign reserves and accumulated an external debt of $19 billion. Western Europe's economic recession following the second 'oil shock' of 1979 contributed to Yugoslavia's balance-of-payments deficit, dried up the influx of 'petrodollars' which were keeping the economy afloat, and stemmed the flow of 'guest worker' remittances. Yugoslavia's failure to adjust to changing world economic trends was compounded by years of economic mismanagement and accumulated inefficiencies. From 1983 shortages of food and basic commodities forced the government to issue ration tickets and, by 1985, the population living below the poverty line increased to 25%, unemployment reached 14%, while inflation skyrocketed to 80%.[5]

Both international financial institutions and many Yugoslav experts considered that a major cause of the economic decline was 'the gradual shaping up of six "national" economies within the system, which effectively excluded integrative and reintegrative forces'.[6] The

---

[4]See Harold Lydall, *Yugoslavia in Crisis*, Oxford, 1989; David A. Dyker, *Yugoslavia: Socialism, Development and Debt*, London, 1990; and Susan Woodward, *Socialist Unemployment: The Political Economy of Yugoslavia, 1945–90*, Princeton, 1995.

[5]Susan Woodward, *Balkan Tragedy*, Washington, DC, 1995, pp. 52–7.

[6]Vesna Bojičić, 'The Disintegration of Yugoslavia: Causes and Consequences of Dynamic Inefficiency in Semi-command Economies', in David A. Dyker and Ivan Vejvoda (eds), *Yugoslavia and After*, London, 1996, p.34. See also Milica Žarković-Bookman, 'The Economic Basis of Regional Autarchy in Yugoslavia', *Soviet Studies*, XLII/1, 1990, pp. 93–109. For a contrasting view see Ivo Bićanić, 'Fractured Economy' in *Yugoslavia and After*, op. cit., pp. 120–41.

'de-étatisation' of the economy announced by the reforms of the 1960s had stopped at the level of the republics and provinces, leaving economic management in the hands of highly politicised local and regional bosses, closely cooperating with their respective leaderships. Until 1980 the Federal Executive Council had managed to 'broker' among the different regional interests, aided by the inflow of foreign credits and Tito's authority. After Tito's death, however, the largely 'confederalised' structure set up in the 1970s began to expose itself as unworkable. The Constitution of 1974 had effectively replicated the Party-state model on the local level and endowed the federal units with a jealously guarded 'proto-statehood',[7] so that by the 1980s, even assessing the dimensions of the economic crisis was impeded by the lack of accountability of the regional leaderships to the centre: the International Monetary Fund thus could not get a figure for total outstanding debt from the Yugoslavs because the various republic and province authorities had borrowed money without bothering to tell each other or the Federal Executive Council![8] The system of decisionmaking by consensus on the federal level and the locally-controlled implementation of reforms effectively blocked any genuine changes. It became increasingly clear that resolving the economic crisis would have to go hand-in-hand with political reform.

In this context of generalised social and economic distress, Serbia's situation was closer to that of the less developed republics than to Slovenia and Croatia. For example, 'inner' Serbia's unemployment rate in the 1980s remained at 17–18%, while Slovenia maintained near full employment until 1989 and Croatia's rates stayed under 10% throughout.[9] In May 1984 the Serbian press reported that a new wave of rural exodus towards Belgrade was beginning, although a poll undertaken in the city the previous year showed that only 16% of Belgraders felt they could cover their living expenses with their earnings, while 46% said they could do so only with great difficulty and sacrifices.[10] In addition, economic planners also disclosed that, although Serbia had fallen below average in all relevant indicators, Serbia's contribution to the federal budget remained calculated on the premise that it was a developed republic.[11] By March 1985 even

---

[7]Ivan Vejvoda, 'Yugoslavia 1945–91—From Decentralisation Without Democracy to Dissolution' in *Yugoslavia and After*, op. cit., p. 15.

[8]Flora Lewis, 'Reassembling Yugoslavia', *Foreign Policy*, 98, 1995, pp. 140–1.

[9]Woodward, *Balkan Tragedy*, op. cit., pp. 51–3.

[10]*NIN*, 30 Oct., 1983, pp. 12–14, and *Politika*, 6 May 1984.

[11]*Politika*, 6 May 1984.

the federal parliament openly acknowledged that Serbia was falling behind economically.[12]

Serbia's leadership became the champion of the federal government's 'Economic Stabilisation Programme' of 1983, which called for both the continued 'de-étatisation' of the economy and the promotion of 'our common interests'.[13] Although genuinely convinced that economic reform and political reintegration went hand in hand, Serbia's communists also saw in this strategy a chance to resolve their own overarching internal problem—the question of the republic's territorial integrity. As a prominent member of the Serbian Central Committee noted in 1982, 'maybe the criticism of the centrifugal tendencies in our society is louder in Serbia than elsewhere, but this is because such tendencies have put into question the unity of our republic, which is not the case with any other republic'.[14] In the Serbian leadership there was a deep sense of injustice at the fact that 'Serbia was cut in three' while all the republics were becoming internally more unified and centralised.[15] These grievances had already been outlined in an internal Party document in 1977, known as the 'Blue Book', which proposed to reintegrate (though not abolish) the autonomous provinces, but which had been rejected by the other federal units and Tito himself.[16]

The raising of Kosovo and Vojvodina to the level of republics in all but name during the 1970s, while formally maintaining them as part of the republic, effectively made Serbia a Yugoslavia in miniature.[17] On the one hand, the provinces—like the Yugoslav republics—received all the trappings of statehood, such as their own legal, political and education systems, national symbols and institutions, police force and even territorial armies, the right independently to change their constitutions, pursue relations with other countries and have veto power in the federal decisionmaking bodies.[18] The main difference

---

[12]*NIN*, 10 March 1985, pp. 14–15.

[13]*NIN*, 30 May 1982, p. 14. See also Woodward, *Balkan Tragedy*, op. cit., pp. 58–72, and Dennison Rusinow, 'Nationalities Policy and the "National Question"' in Pedro Ramet (ed.), *Yugoslavia in the 1980s*, Boulder, CO: 1985, pp. 144–5.

[14]Ibid., p. 15.

[15]Ivan Stambolić, *Put u bespuće*, Belgrade, 1995, p. 57.

[16]Although the existence of the document was no longer a secret after the mid-1980s, it was only published in Belgrade in 1990. (See Veljko Vujačić, 'Institutional Origins of Contemporary Serbian Nationalism', *East European Constitutional Review*, V/4, 1996, pp. 51–61, and D. Jović, op. cit., pp. 157–62.)

[17]This point is well made by D. Jović, op. cit., pp. 157–8.

[18]Vejvoda, op. cit., pp. 15–16.

between the republics and the provinces was the former's right to secession, which the latter did not have. Even this was problematic, however, due to the constitution's lack of clarity: was the right to secession reserved for the republics or for the 'constitutive nations' of Yugoslavia (Serbs, Croats, Slovenes, Montenegrins, Macedonians and Muslims)?[19]

On the other hand, the provinces still nominally remained a part of Serbia, which meant that, in practice, consensus was required between all three for all decisions pertaining to the republic and even just to 'inner' Serbia. Affirming their independence, the representatives of Vojvodina and Kosovo not only consistently voted against Serbia in federal bodies and refused any consultation with Serbia's leadership in their affairs, but they also blocked decisions on the level of the republic, making it impossible to pass a number of vital laws and implement economic reform.[20] In a situation of worsening economic crisis, some sort of constitutional clarification of this incongruence was required: either the subordination of the provinces to the republic, or a formal acknowledgement of the prevailing practice by the creation of three completely independent units.

The unrest that broke out in Kosovo in the spring of 1981, whose key demand was the creation of a 'Kosovo Republic', provided an excellent opportunity for Serbian communists to press for their preferred solution: reducing the autonomy of the provinces. A three-day plenum of the Serbian Central Committee in December 1981 pitted the leaderships of the republic and the provinces against each other.[21] While Serbia's leaders condemned 'the rise of 'autonomist' exclusivity' and demanded that the provinces recognise that they are the republic's constitutive units, Vojvodina's representatives warned that any policy 'which sees the solution in a change of the established constitutional relations is unacceptable'.[22] This Vojvodinian defence of its independence showed to what extent a federal unit could develop its own and, in this case non-ethnic, form of nationalism (officially called 'étatism').[23] With a generational change in the Serbian Party elite and Ivan Stambolić's rise to power in 1984, the Serbian leadership

[19]Vojin Dimitrijević, 'Sukobi oko ustava iz 1974' in Popov (ed.), *Srpska strana rata*, op. cit., pp. 447–72.

[20]On these conflicts see D. Jović, op. cit., p. 159.

[21]The Kosovo leadership was more subdued due to the pressures on it following the 1981 demonstrations.

[22]*NIN*, 3 Jan. 1982, p. 28.

[23]The Vojvodinian leadership was predominantly ethnically Serbian.

became increasingly assertive on the issue of the republic's unity, although it maintained its commitment to achieve this only through negotiation and internal Party consensus.[24] At first Serbian communists did not dare question the constitution of 1974 *per se*, but condemned the 'false interpretation of autonomy' by the provinces.[25] By 1985, however, Stambolić was openly calling for constitutional change in the defence of 'the interests of the Serbian people', most importantly, the right of the Serbian nation 'to create its own state, like the other nations of Yugoslavia'.[26]

As before, the Serbian leadership's call for its republic's reintegration was blocked, not only by the provinces but also by other republics, particularly Slovenia and Croatia, who saw it as the first step towards recentralisation of the federation and a loss of the gains made since the 1960s. Slovenia, which led the 'confederalist' camp since the 1971 crackdown on the Croatian 'spring', also increasingly began to see Yugoslavia as more of a liability than an asset. It was opposed to a further influx of workers from the 'south' and wanted to avoid any higher contributions to the Federal Fund, even renewing the demand for the local retention of foreign currency holdings.[27] Politically, the Slovenian Party also resisted any infringements upon its sovereignty. In 1981 Milan Kučan, the rising star of the Slovenian Party and later the republic's first democratically elected President, argued that, although the federal units acted 'as states and not as self-managing communities', it was necessary to maintain consensus-based decision-making in federal bodies to 'guarantee equality and sovereignty of republics and provinces'.[28] In April 1982 the Slovenian Central Committee issued a clear warning to its Yugoslav partners that 'any attempt to change anything in the present system would mean a grave danger for our unity'.[29]

By 1983 the press began to reveal the depth of the divisions within the leadership. Although in its subsequent meetings the Central Committee adopted a set of resolutions to strengthen the powers of the federal institutions and openly admitted 'dissatisfaction with the situation', it nevertheless stopped short of proposing a different method of decisionmaking or a redistribution of authority between the republics

[24]Stambolić, op. cit., pp. 59–61.
[25]*NIN*, 27 Dec. 1981, p. 19.
[26]*NIN*, 8 Sept. 1985, p. 14.
[27]Woodward, *Balkan Tragedy*, op. cit., pp. 61–2.
[28]*Komunist*, 17 Dec. 1981.
[29]*NIN*, 25 Apr. 1982, p. 8.

and the federation.[30] By the end of 1985 the debates on political and economic reform both in the Republic of Serbia and on the federal level had reached a stalemate, as was made clear by the increasing number of temporary measures undertaken by the Federal Executive Committee, the paralysis of the collective presidency and the inability of the Federal Assembly to pass important laws.[31]

This growing political polarisation was mirrored in the cultural sphere. The subordination of scholarship to political needs was a problem already endemic to the Yugoslav system. In the period immediately following the Second World War, Yugoslav historiography, like all other disciplines, had been put in the service of the revolution. In line with the adoption of Soviet methods, 'history was made to begin when the Communist Party went over to the resistance in 1941. All the rest was prehistory leading to that event'.[32] Although the ruling communists allowed the pre-war historical establishment to continue its work on certain periods (notably Byzantine and Medieval history) without significant interference, the study of modern history was strictly controlled. The 1948 break with the Soviet Union, however, cut short the subordination of Yugoslav scholarship to the Soviet model, allowing progressive liberalisation to take place. The establishment of cooperation with Western countries also made Yugoslav historians familiar with Western historical methods and ideas and allowed numerous opportunities for study abroad and for international exchanges.

However, despite these changes ideological and methodological restrictions remained:

The Yugoslav communist regime never renounced its Marxist direction in all areas of culture, including historiography, although it contented itself with little ideology. No polemics were allowed on basic and universal principles of Marxist methodology (although their vulgarisation in other socialist countries could be denounced), certain conventions of terminology and periodisation had to be observed, social and economic themes were favoured, especially the history of the workers' and socialist movements, while party and military history were fostered in special, parallel institutions.[33]

[30]Burg, 'Political Structures', op. cit., p. 19.

[31]For example, in 1983 only eight of the twenty-five major laws considered by the Federal Assembly were passed. The other seventeen had to be shelved. (Pedro Ramet, 'Apocalypse Culture and Social Change in Yugoslavia' in *Yugoslavia in the 1980s*, op. cit., p. 9)

[32]Stevan K. Pavlowitch, *The Improbable Survivor*, London, 1988, p. 129.

[33]Sima Ćirković, 'Historiography in Isolation: Serbian Historiography Today', *Helsinki Monitor*, special issue, 1994, p. 37.

Even after liberalisation, several 'holy cows' had to be observed in the writing of history: first, the inherently positive value of Yugoslav unification as the accomplishment of the 'historical strivings' of the different Yugoslav peoples; second, the negative nature of the interwar Yugoslav regime, depicted as a 'monarcho-fascist dictatorship' and subject to 'Greater Serbian hegemony' (supported by other non-Serbian 'bourgeoisies'); and, third, the official interpretation of the 'war of national liberation' and the communist revolution.

During the phase of 'socialist Yugoslavism' in the 1950s, a series of joint projects were sponsored to promote Yugoslav unity, notably the launching of the *Encyclopedia of Yugoslavia*, under the directorship of Croatia's most prominent writer Miroslav Krleža. With the onset of decentralisation, however, republican and provincial historians increasingly gave primacy to their own 'national' histories and, from the end of the 1960s 'it became increasingly clear that the unity of Yugoslav historiography was dependent on regime unity'.[34] Although initially political decentralisation was accompanied by a freeing of scholarship from political control, after the purges of the 'liberal' republican leaderships in the early 1970s the situation changed again, as the combination of decentralisation and reimposed dogmatism effectively subordinated official historiography to the interests of the Party leaderships of the different federal units. The growing tendency to limit work to institutions sponsored by the individual republics or provinces compounded the problem of establishing universal scholarly criteria for historical study and promoted local Party intellectuals of dubious qualifications to positions of prominence.

As historians increasingly served local Party interests and legitimised their own national 'proto-states', common Yugoslav nation-building projects suffered. Both the *History of the Peoples of Yugoslavia* and the *History of the Communist Party/League of Communists of Yugoslavia* came to a standstill already in the early 1970s, replaced by officially sponsored projects for new histories of the various Yugoslav peoples and their 'proto-states'.[35] By the 1980s the disagreements surrounding these

[34]Ivo Banac, 'Historiography of the Countries of Eastern Europe: Yugoslavia', *American Historical Review*, XCVII/4, 1992, p. 1086.

[35]See the letter to the editor by Slovenian historian Bogo Grafenauer in *NIN*, 24 Apr. 1983, p. 4. The *History of the Peoples of Yugoslavia*, of which Grafenauer was editor, got stuck on the volume dealing with the 19th century, when the different South Slav national movements arose. The divergent scholarly visions, particularly between Croatian, Bosnian and Serbian historians, are also captured in the polemic over the

projects were given increased public airing thanks to the liberalisation of the press. This transparency, in turn, radicalised the positions of the different participants, who were now aware that they were not only catering to their respective leaderships but to public opinion in their federal units. In the course of the post-Titoist decade, these divisions reached their paroxysm, as was evident in the vicissitudes of the most ambitious and most publicised common enterprise, the second edition of the *Encyclopedia of Yugoslavia*.

Begun in 1975, this revised version of the '*Yugoslavica*' was hailed by the federal leadership as a 'historical milestone both from a cultural and from a social viewpoint'.[36] Yet from the start the project was plagued by the necessity of reconciling the divergent positions of all the different republican and provincial committees. As one of the editors of the project, Belgrade historian Sima Ćirković, later noted, 'the greatest sin of the *Encyclopedia* was the acceptance of dividing history along republic and province borders, instead of showing, in accordance with the facts, that three, five or six centuries ago divisions were of a different nature'.[37] The initial negotiations dragged on until the end of 1979, when participants finally reached agreement on financing and the *Encyclopedia* entries. The result of this first set of political compromises was an expensive and ambitious project, which was to publish six parallel sets in all the languages and alphabets of the Yugoslav 'nations and nationalities', along with a condensed two-volume version in English, amounting to a total of more than 80,000 complete sets and 850,000 volumes.[38]

When the first volume of the *Encyclopedia* appeared at the end of 1980, it immediately gave rise to heated polemics. The main problem concerned the entries 'Albanians' and 'Albanian-Yugoslav Relations' written by Kosovo Albanian historians and officially approved by the Presidency of the Province Committee of the League of Communists of Kosovo.[39] As the Italian historian Marco Dogo has noted, Kosovo Albanian historiography contained 'trends and vices which anticipated Serbian developments by fifteen years' and presented 'an important

1972 *History of Yugoslavia*. (See Michael Boro Petrovich, 'Continuing Nationalism in Yugoslav Historiography', *Nationalities Papers*, VI/2, 1978, pp. 161–77)

[36]1976 declaration of Josip Vrhovec, member of the Central Committee of the LCY and, in 1984–9, Croatia's representative to the Federal Presidency, reprinted in *NIN*, 3 Aug. 1986, p. 18.

[37]*NIN*, 26 July 1991, p. 20.

[38]*NIN*, 3 Aug. 1986, p. 18.

[39]Ibid., p. 19.

and complex case of selective history-writing for the sake of nation-building'.[40] The *Encyclopedia* texts put forward a claim which had gained common currency among Albanian scholars since the early 1970s, that Albanians were the descendants of the ancient Illyrians and were therefore the true autochtons of present-day Albania, Kosovo and western Macedonia, present before the Slav migrations of the 7th century. Non-Albanian historians have criticised the 'Illyrian thesis' for lack of conclusive evidence and because of the 'implicit, as well as more explicit, Albanian territorial claims connected to the Illyrian heritage'.[41]

Albanians were not the only ones seduced by romantic visions of the nation. Ethnogenesis and national heroes were also the preoccupation of Montenegrin and Bosnian scholars, the former eager to differentiate their nation from the Serbian and the latter to promote an independent Muslim national identity and 'state tradition' vis-à-vis Serbia and Croatia.[42] The *Encyclopedia* entries 'Montenegro' and 'Bosnia-Hercegovina' thus also caused interminable debates. The most important bones of contention concerned claims by Montenegrin scholars that their nation descended from the ancient Docleans, who preceded the Slav settlers, the promotion of new 'national' languages ('Bosnian' and 'Montenegrin'), as well as the 'national' attribution of historical and cultural figures.[43] By August 1986 an article in the Belgrade weekly *NIN* noted that 'experience has unequivocally con-

---

[40]Marco Dogo, 'National Truths and Disinformation in Albanian-Kosovar Historiography' in Ger Duijzings, with Dušan Janjić and Shkelzen Maliqi (eds), *Kosovo-Kosova. Confrontation or Coexistence*, Nijmegen, 1997, p. 34.

[41]Sima Ćirković 'Images of History: Same Objects, Different Perspectives' in ibid., p. 26.

[42]Macedonian intellectuals were just as prone to nationalist legitimation through historiography, but this issue did not come up in the debates on the Encyclopedia simply because of the alphabetical order of entries (on Macedonian historiography see Pavlowitch, *The Improbable Survivor*, op. cit., p. 130). Montenegro and Vojvodina were treated, however, because 'Montenegro' is *Crna Gora* in Serbo-Croatian and therefore under the letter 'C', while 'V' is the third letter of the Cyrillic alphabet.

[43]For example, Montenegrin scholars denied that Petar Petrović-Njegoš, Montenegro's 19th-century ruler whose poetry was also essential to the forging of Serbian national identity, could be included in more than one—their own—entry. (*NIN*, 4 July 1982, p. 31, and 16 May 1982, pp. 34–5) The question of 'appropriation' of Bosnian writers had already come up in 1972, over Predrag Palavestra's book *Posleratna srpska književnost*. The fact that Palavestra included several Muslim writers in his book (with their permission), was interpreted as a negation of an independent Muslim identity. (Interview with the author, 12 Aug. 1997. For the Bosnian board's standpoint on the attribution of literary figures see *NIN*, 30 Oct. 1983, pp. 22–3.)

firmed that the '*Yugoslavica*'—if it continues to be worked on in the same fashion as up to now—will resemble more a sum of political compromises than a collection of scholarly portrayals of ourselves and our past.'[44]

The obsession with 'national' rights and entitlements, which kept delaying the completion of the Encyclopedia volumes and incurring ever greater expenses, is best illustrated by the dispute between Montenegrin representatives and the central board over the entry for an obscure medieval ruler, Vojislav of Zeta. The central board received two texts for Vojislav: one by Sima Ćirković, the author of the entry in the first edition of the *Encyclopedia*, who simply adapted his original text according to the criteria established for the new edition (as was the general rule for minor entries) and one by Montenegrin historian and academician Pavle Mijović, which was much longer and hailed the 11th-century prince as a Montenegrin national hero. The Montenegrin scholars argued that the preparation of the text on Vojislav, whose principality was on the territory of today's Montenegro, 'is the obligation and the right of the Montenegrin board' and that 'renouncing Vojislav means renouncing the integrity and continuity of Montenegrin history and culture'.[45] The central board stuck to its guns and the dispute was finally resolved in its favour, but not before February 1987, causing a year's delay and additional costs for an entry of not more than fifteen lines.[46]

In 1984 the struggle for power between the political leadership of Serbia and those of the two autonomous provinces also found its way into the Encyclopedia. The question concerned not so much the content of the entries for Serbia and the two provinces, but the form: should Vojvodina and Kosovo have their own separate entries or should they be subsections under the entry for Serbia? This issue of little scholarly value was of considerable political importance for both sides because it determined the relationship between the republic and the provinces, hotly debated in government and Party organisations. The central board of the *Encyclopedia* managed to achieve a compromise, by which the provinces would have their own, relatively brief, entries, but would also be cited more fully under the entry for Serbia. In 1983, however, the Vojvodina editorial board decided to publish

[44]*NIN*, 3 Aug. 1986, p. 18.

[45]Sreten Asanović and Ratko Djurović, members of the Montenegrin board, quoted in *NIN*, 27 July 1986, p. 22.

[46]*Danas*, 18 Aug. 1987, pp. 40–2.

its entry as a separate pamphlet 'for use in schools and scholarly institutions', provoking a reaction from the Serbian board, which argued that this act 'has left the impression in public opinion that the accepted principles on the presentation of the S[ocialist] R[epublic of] Serbia are being abandoned' and that it threatened the 'equal presentation of S.R. Serbia in relation to the other republics'.[47] As a result, a new debate erupted concerning the size and importance of each of the entries, with each side trying to 'bid' for their preferred number of lines for the separate province entries in an atmosphere that resembled an auction. In 1986 the Serbian board, 'after consultation with the republic's highest political instances', once again questioned the very principle of granting the provinces separate entries.[48] Following a series of changes in the editorial boards of the republican and provincial organisations in early 1987, the conflict was temporarily resolved. Serbia's new editorial board, under Sima Ćirković, accepted in principle the original provision for both separate entries for the provinces and sub-entries under the republic heading, still awaiting the drafts of the entries 'Kosovo' and 'Serbia' for a final decision.[49]

Due to the constant problems and growing awareness that the Encyclopedia was coming to a standstill, a complete renegotiation of the 'Agreement on the Preparation and Financing of the second edition of the *Encyclopedia of Yugoslavia*' took place in mid-1987. It was announced at this point that only seventeen of the planned seventy-two volumes (of each collection) had been completed and that, 'in the next thirteen years, a huge sum of money is needed [to finish the project], more than what was spent so far and adding another 50%. In total, we are speaking of $40 million, with each volume costing $3 million'.[50] Furthermore, in the same year the *Encyclopedia* faced its greatest stumbling-block—the entry for Yugoslavia, considered the 'central theme and moving spirit of the entire project'.[51]

The main problems for the central editorial board was to find specialists willing to write the different texts of this 480-page entry and able to provide a synthesis acceptable to all the federal units. None of the proposed historical texts was accepted in its first version, due to criticisms coming mainly from the ranks of Serbian scholars, who

---

[47]Quoted in *NIN*, 10 Jan. 1988, p. 29.
[48]*NIN*, 22 Feb. 1987, p. 32, and *Danas*, 31 March 1987, pp. 39–41.
[49]*Danas*, 15 March 1988, pp. 33–5.
[50]Quoted in *Danas*, 18 Aug. 1987, p. 42.
[51]*Danas*, 17 Oct. 1989, p. 35.

had by now gone through a full-scale revision of the official version of Yugoslavia's history.[52] The Slovenian historians Janko Pleterski and Ciril Ribičić were attacked for their respective portrayals of the interwar Yugoslav state and of the constitutional development of postwar Yugoslavia, while the Croatian historian Dušan Bilandžić was criticised for his presentation of the 'War of National Liberation and the Socialist Revolution'.[53] By the time the volume containing the entry 'Yugoslavia' finally came out in 1990, the Belgrade press carried the news under titles such as 'Whose truth are we talking about?'[54] and the question of continued financing of the project was a recurrent topic on the republic's agenda.[55] Finally, in 1991, as the Yugoslav state was approaching its own demise, the central board of the Encyclopedia formally took the decision to discontinue work on the project.

Concurrently with the slow death of the *Encyclopedia of Yugoslavia*, the 1980s witnessed the birth of individual, politically backed projects of separate Slovenian, Montenegrin and Vojvodinian 'national' encyclopedias. The Academy of Sciences and Arts of Vojvodina supervised work on the province encyclopedia—facetiously called the *Autonomica* in the Belgrade press—with the aim of presenting 'the historical and contemporary' autonomous province.[56] The Montenegrin and Slovenian projects were more ethno-national in character, the Montenegrins having set up their own Lexicographical Institute for the purpose. When the first volume of the *Encyclopedia of Slovenia* appeared in 1987, a Slovenian reviewer, Ivan Cesar, hailed it as a book 'about who Slovenes are and must be, an inestimable source for an introduction to and experience of their own identity'.[57] He noted further that 'the publication of a national encyclopedia is in and of itself proof of national pride and conscience, as well as of a cultural atmosphere in this nation and a political maturity which shows that the expression of one's own identity—through work on an encyclopedia—does not threaten anybody else.'[58] In Serbia too a team of collaborators was chosen to work on a separate encyclopedia, but

[52]See below.

[53]*Danas*, 17 Oct. 1989, pp. 35–6.

[54]*Intervju*, 26 Oct. 1990, p. 29.

[55]The first proposal to discontinue the project was made in the Serbian Parliament in July 1989. Disagreeing with it, Sima Ćirković resigned as the director of Serbia's editorial board (*NIN*, 17 Nov. 1989, pp. 45–7).

[56]*NIN*, 17 Oct. 1982, p. 29.

[57]*Danas*, 22 Dec. 1987, p. 48.

[58]*Danas*, loc. cit.

the project had trouble getting off the ground because the scholars could not decide whether to create an encyclopedia for 'Serbia', the republic, or for 'Serbs', the nation.[59]

The crisis of common history, illustrated by the problems of the *Encyclopedia of Yugoslavia* and the other common projects, translated itself to all instances of inter-republican cooperation and exposed to what extent any sense of Yugoslav unity had become lost. Already at the Eighth Congress of Yugoslav historians held in 1983 it was possible 'to predict a scholar's polemical arguments by his national origin'.[60] By the time the Ninth Congress was held four years later, the situation had only worsened: the most controversial 'national' historians did not even appear. The two principal speakers at the congress, Belgrade historian Sima Ćirković and his colleague from Ljubljana, Janko Pleterski—who were both involved in the *Encyclopedia of Yugoslavia*—had no choice but to recognise how far the basic assumption of Yugoslavia's unification in 1918 as a positive and viable phenomenon had been eroded.[61]

'De-Titoisation' and the revision of history in Serbia: Yugoslavia reconsidered

Belgrade's news weekly *NIN* characterised the year 1983 as that of 'the outburst of history'.[62] The reasons for this upsurge of historical inquiry were rooted in the crisis of the present. As the Zagreb political scientist Jovan Mirić noted in his best-selling 1984 book *The System and Crisis*: 'When a society is confronted with a crisis, it usually turns to its foundations; it examines and reconsiders its basic principles.'[63] In terms of both the intensity of cultural activity and the progressive revival of nationalism, the reappraisal of the past that permeated all levels of Yugoslav scholarship, culture and media in the 1980s was comparable to the cultural streamings of the 1960s. Yet the extent of

[59]*NIN*, 17 Oct. 1982, p. 30. In the end, the project became concrete only in 1993 and then as three separate projects (see *Vreme*, 18 Apr. 1994, pp. 39–40).

[60]*NIN*, 30 Oct. 1983, p. 24.

[61]*Danas*, 6 Oct. 1987, p. 36, and *NIN*, 4 Oct. 1987, pp. 30–2.

[62]*NIN*, 10 July 1983, pp. 28–30, and 7 Aug. 1983, pp. 28–9.

[63]Jovan Mirić, *Sistem i kriza* (1984), Zagreb, 1985, p. 15. The book saw three editions in the first year of its publication and was serialised in both *NIN* and *Borba*, sparking many reactions by Yugoslav politicians and intellectuals (see *NIN*, 28 Oct. 1984, p. 20, and 16 Dec. 1984, p. 14). A Serb born in the Krajina in 1934, Mirić later became well-known critic of the resurgent nationalism of both Serbs and Croats.

historical revisionism and its challenge to communist rule went beyond anything that the country had experienced before. Although the resurgence of history affected all parts of Yugoslavia, it is in Serbia that it took on the most extensive, most all-encompassing and most radical character, due to the return of greater liberalism in the republic, as well as the more powerful impact of the economic crisis and the disintegrative processes in the country. Serbian intellectuals' re-examination of the past and demystification of the communist period were marked by an overwhelming sense of disappointment with the common state. This emerging anti-Yugoslavism went beyond anything that had been witnessed during the debates of the previous two decades.

The floodgates of historical revisionism were opened by the unlikely figure of Vladimir Dedijer, the official chronicler of the Partisan struggle during the Second World War and Tito's hand-picked biographer.[64] Dedijer's *Novi prilozi za biografiju Josipa Broza Tita* (New Contributions for the Biography of Josip Broz Tito) of 1981 was an official project sanctioned by Tito himself and was probably not meant to be a revisionist biography.[65] Nevertheless, his disclosures made it impossible to defend the infallibility both of the revolution and its leader and gave rise to a full-scale reinterpretation of the history of the Yugoslav communist movement in the interwar and wartime years.[66]

Dedijer's book provided a new vision of Tito himself—a more 'human' Tito behind the facade of the great leader—and thus struck an irremediable blow to the personality cult that had been developed around Yugoslavia's late ruler. It revelled in piquant details of Tito's personal life and put into question his role in the arrests of Moscow-based Yugoslav communists during the Great Purge. It also showed that Tito had personally participated in the 1914 Austro-Hungarian attack on Serbia, which later gave rise to allegations that Yugoslavia's communist leader had always been an 'anti-Serb'.[67] Dedijer's disclosures sparked a barrage of gossip and rumour about Tito, ranging from

---

[64]For Dedijer's career see Stevan K. Pavlowitch, 'Dedijer as a Historian of the Yugoslav Civil War', *Survey*, XXVIII/3, 1984, pp. 97–8.

[65]Pavlowitch, *Tito,* op. cit., p. 90. Ivo Banac, on the other hand, portrays Dedijer as a conscious revisionist, who 'delighted in breaking every taboo', merely 'maintaining the appearance of amity for his subject' (Banac, 'Historiography', op. cit., p. 1093).

[66]Vladislav Marjanović, 'L'Historiographie contemporaine serbe des années quatre-vingt. De la démystification idéologique à la mystification nationaliste' in Antoine Marès (ed.), *Histoire et pouvoir en Europe médiane*, Paris, 1996, p. 144.

[67]Vladimir Dedijer, *Novi prilozi za biografiju Josipa Broza Tita*, II, Rijeka, 1981, pp. 308, 332–4, and 246.

allegations that he was a Freemason to stories of family squabbles over his inheritance, so that by September 1984, a new law was promulgated to protect 'the use of [Tito's] image and legacy'.[68] As Stevan Pavlowitch noted in his 1992 biographical essay on Tito, 'By the time of the tenth anniversary of his death, not only was he being depicted as greedy, vainglorious and mendacious, but all of the ills of Yugoslavia and of its component ethnic communities were attributed to him, and he was no longer referred to as Tito. He was plain Josip Broz.'[69]

Dedijer also provided a number of new disclosures that radically put into question official portrayals of the Yugoslav communist movement and the Partisan struggle. First of all, he referred to the Comintern's promotion of the break-up of Yugoslavia before 1935, its acceptance of the creation of the Independent State of Croatia in 1941 and its wartime sponsorship of an independent Croatian Communist Party.[70] These disclosures inevitably raised the question of what the Yugoslav communists' own stand on the thorny national question had been. Dedijer also made public the unsavoury aspects of the Partisans' wartime struggle, such as the excessive reprisals and summary executions of civilians and fellow-combatants.[71] Finally, for the first time in Yugoslavia, he openly spoke of the Partisan leadership's secret talks with the Germans in March 1943.[72] He not only translated the German military documents on the cease-fire agreement and exposed that they went well beyond a simple exchange of prisoners (which already undercut the claim that the Partisans were the only force in Yugoslavia that had consistently resisted the occupier), but he also showed that the Partisans considered their main enemy to be, not the occupying Axis forces, but the predominantly Serbian Chetniks, the remnants of the defeated Yugoslav army loyal to the government in exile.[73] In this way Dedijer set the stage for a full-scale reinterpretation of the war, now increasingly discernible as more than simply the 'national struggle against the occupier and domestic collaborators'. As the historian Vladislav Marjanović has noted, 'all of a sudden,

[68]*NIN*, 23 June, 1985, p. 21.

[69]Pavlowitch, *Tito,* op. cit., p. 92.

[70]Dedijer, op. cit., pp. 425–31.

[71]Ibid., pp. 719, 722.

[72]Although they were taboo in Yugoslavia, these talks had been noted in Western and émigré Yugoslav historiography, as well as in Milovan Djilas's 1977 autobiography *Wartime*, which only came out in Yugoslavia in 1989.

[73]Dedijer, op. cit., p. 805. See Pavlowitch, 'Dedijer', op. cit., for an elaboration of Dedijer's sources and arguments.

questions of collaboration and treason during the Second World War in Yugoslavia found themselves relativised'.[74]

Dedijer's book was immediately attacked by numerous high-ranking officials, regime intellectuals and veteran organisations, who accused its author of maligning the Yugoslav revolution, insulting Tito's image and putting into question the moral and ethical principles of the Partisans.[75] In January 1982 Dedijer was even accused of being a pawn in an alleged Western policy of destabilising Yugoslavia.[76] Some of the strongest attacks came from Croatia, because of Dedijer's allegations about the nationalist tendencies of leading wartime Croatian communists.[77] The result of the outcry against Dedijer was merely further to stimulate public interest in his book. In January 1982 *NIN* wrote: 'If a book was judged by its commercial success, or by the number of copies sold, and, probably, even by the number of readers, Dedijer's *New Contributions for the Biography of Josip Broz Tito* has been the book of the year.'[78] A number of intellectuals surveyed by *Književne novine* named it the best book of 1981, while *Književna reč* lauded it for exposing the need to reconsider Yugoslavia's modern history.[79]

The publication of Dedijer's controversial book inaugurated a radical reappraisal of the Yugoslav Communist Party's past by a host of writers and scholars in Serbia. As new histories and memoirs began to challenge the official founding myths of Yugoslav communism, both literary and historical endeavours increasingly became focused on three main themes: the brutality employed by the Party against domestic opponents, during both the communist revolution and the 1948 break with the Cominform; the leadership's wartime decisions, which laid the foundations of the Yugoslav federation and its internal borders; and the Party's factional struggles, its relationship with the Comintern and its approach to the national question in the interwar years. Their reappraisal of the past produced a rising sense that the Party had acted as the vehicle of a policy of weakening the Serbs in order to satisfy the aspirations of the other Yugoslav nations, while their historical delegitimation of the communist project increasingly

[74]Marjanović, op. cit., p. 146.
[75]For examples, see *South Slav Journal*, IV/4, 1981–2, p. 2.
[76]Cited in Banac, 'Historiography', op. cit., p. 1094.
[77]See for example the statement by Vladimir Bakarić, Croatia's leading communist and representative to the Federal Presidency, *NIN*, 17 Jan. 1982, p. 19.
[78]Ibid., loc. cit.
[79]*Književne novine*, 640, 21 Jan. 1982, and *Književna reč*, 182, 10 Feb. 1982.

became tied to a critical reassessment of the Yugoslav state it had given birth to in 1945.

One of the first themes to resurface in post–Titoist Yugoslavia was the Party's brutal reckoning with political adversaries and the undemocratic nature of the consolidation of its regime in the 1940s. The most potent symbol of Yugoslavia's 'Stalinism' was the Goli Otok prison camp, created in the Adriatic for individuals who were suspected of pro-Soviet sympathies in 1948. Until the 1980s any reference to Yugoslavia's 'Gulag' was considered unacceptable, although several attempts had been made to broach the subject in the late 1960s and the 1970s.[80] In Serbia the breakthrough came in January 1982 with the publication of Antonije Isaković's novel *Instant 2* (*Tren 2*). Isaković, a renowned writer of short stories about the Partisan wartime experience and vice-president of the Serbian Academy, had already come into conflict with the authorities over the 1967 'Proposal for Consideration'.[81] He wrote *Instant 2* in the late 1970s, but was prevented from publishing it for several years. The novel passed through the hands of twenty-three official readers, Isaković eventually had to add a section to show the 'other side' (a security official's account) and when the book appeared in 1982, it was accompanied by two articles to show the 'context' and 'relativise' its theme.[82] These attempts to diffuse the bombshell effect of the novel's disclosures were promoted by Isaković himself, as well as by other intellectuals, who were afraid of repression and a reversal of the new opening in culture. On receiving of the prestigious *NIN* prize for his book in 1982, Isaković thus argued that he did not consider his treatment of this taboo subject as a negation of the Yugoslav regime and emphasised that his aim was not to rehabilitate the Cominformists, but to engage in a general reflection on the incompatibility of 'noble ends and ignoble means'.[83] The tentative manner in which the author talked about his novel was echoed in public debates on the book.[84]

---

[80]See Milivoje Marković, *Preispitivanja*, Belgrade, 1986, and Oskar Gruenwald, 'Yugoslav Camp Literature: Rediscovering the Ghost of a Nation's Past-Present-Future', *Slavic Review*, XXXXVI/3–4, 1987, pp. 513–28.

[81]See Chapter 1. In 1985 he was head of the committee that drafted the Academy's Memorandum.

[82]Interview of Dec. 1981 in *Auto-svet*, in Isaković, *Govori i razgovori*, op. cit., p. 118.

[83]*NIN*, 16 Jan. 1983, pp. 28–9. The annual *NIN* award for best novel in Serbo-Croatian was inaugurated in 1955. It subsequently became one of the most cherished literary prizes in the country.

[84]See Zoran Milutinović, 'Mimezis u socijalizmu', *Letopis matice srpske*, XXV/1, 1996, p. 446.

As in Dedijer's case, the reaction of the authorities was not to prohibit the book or discussion of the subject. Instead they tried to mitigate its effect by inserting Goli Otok into the larger context of the 1948 Soviet-Yugoslav break. The weekly *NIN* thus published a series on 'The Cominform and Goli Otok' in spring 1982, in which leading Serbian communists argued that 'certain distant events are being taken out of their historical context and maliciously interpreted in order to diminish the greatness of our revolution'.[85] The authors of the articles attempted to justify the excesses of 1948: although the punishment on Goli Otok was cruel and 'in some cases big mistakes were made', these were the result of 'hastiness' and were corrected whenever noticed.[86] 'In the end, most of the prisoners were real Cominformists, traitors to their country and their revolution', they noted, and 'we must not be ashamed even of Goli Otok, because it was the consequence of our people's superhuman striving for liberty'.[87] Throughout the publication of this serial, *NIN* received numerous letters to the editor, showing an inordinate interest in the subject.

All these efforts were incapable of softening the effect *Instant 2* had created in Serbia's reading public. In the novel Isaković vividly described not only the inhumane conditions in the prison camp and the torture and psychological abuse of its inmates, but also the lasting traces of the experience for the former prisoners and the impossibility of reintegration into normal life, leading in some cases even to suicide. He contrasted the harsh treatment meted out to inmates to the fact that 'on the island most prisoners had committed a small crime compared to the sentence they were serving. All this disproportion showed to what extent the conflict of 1948 was cruel and dangerous'.[88] As the literary journal of the Serbian Youth Organisation, *Književna reč*, put it bluntly and more courageously than the established reviewers, this was the first work in Serbian literature to deal directly with the domestic repression that followed the break with the Cominform and much of its interest was in fact not literary but historical.[89] In painting such a horrifying picture of the fate of the Goli Otok prisoners, it inescapably put into question the morality of a system that allowed such inhumanity.[90]

---

[85]*NIN*, 14 March 1982, p. 56.

[86]Ibid., loc. cit.

[87]Ibid., loc. cit. and 28 Feb. 1982, p. 53.

[88]Antonije Isaković, *Tren 2* (1982), Belgrade, 1988, p. 214.

[89]*Književna reč*, 186–7, Apr. 1982.

[90]See Gojko Nikoliš, 'Još jedna varijacija na temu polu-odevenog otoka', *Književna reč*, 188, May 1982, p. 3.

The sufferings of the accused Cominformists became the subject of a veritable flood of publications, theatre and cinematographic endeavours in the 1980s.[91] In November 1983, *Instant 2* was put on as a play at the Student Cultural Centre in Belgrade, followed in 1984 by Dragoslav Mihailović's forbidden 1969 play *When Pumpkins Blossomed*. After the mid-1980s, explicit accounts by former Goli Otok inmates began to appear in Belgrade's bookshops.[92]

The breaking of the taboo of Goli Otok was accompanied by a further reassessment of the repressive and undemocratic nature of Yugoslavia's communist revolution. In 1983 the jurists Kosta Čavoški and Vojislav Koštunica, well-known liberal critics of the regime who had been purged from Belgrade University in the 1970s, broke new ground by publishing an analysis of the Yugoslav Communist Party's take-over of power in the immediate post-war period. Their book, *Stranački pluralizam ili monizam* (Party Pluralism or Monism) was published by the Institute of Philosophy and Social Theory, the stronghold of the Praxists since their ouster from Belgrade University. As Ivo Banac noted in his analysis of Yugoslav historiography, Čavoški and Koštunica 'turned the cheaply printed edition of a thousand copies into a political fire bomb'.[93] The two authors were subjected to a campaign of abuse in the press and were accused of favouring a 'bourgeois' multiparty system and maliciously misinterpreting the Yugoslav revolution.[94]

In their examination of the Communist Party's establishment of hegemony, Čavoški and Koštunica denied the official claim that all the 'bourgeois' political parties had collaborated with the occupier during the war and depicted them instead in a much more positive light, especially the Democratic Party of Milan Grol.[95] They argued that the communists had made a mere pretence of cooperation with the other political organisations, only to subsequently use a variety of unsavoury methods to co-opt or coerce them into submission. Tracing

---

[91]The best known of these is probably Emir Kusturica's film *Otac na službenom putu* (When Father Was Away on Business), which won the 'Golden Palm' at the Cannes Film Festival.

[92]See particularly Miroslav Popović, *Udri bandu*, Belgrade, 1985 and Dragoslav Mihailović's interviews in *Goli Otok* (Belgrade, 1990), first serialised in *Književne novine* in 1988 and 1989.

[93]Banac, 'Historiography', op. cit., p. 1096.

[94]See, for example, *Politika*, 17 Sept. 1983.

[95]Kosta Čavoški and Vojislav Koštunica, *Stranački pluralizam ili monizam*, Belgrade, 1983, p. 43. The two authors were instrumental in reviving the Democratic Party in 1989 (see Chapter 5).

the sources of this strategy to Bolshevik ideology, they noted that the Party's establishment of 'monism' rendered all subsequent changes to the Yugoslav system superficial and compromised its role in building socialism.[96] They also argued that, in trying to substitute a degree of pluralism for genuine democracy, Yugoslavia's 'monist' Party had essentially became federalised into several national parties, which—still undemocratically—pursued their own local 'national' interests.[97]

Other intellectuals critically examined the various aspects of the Yugoslav Party's history, scrutinising the persecution of Trotskyists within its ranks in the 1930s, its failure to harness the popular uprising in Serbia against the German occupier in 1941, as well its policy of forced collectivisation in the 1940s.[98] This reappraisal increasingly focused on the national question, seen as the principal cause of Yugoslavia's post-Titoist crisis. The Zagreb political scientist Jovan Mirić began his book on *The System and Crisis* by highlighting the extent to which the Constitution of 1974 and its application by Tito's successors had deviated from the original principles of the Yugoslav revolution, embodied by the decisions taken at the second session of the Anti-Fascist Council of the People's Liberation of Yugoslavia (AVNOJ) in 1943.[99] However, his Belgrade colleagues went further than that and turned to an examination of the very principles that governed the 1943 federal 'contract', particularly the principle of equality of nations. In a 1986 article Kosta Čavoški openly contested the AVNOJ decisions themselves for violating this principle, and, for the first time since the 1971 Law Faculty debate, he openly raised the question of Yugoslavia's internal borders.[100]

In his analysis Čavoški concluded that a variety of criteria had been used in the drafting of borders, without universally applied principles. As a result of this apparently arbitrary approach, the various Yugoslav nations had not been treated equally. The biggest winners were Slovenes and Macedonians, who both managed to regroup practically all members of their nation in their respective republics.

[96] Ibid., p. 7.
[97] Ibid., p. 166.
[98] Many of these articles were published in *Književna reč* in the first half of the 1980s. For a list of these, see *Književna reč*, 179, 25 Dec., 1981, p. 3. See also Miodrag Milić, *Radjanje Titove despotije. Prilog fenomenologiji jugoslovenske revolucije*, Harrow, 1985, which led to his two-year sentence in the case of the Belgrade Six in 1984 (see Chapter 1).
[99] Mirić, op. cit., pp. 17–22.
[100] On the 1971 debate see Chapter 1.

In addition, Slovenes received an outlet to the sea in Istria, while Macedonia was given a large territory populated by an Albanian majority. In his opinion, Muslims and Montenegrins also had reason to be satisfied. Although Bosnia-Hercegovina—which was recreated in the historical borders of Ottoman province, confirmed by the 1878 Congress of Berlin—did not get the mainly Muslim-populated Sandžak region, it united almost all the other Yugoslav Muslims and received an outlet to the sea. Montenegro was recreated in its pre-1912 borders, which did not include its territorial gains of the two Balkan wars, but it did receive strategically important areas on the Adriatic coast (notably Kotor). As far as Croats was concerned, Čavoški argued, the results were mixed: on the one hand, the Hercegovinian Croats were left outside their 'homeland republic' and Croatia lost Kotor to Montenegro and parts of the Srijem (Srem) to Vojvodina. On the other, the republic united the historically distinct regions of Croatia, Slavonia and Dalmatia (despite Dalmatian communists' demands for autonomy) and received a part of the Vojvodina, all of Istria and a number of formerly Italian islands.[101]

The biggest losers, according to Čavoški, were the Serbs. The Republic of Serbia was recreated in its pre-Balkan war borders (aside from two municipalities that had belonged to Bulgaria until 1913), which meant 'that Serbia's gains in the liberation wars against Turkey and Austria-Hungary from 1912 to 1918 were simply not recognised.'[102] In addition, Serbs did not get autonomy either in Croatia or in Bosnia-Hercegovina, despite having been victims of Ustasha terror in the Independent State of Croatia, whereas Albanians (who had been on the wrong side in the war) received such autonomy in Serbia. In fact, he noted that the borders of the AVNOJ-designated 'inner' part of the republic (without the provinces) almost completely corresponded with those of occupied Serbia during the Second World War, thus implicitly drawing a parallel between the treatment of Serbs by Nazi Germany and the Yugoslav communists.[103] Such reconsiderations went beyond the assessment made ten years earlier, which had focused on the evolution of the Yugoslav system, rather than its origins. Also, the fact that Čavoški was a liberal intellectual, who had

---

[101]Kosta Čavoški, 'Iz istorije stvaranja nove Jugoslavije', *Književna reč*, Dec. 1986, reprinted in *Naša reč*, 383, March 1987, pp. 3–5. On internal borders, see also Banac, *With Stalin Against Tito*, op. cit., pp. 98–110, and for Croatia, Irvine, op. cit., pp. 220–5.

[102]Ibid., in *Naša reč*, 386, June-July 1987, p. 5.

[103]Ibid., pp. 5–7.

previously not concentrated on the Serbian national question as such, was indicative of the mood that was coming to prevail within the Belgrade intelligentsia.

In the crisis-ridden 1980s the primary concern of regime critics became the quest to explain what they considered to be the unequal treatment of Serbs at the very creation of communist Yugoslavia. In this endeavour, they increasingly turned to the Communist Party's pre-war approaches to the national question and its relationship with the Comintern, which until 1935 advocated the break-up of Yugoslavia and cooperation with the various non-Serb national movements including in the early 1930s the Croatian Ustasha.[104] As Wolfgang Höpken has argued, until the post-Tito era, the national question as such was never made an object of serious historical inquiry and Serbo-Croat conflict in the first Yugoslav state was not discussed beyond the crude official line that presented it as a consequence of the Serbian bourgeoisie's desire for hegemony, or as the result of quarrels and arrangements among all the Yugoslav bourgeoisies.[105] This re-examination of the interwar period of the Party's history also concerned regime historians, but it is from the ranks of the intellectual opposition that the most comprehensive reassessment emerged.[106]

In a 1982 interview in *Theoria*, the journal of the Philosophy Society of Serbia, the Praxist Ljubomir Tadić first analysed Yugoslavia's present crisis by referring to the Party's so-called 'Comintern legacy'. He argued that the Yugoslav leadership 'had never seriously brought into question the organisational structure and ideological basis of the C[ommunist] P[arty] inherited from Bolshevism ... It also never critically re-examined the Comintern's policy on the national question in Yugoslavia, but—to the contrary—it realised that policy with some insignificant

[104]For the Yugoslav Communist Party's approaches to the national question in the interwar and wartime periods see Irvine, op. cit., Banac, *With Stalin Against Tito*, op. cit., Shoup, *Communism and the Yugoslav National Question*, op. cit., and Aleksa Djilas, *The Contested Country*, Cambridge, MA, 1991.

[105]Wolfgang Höpken, 'History Education and Yugoslav (Dis-)Integration', in Melissa K. Bokovoy, Jill A. Irvine and Carol S. Lilly (eds), *State-Society Relations in Yugoslavia, 1945–1992*, Basingstoke, 1997, p. 91.

[106]For regime historians' debates on the Party's interwar policy, see *NIN*, 19 Feb. 1984, p. 15; 23 June 1985, pp. 22–4; and 19 Jan. 1986, pp. 31–3. The best example of the new trend is Desanka Pešić, *Jugoslovenski komunisti i nacionalno pitanje (1919–1935)*, Belgrade, 1983. For Croatian historians' responses see *Danas*, 22 March 1988, pp. 24–5.

modifications'.[107] In the course of the decade Tadić elaborated this argument. In a 1986 interview in *Književne novine* he argued that the Party's excessive critique of Serbian unitarism and centralism, which was used to justify the policy of decentralisation, followed 'a scenario prepared in advance':[108]

In the distant historical background of this policy one can discern the dark silhouettes of Austria-Hungary and Turkey, the two imperial powers that disappeared in World War I, as well as the policy on the national question in Yugoslavia of the Comintern and Stalin personally. The common denominator of this heavy historical load and this policy is the struggle against 'Greater Serbian hegemony'. This struggle continues even today ... In this way, in a single stroke, the nearly one hundred and fifty-year battle of [the Serbian] nation has been erased. It is as if ... there had been no Partisan war and Serbian Partisans had not given their proportional and numerically decisive contribution to the destruction of the old Yugoslavia.[109]

In two further articles in 1988 Tadić argued that the creation of national states on Yugoslavia's territory was no less than 'the main goal and programme of the revolutionary and wartime strategy of the CPY', while the building of a socialist society was merely a 'secondary, accessory element'![110] This primacy of national over social aims resulted from several factors: the rise and influence of the Croatian national movement in the first Yugoslav state, the need to find new allies in the struggle for power and the subordination of the Yugoslav Party to the Comintern, which had declared the Kingdom of Yugoslavia an artificial creation of Versailles, in which the Serbs oppressed all other nations. Although Tadić acknowledged that the Serbs dominated the state apparatus and administration in the first Yugoslav state, he did not mention this as having any impact on the Communists' approaches to the national question. According to him, the consistent use of Comintern propaganda had two long-term consequences: the creation of a stereotype of Serbs as an oppressor nation, thus providing for the total neglect of Serbian national rights in communist Yugoslavia,

---

[107]Interview in *Theoria*, 3–4, 1982, in Ljubomir Tadić, *Da li je nacionalizam naša sudbina?*, Belgrade, 1983, p. 128.

[108]Ljubomir Tadić, 'Nacionalne strasti kao zamena za demokratiju', *Književne novine*, 709, 1 May 1986, p. 1.

[109]Ibid., p. 7.

[110]Ljubomir Tadić, 'Kominterna i nacionalno pitanje u Jugoslaviji', *Književne novine*, 760, 15 Sept. 1988, p. 1.

and the promotion of non-Serbian cadres within the Party, who worked for their own national goals.[111] Serbian communists, who were 'brought up in the spirit of internationalism ..., made one concession after another ... [and] almost masochistically subordinated themselves to the Party line and sadistically persecuted real or imaginary Serbian nationalism'.[112] In Tadić's eyes this was the explanation for the Serbs' subordinate and weakened position in post-Tito Yugoslavia. Like Čavoški, Tadić had not until the 1980s taken up the 'defence' of the Serbian nation; his critique of nationalism had always been made from a leftist and 'Yugoslav' position.[113] This shift in his position was paradigmatic of the wider tendencies that were taking over in the Belgrade intelligentsia.

While the Communist Party was rapidly losing legitimacy, a rehabilitation of other actors in Serbia's past gained momentum, as memoirs, speeches and writings of the many 'bourgeois' political figures, military leaders and even King Peter himself flooded the market, along with both hagiographies and more serious scholarly works.[114] The most important project of this time was the attempt to publish the collected works of historian and jurist Slobodan Jovanović, one of the foremost Serbian intellectuals of the 20th century and prime minister of the Yugoslav government in London during the war, later sentenced in absentia by the communists to twenty years in prison.[115] In 1984 two Belgrade publishers entered into a legal battle over rights to the publication, at which point the Belgrade City Committee, headed at the time by an orthodox and vehemently anti-nationalist Slobodan Milošević, put an end to it.[116] The project was revived at the highpoint of the nationalist euphoria at the end of the decade and the twelve volumes of Jovanović's writings finally appeared in 1991.[117]

This reappraisal of Serbian historical figures went hand-in-hand

---

[111]Ibid., p. 5.

[112]Ljubomir Tadić, 'Balkanizacija partizanskog jugoslovenstva', *Književne novine*, 749–50, 1–15 March 1988, p. 8.

[113]For some of the early texts see Tadić, *Da li je nacionalizam naša sudbina?*, op. cit.

[114]For a discussion of these see Marjanović, op. cit., pp. 164–8 passim.

[115]On Jovanović, see Dimitrije Djordjević, 'Historians in Politics: Slobodan Jovanović' in Walter Laqueur and George L. Mosse (eds), *Historians in Politics*, London, 1974, and Aleksandar Pavković, *Slobodan Jovanović: An Unsentimental Approach to Politics*, Boulder, CO, 1993.

[116]See *NIN*, 10 Feb. 1985, pp. 34–5, and Djukić, *Kako se dogodio vodja*, op. cit., p. 83.

[117]*Sabrana dela Slobodana Jovanovića*, I-XII, Belgrade, 1991.

with a general rejection of the ingrained notion of 'Greater Serbian hegemony', one of the cornerstones of communist national policy in the interwar period and part of the Party's historical legitimation as a fundamentally different and progressive unifying force. Initially this myth was dismantled by serious historians, careful of the nuance between 'hegemony' and political domination and interested in a scholarly examination of the issue. Andrej Mitrović, a renowned specialist on modern Serbian history and later a vocal critic of the Serbian nationalist euphoria under Milošević, thus argued that 'Great Serbian hegemony' was an instrument of political propaganda, whose origins could be found in the late-19th-century Habsburg policy and which was revived by the Comintern and the right-wing national movements in the first Yugoslavia.[118] The historian Djordje Dj. Stanković, whose ground-breaking biography of Nikola Pašić—the architect of the centralist Kingdom of Serbs, Croats and Slovenes in 1918—provided a much more nuanced and complex picture of Serbia's veteran statesman, noted in a 1984 interview that the Serbian bourgeoisie clearly enjoyed political supremacy in interwar Yugoslavia, but that it had not created Yugoslavia in order for the Serbs to oppress and exploit other nations.[119] However, these nuances were progressively erased in the public mind as the nationalist momentum gained ground and an alternative vision of a wronged and oppressed Serbian nation became dominant.

It was in literature that the Serbian struggle for national unification of the 19th and early 20th centuries achieved a complete make-over and nobody elaborated this new vision as well as writer Dobrica Ćosić. Nobody wove as masterfully as he did the themes of Serbia's greatness and hubris, its wartime martyrdom and naive belief in 'brotherly' South Slav nations, its constant struggle for 'liberation and unification' and its misplaced investment into the common Yugoslav state. As Ćosić recorded in his journal, all of his characters were the embodiment of the nation with its many faces, as well as carriers of the national destiny as a whole.[120] As the journalist Milorad Vučelić noted in 1987, *Vreme smrti* (*A Time of Death*), Ćosić's epic novel about Serbia's struggle in the First World War, was, for his generation, 'a discovery of history

[118]*Književne novine*, 700–1, 15 Dec. 1985, p. 27.

[119]*NIN*, 24 Apr. 1984, p. 28. See also Djordje Dj. Stanković, *Nikola Pašić i jugoslovensko pitanje*, Belgrade, 1985.

[120]'In every one of my literary heroes I saw the people' (Dobrica Ćosić, *Promene*, Novi Sad, 1992, p. 211).

and a powerful break with the schematic, uninteresting, falsely ideological and one-dimensional portrayal of the past'.[121] *A Time of Death*, which appeared in four volumes in the course of the 1970s, established the novelist Ćosić as the authoritative interpreter of 20th-century Serbian history, with an ever greater reading public unhappy with ideologically conditioned official historiography.[122] It was not uncommon for young scholars to boast 'that they had learned most about the First World War from the novel *A Time of Death*'.[123]

The theme of Ćosić's monumental novel is the experience of the Serbs in the early part of the First World War, from July 1914, when Serbia was presented the ultimatum by Austria–Hungary, to the winter of 1915 and the retreat of the Serbian army across Albania. Ćosić's research was extensive; he provides excerpts from historical documents, newspapers and other sources, and blends fictional characters and real historical figures, which gives the novel a strong flavour of historical authenticity. Throughout his epic Ćosić defines Serbia's wartime drama not only as a heroic enterprise against a much stronger enemy, but also as proof of the nation's tragic destiny to strive for liberty and greatness at the expense of near physical extinction. *A Time of Death* depicts the incredible suffering of the Serbian people during the war, from the hard-won military victories against the overwhelmingly stronger enemy to the decimation of the Serbian youth in battle, from the deadly typhus epidemic and famine of the war years to the difficult wintertime exodus across the hostile Albanian mountains in 1915. In Ćosić's vision Serbs are a small nation whose aspirations not only exceed their means in the face of much more powerful hostile earthly forces, but go against the very laws of heaven.[124]

Throughout this cataclysm Ćosić's protagonists reflect on the treachery of their European allies, who request that Serbia cede hard-won territories to satisfy the demands of other Balkan countries and who are willing to sacrifice them on the battlefield—often without sending aid or ammunition—for the sake of interests over which Serbia has no control. In the words of Ćosić's main character Vukašin Katić, 'friends would not issue demands which are more difficult than those of Vienna's ultimatum ... [and] which, with the territories

---

[121]*Književne novine*, 738, 15 Sept. 1987, p. 3.
[122]Nebojša Popov, 'Srpski populizam', *Vreme* (special edn), 24 May 1993, p. 16.
[123]According to Vida Ognjenović, who was critical of this trend (*Vreme istorije*, 22 March 1993, p. 5).
[124]Dobrica Ćosić, *Vreme smrti*, I, Belgrade, 1972, p. 75.

of an ally, with Serbian territories, compensate the neutrality of Bulgaria and Romania, their future adversaries'.[125] The Allies demand that Serbian forces pursue the enemy troops deep into hostile territory in order to alleviate the pressure on the other fronts, although this means, as the Serbian generals know, that their 'small nation ... would be completely crushed, would destroy itself for the sake of others'.[126] As a result of this impossible offensive the Serbian army, the King and a large civilian population have to retreat across Albania to the Adriatic sea.

The novel ends with this epic journey through hostile territory, whose meaning is captured by Vukašin Katić:

Instead of complying with the law of history by which the defeated and occupied give themselves up to the victor and the betrayed renounce their betrayers, we do the opposite: not accepting defeat, we leave our land and remain faithful to the unfaithful Allies. The whole of Serbia ... is going into exile. We willingly and consciously walk into the unknown; we risk never to return ... [Yet] by not accepting capitulation and by leaving our land in these circumstances and in this way, we are turning our military defeat into a victory over history. This is something only a great nation can do. This greatness is perhaps too costly. Liberty itself does not deserve such a price. This victory will probably not bring us happiness. But we have goals which are greater even than liberty, glory, happiness. We want to unite all South Slavs, defeat the Habsburg Empire, become something different and more valuable to the world than we have been until now'.[127]

In his novel, Ćosić questions the wisdom and desirability of this choice. His protagonists continually ask themselves: 'Will the state that emerges from this war be good and just enough to compensate such over-whelming Serbian sacrifice?'[128] Plenty of evidence is presented to speak against uniting 'with those who are fighting in order for such unification never to take place'.[129] Although some South Slavs in the Austro-Hungarian army do go over to the Serbian side, they never-theless make up almost half of the enemy forces and loyally fight for the empire.[130] In addition, Croats rejoice when they defeat Serbs in battle, taunt them across front lines and sing songs of 'Greater Croatia',

[125]Ibid., IV, 1979, p. 163.
[126]Ibid., III, 1975, p. 319.
[127]Ibid., IV, pp. 563–4.
[128]Ibid., I, p. 46.
[129]Ibid., p. 172.
[130]Ibid., p. 481.

while Serbian soldiers despondently note that 'we thought we were brothers, that we were fighting for our unification'.[131]

In his speech upon becoming a full member of the Serbian Academy of Sciences and Arts in March 1977, Ćosić publicly intimated for the first time that creating Yugoslavia in 1918 had been a costly Serbian mistake. In the century of such great turmoil and tremendous sufferings, Ćosić argued, the Serbian nation had often 'been deceived' and had also 'fooled and blinded itself' to accomplish tasks that went beyond its capabilities. Noting that Serbia had sacrificed almost half of its population during the First World War, he wondered:

What kind of people are we, what kind of a nation, that we die so easily for freedom and remain in our victories without it? How is it possible that some among us, in our own home, have stolen from us what a much more powerful enemy could not take on the battlefield? How can a people so dignified, proud and courageous in war accept to be so humiliated and docile in peace?[132]

Entering the eighth decade of the 20th century, Ćosić argued, Serbs had a duty to reflect upon their history, national and state traditions and their fathers' heroism and suffering. He stated that the most tragic legacy was 'to be constantly considered a culprit for having been a son, a grandson, or simply a descendant of those who, enthusiastically and consistently, consciously and yet mistakenly, waged a war for 'liberation and unification' between 1912 and 1918'.[133] The implication of Ćosić's message was clear: the enterprise of state-creation had been an eminently 'democratic' and legitimate one, in which the whole people participated and for which it shed a tremendous amount of blood—not for the sake of 'imperialist' ambitions or the desire to subdue other nations, but because of its genuine belief in the idea of brotherhood of the South Slavs. With his idea of Serbs having 'won the war, but lost the peace', he implied that the creation of Yugoslavia, instead of a larger Serbian state, had been a mistake.

Ćosić's speech was banned from publication but circulated in *samizdat* form. In 1983 it was finally published, along with his forbidden 1968 presentation on Kosovo,[134] in a collection of essays entitled *Stvarno i moguće* (The Real and the Possible). The first edition of twelve thousand copies was sold out within a few days, sparking renewed

[131]Ibid., II, pp. 91, 102, 160–4.
[132]Dobrica Ćosić, 'Književnost i istorija danas' in Ćosić, *Stvarno i moguće*, op. cit., p. 131.
[133]Ibid., p. 132.
[134]See Chapter 1.

attacks on the author and his publisher and the banning of his book, deemed to be 'the bible of Serbian nationalism'.[135] In January 1984 the Yugoslav Drama Theatre staged a play based on the second volume of *A Time of Death*, entitled *The Battle of Kolubara*. This stage adaptation of a part of Ćosić's novel by his long-time friend, literary critic and playwright Borislav Mihajlović-Mihiz, presented Serbia's victory against the vastly superior Austro-Hungarian forces in this famous battle of December 1914 as resulting from the valour of its peasant army, which 'defends the hearth and children and fights for survival and life', and the Serbs' 'national character', built on courage, disdain for death and the spirit of *inat* (defiance adopted in situations of adversity regardless of the consequences).[136] In the words of one of reviewer, it was 'the victory of morality over arms'.[137] The play provoked impressive reactions from its audience. Not only was it the main event on the Belgrade cultural scene in this period, attracting the whole spectrum of the intelligentsia, but it was completely booked for months on end and every performance was greeted by frenetic applause, exclamations and even tears by an ecstatic audience.[138] Its success inaugurated the proliferation of plays with historical national themes in the years to come.[139]

In the 1980s Ćosić took his reconsideration of Yugoslavia further and combined it with a reflection on the nature of pre-war communism. His 1985 novel *Grešnik* (The Sinner), the first part of his new trilogy *Vreme zla* (A Time of Evil), explores the psychological struggle of Serbia's interwar communists to explain and justify Stalin's pact with Hitler, the Great Purge and the brutal repression of internal dissent in the Party. The communists, as portrayed by Ćosić, are fanatical believers in the new secular religion: in jail, 'comrades tortured comrades [and] in the name of their god, even sinners persecuted sinners'.[140] The protagonist, Vukašin Katić's son Ivan, learns that serv-

---

[135]See Djukić, *Čovek u svom vremenu*, op. cit., p. 262, and *NIN*, 13 March 1983, p. 29.

[136]Dobrica Ćosić and Borislav Mihajlović-Mihiz, *Kolubarska bitka*, Belgrade, 1983, p. 39.

[137]Jovan Ćirilov, *Politika*, 9 Jan. 1984, quoted in *Drugi—o Mihizu*, op. cit., p. 112.

[138]See the reviews in *Borba, Komunist, Politika* and *Danas* in ibid., pp. 112–19, as well as *NIN*, 8 Jan. 1984, p. 37, and *Die Presse*, 7 Aug. 1984.

[139]At the time of Milošević's take-over of power in September 1987, the repertoire in Belgrade theatres included plays such as *The Decline of the Serbian Empire, The Salonika Veterans Speak, The Killing of the Voïvod*, and *The Migration of Serbdom* (Stambolić, op. cit., pp. 156–7).

[140]Dobrica Ćosić, *Grešnik*, Belgrade, 1985, p. 418.

ing the Party involves giving up one's moral integrity and independence of thought and—unable to abandon his own liberal ideals
of truth and justice—becomes 'the sinner'. Rejected by his former
comrades, including members of his family, he is forced to realise that
adherence to communist dogma also demands the betrayal of one's
own family and nation.

Echoing the historiographical theme of the Comintern's anti-
Yugoslav policy in the interwar period, one of the novel's central
questions is how Serbian communists could, 'on the Kremlin's
command, pursue the destruction of Yugoslavia, [their] homeland, for
which [they] had gone to war for several years and for which half of
[their] people died'.[141] The answer given by communist activists is as
simple as it is unscrupulous:

Communists of every country have to find the Achilles' heel of the bourgeoisie;
you do not start a revolution only by class war, without allies. According to
the Comintern, in Yugoslavia, the Achilles' heel of the bourgeoisie is national
inequality and the lack of unity.[142]

Since the interests of the Soviet Union demand collaboration with
'the enemies of the Serbian people' and working for the break-up
of Yugoslavia, Serbian communists prove their total commitment
to the cause by effectively betraying their nation. This betrayal is
compounded, according to Ćosić, by the fact that the Serbs are
surrounded by enemies. Threatened by their 'historical enemies' from
the First World War—Germany, Austria, Hungary and Bulgaria—
they are equally at the mercy of the other nations in Yugoslavia, none
of whom want the common state.[143]

Ćosić's novel not only provides a reinterpretation of the nature
of the communist movement, but contains a reappraisal of the 'Yugoslav
solution' to the Serbian national question. Building on the themes
and technique he established in *A Time of Death*, Ćosić confronts his
fictional character, Vukašin Katić, with two authentic figures, Slobodan
Jovanović and Dragiša Vasić, interwar intellectuals and members of
the Serbian Cultural Club.[144] In the course of their discussion, Vasić

---

[141]Ibid., p. 238.

[142]Ibid., p. 246.

[143]Ibid., pp. 288–94 and 331–6 passim.

[144]The Serbian Cultural Club was created in 1937 as an opposition-minded
think-tank. After the 1939 Agreement, it concerned itself primarily with the
articulation of Serbian national interests. Vasić was a well-known lawyer and writer,
who eventually joined the Chetniks and became an advisor to their commander,
Draža Mihailović. He was killed, probably by the Ustasha, towards the end of the

argues that the 1939 Cvetković-Maček Agreement, which established an autonomous Croatian unit in Yugoslavia, amounts to Yugoslavia's 'Munich'—appeasement of Croatian separatism.[145] Nevertheless, Jovanović continues to advocate Yugoslavia as the only way for both Serbs and Croats to avoid becoming dominated by outside powers. For him, Yugoslavism should not be a 'national idea', aimed at merging the country's diverse peoples, but a 'state idea'—a rational compromise based on common interests.[146] Unlike Vasić, he does not see Croatian aspirations for autonomy as a 'stab in the back', but as a clear signal for Serbs to mobilise and create their own national programme: 'As soon as the Croatian question was opened, so was the Serbian. If Croats want ethnic borders and an ethnic entity, then we, Serbs, must create our own ethnic entity and draw our own borders'.[147] He argues that Serbs should not turn against the Yugoslav state, since they are scattered all over its territory, but that they should work for the satisfaction of their own interests within it.[148]

Vukašin Katić, on the other hand, believes that 'Yugoslavia is the most expensive and most tragic delusion of the Serbian people'.[149] In his view Serbs fought the First World War believing that Croats and Slovenes would see them as liberators, but were soon confronted with the realisation that they were merely considered as new occupiers. Deluded by their own ideas of South Slav brotherhood and fundamentally unable to understand the 'insurmountable difference of religion' and 'the hatred they did not deserve', Serbs fruitlessly defended the common state:

We have sacrificed everything for Yugoslavia—our liberty, democratic institutions, parliamentary life, freedom of the press, and above all, our national identity and our prestige as the most developed Balkan state. We were

---

war. On Jovanović see above, p. 88. On the ideas of the Serbian Cultural Club, see Miodrag Jovičić (ed.), *'Jako srpstvo—jaka Jugoslavija'. Izbor članaka iz 'Srpskog glasa', organa Srpskog kulturnog kluba, 1939–1940*, Belgrade, 1991.

[145]Dobrica Ćosić, *Grešnik*, Belgrade, 1985, pp. 332–3 and 362. On the creation of the *'Banovina* Croatia' by the 1939 Agreement, see Ljubo Boban, *Sporazum Cvetković-Maček*, Zagreb, 1964. The Croatian unit encompassed the pre-war territory of Croatia, most of Slavonia, Dalmatia and parts of Bosnia-Hercegovina and had authority over the economy and trade, social policy, justice, internal administration and, in 1941, the regional police.

[146]Ćosić, *Grešnik*, p. 364.

[147]Ibid., p. 360.

[148]Ibid., p. 364. For Jovanović's ideas on the national question, see *'Jako srpstvo—jaka Jugoslavija'*, op. cit., pp. 45–51, 95–6 and 181–4.

[149]Ćosić, *Grešnik*, op. cit., p. 291.

annihilated by war and left without the strength for peace. And in that peace, we devoted all our political wisdom to solving the Croatian question and put all our national energy into saving a state that could not be saved. A state which is only saved by dictatorship and police ideology ... has no reason to exist.[150]

Katić recognises the Croats' right to their own state and wishes Serbs had let them create one much earlier. In his view, solving the question of borders with the Croats would be a lot less difficult than trying to save Yugoslavia. The author's message is clear: first of all, the victory of communism was a terrible historical mistake, based on lies, injustice, fanaticism and the sacrifice of human life and dignity; second, if, as Vukašin Katić put it, 'Yugoslavia is only possible as a totalitarian state ... [then] we have to choose: do we want freedom and democracy or Yugoslavia?'[151] For Katić in 1939 there was no doubt as to the answer: the disintegration of Yugoslavia, even at the cost of a war, would represent 'the real national liberation of the Serbian people and the beginning of its great renewal and historical recovery'.[152] For Ćosić there did not seem to be one either; in his diary entry for April 1982, he noted that 'the existence of Yugoslavia is irreconcilable with democracy and freedom', but that 'without these it has no reason to exist'.[153] Indeed, in his view, the Serbs had to 'sober' themselves of their traditional Yugoslavism because the country's unraveling had gone too far and forced reintegration would lead only to further 'divisions, enslavement and shame'.[154]

The scathing criticism of the Yugoslav communist movement and the disillusionment with Yugoslav unification were echoed in other works of literature of the time. Slobodan Selenić, the author of the ground-breaking *Memoirs of Pera the Cripple* of 1968,[155] published in 1985 a new novel, *Očevi i oci* (Fathers and Forefathers), in which he told the tragic story of a 'bourgeois' family torn apart by the ideological and political upheaval that characterised the final years of the Kingdom of Yugoslavia and the Second World War. The novel represented a rehabilitation of the old Serbian bourgeoisie with its liberal democratic values.[156] Selenić's protagonist Stevan Medaković—'educated as a

---

[150]Ibid., p. 337.
[151]Ibid., p. 338
[152]Ibid., p. 366.
[153]Dobrica Ćosić, *Promene*, Belgrade, 1992, p. 62.
[154]Ibid., p. 76.
[155]See Chapter 1.
[156]Igor Mandić in *NIN*, 15 Dec. 1985, p. 40.

democrat, a professor who for years taught his students that the right of the minority to equal presentation of its point of view is the first condition of democratic procedure'[157]—stands as an inherently positive and complex literary figure. He is confronted with the unscrupulous totalitarian ideology of the victorious Yugoslav communists, who provide the vehicle by which all that is dear to him is destroyed— his country, his class and finally also his own family. For Medaković the communists are members of 'a kind of religious sect, who operate with a few dogmatic formulas and phrases which they apply with a senseless blindness everywhere and for everything'.[158] Depicting them as primitive and uncouth 'Huns and Visigoths', who revel in 'muddying and destroying, breaking the order ... with the naturalness of the first humans born in the jungle',[159] Medaković nevertheless has to recognise communism's victory over his own liberal values, when his son—a brilliant but deeply troubled youth—is seduced by the movement and is killed as a Partisan volunteer in 1945.

This family drama and the destruction of the old order and the values of the Serbian bourgeoisie also provide the context for a related reflection on the national question and the existential dilemma of the common state. As in Ćosić's *The Sinner*, it is articulated in the course of a conversation between the fictional protagonist Stevan Medaković and the historical figure of Slobodan Jovanović. Medaković refuses to join Jovanović's Serbian Cultural Club because in his view Yugoslavia cannot be saved. The main reason is that 'Croats will not defend Yugoslavia ... because they were always only interested in how to become and remain independent.'[160] Arguing that even the establishment of a 'state within the state' for Croats in 1939 does not satisfy their desire for full independence, Medaković is worried that 'all this proof that Croats do not want Yugoslavia has only increased our thoughtless piedmontism, instead of making at least Serbian intellectuals more reasonable'.[161] Like Ćosić's Vukašin Katić, he evaluates the consequences of creating the common state on the Serbs and comes out with a devastating verdict. Yugoslavia has destroyed all the Serbs' positive traditional values and highlighted the negative aspects of their national character. The royal dictatorship proclaimed in 1929 to preserve Yugoslavia has 'only succeeded in thoroughly

[157]Interview with Selenić, *NIN*, 25 Aug. 1985, p. 33.
[158]Slobodan Selenić, *Očevi i oci* (1985), Belgrade, 1990, p. 236.
[159]Ibid., p. 269.
[160]Ibid., p. 141.
[161]Ibid., p. 143.

destroying Serbian political life and greatly strengthening the national parties of the Croats, Slovenes and Bosniaks'.[162] Serbia's ambitions had simply been too great for its 'civilisational capacity':

> Serbia could swallow Croatia and Slovenia, but it could not digest them. From their 'oppression' in Yugoslavia, we thus see how Croatia and Slovenia are surfacing stronger than ever; from its 'hegemony', Serbia is emerging totally disintegrated.[163]

Although Jovanović continues to insist that the Croats too need Yugoslavia and that the main question is not whether the country should stay together but how, Medaković is not convinced. His own vision of Yugoslavia as a Serbian mistake prevails in the novel.

Both Ćosić's and Selenić's novels were among the most popular of 1985;[164] nevertheless, they remained destined for a more educated readership. The question of Yugoslavia's desirability gained the clearest answer—in plain vernacular of rural Serbia—by the quintessential Serbian peasant in Danko Popović's best-seller of the same year, *Knjiga o Milutinu* (The Book about Milutin). Popović traces Milutin's travails from his participation in the First World War to his imprisonment as a *kulak* by the new communist authorities and his death in jail in communist Yugoslavia. Milutin's common sense and naïveté provide the vehicle through which the main events of the first half of the 20th century are apprehended, and his commentary on the creation of the common Yugoslav state, the corruption and disunity of that state, the resurgence of war in 1941 and the immorality of the new communist authorities, illuminates the absurdity of the struggle and sacrifices of the Serbian people.

In 1914 Milutin goes off to fight for unification with 'our brothers in Austria', taught about the brotherhood of South Slavs and of their common desire for unity. Yet Milutin notices that the Slav brothers 'did not rise up, they did not experience the same as us, they lived and cooperated with their enemies' and that they look upon their 'liberators' with a haughty disdain.[165] He also fights for Macedonia, only to be told half a century later that the Serbs had in fact not

[162]Ibid., p. 147.

[163]Ibid., p. 153.

[164]See *NIN*, 24 Feb. 1985, p. 29, and 8 June 1986, p. 44. Particularly Ćosić's novel achieved very high levels of popularity; it sold out in a record 30,000 copies within a few weeks.

[165]Danko Popović, *Knjiga o Milutinu* (1985), Belgrade, 1986, pp. 42–3 passim.

'liberated' but 'occupied' Macedonia. In the end Milutin gains nothing from the 'large' new state. He only has to pay higher taxes and feels more distant from his king. When it falls apart in 1941 and he hears of the atrocities committed against the Serbs in the Independent State of Croatia, Milutin merely comments that this is proof that 'nobody saw this state as theirs, everyone dug its grave, and now it is dead' and that 'we Serbs should really learn from this and get a bit more intelligent'.[166] He notices that the Partisans, led by a Croat and a Slovene—Tito and Kardelj—raise their insurrection in Serbia, where the Nazi occupiers execute a hundred Serbs for every German, instead of doing it 'where they are from', where the cost to the population is not nearly as high. Watching his son go off to fight and die on the front for the construction of the new communist Yugoslavia, Milutin reflects: 'What is this fatherland of ours worth, that we constantly give it all that is dearest to us?'[167]

The book's overwhelming popularity (it appeared in over twenty editions since 1985, of which seventeen came out by the end of 1986) reflected the changing mood in Serbia. Not only did it seduce an unprecedented number of readers, but it also received considerable critical acclaim from the ranks of numerous intellectuals and reviewers.[168] In accounting for this unprecedented success, author Danko Popović noted that Milutin was not a fiction, but 'our all-Serbian grandfather', whose simple peasant values and moral strength represented an antidote to the sense of uncertainty and crisis.[169] Popović also argued that the book was so popular because 'some historical themes are very topical in our current reality'.[170] The source of the Serbs' current problems was Yugoslavia, in which 'defeated Croatia realised its historical goal, while victorious Serbia remains disunited, without all its Serbian lands', although the Serbian people had 'paid for the illusions, short-sightedness and ignorance of its leading politicians' by perishing in the camps and pits of the Independent State of Croatia.[171] Popović's statement referred to the final link in

[166]Ibid., p. 78.

[167]Ibid., p. 114.

[168]See *NIN*, 10 Aug. 1986, pp. 28–9, and *Književne novine*, 709, 1 May 1986, pp. 8–9, 18.

[169]Danko Popović, *Vreme laži*, Belgrade, 1990, pp. 10–12. For the populist nature of Popović's book, see Mirko Djordjević, 'Književnost populističkog talasa' in Popov (ed.), *Srpska strana rata*, op. cit., pp. 394–418.

[170]Ibid., p. 9.

[171]Ibid., pp. 20–1.

the vision that combined the Communist 'stab in the back' and the Serbs' 'Yugoslav mistake': the theme of genocide.

The theme of genocide: the Second World War revisited

Of all the legitimising myths of the Yugoslav regime, it was the official version of the 'common struggle against the occupier and domestic traitors' during the Second World War that was the most important. A veritable 'policy of memory' was constructed around the Partisan war, giving rise to a host of research institutes and projects, monuments and commemorations, aimed at fostering a common identity among the Yugoslav population and justifying communist rule.[172] The official interpretation of the war contained two principal aspects: first, it relied on a simple dichotomy, presenting the Partisans as 'revolutionaries' and 'liberators' and all other forces as 'counterrevolutionaries' and 'fascists'; secondly, it effectively 'de-ethnicised' the war, by blaming the 'bourgeoisies' of all Yugoslav nations for the crimes that had taken place and by dealing with wartime inter-ethnic conflicts only in terms of superficial reciprocity (all nations had their traitors, all had committed cruelties and none was more or less guilty).[173] In the atmosphere of revision and disclosure in the 1980s, both aspects of the official representation of the war came under attack.

The first challenge to the portrayal of the defeated Chetniks as nothing but traitors and collaborators came in 1983, in a collection of poems entitled *Istočnice* (East Stars) by Ljubomir Simović, published as a supplement with the April edition of *Književne novine*. As a result, the issue was banned and the journal was subsequently discontinued for over a year.[174] Simović was expelled from the Party and subjected to intense pressure from the authorities.[175] Several of the poems presented the Partisan-Chetnik war as fratricide rather than a liberation struggle—not glorious but a personal and national hell. One explicitly commemorated the thirty-eighth anniversary of a battle between Partisans and Chetniks, reflecting on the thousands of dead, all of whom had been killed 'by the hand of a godfather, father, son or

---

[172]Wolfgang Höpken, 'War, Memory, and Education in a Fragmented Society: The Case of Yugoslavia', *East European Politics and Societies*, XIII/1, 1999, p. 197.

[173]Ibid., p. 200, and Höpken, 'History Education', op. cit., p. 92.

[174]See Chapter 1.

[175]*NIN*, 24 Apr. 1983, pp. 35–6, and 3 June 1983, pp. 31–2, and *Danas*, 7 June 1983, pp. 12–15. On *Književne novine's* 'transgressions' see also Chapter 1.

brother'.[176] In the course of the next few years, the notion that the Partisan–Chetnik conflict was symbolic of the divisions within the Serbian nation increasingly gained ground. The most explicit statement of this kind was made at a forum held at the Writers' Association of Serbia in January 1985, by the poet Matija Bećković, one of the 'usual suspects' of the intellectual opposition, whose father had been a Chetnik: 'The civil war was the central event of our history and our fate ... It seems we fought each other most of all. Half a century since the Second World War we still live off digging in our chasms, instead of burying our blood and wounds.'[177] Bećković's plea for Serbs to achieve national reconciliation gained importance over the course of the next several years, becoming the central theme of a part of the political opposition that was created at the end of the decade.[178]

In historiography, it was Veselin Djuretić's 1985 monograph *Saveznici i jugoslovenska ratna drama* (The Allies and the Yugoslav War Drama), that provided the most radical reappraisal of the Second World War and the proscribed Chetniks. Djuretić was the first not to use the communists' ideological prism for the presentation of the war and openly to depart from the official condemnation of all the revolution's enemies.[179] His voluminous study, which was based on abundant documentation from the American and British archives and for the first time included references to Serbian émigré sources, analyses the Allies' transfer of support from the Yugoslav government in exile and the Chetniks to Tito's Partisans. He traces this change of Anglo-American policy to the effectiveness of Soviet propaganda, which deliberately misrepresented the first Yugoslav state as subject to 'Greater Serbian hegemony', diminished the Serbs' suffering in the Independent State of Croatia and exaggerated the extent of Croatian participation

---

[176]'Na Tridesetosmogodišnjicu bitke izmedju Partizana i Četnika na Jelovoj Gori meseca septembra godine 1944' in Ljubomir Simović, *Istočnice*, Belgrade, 1983, p. 14.

[177]Quoted in *Naša reč*, 363, March 1985, p. 19.

[178]Notably of the Serbian Renewal Movement, the largest opposition party (see Chapter 5). On the issue of national reconciliation, see also Budding, 'Serb Intellectuals and the National Question', op. cit., pp. 380–1, and Dejan Djokić, 'The Second World War: Reconciliation Among Serbs and Croats and Irreconciliation of Yugoslavia', paper presented at a workshop on 'Post-Kosovo Balkans: Perspectives on Reconciliation', School of Slavonic and East European Studies/University College London, March 2000.)

[179]Djordje Stanković's review in *NIN*, 29 Sept. 1985, p. 40. Djuretić barely even uses the word 'revolution' in his account of the war.

in the Partisan movement in order to discredit the Chetniks and present Tito's communists as the only viable antifascist force.[180]

Djuretić's aim was to refute the thesis of a symmetrical culpability of Croats and Serbs for war crimes, as well as to show the 'real dimension' of Serbian participation in the liberation struggle.[181] He therefore clearly stated that Serbs provided the vast majority of all the opposition forces, Chetnik and Partisan, because they were subjected to Nazi brutality in occupied Serbia and genocide in the Independent State of Croatia. According to Djuretić, the Chetniks were equally committed to the war against the Axis forces, but were imbued with a 'national realism' concerning the plight of Serbian civilians, the target of excessive German retaliation. They therefore mitigated their actions and sought a *modus vivendi* with the occupier in order to protect the population from reprisal, sinking into ever greater defeatism and collaboration. The Partisans, on the other hand, remained true to their 'revolutionary realism', heedless of the people's suffering, and continued to fight.[182] Backed by the Soviet Union and the Anglo-Americans, Tito was thus able to achieve final victory for his forces. The main losers in the story were the Serbs, who had been victims of both foreign and internal oppression, as well as of Allied betrayal.[183] As his fellow-historian Djordje Stanković put it, Djuretić's desire to break communist propaganda and symmetries thus provided fuel for a new myth of Serbian martyrdom.[184]

Djuretić was not a member of the intellectual opposition kept under surveillance by the authorities. Before publishing his controversial history, he had been an established historian who had collaborated on the compilation of Tito's complete works at the Institute of Contemporary History in Belgrade. He then moved to the Balkanological Institute of the Serbian Academy of Sciences and Arts, headed by Radovan Samardžić, a prominent early-modernist who at

---

[180]Veselin Djuretić, *Saveznici i jugoslovenska ratna drama 1941–1945* (1985), Belgrade, 1992. An exhaustive review of Djuretić's book is provided by Stevan K. Pavlowitch, 'London-Moscow through the Fog of Yugoslavia's Wartime Drama', *Storia delle Relazioni Internazionali*, III/4, 1987, pp. 369–94, and IV/1, 1988, pp. 195–213.

[181]Ibid., II, pp. 472–3. These arguments inevitably provoked bitter recriminations in Croatia. See, for example, Ljubo Boban, 'Srpska ratna drama Veselina Djuretića' in his *Kontroverze iz povijesti Jugoslavije*, I, Zagreb, 1987, pp. 399–441, and *Danas*, 13 Jan. 1987, p. 23.

[182]Djuretić, op. cit., I, pp. 201–8.

[183]Marjanović, 'L'Historiographie', op. cit., pp. 154–9.

[184]*NIN*, 29 Sept. 1985, p. 40.

this time became a member of both the dissident Committee for the Defence of Freedom of Thought and Expression and the group working on the Academy's Memorandum. The Balkanological Institute's publication of his revisionist book has subsequently given rise to allegations that it represented a conscious attempt by the Academy to 'test the ground' for the 'launching' of its controversial Memorandum a year later. On closer inspection, however, this argument appears deeply flawed: first, the Memorandum had not even been written at the time of the publication of Djuretić's book and, second, the Academy did not 'launch' it at all—the Memorandum was stolen and published without its consent, causing the institution considerable problems at the time.[185] Nevertheless, the Academy's presentation of the book amid great pomp and circumstance (at which over 500 people, including many opposition intellectuals, participated) testifies to the change in climate in this important cultural institution and the extent to which an influential core group of nationalist intellectuals was becoming increasingly assertive.

When the regime resorted to repressive action, first putting tremendous pressure on the Academy to distance itself from the historian and expelling both the author and his two official readers from the Party, to then legally prohibit further editions of his book, it mobilised the intellectual opposition, which—as in other cases—defended the author's right to free speech. Instead of discrediting Djuretić, therefore, regime repression only ended up turning the affair into a political confrontation and precluded an informed discussion of Djuretić's ideas. In this way, the contested post-Titoist regime merely contributed to sparking even greater public interest in the book and provided its author with a scholarly renown and legitimacy he may not otherwise have achieved. The book's first two editions immediately sold out and, although the third and fourth were banned, pirated copies circulated in Belgrade, apparently fetching up to $200 on the black market.[186]

Part of the interest in Djuretić's controversial history of the war was undoubtedly contained in his uninhibited portrayal of the mass extermination of the Serbs in the Independent State of Croatia, which became the most potent historical symbol of Serbian victimisation in the latter part of the 1980s. In communist Yugoslavia the issue of

---

[185]See Chapter 4.

[186]Branko Lazitch, 'Espaces de liberté et Yougoslavie,' *Est et Ouest*, 41, Apr. 1987, p. 8.

the wartime treatment of Serbs in Croatia and Bosnia-Hercegovina had been 'effectively buried'.[187] Although it was not a taboo as such, the memory of the genocide was seen as a direct threat to the new Yugoslav state and the 'brotherhood and unity' of its peoples. Because of this, official memorials raised for the 'victims of fascism' never specifically mentioned the ethnic or religious communities subject to the Ustasha extermination policy (Serbs, Jews and Gypsies).[188] Yet the powerful collective memories of the wartime suffering remained firmly ingrained among the survivors, transmitted through family oral history and tales of atrocities which circulated outside the channels of publicly permitted discourse.

Although some controversies about the number of war victims appeared in the 1960s and during the 1971 Croatian 'mass movement', the return of dogmatism in the 1970s prevented any genuine debate about this painful recent history from taking place. When the issue resurfaced in the post-Titoist period, this time in Serbia, it immediately took on an extremely volatile tone. The fact that it was initially treated in semi-fictional form by authors whose families were directly affected by the 'suppressed memories' they described contributed to the emotional charge of this already extremely sensitive subject. As in the case of Goli Otok, the Serbian experience in the Independent State of Croatia was 'opened' in the early 1980s by writers, notably Vojislav Lubarda, Vuk Drašković and Jovan Radulović, who were all originally from Bosnia-Hercegovina and Croatia.[189]

The first of these, Vojislav Lubarda's autobiographical account, *Anatema* (Anathema), published in 1982, documents the author's persecution following the appearance of an excerpt from his unpublished novel *Gordo posrtanje* (Proud Stumbling) in a Sarajevo journal in 1969. The excerpt, reproduced in *Anathema*, recounts the 1941 massacre of local Serbs by Muslim Ustasha in the author's home town in eastern Bosnia, followed by the revenge killings carried out by Serbian Partisans. Lubarda's graphic depiction of the Ustasha massacre is given particular poignancy by the inclusion of himself as a child watching his own father being taken away for execution.[190]

---

[187]Bette Denich, 'Dismembering Yugoslavia: Nationalist Ideologies and the Symbolic Revival of Genocide', *American Ethnologist*, XXI/2, 1994, p. 367.

[188]Ibid., p. 370.

[189]Lubarda was born in 1930 in Rogatica, a town in eastern Bosnia, Drašković in 1946 in Vojvodina into a Hercegovinian immigrant family, and Radulović in 1951 in Polača, a village in the old Military Frontier known as the Krajina.

[190]Vojislav Lubarda, *Anatema* (1982), Gornji Milanovac, 1990, p. 40.

In his text Lubarda broke a number of taboos. First, in his portrayal of the Ustasha massacres, he not only vividly described events he personally had witnessed, but also provided the real names of a number of prominent Muslims from the town who had perpetrated the slaughter; several of these had subsequently joined the Party and achieved positions of power in the local bureaucracy. Second, Serbian Partisan veterans also objected to Lubarda's depiction of their own side in the war as a vengeful 'horde'. Finally, the town of Rogatica itself condemned Lubarda's choice of subject and reproached him for not writing about the 'brotherhood and mutual aid' between Serbs and Muslims in the post-war reconstruction of the town and the building of the 'glorious socialist future'.[191] The end-result was a virulent campaign against the author that cost him his job, prevented him from publishing for ten years and nearly landed him in prison. His description of his travails, which eventually forced him to leave Sarajevo for Belgrade, is supported by reprints of the articles, declarations and political interventions and provides a devastating account of the Bosnian regime's attempts to force his silence. Furthermore, Lubarda's picture of Bosnian reality as characterised by 'hundreds of years of living by the knife'[192] directly undermined the officially espoused slogan of 'brotherhood and unity' and his comments about life in the communist republic implied that ethnic fissures were only papered over by the new regime.

A similar point was made by Jovan Radulović's 1983 play *Golubnjača* (The Pigeon Pit). Set entirely in the 1960s, it depicts a Serbian community in Croatia unable to overcome the trauma left by the wartime massacres and symbolised by the ravine (the 'pigeon pit') into which many locals had been thrown by Croats from the neighbouring village. The continuing chasm between the Serbian and Croatian villagers undermined the claim that the ideal of brotherhood and unity held any substance, while the extreme poverty and backwardness of the two communities cut through the core of communist propaganda about the progress inherent in the 'building of socialism'. The communists are represented in the play by farcical figures of a paedophile schoolteacher and a 'pale' war veteran, whose mechanical repetition of the worn-out slogan 'Long live brotherhood and unity of Serbs and Croats!' is contrasted with the behaviour of the Serbian and Croatian schoolchildren, who mirror the adults' behav-

---

[191]Ibid., p. 72.
[192]Ibid., p. 88.

iour by insulting and threatening each other.[193] Thus Radulović's play not only painted a difficult past and a desolate present, but also a hopeless future.

The fate of *The Pigeon Pit* was representative of the inability of the authorities to curb the propagation of the emergent reappraisal of history and of their losing battle against the budding intellectual opposition. The staging of the play in Novi Sad in autumn 1982 initially went smoothly and received considerable critical acclaim, but after ten performances Vojvodinian authorities branded it as an instance of 'Greater Serbian chauvinism' and banned it because its 'political messages and aims are leading to negative social reactions, and its treatment of relations between nations is unacceptable'.[194] Following the ban, protests from different personalities, groups and institutions followed, with the Writers' Association of Serbia at the forefront of the movement. Finally, the play was put on in Belgrade by the Student Cultural Centre, provoking renewed attacks on the Serbian leadership for 'fostering nationalism' in the republic.[195] Eventually *The Pigeon Pit* went on to be staged in Slovenia, where it played to full houses and even won a prize. Despite the pressure on both Lubarda and Radulović, the two authors continued to be politically engaged. In the 1990s Lubarda was among the founders of the Belgrade-based Bosnian Serb organisation and Radulović even became a minister in the 'Republic of Serbian Krajina' during the war in Croatia.

The third author to revive the painful historical memory of the Ustasha persecution was the journalist and writer Vuk Drašković, who later went on to become the leader of the most important opposition party in Serbia in the 1990s. Drašković based his 1982 novel *Nož* (The Knife) on the true story of the massacre of a Serbian family by its Muslim neighbours in a Hercegovinian village on the Orthodox Christmas Eve in 1942. He had heard this story many times in his childhood, behind closed doors, 'at a time when the great crime against the Serbs could only be whispered about'.[196] In his story a new-born baby, the Serbian family's only survivor, is taken by one of the perpetrators as compensation for the killing of his own son and raised as a Muslim. In his subsequent search for his roots, this young man progressively discovers the truth about his identity

[193]Jovan Radulović, *Golubnjača* (1982), Belgrade, 1993, pp. 94–5.
[194]*NIN*, 19 Dec. 1982, p. 32.
[195]*NIN*, 2 Jan., 1983, p. 40.
[196]Drašković's interview in *Vreme*, 18 July 1998, p. 31.

and the horrifying wartime crime and, at the end of the novel, embraces his Serbian identity.[197]

The fate of Drašković's protagonist is clearly meant to be a symbol of the relationship between Muslims and Serbs. References to the Battle of Kosovo and the conversion of Serbs to Islam under Turkish rule pepper the novel and represent the 'original sin' providing the underlying rationale of the wartime massacres. Because Muslims were Serbs who had adopted the conquerors' faith, they had turned against their brethren to eliminate all traces of their treason:

It is because you have the same blood, because they grew from your seed, that their hatred knows no limits. It is precisely for this reason that there are no bounds to their madness. That [common] origin is the stain on their conscience and their name ...[198]

Although the novel contains a number of sympathetic Muslim characters, who resist the persecution of the Serbs during the war and deeply regret the crimes that were committed in their name, the borderline between victims and villains is clearly drawn. Symbolised by the fate of Drašković's protagonist, the only hope of redemption is for the converts to go back to their 'true', Serbian, identity. The young man's discovery that he is a Serb thus meant that 'there was no longer the feeling of being guilty of something, of being half-foreign in the midst of your own house'.[199] Drašković's public readings from his novel and conferences he gave at this time made his point explicitly and were often met by 'frenetic applause' from his audiences.[200] As a result he was expelled from the Party, dismissed from his job and unable to find work for years.

In the mid-1980s Drašković drew closer to the Serbian Orthodox Church, which itself began to devote ever more attention to the topic of genocide.[201] He was also among the first to raise the idea of the 'brotherhood in suffering' between Serbs and Jews. In 1985 he sent an open letter to Israeli writers, reminding his Jewish 'brothers' that 'every span of Serbian land [was] Jerusalem' and that Serbs and Jews perished in the Second World War 'at the hands of the same executioners, were exterminated in the same concentration camps,

[197]Vuk Drašković, *Nož* (1982), Belgrade, 1990.
[198]Ibid., pp. 13–14.
[199]Ibid., p. 365.
[200]See *NIN*, 20 Feb. 1983, pp. 3–4.
[201]See Radmila Radić, 'Crkva i "srpsko pitanje" ' in Popov (ed.), *Srpska strana rata*, op. cit., pp. 279–81.

slaughtered on the same bridges, burned alive in the same caves and disappeared in the same pits'.[202] Implying that only an independent national state represented salvation, Drašković noted that the creation of the state of Israel had ended Jewish suffering, whereas the Serbian 'Golgotha' still continued. This parallel with the Holocaust gained ground in the intelligentsia, contributing in May 1988 to the creation of a Society of Serbian-Jewish Friendship by Belgrade opposition intellectuals.[203]

As Serbian writers broached the subject of the Ustasha genocide in a new way in the early 1980s, two main themes became central: the number of war victims and the causes of the genocide. The debate on the number of war victims resulted from an exaggerated initial figure provided by the Yugoslav government to the international reparations commission after the war, which later enabled speculation that easily gave rise to nationalist arguments by both Serbian and Croatian intellectuals.[204] In the 1980s two independent studies of Yugoslav war casualties, carried out concurrently by Vladimir Žerjavić, a Croatian scholar, and Bogoljub Kočović, an émigré Bosnian Serb statistician and lawyer, came up with very similar results. Using population censuses of the time, they calculated that the total number of war victims for the country lay just above one million, approximately half of which were Serbian (487,000 according to Kočović and 530,000 according to Žerjavić).[205] Although the proportional losses sustained by the Serbs, Croats and Muslims in the whole of Yugoslavia were in the same range, in the Independent State of Croatia a substantial difference is clear: Serbian losses were 334,000 or around 17% of their total population, while Croatian and Muslim losses were 203,000 (6%) and 75,000 (8.6%) respectively.[206] There is less reliable information on the

[202]Vuk Drašković, 'Letter to Israeli Writers', 17 Dec. 1985, in *Naša reč*, 373, March 1986, pp. 8–9.

[203]See *NIN* 5 June 1988, p. 36. The Society had twenty-one founders, including Dobrica Ćosić, Andrija Gams, Pavle Ivić, Mihailo Marković, Ljubomir Tadić, Matija Bećković, Predrag Palavestra, Dragoslav Mihailović, Ljubomir Simović, Boris Mihajlović-Mihiz and Slobodan Selenić. It also aimed to reverse Tito's pro-Arab policy and promote closer ties with Israel.

[204]See Srdjan Bogosavljević, 'Nerasvetljeni genocid' in Popov (ed.), *Srpska strana rata*, op. cit., pp. 159–70. For an explanation about the source of these high figures see Vladeta Vučković in *Naša reč*, 368, Oct. 1985, pp. 2–3.

[205]Bogoljub Kočović, *Žrtve drugog svetskog rata u Jugoslaviji*, London, 1985, and Vladimir Žerjavić, *Gubici stanovništva Jugoslavije u drugom svjetskom ratu*, Zagreb, 1989.

[206]These are Kočović's figures, in ibid. Proportionally, Jews and Gypsies suffered the greatest losses (around 80% of their pre-war population for the former and

numbers that perished in the Ustasha concentration camps. Žerjavić has estimated that approximately 83,000 people died in Jasenovac, the largest camp, of whom more than half were Serbs.[207]

With the publication of these two independent yet similar assessments, one would have expected the debate on the war losses to have been laid to rest. This may have been so if it had really just been about numbers. Yet, the issue of war losses, which became particularly focused on Jasenovac as the symbol of Serbian suffering in the Independent State of Croatia, was intrinsically tied to the more controversial questions concerning the nature of Ustasha policy itself, its historical roots, the extent of its support by the Croatian (and Bosnian Muslim) population and its uniqueness in the context of the generalised civil war in Yugoslavia. As Robert Hayden has noted, for Serbian nationalist intellectuals, exaggerating the Serbian dead, particularly in Jasenovac, would inevitably break the officially established 'symmetry' of victimisation and villainy in the war and feed into the notion of Croatian 'betrayal', whereas for Croatian nationalists, inverting the numbers equation, provides the logic that 'there were few bodies, hence no genocide, hence nothing to be sorry about'.[208]

The contestation of the excessive official figures that began in Croatia in the 1960s was in and of itself a valid historical enterprise. However, the problem lay in the way this task was undertaken by intellectuals of the Croatian 'mass movement', who not only excessively reduced the war losses, particularly those of the Serbs, but tied this project to a wider 'rehabilitation' of Croatian history, including an attempt to 'relativise' the Ustasha experience.[209] After the 'mass movement' was suppressed in 1971, Croatian 'nationalists' continued to argue in smaller gatherings or interviews with foreign journalists that Croatian and Serbian war losses were approximately equal and

---

around 30% for the latter). Žerjavić's estimates for the number of Serbs and Croats killed in the Independent State of Croatia are almost identical to Kočović's. His figures for Muslims are slightly higher.

[207]Vladimir Žerjavić, *Opsesije i megalomanije oko Jasenovca i Bleiburga*, Zagreb, 1992, p. 72.

[208]Robert Hayden, 'Balancing Discussion of Jasenovac and the Manipulation of History', *East European Politics and Societies*, VI/2, spring 1992, p. 208. See also Hayden's debate with two Croatian historians, Ljubo Boban and Anto Knežević, in ibid., VI/2, spring 1992, pp. 207–12, VII/1, winter 1993, pp. 155–67, and VII/3, fall 1993, pp. 577–82.

[209]See, for example, Vlado Gotovac's statement about the efforts of the 'mass movement' in *Danas*, 17 Dec. 1991, p. 32.

maintained that, although the Independent State of Croatia was a 'black mark' in Croatian history, all nations, if they regarded themselves honestly, 'have their black marks'.[210]

The most open contestation of the official figures came from Franjo Tudjman, a former Partisan general turned historian who became Croatia's first democratically elected President in 1990. In his second trial in February 1981, Tudjman argued that the total figure for Yugoslavia's war dead was no more than 800,000, that Croatia had lost around 185,000 of whom 'a vast majority were Croats' and that the number of people who had died in *all* the camps of the Independent State of Croatia was not more than 60,000. The bloating of these figures was, in his opinion, an attempt to impose a collective 'guilt complex' on the Croatian nation and to keep it subjugated to the 'centralist-unitarist forces' in Belgrade.[211] In his 1989 book *Bespuća povijesne zbiljnosti* (Impasses of Historical Reality)[212] Tudjman minimised the Ustasha extermination campaign against Serbs, by arguing that the wartime 'Greater Serbian' programme of the Chetnik movement was 'no less radical'[213] and that 'throughout history there have always been attempts at a 'final solution' of foreign or dissimilar racial and ethnic or religious groups', so that 'every attempt at establishing the nature of all forms of genocidal acts in one historical period alone is a futile task'.[214] In his eyes, the fundamental precondition for settling the Croatian-Serbian differences and overcoming the 'Jasenovac myth' lay in 'rationally and soberly' assessing historical causalities, 'accepting' the national identity of both Serbs and Croats and recognising 'that each of the two has the right to self-determination and *its own state*'.[215]

As Tudjman and other Croatian nationalists attempted to minimise the figures and the importance of the Ustasha extermination

---

[210]See the interviews by Marko Veselica and Vlado Gotovac in Katich (ed.), *So Speak Croatian Dissidents*, op. cit., pp. 110 and 48 respectively.

[211]Tudjman's defence speech in ibid., pp. 122–6.

[212]Franjo Tudjman, *Bespuća povijesne zbiljnosti* (1989), Zagreb, 1994. The American edition of this book is entitled *Horrors of War* (New York, 1996). Although the editor's note warns that this edition was 'substantially revised', it actually not only leaves out the contentious passages on the Holocaust, but in some cases changes their very meaning. (For example, compare p. 114 to the Croatian edition, p. 207.)

[213]Ibid., pp. 158–60. For a refutation of this argument, see Denich, op. cit., p. 375. On Ustasha ideology and extermination policy see A. Djilas, *The Contested Country*, op. cit., pp. 103–27, and Fikreta Jelić-Butić, *Ustaše i NDH*, Zagreb, 1977, pp. 158–87. On Tudjman, see Jill A. Irvine, 'Ultranationalist Ideology and State-Building in Croatia, 1990–1996', *Problems of Post-Communism*, July/Aug. 1997, pp. 30–43.

[214]Ibid., p. 233.

[215]Ibid., p. 687 (emphasis added).

of the Serbs, in order to remove the stigma from their own project of Croatian independence, their Serbian counterparts were doing the opposite, magnifying Serbian war losses even beyond official statistics, thus feeding nationalist visions of Serbian victimisation. Already in the early 1980s Vladimir Dedijer stated that between 480,000 and 800,000 people had been killed in Jasenovac alone, while Velimir Terzić, another general turned historian, argued that over one million Serbs had died in the camp.[216] Testifying to the surge of interest in the subject, from 1986 onwards a series of new histories appeared in Serbia on various aspects of the Ustasha extermination policy, while poets and writers produced works that vividly evoked wartime massacres of Serbs in the Independent State of Croatia.[217]

Although the theory of the Croatian (and Muslim) betrayal of the Serbs had arisen in the early 1980s, it was not until 1986 that an article directly on the subject of the 'continuity' of Croatian 'genocidal intentions' towards the Serbs appeared. The author of this text, published in *Književne novine*, the main journal of Serbia's intellectual opposition, was Vasilije Krestić, a professor at Belgrade University, director of the Serbian Academy's historical archives and member of the 'Memorandum' committee. Krestić had distinguished himself as a historian of the 19th century, focusing primarily on Serbian-Croatian relations, the 'Yugoslav idea' and national intellectual currents of the time.[218] In 1983 he had published a collection of articles on *Serbo-Croatian Relations and the Yugoslav Idea 1860–1873*, where he already argued that the most prominent 19th-century Croatian proponent of Yugoslavism, Bishop Juraj Strossmayer, in fact merely sought the unification of the Croatian 'political nation', using the Yugoslav idea as a cover.[219]

[216]Dedijer, op. cit., p. 489, and Velimir Terzić, *Slom Kraljevine Jugoslavije*, II, Belgrade, 1983, p. 610 and *Intervju*, 5 Aug. 1983, p. 9.

[217]In historiography, these were, most importantly, Viktor Novak, *Magnum crimen* (1948), Belgrade, 1986, and Branimir B. Stanojević, *Alojzije Stepinac: zločinac ili svetac?*, Belgrade, 1986, on the role of the Catholic Church and a vast collection of documents, collected by Antun Miletić in *Koncentracioni logor Jasenovac*, I–III, Belgrade and Jasenovac, 1986–7. Literary works include poems by Stevan Raičković commemorating two of the worst Ustasha massacres of Serbs during the war, in the villages of Glina and Prebilovci, in *Suvišna pesma. Devet fragmenata o genocidu sa predgovorom i komentarima*, Belgrade, 1991, and Slobodan Selenić's novel *Timor mortis*, Sarajevo, 1989, which also evokes the Glina massacre.

[218]Less than two weeks after the appearance of Krestić's contentious article on the 'genesis' of the genocide, the far-reaching public scandal concerning the Memorandum broke out.

[219]Vasilije Krestić, *Srpsko-hrvatski odnosi i jugoslovenska ideja 1860–1873*, Belgrade, 1983, pp. 119–52 and 'Zmaj i Štrosmajer', *Književne novine*, 713–14, 1 July 1986, p. 13.

In his 1986 article 'On the genesis of the genocide of the Serbs in the Independent State of Croatia', Krestić devoted no space to the actual creation of the Ustasha movement or the period of the first Yugoslav state, but focused instead on 'deeper causes', reaching back as far as the 16th and 17th centuries.[220] Noting that from the moment Serbs settled in the territories of present-day Croatia, they were subjected to pressures to become serfs and Uniates by the local elites, he stated that, already 'at the dawn of the 18th century, Croatian feudal circles were—for reasons of class and religious antagonism—ready for genocide against the Orthodox Serbian population which had immigrated to their lands'.[221] He argued that this policy continued throughout the 19th century, as all Croatian intellectual and political elites worked to create an ethnically pure 'Greater Croatian' state. Krestić argued that the 'genocidal idea' had matured fully in Croatian bourgeois society already before the First World War and that this 'programme' had merely been deferred until the next war. All in all, he concluded, the Ustasha genocide against Serbs was inherent in their 'centuries-long cohabitation', and its long 'gestation' had allowed for the creation of a wide basis in Croatian society and was 'deeply rooted in the consciousness of many generations'.[222]

Both Krestić himself and Miodrag Perišić, editor of *Književne novine*, rejected the barrage of accusations that were heaped upon the historian in the official media, and Krestić affirmed that he had never accused 'the whole Croatian people' of being genocidal, but had spoken only of the Croatian 'bourgeoisie' and its political parties.[223] Although he did win a court case against a journalist who accused him of claiming that Croats were 'genetically genocidal', his remonstrations could not acquit him of the accusation that he had endorsed an extreme intentionalist vision of Croatian 'genocidal tendencies'. That he completely ignored Croatian grievances in the interwar state which contributed to the rise of extremism before 1941, and did not examine the Ustasha ideology itself, or the question of how much support the Ustasha regime actually had in the Croatian traditional elites and population, were already grave omissions for any examination of the 'genesis of genocide'. In addition, his claim

[220]Vasilije Krestić, 'O genezi genocida nad Srbima u NDH', *Književne novine*, 716, 15 Sept. 1986, p. 1.

[221]Ibid., loc. cit.

[222]Ibid., pp. 4–5.

[223]See Perišić's editorial in *Književne novine*, 718, 15 Oct. 1986, p. 2, and Krestić's reply to critics in 720, 15 Nov. 1986, pp. 6–7.

about a centuries-long continuity of genocidal 'intent' among all Croatian elites implied that the mass extermination of Serbs was an inevitable ('inherent') phenomenon and left a clear message that Serbs in Croatia could never be safe—either in the past or in the present.

From the summer of 1988 genocide became a central theme in the media and particularly in the yellow press, using explosive language, vast generalisations and reproducing photographs from the war showing dead and mutilated bodies for full shock effect.[224] Instead of working to calm spirits and provide a more measured scholarly approach to the subject, Serbia's most important cultural institution and one of centres of the intellectual opposition, the Academy of Sciences and Arts, played into this media orgy. At a widely publicised conference dedicated to Jasenovac in November 1988 participants enumerated one after the other the horrendous ways in which Serbs had been killed and tortured by the Ustasha, from the instances of Serbian villagers being burned alive in their Orthodox churches to 'bloody orgies' and 'the breaking of legs and arms, gouging of eyes, cutting of tongues and noses, hammering of nails into skulls and brains, the nailing of hoofs on people and mass rape of virgins'.[225]

Along with this insistence on the gory details of the Ustasha terror, many speakers accused the communist regime for its 'complicity of silence'. In an interview preceding the conference, former diplomat Milan Bulajić, one of the advocates of 'maximalist' figures on the war dead, asked why the Partisans had not tried to liberate the inmates of Jasenovac or attack prisoner transports to the camp?[226] The implication of his question was quite clear: it confirmed that the Yugoslav communists had been anti-Serbian, or at least did not consider the defence of the Serbs as a worthy task. In his presentation at the conference, Bulajić lamented that Jasenovac now resembled a 'golf course' and protested against the maintenance of the taboo on the 'real' number of victims of the genocide.[227] Other participants demanded why no compensation had been paid to the victims of

---

[224]See Zoran M. Marković, 'Nacija—žrtva i osveta' in Popov (ed.), *Srpska strana rata*, op. cit., pp. 647–50.

[225]See *NIN*, 27 Nov. 1988, p. 27.

[226]*NIN*, 17 July 1988, p. 26.

[227]*NIN*, 27 Nov. 1988, p. 26. In 1989, Bulajić published a four-volume work, where he insisted on the 'correct' number of victims of 1,700,000 dead and 2,800,000 demographic losses. (Milan Bulajić, *Ustaški zločin genocida*, I-IV, Belgrade, 1989) He also entered into a bitter polemic with Vladimir Žerjavić over the latter's results on the war victims (see Žerjavić, *Opsesije*, op. cit., pp. 23–33).

Ustasha terror and why no Ustasha had been tried for genocide in association with Nuremberg. Vladimir Dedijer, the organiser of the conference, directly accused Vladimir Bakarić, Croatia's leading post-war communist, of keeping some 'important documents' concerning the Ustasha crimes under lock and key.[228] A month later, in December 1988, a delegation of the Academy visited Jasenovac, receiving full coverage in the Serbian media.

In his assessment of the causes of the outbreak of war in Yugoslavia in 1991 the American scholar Dennison Rusinow noted the importance of 'collective existential fear, refracted from group to group until almost all were affected'.[229] This belief that the national community was threatened by extinction—which existed in all contemporary Yugoslav nationalisms but was most prevalent in the Serbian—originated in the revision of history of the 1980s, particularly in the theme of genocide contained in the new nationalist vision forged within the Belgrade intelligentsia. The revival of the painful historical memory of the wartime massacres of Serbs in present-day territories of Bosnia-Hercegovina and Croatia was, in any case, bound to cut at the very heart of the official communist slogan of 'brotherhood and unity'. Yet the graphic descriptions of the slaughter and mutilation, the exaggerated figures of Serbian victims and the allegations of a 'conspiracy of silence' about the crime all contributed to the increasingly public outrage at the communist 'stab-in-the-back'. When linked to a radically 'intentionalist' explanation of Croatian and Muslim 'genocidal' tendencies, this conspiracy theory assumed even more ominous implications about the impossibility of cohabitation with other Yugoslav nations. The notion propagated by many intellectuals that genocide was 'one of the most important factors determining Serbian history' and even 'the fate of the Serbian people'[230] also provided a potent symbol not only to characterise the past but to explain the present—in particular, the disclosure of the large-scale emigration of Serbs from Kosovo.

[228]*NIN*, 27 Nov. 1988, pp. 26–8.
[229]Rusinow, 'The Avoidable Catastrophe', op. cit., p. 18.
[230]Radovan Samardžić, interview in *NIN*, 30 Apr. 1989, p. 35.

3

THE WATERSHED: INTELLECTUALS AND KOSOVO, 1985–8

In the mid-1980s Serbia's intellectual opposition transferred the focus of its political activism from the struggle for freedom of expression to the so-called 'Kosovo question'. As in the revision of history, this new cause represented a reaction to political events and problems of the post-Tito period. The outburst of Albanian nationalism in 1981, accompanied by stories of human rights violations and forced Serbian emigration from Kosovo, were met by what was widely perceived as an inadequate and undemocratic response by the Yugoslav leadership. This context was extremely propitious for critical intellectuals to step in as a substitute political force; Kosovo represented a cause which allowed them to transcend their existing defence of freedom of speech, embrace a wider human rights issue and—considering the vision of Kosovo as the 'Serbian Jerusalem', a holy land of inestimable importance to national identity—adopt the role of guardians of both universal and national values. By launching their new 'battle' for Kosovo in 1985 the Belgrade activists turned into a *de facto* political opposition, directly challenging state policy and providing an alternative political platform to the Serbian public.

The way the intellectual opposition came to define the 'Kosovo question', however, turned it away from its liberal, universalist aspirations towards a more narrow nationalist agenda. As the established dissident fora mobilised to fight for the rights of Kosovo Serbs, they generally continued to emphasise their commitment to peaceful, democratic means for the resolution of the problem and also defended the civil rights of Kosovo Albanians standing trial for 'verbal crime' and participation in the 1981 demonstrations. At the same time, however, they accompanied their human rights activism with an affirmation of

Serbian national rights to Kosovo and a call to reduce the province's self-rule despite Albanian demographic preponderance in the province. Applying explosive language and a one-dimensional historical interpretation proper to the new nationalist vision, exaggerating claims of Serbian mistreatment in Kosovo and portraying Albanians as collectively guilty of 'genocide', the Belgrade intellectual opposition effectively precluded any genuine compromise on the issue. In their eyes Serbs could only be protected and the 'Kosovo question' resolved by the reassertion of Serbia's control over the province. They argued that the achievement of Serbia's 'statehood' in Yugoslavia would also rectify the 'injustice' that had been perpetuated against the Serbs, who—unlike Yugoslavia's other nations—were the only ones not to have such a state in their republic. In this way—like their Albanian counterparts, who were calling for their own Republic (read state) of Kosovo—they exposed their inability to move beyond the established Titoist practice of providing territorial solutions to problems of human and minority rights and the 'model of ethnic domination' that had characterised such solutions until then.

Defining the Kosovo question, 1981–5

The Albanian revolt of 1981 shook the very foundations of the post-Tito regime and exposed the extent to which the national question had not been resolved. Although Kosovo had functioned as a *de facto* republic since the early 1970s,[1] the unrest reflected 'the pent up feeling of frustration, universal among Kosovars, for failing to have their province promoted to republican status ... [which] was interpreted as discrimination against them as Albanians by South Slavs'.[2] The

---

[1]Kosovo had received the right to nominate its own government and representatives to federal decisionmaking bodies (including veto power), along with the right to fly the Albanian flag alongside the Yugoslav and pursue virtually independent foreign relations, cultural and trade links with Albania. Kosovo got its independent Albanian-language university, Albanological Institute and, as of 1978, an Academy of Sciences and a Writers' Association. Albanians were also given preferential treatment in state employment in the province—see Ramet, *Nationalism and Federalism*, op. cit., pp. 192–4. This was acknowledged by the Kosovo leadership of the time. See Azem Vllasi's interview in Momčilo Petrović, *Pitao sam Albance šta žele*, Belgrade, 1996, p. 47).

[2]Arshi Pipa, 'The Other Albania: a Balkan Perspective', *South Slav Journal*, VIII/1–2, spring-summer 1985, p. 20. On the 1981 demonstrations see also Julie A. Mertus, *Kosovo. How Myths and Truths Started a War*, Berkeley, CA, 1999, pp. 17–93.

grassroots nature of the movement, which escaped communist control, in fact frustrated the Kosovo political leadership's realisation of its long-term project to achieve the status of a republic for the province.[3] The demonstrations considerably reduced the manoeuvrability of the province's Albanian leadership, while enabling Serbian politicians, long unhappy with the constitutionally untenable situation in the republic, to demand a revision of the provinces' autonomy. The mass purges of both the leadership and the intellectual elites from the Kosovo Party, along with the temporary introduction of martial law and a host of long-term repressive measures, only confirmed the Albanians' alienation from Yugoslavia. More than 1,600 Albanians were tried and imprisoned, of whom over 400 were minors, and throughout the post-Tito decade Albanians made up around 80% of the total number of political prisoners in Yugoslavia.

A related phenomenon that came into the open in the aftermath of the 1981 events was that Serbs and Montenegrins had been constantly emigrating from Kosovo, particularly since the 'Albanianisation' of all instances of power in the province after 1966.[4] According to official statistics, approximately 105,000 Serbs and Montenegrins left the province between 1941 and 1981, of whom more than half emigrated after 1961.[5] Another 26,000 Serbs left between 1982 and 1988, which brought the total number of emigrants to one-third of the original population.[6] Due to this continuous emigration and the difference in birth-rates between Kosovo Serbs and Albanians, the proportion of Serbs in the population of the province diminished

[3]Mahmut Bakalli, Kosovo's leading communist purged in 1981, in *Pitao sam Albance šta žele*, op. cit., p. 20.

[4]For the sake of concision, we will continue to refer only to the emigration of Serbs, which included that of the Montenegrins. This is not meant to imply that Montenegrins are Serbs.

[5]Srdjan Bogosavljević, 'Statistička slika srpsko-albanskih odnosa' in *Sukob ili dijalog*, Subotica, 1994, p. 23.

[6]Marina Blagojević, 'Iseljavanje Srba sa Kosova: Trauma i/ili katarza', in *Srpska strana rata*, op. cit., p. 236 and Branko Horvat, *Kosovsko pitanje*, Zagreb, 1989, p. 157. Horvat noted that, before 1988, Albanians also emigrated from the province, but much less so in relative terms. Official statistics corroborate this: of the 4562 individuals who left the province between June and December 1983, 54.9% were Serbs and Montenegrins and 24.3% were Albanians (*NIN*, 25 March 1984, p. 13). After the reassertion of Serbian rule over the province, these proportions changed. From 1989 to 1993 around 7,200 Serbs and Montenegrins and 9,700 Albanians emigrated from Kosovo (Blagojević, op. cit., p. 237).

progressively over time. Whereas it had remained stable between 1931 and 1961 at around 23–27% (with Albanians making up approximately 60–67%), in the 1960s this equilibrium was clearly broken, with the proportion of Serbs being reduced to 13.2% in 1981.[7] Neither Albanians nor Serbs have contested the high Albanian birth-rate, the emigration of Serbs and the decline of the Serbian population in proportion to the Albanian, although there have been some differences in the figures cited.[8] It is the causes of the emigration that have provided the subject of greatest controversy.

Two polarised arguments were given to explain the causes of Serbian emigration.[9] The first one, coming from the Albanian side, was that Serbs were simply leaving for economic reasons. The Kosovo writer Rexhep Qosja argues:

> The underdevelopment of Kosovo, limited possibilities of employment, low wages, poor quality of life, a better life in Serbia, along with better pay, family relations and the desire to be with children who married outside Kosovo— all these are reasons which conditioned migrations of Serbs and Montenegrins and others, from Kosovo.[10]

According to this view, Serbs were simply leaving the province to seek employment opportunities and a better life elsewhere. Kosovo was by far the poorest part of Yugoslavia and felt most acutely the consequences of the economic recession. In 1984 Slovenia's gross domestic product was over seven times higher than Kosovo's, equivalent to the discrepancy between the United Kingdom and Northern Africa.[11] In addition, Albanian scholars have claimed, the loss of privileges that Serbs enjoyed in the province until 1966 and 'their unwillingness to accept equality with Albanians' induced many of them to leave.[12]

---

[7] Blagojević, op. cit., pp. 234–6 passim, and Bogosavljević, op. cit., p. 17. Between 1953 and 1991, the Kosovo Albanian birth-rate remained between 6.32 and 6.16 children per woman, while that of Serbs in the region fell from 5.92 to 2.78.

[8] Kosovo Albanian demographer Hivzi Islami provides a smaller number of Serbian emigrants: 52,000 between 1966 and 1981 and another 20,000 between 1981 and 1994 (Hivzi Islami, 'Demografska stvarnost Kosova', in *Sukob ili dijalog*, op. cit., p. 47). An unofficial number that circulated in Belgrade was of 200,000 emigrants between 1966 and 1986.

[9] See the survey in Tonci Kuzmanić and Slavko Gaber (eds), *Kosovo-Srbija-Jugoslavija*, Ljubljana, 1989, pp. 320–1.

[10] Rexhep Qosja, *Nezaštićena sudbina*, Zagreb, 1990, p. 146.

[11] Horvat, op. cit., p. 136.

[12] Islami, op. cit., p. 46.

Serbs, on the other hand, argue that emigration was due mainly to pressures and discrimination. From 1982 on, the increasingly uncensored Serbian press reported emigrating Kosovo Serbs' stories, most of which followed a similar pattern:

We did not leave for economic reasons, we had large farms. Most of us left due to conflicts with our Albanian neighbours. Their cattle destroyed my crops for years. My children were beaten on their way to and from school ... Slowly [the other Serbian villagers moved out and] I was left alone. Then came the problems at work and I was declared redundant twice. In the end I couldn't take it any more. I closed up my five-room house, left behind ten hectares of fields and forest and came [to Serbia] to sublet a flat. I tried to sell my farm, but my neighbours are scaring away all potential buyers. I have estimated my land and buildings at 270 million dinars—they will only give me 90 million. I am here, so my neighbours cut my forest, their cattle grazes on my fields and now they don't even have to buy my farm.[13]

These two arguments were mirrored in official investigations of the causes of emigration. Two studies carried out at approximately the same time (1982–3) produced very different conclusions. An investigation by a Kosovo Province Committee working group showed some evidence of discrimination, but concluded that the main causes of emigration were social and economic,[14] while a study by a working group of the Serbian Parliament and the Federal Executive Council (FEC) claimed that emigration was the result of 'a political atmosphere and the use of vandal methods with the aim of creating an "ethnically pure Kosovo"'.[15] Of the 5,000 heads of emigrant Kosovo Serb families who were interviewed, only 1.4% did not say they had left under pressure.[16] Both documents were debated in the Federal Parliament in October 1982 and while Albanian delegates criticised the findings of the Serbian/FEC working group for accepting uncritically the Kosovo emigrants' statements, Serbian delegates discredited the findings of the Kosovo commission because they relied on unreliable official sources in the province. They argued that people most often did not state the real reasons for wishing to emigrate when requesting relocation permits, due to the bias of the authorities and the tremendous complications this could create for them.[17] Both studies were kept

---

[13]*NIN*, 22 November 1981, p. 20.
[14]*NIN*, 14 March 1982, pp. 10–11.
[15]Quoted in *Naša reč*, 341, January 1983, pp. 16–17.
[16]*NIN*, 10 October, 1982, p. 17.
[17]*NIN*, 31 October 1982, p. 16 and 11 December 1983, p. 3.

'top secret', but photocopies circulated in Serbia and findings were leaked to the press. The émigré journal *Naša reč*, which was widely read by the Belgrade intelligentsia, even published excerpts from the Serbian Parliament's document.

In 1985 two Belgrade sociologists undertook an independent survey under the auspices of the Serbian Academy of Sciences and Arts. Their results, published in 1989, corroborated the vision of emigration under pressure. Of a representative group of over three thousand Serbian emigrants from Kosovo, only a quarter cited economic factors as the causes of their resettlement in Serbia. They generally had a relatively advantageous material and social situation in Kosovo, were rooted there and many even spoke Albanian. Most of the questioned pointed to discrimination as the main cause of emigration: half cited oral threats and a feeling of insecurity, a third mentioned threats and beatings of their children and difficulty in obtaining education in Serbo-Croatian. A quarter cited employment problems, but always in reference to discrimination (different criteria applied to Serbs and Albanians in hiring practices, favouritism of Albanians in the workplace, few possibilities of promotion for Serbs etc.). Around 11% referred to material damage (arson, killing of farm animals, desecration of monuments etc.) and acts of physical aggression (assault, rape and murder), often stating that the authorities had not undertaken anything for their protection despite their requests. The police and local courts were often accused of covering and colluding with the perpetrators. The researchers concluded that a 'pyramid' of factors had pushed the Serbs to leave, ranging from a relatively limited number of direct acts of physical aggression to a vast base of discriminations and threats creating a charged atmosphere and a feeling of insecurity.[18]

A second study undertaken by an independent commission directed by lawyer Srdja Popović, a liberal intellectual and defence counsel in many political trials, re-examined the causes of Serbian emigration at the end of the decade, when the nationalist hysteria in Serbia had reached a highpoint. The commission included Vesna Pešić and Ivan Janković, members of the Committee for the Defence of Freedom of Thought and Expression, Svetlana Slapšak, president of the Committee for the Defence of Freedom of Creation of the Writers'

---

[18]Marina Blagojević and Ruža Petrović *Seobe Srba i Crnogoraca sa Kosova i Metohije*, Belgrade, 1989. An overview of the findings can be found in Blagojević, op. cit.

Association of Serbia from 1986–9, and human rights campaigners Nataša Kandić, Dejan Janča and Tanja Petovar, all of whom later became prominent anti-war activists in Serbia. The study included analyses not only of the causes of emigration, but also of crime rates in the province and of the language used in reporting on Kosovo by Belgrade's main newspaper, *Politika*. Although the commission showed (on the basis of official statistics) that there was little substance to the allegations of mass physical aggression and rape, which had by this time become the prevalent ingredient of public discourse on Kosovo,[19] it confirmed that Kosovo Serb emigration was provoked above all, by the 'model of domination' incarnated by the League of Communists. The report argued that the Party represented the vehicle of ethnic domination in all parts of communist Yugoslavia, which meant that in Kosovo—as elsewhere—the ethnic group which controlled the Party apparatus at a particular time (Serbs from 1945 to 1966, Albanians from 1966 to 1988 and Serbs again from 1989) discriminated against members of the other ethnic community, using all the instances of power: the administration, legal system, media, security apparatus and education.[20]

In view of this research, there was a case to be made for the definition of the Kosovo question as a problem of democracy and human rights, both for the Albanians who were imprisoned for demanding a republic and the Serbs who were victims of discrimination.[21] Yet the Serbian leadership's response was—as Ivan Stambolić himself later admitted—'hesitant, disunited, ... clumsy and even fearful', aware that the situation was 'untenable' but too afraid of a possible backlash in Serbia and of being labelled nationalist by other leaderships in Yugoslavia.[22] Behind closed doors it concentrated on a strategy of constitutional change, which aimed to bring the provinces under Serbia's jurisdiction and necessitated consensus-building with Serbia's reluctant partners in the collective Federal Presidency, as well as approval from the province leaderships themselves.[23] At the same time it tried to placate public

---

[19]Srdja Popović, Dejan Janča and Tanja Petovar (eds), *Kosovski čvor: drešiti ili seći?*, Belgrade, 1990, pp. 34–46 passim. On the 'nationalist rape' hysteria in Serbia see Wendy Bracewell, 'Rape in Kosovo: Masculinity and Serbian Nationalism', *Nations and Nationalism*, VI/4, 2000, pp. 563–90.

[20]*Kosovski čvor*, op. cit., p. 22.

[21]Blagojević, op. cit.

[22]Stambolić, op. cit., pp. 81–4, 174.

[23]See Chapter 2.

opinion by unsuccessful attempts at window-dressing, such as the creation of a Commission for the Prevention of Emigration of Serbs and Montenegrins in 1981 whose results were negligible. Confronting Albanian demands for a 'Kosovo Republic' and the Serbs' allegations of persecution 'would have required acknowledgement that a conflict existed and would have destroyed the illusion of peace, equality and a balanced order—the 'brotherhood and unity' that the political leadership considered indispensable'.[24] Instead, officially the Albanian revolt of 1981 was portrayed as a 'counter-revolution' which had resulted from 'bureaucratism' and the 'infiltration of the class enemy' (with collusion from hostile outside forces) and which had to be fought by 'differentiation' of the unhealthy from the healthy elements within the Party.[25] Continuous trials and imprisonment of Albanian 'irredentists' not only failed to stem the Serbian emigration from the province, but antagonised the Albanian population even more.

The clumsy and undemocratic response of the province, republic and federal governments provided a classical example of a situation ripe for intellectual activism: the presence of a burning social, political or national issue which appealed to matters of higher moral principle, combined with the absence of a political context that could bring about genuine change. In the view of the Belgrade intellectual opposition, Ivan Stambolić was an apparatchik whose commitment to solve the Kosovo problem was purely formal. Although he was working to introduce market reforms in the economy and a revision of the constitution, his constant references to outdated symbols, combined with the continuing (though weaker) censorship and repression in the cultural sphere made it impossible for him to gain the sympathies of reform-oriented intellectuals. In their view the regime's mismanagement of the Kosovo problem was simply further proof of its undemocratic character. As Dobrica Ćosić put it in 1989,

If we had had a state based on the rule of law and a democratic approach to the Kosovo question and the situation of the Serbs, if our national oligarchies had had political sense, a conscience and enough courage, at least in 1981, if not in 1968, to speak out about the persecution of Serbs ... and call upon the

---

[24]Slavko Ćuruvija and Ivan Torov, 'The March to War (1980–1990)' in Jasminka Udovički and James Ridgeway (eds), *Yugoslavia's Ethnic Nightmare*, New York, 1995, p. 79.

[25]See, for example, the interview with Sinan Hasani, the Kosovo Albanian Deputy President of the Federal Parliament, *NIN*, 5 July 1981, p. 22.

Yugoslav government ... to guarantee fundamental civil rights, if this question had not been perceived as purely a Serbian one, but as a democratic and Yugoslav one, I am sure that Yugoslavia would not have sunk into the agony in which it is today.[26]

In this sense, Kosovo provided an excellent opportunity to expand the intelligentsia's struggle for freedom of expression to include a wider notion of minority and human rights and 'offered a chance for all democratically-oriented intellectuals to honour legitimate complaints by the Serbian population in Kosova, while still supporting the autonomy of the Albanians and hastening the political liberalisation of Serbia as well as Yugoslavia in general'.[27]

A few initial signs seemed to indicate that this could take place. Two months before the unrest in Kosovo in 1981, a novel by the Belgrade writer Slobodan Selenić entitled *Prijatelji* (*Friends*) won the prestigious *NIN* prize. The recognition awarded to this story of a friendship between a Serb and an Albanian represented a challenge to the prevalent negative stereotype of Albanians in Serbia.[28] Even after the demonstrations, the petition of over a hundred university students from Belgrade, Zagreb and Ljubljana protesting the trials and imprisonment of Albanian students indicated inter-ethnic solidarity against police repression.[29] In November the same year the exiled dissident Mihajlo Mihajlov stated in an interview with the émigré journal *Naša reč* that 'sooner or later the Serbian people will have to reconcile themselves with the fact that Kosovo is ethnically Albanian today ... [and] like it or not, in our times the ethnic argument carries greater weight than the historical.'[30] In an article published in the same journal in the summer of 1982, Milovan Djilas traced the origins of the Kosovo crisis to the general tendency of republican and provincial communists to play the national card as a substitute for democracy. He argued that the regime could temporarily 'stifle the unrest in Kosovo with force and propaganda, but not eradicate it'. For Djilas only free discussion and democratic political organisation could create a wider range of political platforms on the Kosovo problem and increase the

---

[26]Ćosić quoted in Djukić, *Čovek u svom vremenu*, op. cit., p. 200.
[27]Ćuruvija and Torov, op. cit., p. 83. 'Kosova' is the Albanian name for Kosovo.
[28]Slobodan Selenić, *Prijatelji*, Novi Sad, 1980. Selenić undertook extensive research into Albanian customs, language and oral history for the book.
[29]In Magaš, op. cit., pp. 13–14.
[30]*Naša reč*, 329, Nov. 1981, p. 2.

chances of finding a solution. 'In any case', he concluded, with more dialogue 'there would be less violence, less hatred and hopelessness.'[31]

Despite these early signs of the Kosovo question being linked to systemic change and democratic values, ultimately the way in which it was defined by Serbian intellectuals and cultural and religious institutions showed that, for Serbs, much more than human rights was at stake. The reason for this lay in the very nature of Kosovo as a traditional national symbol and the Serbs' quasi-religious reverence for this region as a holy land inextricably linked to their sense of national identity. The Kosovo legend, which lies at the heart of this identity, is based on the historical account of the defeat of the Serbian army by the Ottoman forces in the Battle of Kosovo on 28 June 1389, during which both the Serbian leader Prince Lazar and the Ottoman Sultan Murad were killed and the Serbian aristocracy was wiped out. For Serbs, the legend of this battle, which in popular consciousness marked the beginning of 'the long Turkish night', is 'a tale of human destiny on earth and in the universe, of sin, sacrifice, salvation and resurrection'.[32]

The potent symbolic power of the Kosovo ethic not only sustained a sense of ethnic identity among the Serbian peasantry during the centuries of Ottoman rule, but played an important role in Serbian self-perceptions during the wars of national liberation. The idea of 'avenging Kosovo' and returning to the holy land, sustained by the Serbian Orthodox Church and the teachings of the epic songs during the centuries of Ottoman rule, was combined in the 19th Century with the rise of modern nationalism and figured strongly in the Serbian ideal of liberation from foreign occupation and unification in an independent state.[33] During the Second World War, Tito's Partisans referred to this traditional theme in forging support for their movement and the struggle against the much more powerful Axis occupiers. The Kosovo legend affected even atheist Serbian communists; according to Milovan Djilas, the reception of the 1948 Cominform Resolution on 28 June, the anniversary of the Battle of Kosovo, 'cut into the

---

[31]Milovan Djilas, 'Kosovo, Danas', *Naša reč*, 336, June–July 1982, pp. 2–3.

[32]Aleksandar Petrov, 'Kosovo—sveta priča srpskog naroda' in *Srpsko pitanje*, op. cit., p. 46. On the Kosovo legend and its importance in the forging of Serbian national identity, see Olga Zirojević, 'Kosovo u istorijskom pamćenju' in Popov (ed.), *Srpska strana rata*, op. cit., pp. 201–31 and Thomas A. Emmert, 'Kosovo: Development and Impact of a National Ethic' in John Ackerman, Ivo Banac and Roman Szporluk (eds), *Nation and Ideology*, Boulder, CO, 1981, pp. 61–86.

[33]For a vivid account of the experience of the reconquest of Kosovo in 1912, see Emmert, op. cit. p. 76.

hearts and minds of all us Serbs. Though neither religious nor mystical, we noted, with a certain relish almost, this coincidence in dates between ancient calamities and living threats and onslaughts'.[34] In the 1980s the perception of a renewed and perhaps definitive 'loss' of Kosovo, combined with the conviction that this was the product of pressures and forced Serbian emigration, had an emotional value that went well beyond any rational assessment of reality or national interest.

In view of its traditional role as the guardian of Serbian identity, it comes as no surprise that the first institution to mobilise in the 'defence' of Kosovo in the 1980s was the Serbian Orthodox Church. In February 1982 several priests demanded in an open letter to the Patriarch that the Church break its silence and take action to prevent the 'extinction' of the Serbian people in the province.[35] In April the same year a second, more explicit letter followed suit, signed by twenty-one priests, monks and nuns, including three prominent younger bishops, Atanasije Jevtić, Amfilohije Radović and Irinej Bulović, who soon became the most radical proponents of Serbian national rights within the Church.[36] Their 'Appeal for the Protection of the Serbian Population and Their Sacred Monuments in Kosovo' presented 'the real essence of the Kosovo problem' as a moral and existential issue:

The Serbian people do not have a word more precious than Kosovo, nor a reality more valuable, nor a greater shrine, past, present or future, than is the reality and shrine of Kosovo. For the Serbs, the question of Kosovo is not simply a biological question or just a question of a 'region' or 'province' or a 'republic'. It is something incomparably greater and loftier than that ... The question of Kosovo is a question of the spiritual, cultural and historical identity of the Serbian people ... Kosovo is our memory, our hearth, the focal point of our existence. And to take away a people's memory is to slay that people and annihilate it spiritually.[37]

Linking historical experience to the present, the letter portrayed the emigration of Serbs from Kosovo as merely the last stage of 'the policy from the Bosphorus' aimed at wiping out 'the last remnants of

---

[34]Milovan Djilas, *Rise and Fall*, New York, 1985, p. 201. Apparently, Djilas also saw Lazar's choice of the heavenly kingdom as an inspiration to continue writing his articles in late 1953, which led to his fall from power.

[35]In *Naša reč*, 336, June-July 1982, pp. 15–16.

[36]All three had gained their doctoral degrees in theology in Athens and were professors at the Belgrade Theology Faculty. They were increasingly active on the Belgrade cultural and intellectual scene, taking part in public debates. In 1985, all three were admitted to the Serbian Writers' Association.

[37]In *South Slav Journal*, V/3, autumn 1982, pp. 50–1.

the cross and the last pockets of resistance of the Serbian people in Kosovo', whose executioners were Muslim Albanians. In urgent terms, the letter warned that a 'planned, premeditated *genocide* [was] being carried out against the Serbian people' in the region and that 'suddenly Kosovo is ceasing to be ours and we are ceasing to be what we are'.[38] The struggle depicted by the petition was a contest between the cross and the crescent, good and evil and, by implication, civilisation and barbarism.

In the course of the following years, the Serbian Church directly linked the present emigration of the Kosovo Serbs to other historical traumas, such as the wartime losses in 1914–18 and the 1915 retreat through Albania and, in particular, the extermination of Serbs by the Ustasha during the Second World War. In June 1982 Bishop Atanasije Jevtić, one of authors of the petition, openly referred to the persecution of Serbs by 'Albanian Nazis' in an article in the Church journal *Pravoslavlje* (Orthodoxy).[39] At the end of 1983 the journal began a series of articles by Jevtić, which represented a morphology of massacres of Serbs throughout history, linking the persecution of Serbs in Kosovo during the Ottoman period to the experience of the wartime Independent State of Croatia. In this series, the continuity of 'genocide' went hand in hand with the themes of martyrdom and of being a chosen people. In addition, Bishop Atanasije was defining the mission of the Church for the 1980s: to resume its traditional role of protecting the Serbian nation and keeping alive its historical memory and identity. By 1987—attesting to the radicalisation of the Church—even the moderate Patriarch German spoke of the 'genocide' being perpetrated against Serbs in Kosovo.[40]

Remarkably, the Kosovo question was largely absent from the Serbian intellectual scene before 1985. It had remained a taboo subject ever since Ćosić's famous speech of 1968 and too dangerous for critical intellectuals to raise publicly even in the comparatively liberal early 1980s. The defence of freedom of speech and historical preoccupations, which did not directly concern themselves with the content of state policy as such, provided a more natural rallying point for political mobilisation.[41] When the Kosovo question was first raised, therefore, it appeared as part of the wider quest for historical 'truth' in the usual way that taboo political subjects were broached—by the

---

[38]Ibid., pp. 51–2 passim (emphasis added).
[39]*Pravoslavlje*, 366, 15 June 1982, quoted in Radić, op. cit., p. 270.
[40]*NIN*, 18 Jan. 1987, p. 18.
[41]See Chapter 1.

publication of a revisionist history. The author of the influential historical study called *Knjiga o Kosovu* (Book about Kosovo), which was published among the numerous revisionist writings of 1985, was Dimitrije Bogdanović, a respected scholar of medieval Serbian literature and a member of both the Serbian Academy of Sciences and Arts and the Committee for the Defence of Freedom of Thought and Expression. Significantly, Bogdanović also had a degree in theology and was involved in the Serbian Church's activities on Kosovo.[42] His book became the widely-cited source on the Kosovo question in the Serbian intelligentsia and the main reference in reflections and debates on the subject.

In essence this book represented a response to the historical debates with Albanian scholars over the 'identity' of Kosovo, which had suffocated progress on the *Encyclopedia of Yugoslavia* in the 1980s.[43] Bogdanović's *Book about Kosovo*, however, went further than simply criticising the controversial foundations of the 'Illyrian thesis' prevalent in Albanian scholarship. Characterising the Albanian claims to ancient Illyrian ancestry as not only historically unjustified, but as 'an essentially racist thesis', Bogdanović stated instead that it was 'a historical fact' that 'Kosovo is a Serbian land'.[44] He argued that Kosovo had had a homogenous Serbian population from the Middle Ages until the 18th century and that the 'colonisation of Serbian lands' by Islamicised Albanians had left a 'bloody trail on the Serbian historical consciousness'—a 'dark picture' that could not be erased.[45] Albanians were 'a foreign element', who 'forcibly in stages infiltrated and appropriated for themselves the lands of Kosovo and western Macedonia from their Slavic inhabitants'[46] and embarked on a full-fledged and planned 'genocide' of Serbs between 1878 and 1912—the final straw that definitively broke the ethnic balance in Kosovo.[47]

Book about Kosovo wanted to portray Serbs as the sole victims of historical persecution. It thus sought to counter Albanian claims of victimisation under Serbian rule during the period of the interwar

[42]See, for example, Bogdanović's 1986 lecture at the Serbian Patriarchate in Belgrade, in Dimitrije Bogdanović, *Knjiga o Kosovu* (1985), Belgrade, 1990, pp. 446–51.

[43]See Chapter 2.

[44]Bogdanović, op. cit., p. 318.

[45]Ibid., p. 179.

[46]Ibid., pp. 124–76 passim.

[47]Ibid., pp. 324–5. 1878 saw the creation of the League of Prizren as the core of the Albanian national movement, and 1912 the First Balkan War and the Serbian reconquest of Kosovo.

Kingdom of Yugoslavia. Albanian intellectuals argued that the 'Greater Serbian bourgeoisie' pursued a policy aimed at 'recolonising' Kosovo with Serbs and Montenegrins and forcing out the Albanian population by a variety of measures, including the expropriation of land by an unjust and exploitative agrarian policy, 'permanent terror' and attempts to deport them out of Yugoslavia.[48] They particularly referred to Yugoslavia's negotiations with Turkey in 1938 to resettle 40,000 'Turkish' families from Kosovo and a 1937 presentation on 'The Expulsion of Albanians' to the Serbian Cultural Club by historian and academician Vaso Čubrilović, which described Albanians as 'a wild and untrustworthy element', a 'hardy, resistant and prolific race' incapable of assimilation, and advocated a 'mode of evacuation' that ranged from 'private initiative' and a variety of state pressures to 'secretly raising Albanian villages and settlements to the ground'.[49]

Both texts reflected the broader anti-Albanian climate in Serbia of the 1930s and a desire to 'solve' the 'Kosovo question' by mass deportation. Nevertheless, it is important not to exaggerate the impact of either text. The unsavoury Čubrilović speech was neither published nor translated into an officially adopted policy, but represented a private individual's opinion presented to a non-state body. The Turkish-Yugoslav Convention was only in the process of negotiation and was never implemented.[50] In reference to the agrarian policy, Italian historian Marco Dogo argues that Kosovo at this time was an underpopulated region with plenty of unclaimed land, so that the land expropriated from Albanians represented only a small fraction of the total. Furthermore, the number of Serbian colonisers who settled in Kosovo in the interwar period was too small to alter the demographic reality in the region.[51] Although there had been real discrimination against Albanians in the Kingdom of Yugoslavia, from this perspective, Bogdanović's claim that the negative aspects of the interwar period had been greatly exaggerated in Albanian scholarship, seems reasonable.[52]

[48]See, for example, Ali Hadri, 'The Position and Condition of Kosova in the Kingdom of Yugoslavia (1918–1941)', *Gjurmime Albanologjike* (Prishtina), 2, 1968, reprinted abridged in *The Truth on Kosova*, Tirana, 1993, pp. 127–39.

[49]For both see Robert Elsie (ed.), *Kosovo in the Heart of the Powder Keg*, Boulder, CO, 1997, pp. 400–34. On the Serbian Cultural Club, see Chapter 2, p. 103.

[50]Dogo, op. cit., p. 37, and Stevan K. Pavlowitch, *The Balkans, 1804–1945*, pp. 273–4.

[51]Ibid., pp. 35–8.

[52]Bogdanović, op. cit., p. 227.

Yet, in his section on the interwar period, Bogdanović went considerably further than that. He justified the royal government's plans to resettle Albanians in Turkey and the policy of colonising Kosovo by Serbs, by characterising them as merely an attempt 'to redress the ethnic and national balance in this area and to improve the situation of the Serbian people, which had been marked by chronic violence'.[53] He also denied any conscious attempt of the Serbian authorities to use the agrarian reform to discriminate against the Albanians. For him, the reform simply aimed at ending feudal relations, although he did concede that it allowed misuse. While he did include a chapter on the emigration of Albanians from interwar Yugoslavia, he attempted, through the use of selective facts, to minimise the issue. He did not examine the existing debate on the extent of emigration, but simply gave a relatively conservative figure of 45,000 emigrants—specifying that they were 'not only Albanians, but also ethnic Turks and Gypsies'— and noted that Serbs had also emigrated during this period.[54]

Finally, Bogdanović did not mention the Čubrilović proposal, but merely made a vague reference to another debate in the Serbian Cultural Club in May 1938, where it was proposed 'that Albanians from Yugoslavia emigrate to Albania or Turkey after this was worked out through diplomatic channels, in the same way that Bulgaria, Romania and Greece had satisfactorily solved their problem with their own Muslim populations'.[55] While he correctly concluded that neither the Serbian colonisation nor the emigration of Albanians were significant enough to alter the ethnic balance in the province, from this he extrapolated that 'there cannot be a symmetry of responsibility between these twenty years of 'Greater Serbian hegemony' and the '200 years of Albanian terror against the Serbian people'.[56] With this attitude, he effectively undermined the Albanians' historical memory of past repression and the effect that the disclosures of interwar Serbian approaches to the Albanian 'problem' were having, not just on intellectuals, but on ordinary people in contemporary Kosovo.[57]

Like many of his colleagues, rather than interpreting the federal arrangement of communist Yugoslavia as a response to Serbian political

[53]Ibid., p. 229.
[54]Ibid., pp. 237–9.
[55]Ibid., p. 239.
[56]Ibid., p. 318.
[57]See, for example, the 'Letter from an Albanian from Gnjilane', in Horvat, op. cit., p. 239.

domination of the first Yugoslav state, Bogdanović viewed it as the result of the 'anti-Serbian' interwar Comintern policy.[58] According to him, the granting of autonomy to Kosovo and Vojvodina was unjustified because of the participation of the Hungarian and Albanian minorities in the wartime dismemberment and occupation of the country and the 'genocide' against Serbs and had the ultimate purpose of keeping Serbia weak. He argued that the communist regime was less concerned with ensuring 'the right of minorities to a political existence in the new state' than with the desire 'to eliminate any possibility of recreating Serbia in its previous political concept ... [and] its leading role'.[59] The decentralising constitutions of 1963 and 1974 merely took this a step further, creating the context in which 'Greater Albanian nationalism' could flourish. In his view, Albanian nationalists, in collusion with the Kosovo authorities, were pursuing a policy of 'ethnic cleansing', which, along with their high birth-rate, served 'the main goal of creating a platform for the internationalisation of the 'Kosovo problem' in the definitively changed demographic and ethnic context'.[60] Bogdanović concluded that the essence of the Kosovo problem throughout history had remained the same—it was 'the right of the Serbian people to live on its own territory'—and he warned that, if the Serbs' historical experience in Kosovo was not taken into account, the results of the 'continuous genocide' against them would be legally sanctioned.[61]

Bogdanović's study of the Kosovo question had a purpose beyond pure intellectual inquiry. It attempted to justify by a combination of historical and moral arguments the Serbian claim to Kosovo and, in his own words, to defend 'Yugoslavia's territorial integrity, threatened and undermined by Albanian nationalism'.[62] Furthermore, Bogdanović urged the government to act quickly, before the problem became 'internationalised', reflecting a fundamental distrust in any outside mediation on the issue (which was bound to give precedence to the Albanian 'demographic' claim to Kosovo) and foreshadowing the attitude that many Serbian intellectuals would adopt as the Yugoslav state moved further towards disintegration in the following years. Implicit in this nascent siege mentality was the notion that unity and

[58]See Chapter 2.
[59]Bogdanović, op. cit., p. 293.
[60]Ibid., pp. 309–10.
[61]Ibid., p. 334.
[62]Unpublished letter to the editor of *Politika*, 13 Dec. 1985, in Bogdanović, op. cit., p. 369.

cooperation—of the whole Serbian nation as well as of its intellectual, spiritual and political elites—was the only salvation. Yet the Serbian leadership of the time rejected Bogdanović's recommendations and the vision he provided as 'an example of right-wing history' and a 'book of destruction'.[63] This official attitude confirmed that no convergence between the intelligentsia and the Stambolić regime was possible.

In January 1985 Bogdanović's ideas appeared in condensed form in an interview with *Književne novine*, which accompanied the imminent publication of his book by the Serbian Academy of Sciences and Arts. This interview in the intellectual opposition's main journal resulted in a displacement of the polemic with Albanian scholars from the realm of state-sponsored projects, such as the *Encyclopedia of Yugoslavia*, to the arena of dissident politics. The debate that raged on the pages of *Književne novine* between Bogdanović and his Albanian critics over the next six months represented a 'dialogue of the deaf', with each side insisting on its own, exclusive vision of history and trying to outmatch the other in claiming the status of victim for its own nation. Kosovo historians condemned *Book About Kosovo* as being 'in the spirit of bourgeois Greater Serbian historiography', reaffirmed the Illyrian thesis, criticised Bogdanović for negating the 'patriotic and freedom-loving tradition of the Albanian people' and argued that bad relations between Serbs and Albanians in the past were due to the militaristic and bourgeois elites shaping Serbian policy at the time.[64] Bogdanović replied by denouncing the 'continuous planned and synchronised campaign of certain Albanian intellectuals against the Serbian people and its presence in Kosovo' and asked: 'Where are these [intellectuals] leading research, culture and the whole of the Albanian people? ... Isn't this Nazism?'[65]

Concurrently Bogdanović's book was presented with great pomp and circumstance in both the Serbian Academy and in the Writers' Association, despite the Serbian regime's disapproval. Excerpts from the book were regularly read out during the numerous public manifestations that took place in these Belgrade institutions. During an important three-day discussion on books on Kosovo held in the Writers' Association in March 1986, *Book about Kosovo* not only provided the

[63] *Politika*, 13 Dec. 1985.
[64] *Književne novine*, 688, 15 May 1985, p. 4.
[65] *Književne novine*, 689, 1 June 1985, p. 3.

centre of attention, but was also sold in the hallway. This event marked the first instance of a new coalition being forged around the Kosovo question between members of the intelligentsia, the radical strain in the Serbian Church (Bishop Atanasije Jevtić presented his book of articles from *Pravoslavlje*) and a few politicians (members of the Federal Parliament Batrić Jovanović and Zarija Martinović) backing the Kosovo Serbs.[66] Rejecting the designations used by official instances and media, the participants demanded that the 'right vocabulary' be applied to define the Kosovo question: 'Nazi separatists' instead of 'irredentists', 'chauvinism' instead of 'nationalism' and 'genocide' instead of 'emigration'.[67] The final evening resounded with condemnations of the government's inaction and culminated in a statement by literary critic Zoran Gluščević, who argued, on behalf of all writers, that they must 'call the leadership to responsibility'. As the holders of the 'real truth' about Kosovo, intellectuals had the moral obligation to 'step in' where politicians had failed and to assume the 'defence' of Serbian nation.[68]

Defending the Kosovo Serbs, 1985–7

While Bogdanović's version of history provided the framework for the definition of the Kosovo question in the 1980s, it was the particularly sordid affair of a Serbian peasant, who was allegedly 'impaled' with a bottle by two Albanians, that sparked the Belgrade intelligentsia into action. On 1 May 1985 Djordje Martinović, a peasant from the Kosovo town Gnjilane, came to the local hospital with serious internal injuries caused by the violent insertion of a glass bottle into his rectum. He claimed to have been attacked by two masked men speaking Albanian as he was working in his field. While in hospital in Prishtina he was interrogated several times by province authorities, and a week later an official declaration was issued asserting that Martinović had hurt himself in an act of masturbation. Following further interrogations in Belgrade, where Martinović was transferred,

---

[66] *Večernje novosti*, 6 March 1986.

[67] *Borba*, 6 March 1986. A lone voice against the use of the term 'genocide' in regard to Kosovo was that of the writer Milovan Danojlić, who was president of the Committee for the Defence of Freedom of Creation in 1984 (see *Književna reč*, 286, 10 Oct. 1986, p. 2).

[68] Zoran Gluščević, 'Situacija na Kosovu' in *Kosovo i nikad kraja ...*, Belgrade, 1989, pp. 11–14 passim.

he eventually signed a deposition to this effect. Despite the official version of events and the contradictory evidence from medical experts in Prishtina and Belgrade, it was generally believed in Serbia that the authorities had, in fact, fabricated the story of self-mutilation to hide the extent of the abuses of Kosovo Serbs from the public.[69] Martinović's case, which combined potent images of Serbian suffering under the Turks and of violated Serbian masculinity by the primitive, brutal and oversexed Albanian became the central symbol of the Kosovo question.[70] It captured the notion of historical continuity, the fear of Albanian demographic victory and the vision of Serbian victimisation.

The most prevalent image of Martinović, propagated in the Belgrade intelligentsia, was that of a martyr whose sufferings symbolised the fate of the Kosovo Serbs as a whole. In an article on the case in a popular Belgrade weekly, satirist Brana Crnčević called the attack on Martinović 'Jasenovac for one man' and demanded that the Orthodox Church proclaim him 'a martyr and a saint'.[71] The poet Stevan Raičković portrayed Martinović as a 'martyr with a crown of thorns' and drew a parallel to Ottoman impalement of Serbs, while his colleague Milan Komnenić, who published a collection of poems on Serbian migrations from Kosovo, devoted one poem to 'the Bottle of Djordje Martinović'.[72] The most compelling image of Martinović as a Serbian martyr was provided by artist Mića Popović, one of the best-known non-conformist intellectuals. Upon his election as full member of the Serbian Academy, Popović presented the institution with a monumental painting entitled '1 May 1985'. This painting was not only the largest he had ever painted, but also one of the largest of Yugoslav post-war art.[73] Inspired by Jose de Ribera's 17th-century depiction of 'The Martyrdom of St. Bartholomew', it showed Martinović being raised on the cross by Albanians (recognisable by their skullcaps), a bottle pointing towards him ominously. The collusion

---

[69]Djukić, *Čovek u svom vremenu*, op. cit., p. 267. An account of the case is also provided in Mertus, op. cit., pp. 95–121.

[70]For the sexual and gender connotations of the Martinović case, see Bracewell, op. cit.

[71]*Duga*, 10 June, 1985, reprinted in Svetislav Spasojević (ed.), *Slučaj Martinović*, Belgrade, 1986, p. 318.

[72]Stevan Raičković, 'Krvava brazda' (1986) and 'Kapija Šumadije' (1988) in *Suvišna pesma*, op. cit., pp. 29–35, and Milan Komnenić, *Izgon*, Belgrade, 1987, p. 72.

[73]*NIN*, 12 Feb. 1989, p. 43. The painting measured 3 by 3.3 metres.

of the regime is represented by the image of a policeman watching the crucifixion of the Serbian Christ.

On 16 June 1985 the Writers' Association of Serbia held its regular assembly, which quickly turned from literary affairs to Kosovo and the Martinović case. At the assembly, literary critic Zoran Gluščević compared the situation in Kosovo to the 'most frightening fascist experiences of the Second World War' and warned that 'if we, from a purely human point of view, ignore and accept what is going on ..., our role as writers would become so problematic and empty that none of us would even have the right to sign any of our texts'.[74] Reminding the assembly of the role that writers had played in history, particularly in the Dreyfus affair in turn-of-the-century France, Gluščević called upon his colleagues to accept the imperatives of intellectual responsibility and act in defence of Martinović. With an overwhelmingly positive response, the assembly adopted an open letter demanding the creation of a committee under the auspices of the Serbian parliament to investigate the Martinović case.[75] At the same time the Association Presidency adopted a more general declaration on the situation in Kosovo, which represented its first official critique of government policy. In this statement, it condemned the 'hesitations, games and manipulations undertaken in the name of a false social, political and national interest, to cover up the real situation [in Kosovo], the slowness in government action ... [and] the impediments to the free flow of information'.[76]

While radical in the terms used to describe the situation in Kosovo and in the critique of the official response to it, these declarations nevertheless still had relatively modest aims. Serbian writers centred their demands on the immediate establishment of the rule of law in Kosovo, but emphasised their opposition to the introduction of a state of emergency in the province. They also did not initially raise the question of Kosovo's reintegration into Serbia, remaining focused on human rights. In addition, when Borislav Mihajlović-Mihiz proposed to address the protest letter to the 'real' recipient—the Serbian people— this was rejected, showing the continued hesitation of the Writers' Association to challenge the regime and assert itself as an alternative political force in the public sphere.

---

[74]Quoted in *Slučaj Martinović*, op. cit., p. 66.

[75]*Književne novine*, 691–2, 1 July 1985, p. 2.

[76]'Stavovi delegatske skupštine UKS povodom stanja u SAP Kosovo', *Književne novine*, 693, 1 Sept. 1985, p. 5.

It was the increasing assertiveness and mobilisation of the Kosovo Serbs from 1983 onward and their search for support in Belgrade that pushed the intelligentsia into adopting a more active role in the 'defence of the people'. Although Kosovo Serbs managed to gain the rudiments of a social organisation around two local party cells and two emerging leaders, Kosta Bulatović and Miroslav Šolević, their appeals for support from authorities in Serbia encountered little success until 1987. Their leaders did, however, manage to gain access to the novelist Dobrica Ćosić, whose forbidden 1968 speech on Kosovo had gained him near mythical status among Serbs in the province. Ćosić received visits from groups from Kosovo since the early 1980s and maintained, in his own words, 'intense cooperation' with them.[77] In 1985 he helped the Martinović family hire a lawyer and bring charges against the officials who had forced the allegedly false deposition. He also wrote a letter on Martinović's behalf to Serbia's President and the Federal Minister of Defence.[78] Many Serbs saw Ćosić's help as the mark of intellectual integrity and altruism at a time when it was still dangerous to take such positions and he was well known for his support, including at times even financial aid, to individuals whose rights had been violated. Ćosić's critics, on the other hand, have argued that he inspired and organised the Kosovo Serb activists and manipulated their movement before the Serbian leadership under Slobodan Milošević took over in 1987.[79] There is no evidence to support this claim that Ćosić represented the moving spirit behind the activities of the Kosovo Serbs; rather, their movement sprang up locally and was initially an authentic grassroots phenomenon.[80] However, by the mid-1980s Ćosić undoubtedly had a hand in how they presented their demands to the public and oriented their activism. Judging by the language adopted in Kosovo Serbs' petitions—compared to those of Ćosić's Committee for the Freedom of Thought and Expression—he probably directly participated in the wording of these texts.[81]

The first success of Kosovo Serb activists, thanks to backing from within the Belgrade intelligentsia, came later that year. In July 1985 forty non-Albanian writers sent the Writers' Association of Serbia

[77]Djukić, *Čovek u svom vremenu*, op. cit., p. 304.
[78]Ibid., loc. cit.
[79]See, for example, Stambolić, op. cit., pp. 166, 172–4.
[80]Vujačić, *Communism and Nationalism*, op. cit., pp. 221–4, and Tomislav Sekulić, *Seobe kao sudbina*, Priština, 1994, pp. 104–7.
[81]See below, pp. 151–3.

an open letter alleging discrimination against them in the Writers' Society of Kosovo.[82] The signatories complained of 'majorisation' (a term designating consistent outvoting of a minority national group), which had most recently occurred in the appointment of the Kosovo association's president, Hassan Mekulli. Although Mekulli had been rejected by the Serbian members as an Albanian nationalist and they had resigned in protest upon his election, the organisation continued to function as if nothing had happened. The letter also alleged discrimination against non-Albanian writers in conferences, poetry readings and other public manifestations, as well as in the running of the association. Finally, it expounded on the generally difficult conditions facing the minority Serbs in the province.[83]

Relations between Kosovo's and Serbia's writers' associations were already tense since the beginning of the year, when Radio Belgrade unsuccessfully attempted to organise a discussion on their future links. The province organisations refused to participate; the president of the Writers' Society of Kosovo was constantly 'unavailable for comment' and the president of the Vojvodina association said outright that the idea of a single organisation for the republic was dead and did not even merit discussion. On the other hand, the president of the Writers' Association of Serbia, novelist Miodrag Bulatović, expressed desire for closer links and did not exclude the idea of a future unification of the three associations.[84] In April 1985 a direct confrontation between Bulatović and Albanian writers took place at the Congress of the Yugoslav Writers' Union in Novi Sad.[85] At this important event—the first all-Yugoslav meeting of writers in ten years—Bulatović called upon his Albanian colleagues to denounce the 'genocide' and the 'disgusting fascism' being perpetrated against Serbs in Kosovo.[86] The retort from the Albanian side, by writer Rexhep Qosja, was predictable: 'Against whom could Albanians have committed genocide, when they have always, since history knows of them ..., had to fight for their very existence?'[87] In this context the open letter of the forty Kosovo Serb writers—even if not orchestrated by Bulatović himself, as Albanian

---

[82]In fact, only twenty-one were still members of the Kosovo Society; the others had emigrated and joined other organisations.

[83]*Književna reč*, 260–1, July 1985, p. 3.

[84]*NIN*, 20 Jan. 1985.

[85]On this Congress see Chapter 4.

[86]*Književne novine*, 1 May 1985, p. 5.

[87]Ibid., loc. cit.

writers alleged[88]—certainly presented a welcome opportunity to lobby for a change of the status quo. As so many times in the past, disputes in the cultural sphere reflected already existing power struggles in Yugoslavia's political leadership.

After months of constant lobbying by the Writers' Association of Serbia on behalf of the forty petitionists, the transfer of the issue to the presidency of the Yugoslav Writers' Union and the outbreak of a public scandal around the affair, Kosovo's political authorities decided it was time to end the dispute. Under the close personal scrutiny of Kosovo's political leader Azem Vllasi, the Albanian president of the Kosovo association was eventually forced to resign and was replaced by the Kosovo Serb Milenko Jevtović. When the next assembly of the Writers' Association of Serbia took place in February 1986, both presidents of the province organisations were present, hailing the beginning of a new era of cooperation. In addition, Jevtović pronounced himself favourable to the idea of changing the associations' statutes so as to include the province organisations as 'collective members'.[89] Although the Serbian writers had thus won the first battle for the reintegration of Kosovo, it was only a pyrrhic victory. A year later the presidency of the Writers' Society of Kosovo went back to an Albanian and its relations with the Serbian association soured once again.

Whereas the dispute between the writers' organisations spelled out the direction of what was still to come, in the course of 1986 the Belgrade intellectual opposition became drawn into more active involvement on behalf of the Kosovo Serbs, achieving a mass following for this new cause. In September 1985 the Kosovo Serb leaders Bulatović and Šolević organised a petition by over 2,000 Kosovo Serbs, which within a few months gathered more than 60,000 signatures.[90] This petition went well beyond the limits of acceptable political discourse in the mid-1980s and both Serbia's Presidency and Central Committee condemned it as a nationalist platform.[91] Among the fifteen points it set out, most were of a distinctly political nature: the granting to Serbia of the same 'statehood' enjoyed by the other republics in Yugoslavia; the removal of the symbols of Albanian statehood in Kosovo (flag, coat-of-arms etc.); the adoption of Serbo-

---

[88]See Rexhep Qosja's presentation at the Kosovo Academy of Arts and Sciences of 15 Oct. 1985, in Qosja, op. cit., p. 84.

[89]*Vjesnik*, 11 Feb. 1985.

[90]Vujačić, *Communism and Nationalism*, op. cit., p. 224.

[91]Ibid., p. 226.

Croatian as the official language in the province; the eviction of all Albanians who had immigrated from Albania to Kosovo since 1941[92] and the annulment of all sales agreements for Serbian farms. Couched in a language of war—that a part of Yugoslavia was under 'occupation' by 'fascists', who were 'ethnically cleansing' the territory by using 'genocide'—the petition concluded with the statement that 'the menace to Serbs in Kosovo and Metohija means the absolute menace to the Serbian people everywhere'.[93] The 'Petition of the 2016' was sent not only to the state institutions, but also to the Writers' Association of Serbia and the Serbian Academy of Sciences. The reaction in the Belgrade cultural institutions was instant. The text was read out at the annual assembly of the Writers' Association, which 'reacted with great consternation ... [and] concluded that the whole of the Yugoslav public must be acquainted with its contents'.[94] It was thus immediately published in *Književne novine*. Compared with the association's earlier restraint in addressing the public, this new approach indicated a change of policy.

The 'Petition of the 2016' marked the turning point of the Belgrade intelligentsia's activism from civil to national issues, in the same way that the 1981 Djogo affair had led to the spread and radicalisation of the struggle for freedom of speech.[95] In January 1986 a petition of some 200 Belgrade intellectuals demanding the rule of law in Kosovo was sent to the Yugoslav media and all instances of political power. This petition is important for a number of reasons. First of all, it showed that the intelligentsia had decided to accept the role of an alternative political force—an 'opposition', as the regime had so often (wrongly) claimed in the past—with the stated aim of mobilising public opinion and rallying support for genuine change in Kosovo.[96] It openly criticised the Serbian leadership for not fulfilling its role and for being 'deaf to [the nation's] desperate cry and awoken consciousness'.[97]

---

[92]One of the claims of the Kosovo Serbs was that Kosovo's authorities were allowing the free flow of Albanians from Albania across the border, to add to the demographic claim and facilitate the eventual unification of Kosovo with Albania.

[93]'Zahtevi 2016 stanovnika Kosova', *Književne novine*, 700–1, 15 Dec. 1985, p. 2. Metohija is the old Serbian name for the western part of the province, abolished in 1968.

[94]*Književne novine*, 700–1, 15 Dec. 1985, p. 2.

[95]See Chapter 1.

[96]'Zahtev za pravnim poretkom na Kosovu' in *Srpsko pitanje*, op. cit., pp. 260–1. An English translation of the petition can be found in Branka Magaš, *The Destruction of Yugoslavia*, op. cit., pp. 49–52.

[97]Ibid., p. 260.

Second, the petition, which was organised by the Committee for the Defence of Freedom of Thought and Expression, combined the liberal principles that had sparked the earlier struggle for civil and human rights with the nationalist rhetoric concurrently elaborated in the revision of history. On the one hand, its principal demand was the introduction of the rule of law and the respect of 'democratic rights' of both Serbs and Albanians and its signatories emphasised that they equally condemned 'all the injustices that were ever committed from the Serbian side against the Albanian nation'. On the other, it was peppered by references to Serbian victimisation throughout history, a call to end Albanian 'aggression' and the depiction of Serbian emigration from Kosovo as 'centuries-long genocide'. The fact that, in the eyes of the signatories, the Serbian nation was fighting for its 'survival' on its 'own land' also implied that there could be no compromise on the question of control over territory. Underlying the liberal principles was a clear demand for changes in the relationship between the autonomous provinces and the Republic of Serbia and an end to 'the internal undermining of Yugoslavia's borders'.[98] The solution to the Kosovo question was thus perceived not only in terms of democratic change, but also in the return of Belgrade's rule over the province.

Finally, the petition's list of signatories read like a 'Who's Who in Serbia', showing that, in terms of both numbers and importance, the mobilisation for the defence of Kosovo Serbs and the criticism of state policy had clearly surpassed the intellectual activism of the first half of the decade. Signatories included well-known university professors and scholars, members of the Serbian Academy, prominent lawyers and architects, famous artists, writers, actors, film directors and musicians, as well as a number of journalists, retired army generals and two of the three activist Orthodox bishops. All strands of Serbia's intellectual opposition were represented: the 'nationalists', the 'liberals' and the 'new left'. The fact that the list contains a number of intellectuals who later became leading opponents and critics of Serbian nationalism indicates the existence of a consensus in the intelligentsia at this time about the urgency of helping the Kosovo Serbs in the face of government inaction.[99] It also implies that the petition's liberal

[98]Ibid., pp. 261–2 passim.
[99]These include Nebojša Popov, Ivan Janković, Zagorka Golubović, Drinka Gojković, Vida Ognjenović, Olga Zirojević, Biljana Jovanović, Radmila Lazić and Dušan Makavejev, all of whom were later active in the various Belgrade anti-war and anti-nationalist organisations.

veneer was still strong enough to hold together this vast and ultimately shaky coalition.

Another protest letter, issued in June 1986 by the Committee for
the Defence of Freedom of Thought and Expression showed how
human rights had ceased being an end in itself and had become subordinate to the achievement of the national right to Kosovo. Cam-
paigning against the imprisonment of Kosovo Albanians for 'hostile
propaganda', the Committee stated that the trials and imprisonment
of Albanians were not merely infringements upon the right to free
speech, but 'a cynical game in which martyrs are being created on
purpose'. It protested such repression, not only on moral grounds,
but also because 'the creation of an ethnically pure, Albanian Kosovo
is only being facilitated by the excessive punishment of individual
Albanians', since Albanians would blame Serbs for the repression
instead of directing their anger at the real culprits—the Albanian
party and government decisionmakers in Kosovo.[100] The call to end
excessive and unwarranted punishment of individual Albanians thus
reflected the Committee's conviction that the respect of human rights
in Kosovo would render illegitimate the Albanian opposition to the
reintegration of Kosovo into Serbia. A similar position was taken by
the Serbian PEN, in its own petition against the prohibition of books
by Albanian authors in Kosovo in October 1987, which argued that
such measures were counterproductive 'because Yugoslav society
is being portrayed as repressive and police-controlled, while the
Albanian people in Yugoslavia is shown as the victim of the allegedly
'pro-Serbian' state pressure'.[101] The status of victim was reserved solely
for Serbs, serving—along with historical arguments—as moral justification for the return of Kosovo to Serbia.

The emerging consensus on Kosovo within the ranks of the critical intelligentsia was confirmed in the course of a new set of protest
evenings held at the Writers' Association in spring 1986, following
the imprisonment of Novi Sad professor Dragoljub Petrović for an
article written in *Književne novine*.[102] Although neither the controver-

---

[100]Communiqué 22, 20 June 1986, *Odbor za odbranu slobode misli i izražavanja*,
op. cit., p. 74.

[101]*Književna reč*, 309, 10 Nov. 1987, p. 2.

[102]Petrović's article, for which he was sentenced to sixty days in prison, denounced
the corruption in the party, both during the period of Partisan warfare and in post-
war Yugoslavia, implying that this was responsible for the crisis in the country (Dragoljub
Petrović, 'Pomirimo prijatelje—neprijatelji su smireni', *Književne novine*, 636, 15 Oct.
1985, p. 6).

sial text, nor the theme of the evenings—'Repression and Creation'—
had anything to do with Kosovo, they took place against the background of heightened activism by Kosovo Serbs and their adoption
of a new strategy of coming to Belgrade to voice their grievances.
'The old grizzled Serbs in their poor peasant garb and distressed Serb
mothers who travelled to the rallies became potent symbols of the
suffering of the Serbs and the Party's indifference to their plight'.[103]
For most members of the Belgrade intelligentsia, it was their first
personal encounter with the Kosovo Serbs and their first direct experience of hearing their stories. Although a news embargo was placed
by the authorities on the first visit by a delegation of 100 Kosovo
Serbs to the Federal Parliament in February 1986, a journalist who
had been there reported on it at the protest evening on 10 March.[104]
Kosta Bulatović, one of the Kosovo Serb leaders, personally participated in the next protest evening, as did a fourteen-year-old boy
from a Kosovo village whose father had been murdered in 1982 and
who had been severely beaten himself a few months earlier.[105] Djordje
Martinović's lawyer also took part and told of his client's suffering
and mistreatment at the hands of the authorities.

The attendance at these protest evenings was higher than ever
before. Over 1,000 people were reported at the early March evening
at which Dobrica Ćosić spoke, most of whom had to remain outside
in the winter cold to follow the proceedings from the garden.[106] This
was Ćosić's first address to such a large audience since his fall from
grace in 1968 and represents an all-encompassing critique of Yugoslavia's
undemocratic system. Noting that the protest meetings of writers and
intellectuals had gone beyond the mere defence of freedom of speech
and were now a reaction to the country's problems more generally, he
called upon his fellow-intellectuals to promote 'a culture of democracy,
dialogue, opposition to violence and non-acceptance of the status
quo' and to work to prevent that 'the emotions of politically bitter,

[103]Aleksandar Pavković, *The Fragmentation of Yugoslavia*, London, 1997, p. 83.

[104]*Corriere della sera*, 15 March 1986. The embargo was soon lifted by the Yugoslav
leadership, and by the end of March the media were extensively reporting on the
meeting between the Kosovo Serbs and the President of the Federal Parliament.
NIN even provided detailed documentation of the grievances of the Kosovo Serbs
(*NIN*, 23 March–13 Apr. 1986).

[105]*The Times*, 26 March 1986. Apparently an unnamed Serbian artist took the
boy's family into his house in Belgrade and gathered the equivalent of more than
£2,000 in donations.

[106]Gruenwald, 'Yugoslav Camp Literature,' op. cit., p. 518.

desperate masses ... [lead to] violence, bloodshed and destruction'.[107] Regarding Kosovo he warned that 'our epic tradition, our celebrated self-destructive explosions of anger, which in the past ended in national tragedy' were not an effective way of changing the status quo.[108] In his view the main question facing Serbia's intellectual opposition was how to resist violence by nonviolence. His answer was eminently democratic: through dialogue with opponents, civil disobedience against regime repression, peaceful resistance (strikes, petitions, public protest) and by actively promoting the creation of a democratic public opinion.[109]

Whereas Ćosić at this time represented the voice of tolerance and moderation, other more radical strands in the intellectual opposition were concurrently gaining ground. The most explosive speech was given by novelist Vuk Drašković on 7 April, the last protest evening held to mark the release of the condemned Novi Sad professor from prison. Noting that the freed intellectual had merely substituted 'one cell for another', Drašković wondered how the freedom of Professor Petrović or anybody else in Yugoslavia could be celebrated when the 'collective cry of Serbian slaves and martyrs' in Kosovo was echoing 'in our ears, if not in our hearts and minds'.[110] Reminding his audience that Britain had gone to war to defend the relatively insignificant Falkland Islands—'although nobody impaled the English farmers, burned their churches, stole their land and desecrated their tombs'—he asked how the Serbs could be 'on their knees, raising their hands in the air and baring [their] necks to the usurper's sword', when Kosovo, 'our Zion, our cursed and damned Jerusalem, the heart of our culture, the foundation of our epic tradition and our national identity' was being lost without a fight.[111] Less than two years later, Drašković was to argue that it was time for Serbs to stop 'turning the other cheek' and to remember that 'Christ knew how to break out in fury and even to use his whip in the Temple of Jerusalem'.[112]

In April 1986, the regime committed one of its biggest mistakes

---

[107]Dobrica Ćosić, 'Šta da se radi?', 3 March 1986, in Ćosić, *Stvarno i moguće*, op. cit., pp. 148–50 passim.

[108]Ibid., p. 153.

[109]Ibid., p. 154.

[110]Vuk Drašković, 'Svi smo u zatvoru', in Drašković, *Koekude Srbijo*, op. cit., p. 17.

[111]Ibid., pp. 13–14.

[112]*Glas crkve*, Christmas issue, Jan. 1988, in Drašković, *Koekude Srbijo*, op. cit., pp. 49–50.

when it arrested Kosovo Serb leader Kosta Bulatović for 'verbal offence' while the protest evenings were taking place. This new act of repression symbolised for Belgrade intellectuals the perfect marriage between their struggle for free speech and the plight of the Kosovo Serbs.[113] A tide of petitions swamped the authorities, while more than ten thousand Kosovo Serbs gathered to protest in front of Bulatović's house. Realising its blunder, the government released the activist three days later and Ivan Stambolić personally travelled to Kosovo Polje to calm the situation.[114] His visit had little effect; on the day of the last protest evening, a new group of over 500 Kosovo Serbs travelled to Belgrade once again to present their demands and were greeted by applause from Belgraders as they marched down the streets of the capital.[115] The regime's retreat in the face of popular pressure and the overwhelming reception given to the Kosovo activists in the capital confirmed in the eyes of the opposition intellectuals that they were in reality the genuine 'democratic' representatives of the people.

The regime's ineffectual response—branding the Writers' Association 'an on-duty address for Kosovo's problems' and characterising the protest evenings as 'an attempt by a group of nationalists active in Belgrade to use the coming of citizens from Kosovo Polje for their own ends'[116]—showed its impotence in the face of rising discontent. By this time, Serbia's boldened intellectual opposition was issuing its own warnings to the government. Over the following year a barrage of increasingly radical articles against the regime appeared in *Književne novine*. In April the journalist Milorad Vučelić, who later became one of Milošević's most important propagandists and director of Radio-Television Serbia, warned that 'political trust is not something that is given forever and clearly in the coming years it will have to be earned before the people'. He also stated that 'a part of the intelligentsia will, in the absence of the real carriers of initiative, propose programmes and measures which are usually the prerogative of the political authorities'.[117] Less than two months later, the journal reported in detail

---

[113]Among the materials confiscated from Bulatović was Dimitrije Bogdanović's *Book About Kosovo* and the January 1986 Kosovo petition of over 200 Belgrade intellectuals (*NIN*, 13 Apr. 1986, p. 15).

[114]*NIN*, 13 Apr. 1986, p. 15.

[115]Ibid., p. 18.

[116]Slobodan Milošević, Stambolić's right-hand-man at the time, quoted in *NIN*, 27 Apr. 1986, p. 14.

[117]Milorad Vučelić, 'Kosovo—drama moći i odgovornosti,' *Književne novine*, 708, 15 Apr. 1986, p. 3.

about the mass descent upon Belgrade of over 3,000 Kosovo Serbs from the village of Batusi, who were threatening to emigrate collectively since their demands had not been fulfilled. The article, entitled 'Yugoslavia, save us', was accompanied by a new text by Vučelić, who called for the rehabilitation of 'people who had warned about this anti-Yugoslav aggression in time and had been politically excommunicated in consequence'.[118] Directly throwing down a gauntlet before the regime, the editors of *Književne novine* published for the first time Dobrica Ćosić's banned 1968 speech, confirming the novelist's centrality to the growing opposition to the regime. This time there was no attempt to ban the journal or the contentious issue.

In the course of the 1980s the Writers' Association of Serbia swelled to include almost six hundred members. In June 1986 it elected a new presidency of prominent anti-regime spokesmen and publicly labelled nationalists, made up of several members of the Committee for the Defence of Freedom of Thought and Expression (Matija Bećković, Dragoslav Mihailović and Dobrica Ćosić), the provocative former president of the Association, Miodrag Bulatović, as well as Antonije Isaković, the coordinator of the Serbian Academy's committee on the Memorandum, and several poets who had distinguished themselves by using Kosovo and historical themes in their poetry (Aleksandar Petrov, Milan Komnenić, Ljubomir Simović, Slobodan Rakitić and Rajko Petrov Nogo). The newly-elected presidency announced its unequivocal support for the Committee for the Defence of Freedom of Creation functioning within the association and adopted all its protest letters. It also declared that it would open up the organisation to intellectuals who were not writers and that, from now on, the association would concern itself with wider social and political issues.[119] Judging by its programme, the new presidency seemed to be set on turning the writers' association into a *de facto* opposition party.

In the spring of 1987, the association organised a new series of protest evenings, this time explicitly dedicated to Kosovo. Its stated aim was to mobilise support for the Kosovo Serbs 'with book and spoken word'.[120] Writers read out their work inspired by Kosovo and poets recited their odes to Kosovo Serbs who had been victims of aggression, particularly the 'impaled martyr' Djordje Martinović; others

---

[118]*Književne novine*, 713–14, 1–15 July 1986, p. 5.
[119]*Politika*, 22 July 1986.
[120]'Programska načela UKS', *Književna reč*, 303–4, July 1987, p. 5.

read out excerpts from historical writings, including the inevitable *Book About Kosovo*. The usual array of Orthodox priests and intellectuals presented the different aspects of the 'genocide' of Kosovo Serbs. The former association president Miodrag Bulatović openly named Kosovo politicians whom he held responsible for this disastrous situation.[121] Once again it was Dobrica Ćosić who led the most attended evening of the cycle. This time, he directly linked the fate of Kosovo with the fate of the federation as a whole, 'since in Kosovo, it is not only Kosovo that is failing; it is Yugoslavia'.[122] Confirming the bitter disappointment with the common state evident in his historical novels, Ćosić wondered:

Why are so many writers, intellectuals, most of the intelligentsia—along with wider segments of society of all Yugoslav nations, particularly in Croatia and Slovenia—so indifferent and even malicious towards the plight of the Serbian people in Kosovo, while they are not indifferent and malicious towards the plight of any tribe on our planet?[123]

The accusation of betrayal by the other Yugoslavs, a central theme in the post-Titoist revision of history, was now being applied to a contemporary situation. For many in the Belgrade intelligentsia Yugoslav solidarity with their own struggle for Kosovo had become the measuring stick of the common state's very capacity for survival and, by this time, it had become clear that intellectuals from other republics had not lived up to expectations.

Seeking solidarity: Kosovo and Yugoslavia, 1986–8

In their quest for support in Yugoslavia, Serbian intellectuals saw Kosovo looked particularly towards Slovenes, whom they considered traditional allies.[124] They were therefore genuinely surprised and shocked at the reaction of Slovenian intellectuals, who—once they reluctantly decided to speak out—generally discounted not only the more extreme Serbian claims, but refused to acknowledge that there was any truth to the allegations of human rights violations against the Kosovo Serbs. For the Slovenes admitting that there was

---

[121]Miodrag Bulatović, 'Open Letter to Fadilj Hoxha', *Naša reč*, 387, Aug.–Sept. 1987, pp. 2–5.
[122]Dobrica Ćosić, 'Koliko smo sami krivi?', *Književne novine*, 733, 1 June 1987, p. 4.
[123]Ibid., loc. cit.
[124]On the relations between Serbian and Slovenian intellectuals see Chapter 4.

a problem opened the possibility of changes to the constitutional framework and thus an assault on the established order they favoured, while the rising hysteria with which Serbs approached the Kosovo question appeared distinctly unsavoury and even threatening. For Serbian intellectuals, on the other hand, the lack of support for their own version of the truth represented a betrayal, which only confirmed their deep disappointment with the common Yugoslav state.

Already in its first declaration on Kosovo in June 1985, the Writers' Association of Serbia stressed that the situation in the province had reached a level that was 'alarming for the whole of Yugoslav society' and noted that this issue was not being given the importance it deserved in the rest of the country.[125] In Serbia the general perception was that other republics had not reacted appropriately to the news about the human rights violations against the Kosovo Serbs. At first, criticism was directed at the media reporting on Kosovo in Croatia and Slovenia. As early as 1982 a heated polemic took place on the pages of *NIN*, after the weekly reprinted an article on the emigration of the Serbs from Kosovo from the Croatian daily *Vjesnik*. The article, which appeared on 24 July 1982, was written by Nadira Avdić-Vllasi, the wife of the Kosovo politician Azem Vllasi, who took over the province leadership after the crackdown in 1981. It presented the emigration of the Serbs as the result of 'the collaboration' of Albanian and Serbian nationalists; while Albanian extremists were trying to create an 'ethnically clean' Kosovo, they were being assisted by Serbian nationalists, who urged people to submit requests to leave the province so as to discredit the new leadership and create an anti-Albanian panic. Avdić-Vllasi argued that Serbian extremists sometimes set fire to Serbian properties and pressured young women to state that they had been raped in order to incriminate Albanians.[126] For her, better employment opportunities in Serbia represented the main cause of emigration, although she did admit that 'cooler relations' between the two communities were an additional factor.[127] The accompanying *NIN* editorial comment essentially branded the article an attempt at disinformation—a 'strange vision of emigration'.[128]

A first reaction came from Slovenian communist politician France

[125]'Stavovi delegatske skupštine UKS povodom stanja u SAP Kosovo', op. cit., p. 5.
[126]*NIN*, 1 Aug. 1982, p. 2.
[127]Ibid., p. 6.
[128]Ibid., loc. cit.

Klopčič in the form of a letter to the editor. Klopčič lauded Avdić-Vllasi's text and noted that, 'characteristically', it was in the Zagreb and not the Belgrade press that a more objective approach to Kosovo was to be found. He did not understand the disproportionate concern in Serbia about the emigration of the Serbs from Kosovo. He justified Albanian nationalism as a reaction to past injustice and noted that, in Slovenia, Albanians were welcome and well-seen, because they were 'hard-working, conscientious, calm, unburdened by differences, and—they even learn the Slovenian language'.[129] He stated that it was not surprising that Slovenes generally had a calmer and more objective vision of the Kosovo question, because they belonged to a nation that 'never in its history oppressed other nations'. He cautioned that he was not the only one in Slovenia to think that way, and that many Slovenes had 'other questions about Kosovo' which had not yet been answered.[130] The response to Klopčič's letter was overwhelming; by the end of August 1982, the *NIN* editorial board announced that it had sparked a total of 177 replies, the vast majority of which expressed shock and disapproval.[131]

A similar reaction followed the news of Djordje Martinović's 'impalement' in May 1985. On 9 May *Vjesnik* brought another commentary by Nadira Avdić-Vllasi, referring to the official statement that Martinović's injuries were self-inflicted: 'It is not the moment to speak of the psyche, character or honesty of a man who, using the pretext of the activity of Albanian nationalists, carried out an equally shameful act as the one he ascribed to them.'[132] The Zagreb weekly *Danas*, in an article written by the journal's editor himself, reiterated this standpoint; it explained Martinović's allegations of having been attacked by Albanians as simply an attempt to 'avoid being branded by shame in his community' and condemned the acceptance of his claims by 'unqualified persons' who continued to 'stubbornly refuse the truth'.[133] This official version of events was backed by a commission of medical experts under the direction of Slovenian academician and forensic medicine specialist Janez Milčinski. Countering an earlier assessment by a team of experts in Belgrade, who had argued

---

[129]*NIN*, 15 Aug. 1982, p. 2.
[130]Ibid., p. 3.
[131]*NIN*, 29 Aug. 1982, p. 2. Apparently, only one anonymous respondent agreed with Klopčič.
[132]*Vjesnik*, 9 May 1985, in *Slučaj Martinović*, op. cit., p. 302.
[133]*Danas*, 2 June 1985, in ibid., pp. 310–11.

that the severity of Martinović's injuries 'could only have been carried out by at least two or more individuals' and not by self-mutilation, the Milčinski team concluded that both were possible.[134] While among the Belgrade intelligentsia Martinović was treated as a martyr impaled on a modern-day stake, in the northern republics the reigning opinion was that the Martinović case was just a pretext for nationalist mobilisation to change the constitution. Similarly, while Serbs saw the mobilisation of their Kosovo co-nationals as the righteous struggle of the oppressed, in the Slovenian press their strategy of coming to Belgrade to voice their grievances was characterised as 'trains of nationalism'.

It was particularly intellectuals in Slovenia who were the greatest source of disappointment for the Serbs. In December 1984 a book entitled *Albanians* was published in Ljubljana by the Cankar Endowment, a prestigious Slovenian cultural institution.[135] According to the editors, the publication of the book was motivated by the Slovenian public's insufficient knowledge of the Albanians and by the heightened interest in the subject after 1981. They had therefore given the Kosovo Academy of Sciences and Arts the supervision of the book, 'to give Albanians the opportunity to speak out ... especially out of a sense of justice, because they have not yet had a chance to do so'.[136] The book thus essentially presented Albanian visions of history and was interpreted in Belgrade as directly condoning Albanian nationalism and taking an overtly anti-Serbian stand over Kosovo. Dimitrije Bogdanović, the author of the as yet unpublished *Book about Kosovo*, agreed to contribute an article, but unsuccessfully tried to withdraw his contribution once he discovered 'what kind of a book it was'.[137] In an interview with the newspaper *Borba* Bogdanović stated:

[134]Medical opinions, signed by Prof. Dr Naum Gutevski, Belgrade, 10 Oct. 1985 and Prof. Dr Janez Milčinski, Ljubljana, 15 Nov. 1985, in ibid., pp. 456–60. The Belgrade team of experts, which included two doctors from Belgrade, and one each from Ljubljana, Zagreb and Skoplje, concluded that the injuries had been caused 'by a strong, brutal and sudden insertion or jamming of a 500 ml. bottle, or rather, its wider end, into the rectum' and that the strength necessary to inflict such injuries was too great for self-mutilation to be possible. The Milčinski commission, on the other hand, concluded that Martinović could have inserted the bottle on a stick, which he had pushed into the earth, and had slipped during masturbation, his body's weight breaking the bottle in his rectum.

[135]The Cankar Endowment building in Ljubljana was the counterpart to the Writers' Association of Serbia—the key place for the propagation of both democratic and nationalist ideas in the 1980s.

[136]Quoted in *NIN*, 16 Dec. 1984, p. 29.

[137]*Politika*, 11 Dec. 1984, p. 11.

Really, I do not know in what sense it can be called a virtue 'not to have an emotional reaction' in Slovenia in the face of Albanian mystifications, the attack on Yugoslavia and the genocide against the Serbian people in Kosovo. I'd like to believe in the contrary; that in Slovenia, the sense of historical truth and justice, along with—dare I say it—Yugoslav solidarity, has not died out. How would it be if somebody in Yugoslavia—free of any emotion—published a book expounding the well-known Bulgarian thesis on Macedonia and Moravian Serbia? Or a book by the Italian irredentists on Dalmatia, Istria, the Slovenian coast and the Julian region? Such 'objectivity' is absurd and has no relation to scholarship ...[138]

NIN too asked whether it was possible that the eminent Slovenian institution did not know that the Kosovo Academy was 'infected with the nationalist and irredentist virus'.[139]

The real test of solidarity came in 1985 during the Serbian intellectuals' activism concerning the resignation of the forty non-Albanian writers from the Writers' Society of Kosovo. The Writers' Association of Serbia requested from the president of the Yugoslav Writers' Union, the Slovenian writer Ciril Zlobec, to hold an emergency special assembly.[140] The meeting, held in Ljubljana on 16 July, did not bring the Serbs the hoped for results, however. Instead of resigning under pressure as they had expected, Hassan Mekulli, the president of the Writers' Society of Kosovo, criticised the fact that his institution had not been given enough time to deal with the matter on its own and accused the Writers' Association of Serbia of trying to foment discord.[141] In addition, the Serbian delegation received only muted support from most of the other participants, who noted that although the day's subject was Albanian nationalism, Serbian 'revanchism' was no less of a problem.[142] Without being specific, the assembly condemned all forms of discrimination in the province, recommending to the Kosovo Society to hold its own discussion about the open letter. When the promised discussion did not take place, the president of the Writers' Association of Serbia sent another letter to the Presidency of the Yugoslav Writers' Union, calling upon it not to accept 'this policy of *fait accompli*'.[143] When still nothing

[138]*Borba*, 8 Jan. 1985.

[139]*NIN*, 16 Dec. 1984, p. 29.

[140]Miodrag Bulatović, the president of the Writers' Association of Serbia, had had a serious run-in with Zlobec at the Writers' Congress in Novi Sad two months earlier (see Chapter 4).

[141]*Književne novine*, 693, 1 Sept. 1985, p. 3.

[142]Ibid., pp. 3–6.

[143]*Književne novine*, 697, 1 Nov. 1985, p. 2.

happened, at the next meeting of the presidency the Serbian delegation insisted once again that measures be taken against the Kosovo Society, at which point the Albanian delegates walked out in protest. This time Ciril Zlobec, the Union's president, openly blamed the clash on the 'uncompromising, accusatory tone' adopted by the Serbs, while the presidents of the associations of Montenegro and Croatia, Jevrem Brković and Marija Peakić-Mikuljan, sided with the Albanians.[144]

These quarrels first became public in summer 1986, when an acerbic polemic erupted between Serbian Praxist Ljubomir Tadić and Slovenian sociologist Dimitrij Rupel, who in 1990 would become independent Slovenia's first foreign minister, following an interview that Tadić gave to *Književne novine*, where he denounced the anti-democratic decentralisation ('re-feudalisation') of Yugoslavia and characterised the Kosovo problem as 'only the unavoidable consequence of turning the Yugoslav federation into a confederation'.[145] In a subsequent interview in the popular Belgrade bimonthly *Duga*, Rupel, referred to Tadić's statements as typical of the 'problematic' Serbian position on Kosovo and the Yugoslav state:

When Tadić speaks of national bureaucracies and étatism, I understand that he is concerned about Kosovo. But when a Slovene reads this, he perceives it as an attack on Slovenian statehood, which is guaranteed by the constitution and which we refuse to discuss because it is a *conditio sine qua non*. I judge such standpoints as unitarist pressure.[146]

Initially reluctant to discuss Kosovo in greater detail, Rupel nevertheless gave in to the persistent questioning of the *Duga* journalist, exposing to what extent 'we in Slovenia see the Kosovo problem differently than you do in Belgrade'. To him Albanian nationalism represented a response to state oppression under Ranković in the first half of the post-war period. It was no different from other Yugoslav nationalisms and thus undeserving of the harsh repression meted out following the 1981 demonstrations. Rupel expressed his concern for the human rights breaches in Kosovo—but, in his opinion, these

---

[144]*NIN*, 17. Nov. 1985, pp. 33–4. This affair first exposed the split within the Montenegrin association between those members who considered themselves Serbs and supported the actions of the Writers' Association of Serbia and those, like Brković, who supported Montenegrin independence and allied themselves with intellectuals in Croatia and Slovenia (see Chapter 4).

[145]Ljubomir Tadić, 'Nacionalne strasti kao zamena za demokratiju', *Književne novine*, 709, 1 May 1986, p. 7.

[146]*Duga*, 322, 22 June–11 July 1986, p. 39.

were experienced exclusively by imprisoned Albanian youths who had demanded a 'Kosovo Republic'. He refused to acknowledge that Serbs were emigrating from the province under pressure and he compared their claims—for which 'no reliable facts' existed—to those made by the English in India, who used to accuse the Indians of arson and other crimes: 'I have sympathy for the English, but they were in a foreign country; Kosovo is not exactly a foreign country, but the majority of the population is Albanian.' Implicitly dismissing the Serbian claim to Kosovo, Rupel also drew a parallel to the Slovenes having to accept that Trieste and Klagenfurt were 'no longer' theirs.[147]

Rupel's interview 'caused a storm of reactions and perhaps one of the greatest polemics in the Yugoslav press since the Second World War'.[148] *Duga* received numerous letters to the editor, containing expressions of disbelief and anger at the Slovene's perception of the situation in Kosovo. The polemic that resulted between Tadić and Rupel after this interview eventually led to their both being officially denounced for nationalism and the dismissal of the journalist who had originally interviewed Rupel.[149] The heightened tone of the debate exposed that the underlying issue for both intellectuals was the constitutional arrangement of the common state. Whereas for Tadić the solution to the Kosovo problem was inextricably tied to that of the Serbian question in Yugoslavia more generally and was to be found in the promotion of a recentralisation of the federation, for Rupel, such a solution was 'unitarism' and an infringement on Slovenian sovereignty. Tadić thus accused Rupel of seeing the Kosovo question exclusively from the position of Slovenian national interest—'it would be better if he reasoned more from the principle of justice and less from a national standpoint'[150]—and accused him of using the Albanian revindications in Kosovo to 'guarantee the existing national and state status of Slovenia and the continued existence of the Yugoslav confederation created in 1974'.[151] Rupel retorted that Slovenes could only accept a Yugoslavia which was 'an appropriate framework for the development and flourishing of their own national community'

[147]Ibid., pp. 39–40.

[148]Snježana Milivojević, 'Nacionalizacija svakidašnjice' in *Srpska strana rata*, op. cit., p. 671.

[149]The journalist, Zdenka Aćin, later became the editor-in-chief of the weekly *Intervju*.

[150]*Duga*, 323, 12–25 July 1986, in Tadić, *Da li je nacionalizam naša sudbina?*, op. cit., pp. 186–7 passim.

[151]*Duga* 327, 6–19 Sept. 1986, in ibid., p. 191.

and emphasising that he totally supported the definition of Slovenia as a state and a voluntary member of the federation, which was provided by the 1974 Constitution.[152]

By the spring of the following year, relations between Serbian and Slovenian intellectuals had become even more strained.[153] During the protest evenings held in May and June 1987 in the Writers' Association of Serbia, 'On Kosovo—for Kosovo', a number of writers denounced what they considered to be the pro-Albanian stand of the northern republics. The poet and playwright Ljubomir Simović made a direct correlation between the bottle with which Djordje Martinović had allegedly been 'impaled' and a bottle sent by an employee of the Albanian embassy in Belgrade to the journalist at the Ljubljana newspaper *Delo* who had written about the Kosovo Serb 'trains of nationalism'. Simović concluded that the Belgrade intelligentsia's 'appeal for the 'Yugoslavisation' of the Kosovo problem' was 'nothing more than another of our illusions and self-deceptions'.[154] The literary critic Zoran Gluščević focused his two presentations on the theme of betrayal, entitling the first 'Why Judas betrayed Christ'.[155]

These criticisms were accompanied by an official demand of the Association for a joint declaration to be adopted by the Yugoslav Writers' Union at its annual conference in Varaždin—a declaration that would represent 'a concrete contribution to brotherhood and unity' by including a statement on the situation in Kosovo, specifically using the term 'genocide' to define the pressures against the Serbs in the province.[156] In the end the statement that was adopted, however, contained a more mitigated wording, expressing concern with 'the undiminishing and tragic process of emigration of a part of the Serbian and Montenegrin nations from Kosovo under pressure from Albanian nationalists and separatists' and condemning 'all violence and persecution committed against any person or people, here and now, today and in the future'.[157] Even this declaration required considerable handwringing and, in the eyes of the Union's other members, went a long way towards meeting the demands of the Serbs. Yet Serbian writers saw it as a way for the rest of the Yugoslavs to 'amiably

[152]*Duga*, 325, 9–22 Aug. 1986, pp. 36–8 passim.
[153]Mainly concerning the election to the presidency of the Yugoslav Writers' Union (see Chapter 4).
[154]*Književne novine*, 1 June 1987, pp. 4–5.
[155]In Zoran Gluščević, *Kosovo i nikad kraja*, Belgrade, 1989, pp.
[156]*NIN*, 28 June 1987, p. 30.
[157]Quoted in ibid., p. 31.

get rid of this problem' and avoid the use of the term 'genocide'. To add insult to injury, in October 1987 the Slovenian Writers' Society invited only Albanian writers from the Writers' Society of Kosovo to present their work in Ljubljana and thus allow Slovenes to become 'better acquainted' with Albanian literature, despite the protests of the Kosovo organisation's Serbian members.[158] In the Writers' Association of Serbia this invitation was perceived as a blatant disregard of its struggle to achieve 'equal rights' for the Kosovo Society's Serbian members and it bitterly reminded the Slovenes that 'not only Albanian literature' existed in Kosovo.[159]

The greatest shock and consternation in Serbia were caused by a series of 'Letters to a Serbian Friend' by the Slovenian writer Taras Kermauner, published in the Belgrade press in the course of 1987. Arguing that Serbs were emigrating simply because they 'did not want to live in the village anymore',[160] Kermauner wondered: 'Why must Albanians, who need more and more living space, remain in Yugoslavia at any price?'[161] He argued that the 'excessive birthrate' of the Albanians meant that they would need ever more *Lebensraum*, and if they did not 'transform themselves from within' they would become 'aggressive, like overbred rats or ants' and turn to war,[162] or perhaps even 'move across Serbian territory to the northwest, to Slovenia and Croatia'.[163] It was better for all concerned if the Serbs gave up their 'blood and soil' ideology and relinquished the province. They also had to understand that Slovenes would not support them on Kosovo, but would rather try to remain 'equidistant' from both sides in the conflict and 'pursue in relation to [the rest of] Yugoslavia our independent— foreign—policy'.[164] With this declaration, which was seen in Serbia as largely representative of Slovenian public opinion, the chasm that had emerged over Kosovo between the two republics appeared unbridgeable.

While the breakdown of dialogue with Slovenian intellectuals could partly be blamed on the latter's exclusive defence of their own 'national interest', it was very clear by 1988 that Belgrade intellectuals

[158]Similar invitations were also extended to Macedonian and Croatian writers. For more on this, see Chapter 5.

[159]*Danas*, 3 Nov. 1987, pp. 42–3.

[160]Second letter, *NIN*, 26 July 1987, p. 23.

[161]Sixteenth letter, *NIN*, 6 Sept. 1987, p. 20.

[162]Thirteenth letter, *NIN*, 6 Aug. 1987, p. 7.

[163]Sixteenth letter, *NIN*, 6 Sept. 1987, p. 20.

[164]Ibid., loc. cit. For Kermauner's other arguments see Chapter 4.

were incapable of any rational discussion on Kosovo at all. The experience of Branko Horvat, a renowned Zagreb economist of a clearly 'Yugoslav' orientation, who essentially agreed with the critique of 'confederalisation' emanating from the ranks of the Belgrade intelligentsia, serves as a case in point.[165] Horvat had already on numerous occasions blamed Yugoslavia's crisis on the extreme decentralisation of the country, which had earned him the label of 'unitarist' in Croatia, and in that sense he could not be accused, as the Slovenes were, of supporting the status quo or of being a 'separatist'.[166] He presented his vision of the Kosovo question in three articles published in *Književne novine* in Spring 1987, after devoting considerable research to the issue. Noting that so far 'direct, open dialogue between intellectuals [had] totally been remiss', he argued that 'on the one side, there are criticisms, reproaches, sermons and even direct attacks, to which the other side responds by denial, often mixed with insincerity'.[167] He said that he felt genuinely concerned by what he agreed was an all-Yugoslav problem and hoped that by publishing his analysis of the Kosovo question, he would spark reflection and dialogue between Yugoslav intellectuals that would lead to greater understanding and a durable, rational solution.

For Horvat there were essentially three aspects to the Kosovo problem. The first of these was the emigration of the Serbs from Kosovo, and he noted that the Yugoslav federation had failed to protect the minority from discriminatory pressures and that the inaction of the administration and the courts had left the people to their own devices, 'as in Turkish times'. He suggested to resolve this problem by creating groups of inspectors, lawyers and court personnel from the rest of

[165]Horvat had already distinguished himself by protesting the official witchhunt against the Serbian Academy following the unauthorised publication of its draft 'Memorandum' in September 1986. Although he disagreed with the 'Memorandum's' nationalist claims, he acknowledged that the document was unfinished and thus implicated only its authors, and not the institution as a whole. He also defended the right of all individuals to free speech (see *Književne novine*, 725, 1 Feb., 1987, p. 3).

[166]In a 1988 interview, for example, Horvat blamed Yugoslavia's 'confederate' structure for the outburst of Albanian nationalism in 1981: 'With the Constitution of 1974, and in practice even before, we began to turn Yugoslavia into a confederation, where each member had it sovereignty and its state ... Then we proclaimed the principle that each [Yugoslav] nation had its own state, and of course the Albanians wanted theirs too. It is not their fault they live in Yugoslavia' (*Start*, 497 and 498, 6 and 20 Feb. 1988, in *Kosovsko pitanje*, op. cit., p. 262).

[167]Branko Horvat, 'Tri aspekta kosovskog problema', *Književne novine*, 730, 15 Apr. 1987, p. 13.

Yugoslavia, who would supervise the establishment of the rule of law in the province, and by establishing the post of an impartial ombudsman to deal with complaints by individual citizens.[168] The second, related aspect of the Kosovo problem was, according to Horvat, the revival of Serbian nationalism. He noted that, under the pretext of defending the Kosovo Serbs, 'some old accounts [were] being settled' and the issue was being used to make claims about the 'inequality' of Serbs in Yugoslavia. In his view, the fact that Serbs and Montenegrins were genuinely persecuted made a response to such claims more difficult, yet the similarities between the Serbian situation and the nationalist upsurge in Croatia in 1971 promised to turn Kosovo into 'the detonator of a new nationalist explosion'.[169]

Horvat defined the third aspect of the Kosovo problem as the problem of integrating the Albanians in Yugoslavia. He disagreed with the official characterisation of the 1981 revolt as a 'counter-revolution'; it had been a 'traditional national revolt', typical of a 'young' nation searching for its identity. In this sense the demand for a 'Kosovo Republic' did not merit police repression—it represented a political demand that was totally legitimate in a federal state[170]—but the demand, was not rational, since—other than in name—Kosovo had in fact been functioning as a republic. However, it did indicate that the Yugoslavs had not managed to prove to the Albanians that Yugoslavia was the federation of all peoples who lived there and not the state of the South Slavs only. For Horvat even the goal of Albanian national unification was not unacceptable, as long as it did not infringe upon the same right for others. He noted that this demand was no different from those of the Serbs and the Croats in the past and argued that there were three possible outcomes: either Albanians would realise their political autonomy within Yugoslavia—in a province or a republic—and give up the goal of national unity; or they would want to secede and join Albania; or they could work to create conditions for an eventual 'Balkan Federation' which would include Albania. Horvat saw this last outcome as neither impossible nor undesirable. He argued that a Balkan Federation represented the same solution to the Albanian question as Yugoslavia was for the Serbian and Croatian ones.[171]

---

[168]Ibid., loc. cit.
[169]Ibid., loc. cit.
[170]Ibid., loc. cit.
[171]Branko Horvat, 'Kosovo-Republika?', *Književne novine*, 732, 15 May 1987, pp. 13–14, and his reply to critics, *Književne novine*, 740, 15 Oct. 1987, pp. 6–7.

It allowed the nation to be unified in one state, without denying that same right to other nations intermingled with it on the same territory.

Although, unlike his Slovenian colleagues, Horvat did acknowledge the legitimacy of Serbian concerns about the Kosovo Serbs (without, however, accepting the terminology of 'genocide' or the other exaggerations) and could not be accused of 'ignoring their plight', he nevertheless dealt with this problem in its logical framework of human rights, without legitimising Serbian claims to ownership of territory. By raising the issue of Serbian nationalism as an offshoot of the Kosovo question and by contesting the link that the Belgrade intelligentsia had made between the Kosovo question and the Serbian question as a whole, Horvat knowingly opened himself to attack from Belgrade intellectuals. By defining the Kosovo question instead as an 'Albanian question'—the issue of Albanian statehood and national unity—he essentially hit the nail on its head. Not only was this the real, underlying concern of the Albanian intelligentsia (rather than merely human rights), but the acceptance of the legitimacy of this demand represented the real test of democracy for the Belgrade intelligentsia. Could Serbian intellectuals accord to Albanians the right to demand what they were essentially claiming for their own nation?

The answer was quick to come and, once again, it proved the exclusiveness of the Serbian vision of Kosovo. One of the editors of *Književne novine*, Milorad Vučelić, lamented that after years of 'silence and indolence of a large part of the Yugoslav 'critical intelligentsia', now 'finally' Branko Horvat had spoken out, but that he did so only to warn of Serbian nationalism and to define the Kosovo question as an Albanian and not a Serbian one.[172] Vučelić accused Horvat of adopting a double standard; when dealing with Albanians, Horvat was bending over backwards to find ways to meet their allegedly 'legitimate' rights, including the utopia of a Balkan Federation, but 'when it is a question of the Serbian revolt against persecution, then he calls it nationalism'.[173] The writer Zoran Avramović also rejected Horvat's definition of the problem, arguing that any empirical investigation would show that there was no discrimination against Albanians in Yugoslavia and—since there was no oppression or denial of rights—one could not speak of a 'national revolt'. Instead, the term

[172]Ibid., pp. 3–4 passim.
[173]*Književne novine*, 741, 1 Nov. 1987, p. 3.

to be used was 'violence with elements of genocide by one part of the Albanian people against Serbs and Montenegrins', and Avramović joined in criticising Horvat for not condemning the silence of the Albanian intelligentsia.[174] The historian Branko Petranović asked why Horvat was turning violent, nationalist Albanians into victims and chastised him for not realising that for Serbs, Kosovo was more than just a question of demography and numbers.[175] In the end none of Horvat's respondents found it in themselves to reply to the Zagreb economist's essential question—did the Kosovo Albanians deserve to have the same right to 'statehood' as other Yugoslavs? The implication was clearly that they did not, that they had to be content with the status of a national minority in a Serbian 'state'.

While in its first stage the debate—which took place on the pages of *Književne novine* and not in the popular press—remained generally of a courteous and more scholarly nature,[176] it contained the seeds of what was to become a campaign of abuse against Horvat in Serbia the following year, at the height of Milošević's 'happening of the people'. In his critique Milorad Vučelić already insinuated that Horvat's complaint of lacking accurate information on Kosovo and its history was a deliberate ploy:

Today, only those who do not want to be informed are uninformed about Kosovo, or those who need 'uninformedness' as an alibi for silence or for a false and allegedly objective discourse; such lack of information is, in reality, 'a certain kind of politics'.[177]

When, in the spring of 1988 Horvat gave an interview to the Kosovo journal *Rilindja*, stating his standpoint along the same lines as before, the dam burst.[178] While no Serbian newspaper translated the interview—which had only appeared in Albanian and was not read by the majority of Horvat's detractors—a whole series of accusations against Horvat appeared in the Belgrade press: that he was propagating the break-up of Yugoslavia, that he had been 'bought' by the Albanian government and was participating in the 'special

[174]*Književne novine*, 733, 1 June 1987, p. 19.
[175]*Književne novine*, 741, 1 Nov. 1987, p. 6.
[176]One of Horvat's critics, journalist Miloš Mišović, even expressed his 'great respect' for Horvat and for his call for a 'reasoned, calm debate' (*Književne novine*, 731, 1 May 1987, p. 5).
[177]*Književne novine*, 732, 15 May 1987, p. 3.
[178]This interview can be found in Horvat, *Kosovsko pitanje*, op. cit., pp. 269–81.

war' against his country and even that he had been involved in shady financial transactions.[179] The Kosovo leadership intervened to diffuse tension, the journalist who had interviewed Horvat—the younger Albanian intellectual Veton Surroi, who later became a leading liberal voice on the Kosovo Albanian political scene—lost his job and his Party membership, and *Rilindja* published a statement condemning Horvat's views and distancing itself from the interview.[180] In addition, Horvat received numerous anonymous letters from Serbia, accusing him of being an Ustasha and threatening his life.[181]

A number of Serbian intellectuals participated in the witchhunt by making public statements against Horvat, and his lecture in Belgrade in April 1988 was disrupted by a group of militants led by the extremist nationalist intellectual Vojislav Šešelj.[182] In the summer of 1988 two special issues of the popular bi-monthly *Duga*, entitled 'The Truth about Kosovo', were organised by Milorad Vučelić and another journalist as a 'response' to Horvat's book, which had appeared that spring. In these issues a number of Horvat's former critics published renewed attacks on the Zagreb economist. At the end of the whole debate the historian Branko Petranović concluded that Horvat was merely 'trying to continue the political hypnosis' by which the Serbs had been kept subjugated, but that he had been 'uncovered from the start' and that his 'pseudo-humanism' towards the Albanians was being paid for 'with the lives of a whole other nation'.[183] As Horvat noted in his final reply to his Serbian critics, the answer to the question about the 'silence' of Yugoslav intellectuals on the Kosovo issue had become more than obvious—the mentality that was reigning in Belgrade was one of 'either you are with the Serbs and you have to justify everything they do, or ... you are against them'.[184] In this context, national 'betrayal' of the Serbs was almost guaranteed; in the second half of 1988, nationalist hysteria in the republic had swallowed all reason and all moderation.

Whereas in mid-decade the raising of the Kosovo question rep-

[179]*Danas*, 17 May 1988, p. 24 and Horvat's letter to the editor of 19 July 1988, p. 30.

[180]Reprinted in *NIN*, 12 June 1988, pp. 14–15.

[181]This was a particularly offensive accusation, considering that both of Horvat's parents had been killed by the Ustasha during the war as Jews.

[182]Ibid., pp. 30–1.

[183]Letter to the editor, *Duga*, 380, 17–30 Sept. 1988, p. 78.

[184]*Duga*, 3 Sept. 1988, reprinted in Horvat, *Kosovsko pitanje*, op. cit., pp. 305–6.

resented 'the rejection of a long established political norm and the "freeing" of speech on a taboo theme',[185] by 1988 it effectively meant the end of dialogue and the 'muzzling of speech' on this issue from any standpoint other than the nationalist one. The final attempt at a discussion between Serbian and Albanian intellectuals confirmed the apparent dead end to which their respective nationalisms had brought them. Both groups of participants appeared monolithic in their exclusive claims to Kosovo and to the status of victim for their nation. As the Zagreb weekly *Danas* pointed out, 'Serbian writers ... wanted a discussion on Kosovo and the tragic fate of the Serbian and Montenegrin people, of exodus, while Albanian writers wanted a discussion of situation of Albanians in Kosovo and Yugoslavia.'[186] From the start there was little common ground and certainly no spirit of compromise.

The Albanian writers based their claims to the province on the inevitable Illyrian thesis and portrayed both the history and the present as a story of constant victimisation of the Albanian people.[187] Previously subjugated by the 'Greater Serbian bourgeoisie', even in socialist Yugoslavia Albanians were victims of a 'Serbian-Macedonian-Montenegrin agreement' to keep them oppressed.[188] Until 1966 Albanians were subject to the continuation to the Serbian 'policy of forced emigration' and only the fall of Ranković provided respite from incessant suffering and inequality. At this point, however, Serbs— who did not want to give up their privileged position—started spreading stories about the alleged emigration under pressure in an attempt to deny Albanians equality and ensure Serbian domination in Kosovo.[189]

Serbian writers, on the other hand, argued that, Kosovo was 'a holy place and the highest spiritual symbol only to Serbs' and that now 'the last remnants of the Serbian nation' were leaving Kosovo due to the 'terrifying anti-Serbian spirit and attitude that has been

---

[185]Gojković, op. cit., p. 373.

[186]*Danas*, 3 May 1988, p. 37.

[187]See particularly the presentations by Ibrahim Rugova, Besim Bokshi, Jusuf Buxhovi and Rexhep Qosja in *Književne novine*, 753, 1 May 1988, pp. 3–4, and *NIN* 15 May 1988, p. 40. Rugova's, Bokshi's and Qosja's presentations can also be found in Harillaq Kekezi and Rexhep Hida (eds), *What Kosovars Say and Demand*, Tirana, 1990, pp. 125–7, 234–7 and 116–20 respectively.

[188]See Qosja, op. cit., pp. 141–53.

[189]Rugova, in *Književne novine*, op. cit., p. 3, and Qosja, op. cit., p. 147.

created for decades among Albanians'.[190] The Serbs were the ones who were continuously persecuted, first under Turkish rule and later by others, influenced by the 'Catholic-inspired' myth of 'Greater Serbian hegemony'—a myth that underlay also the anti-Serbian attitudes and the lack of sympathy of the other Yugoslavs for the Kosovo Serbs.[191] The Serbs themselves were in no way to blame; when Serbia 'liberated' Kosovo in 1912, King Peter offered brotherhood and equality to the Albanians, but they responded by violent revolt and massacres. Similarly, when the first Yugoslav state fell apart in 1941 the Albanians began a 'Third Balkan War', which had never ceased.[192] Finally, the fall of Ranković in 1966 was not the beginning of Albanian equality in Yugoslavia, as the Albanian intellectuals claimed, but the victory of the 'confederate' conception so detrimental to the Serbs.[193]

By the end of the first day both sides judged the meeting to be a complete failure; in their irreconcilable visions of history and of the present, there was simply no basis for discussion. As the Albanian writer Agim Malja pointed out, his side felt like Don Quixote fighting windmills, and this encounter was only making the already strained relations between Serbs and Albanians worse.[194] For the Serbian poet Milan Komnenić this lack of mutual understanding was even more fundamental. His presentation, which won the most enthusiastic applause in the auditorium, began with the declaration:

Gentlemen, we are at war. Since we already know that, why are we trying to hide it. A part of the Albanian nation—I do not know how large—has begun, without declaration, a war against the Serbian people. And if this war is not being fought by arms, it is in spirit ... As far as I am concerned, you can talk to me for centuries, I do not believe anything you say.[195]

Reluctant to come to the meeting in the first place, the Albanian participants announced after the first day that they would leave early. Two weeks later Ibrahim Rugova, president of the Writers' Society of Kosovo, sent a letter to the Writers' Association of Serbia indefinitely postponing the continuation of the meeting, planned for the end of

[190]Aleksandar Petrov and Radosav Stojanović, in *Književne novine*, op. cit., p. 1 and 3 respectively.
[191]Radovan Samardžić and Jovan Deretić, in ibid., pp. 4–5.
[192]Živorad Stojković, in ibid., p. 6.
[193]Aleksandar Petrov, in ibid., p. 1.
[194]Agim Malja, in ibid., p. 5.
[195]Milan Komnenić, in ibid., p. 4.

May in Prishtina.[196] In September 1988 all the Serbian members of the Writers' Society of Kosovo resigned, and the Writers' Association of Serbia broke off relations with its Kosovo counterpart. Instead of being destroyed by this move, the Writers' Society of Kosovo 'found itself promoted to the status of the beacon for the mobilisation of national forces' and Rugova became the leader of the Albanian resistance.[197] Serbian intellectuals meanwhile found themselves at loggerheads with their counterparts in most of the other Yugoslav republics.

[196]*NIN*, 22 May 1988, p. 32.
[197]Shkelzen Maliqi, 'The Albanian Movement in Kosova', in *Yugoslavia and After*, op. cit., p. 144.

4

SERBS AND SLOVENES: 'NATIONAL INTERESTS' IN CONFLICT, 1980–8

In an interview which he gave in August 1989 Predrag Palavestra, president of the Serbian PEN association and one of the founders of the Committee for the Defence of Freedom of Thought and Speech, told of his disappointment with the trajectory of the Yugoslav intellectual dissidence:

A decisive role in our process of liberation [from communist ideology] was played by two great democratic fires that were lit in Belgrade and Ljubljana. Until yesterday these fires warmed all those in Yugoslavia who believed in the future, but now they have escaped from the intellectuals' control. These fires of freedom and democracy have become antagonistic and divided, and have turned into recalcitrance and madness.[1]

In his view, critical intellectuals in Belgrade and Ljubljana had spearheaded the democratic revival in Yugoslavia in the post-Tito period, but had lost their way and had given in to divisive pressures. Palavestra implicitly placed most of the blame for this state of affairs on the Slovenian intellectuals, who not only misunderstood the Serbian question in Kosovo, but who had also demonstrated that 'they did not want to join us in anything—even on the path to freedom!'[2] Palavestra's interview was representative of the expectations vis-à-vis the Slovenes held by many in Belgrade in the first half of the 1980s and of the disappointment felt when the desired response was not forthcoming. It is this sense of betrayal that reinforced Serbian intellectuals' attitudes towards Yugoslavia in the second half of the post-Tito decade.

---

[1]Predrag Palavestra, 'Dva plamena demokratije', *Delo*, 5 Aug. 1989, in Predrag Palavestra, *Književnost i javna reč*, Požarevac, 1994, p. 80.

[2]Ibid., pp. 81–4 passim.

From mid-decade both Serbian and Slovenian nationalism began to adopt more radical forms, as shown by two texts that appeared within four months of each other—the draft 'Memorandum' of the Serbian Academy of Sciences and Arts and the 'Contributions for a Slovenian National Programme' published by the Ljubljana journal *Nova revija*. While the *Nova revija* intellectuals' presentation of the Slovenian question took overtly secessionist tones, the unfinished 'Memorandum' still provided lip service to the idea of reforming Yugoslavia, but the same time it was 'anti-Yugoslav' in the way it tied together the various themes of the Serbian nationalist revival in a repository of grievances against the common state. The irreconcilable attitudes on what kind of association between Yugoslav nations was desirable, which appeared in the 'Memorandum' and *Nova revija*, laid the foundation of incompatible national programmes drafted in early 1988 during a renewed public debate on constitutional change.

Marching together, moving apart, 1981–6

In the first half of the 1980s Slovenia went through its own democratisation process. In this, one of the most liberal Yugoslav republics, two kinds of dissident activism dominated. One was a vigorous 'Alternative Scene', which arose in the early 1980s from a combination of rock bands, art groups and single-issue new social movements (for pacifism, environmentalism, feminism and gay rights), which came together in 1983 under the auspices of the relatively independent official Slovenian youth alliance.[3] The main vectors of the Alternative's ideas were the youth alliance's weekly *Mladina* (Youth), which later became Slovenia's foremost political magazine, and the radio station of Ljubljana University, Radio Študent, which played punk rock and other 'subversive' music and discussed the issues defended by the new social movements. Many of the Alternative's activities and slogans were characterised by an impish irreverence for Yugoslavia's 'sacred' symbols and myths. Through its autonomous media the youth movement poked fun at the untouchable Yugoslav People's Army,

---

[3]See Tomaž Mastnak, 'From Social Movements to National Sovereignty' in Jill Benderly and Evan Kraft (eds), *Independent Slovenia: Origins, Movements, Prospects*, London, 1994, pp. 95–108, and his 'Civil Society in Slovenia: From Opposition to Power' in Jim Seroka and Vukašin Pavlović (eds), *The Tragedy of Yugoslavia: The Failure of Democratic Transformation*, London, 1992, pp. 49–66, as well as Jozef Figa, 'Socializing the State: Civil Society and Democratization from Below in Slovenia' in *State-Society Relations in Yugoslavia*, op. cit., pp. 163–82.

demanded the 'right to alienation' and generally showed disrespect for the 'image and legacy' of the deceased President Tito. Over the course of the decade the new social movements achieved a degree of importance and recognition in the republic. Their initiatives for the creation of independent labour unions, the introduction of civil instead of military service, the dismantling of nuclear power stations and the abolition of 'verbal offence' and the death penalty progressively gained public support. The extent and organisation of the Slovenian Alternative had no equivalent elsewhere in Yugoslavia.

The second form of activism was that of the critical intellectuals, who—like their Serbian counterparts—initiated a process of demystifying the past. Once again, writers and social scientists were at the forefront of these activities, while Slovenian historians generally remained on the sidelines.[4] They provided a new vision of the 'national liberation struggle' of the Second World War and broached taboo subjects concerning communist repression of political opponents.[5] Whereas the Alternative focused on social rather than national issues for most of the decade,[6] critical intellectuals raised the national question in conjunction with their efforts to promote democratisation. As in Serbia, the subject of 'national reconciliation' also came to the fore. Sociologist Spomenka Hribar thus publicly referred to the Partisans' massacre of Slovenian homeguard prisoners of war at Kočevski Rog in May 1945. Her advocacy of 'the *a priori* and *de facto* equality of all members of our ... Slovenian motherland' regardless of their wartime allegiance, led to her expulsion from the League of Communists 'for trying to rehabilitate Slovenian fascists and collaborators'.[7]

Slovenia's critical intellectuals had two main centres; one was a group of writers, philosophers and sociologists gathered around the

[4]Peter Vodopivec, 'L'historiographie en Slovénie dans les années 80' in *Histoire et pouvoir en Europe médiane*, op. cit., pp. 127–37.
[5]A less heroic vision of the Partisan war was provided by Vitomil Zupan's novel *Minuet za gitaru* (Minuet for the Guitar). Other authors broke the taboo of Goli Otok, notably Branko Hofman in the *Noč do jutra* (Night until Dawn) and Vitomil Zupan in his autobiographical novel *Levitan*. A third subject was the 1947 treason trials of former inmates of the Dachau prison camp accused of spying for the West, treated in autobiographical novel *Umiranje na obroke* (Dying in Instalments) by Igor Torkar (a.k.a. Boris Fakin).
[6]Until the '*Mladina* affair' of 1988, which brought together the youth movement and the intellectual opposition in the defence of Slovenian national interests. (See Chapter 5)
[7]Interview in *Književne novine*, 693, 1 Sept. 1985, p. 12.

journal *Nova revija* (New journal) and the other was the Slovenian Writers' Society. *Nova revija* appeared in May 1982 as an independent journal of 'critical intellectuals and sceptical writers' after two years of wrangling with the republic's political authorities. The journal's aim, according to sociologist Dimitrij Rupel, one of its founders, was threefold: to promote cultural modernisation, to work towards the establishment of Western-style democracy in Slovenia and to promote the formation of an independent national state.[8] It played an important role in the process of de-Titoisation in Slovenia, while its publication of 'Contributions for the Slovenian National Programme' in January 1987 provided the first coherent overview of the Slovenian national question. Many of the journal's contributors later became leading political actors of independent Slovenia.[9]

The second important institution was the Slovenian Writers' Society. As Rudi Šeligo, one of its presidents, put it, 'After 1980 the Society achieved a very high degree of autonomy vis-à-vis the political organisations ... and in this way gained prestige and became an important moral force in Slovenia.'[10] It gained prominence in the immediate post-Tito years as the champion of Slovenian cultural rights and initiatives to bring Slovenia 'back into Europe'. This nostalgia for Europe arose among members of the Slovenian literary elite partly as a result of the cultural exchanges that took place in the 1980s in the context of Alpe-Adria, a regional organisation which included parts of Austria, Hungary, Italy and Germany and the Yugoslav republics of Slovenia and Croatia. As the writer and literary critic Ciril Zlobec noted, such cultural cooperation was taken very seriously and awakened 'the need to prove our sovereignty and creative worth'.[11]

As in a number of countries of the Soviet Bloc, the notion of 'Central Europe' became the symbol of Slovenia's national revival, with the Yugoslav 'Balkans' replacing 'Asiatic' Russia as the alien 'Other'. Inspired by Milan Kundera's 1985 article on 'The Tragedy of Central Europe', Slovenian intellectuals saw in this idea the promise of a 'return to civilisation and the exit from historical anonymity'.[12] As the writer

---

[8]Dimitrij Rupel, 'Slovenia's Shift from the Balkans to Central Europe' in *Independent Slovenia*, op. cit., p. 186.

[9]As the leaders of the opposition coalition DEMOS (see Chapter 5).

[10]*Danas*, 21 Apr. 1987, p. 38.

[11]Zlobec, op. cit., p. 17.

[12]According to Drago Jančar, Kundera's text 'expressed something that had for a long time been not only in our hearts, but on the tips of our tongues' (Milan Kundera, 'The Tragedy of Central Europe', *New York Review of Books*, 26 Apr. 1984,

Drago Jančar put it, 'Central Europe' gave Slovenes an 'entry ticket' into Europe and the possibility for independent cultural affirmation:

> We felt that we were overcoming the pointless European ideological divide, national borders, state jurisdictions ... We could talk without having to deal with people whose eyes are bloodshot with history and national hatreds. The differences, pluralism of worldviews, smallness, multilingualism; the whole of that cultural Babylon... we saw as a value and the fertiliser from which grew a new hope.[13]

The opening towards 'Central Europe', however, made many Slovenian intellectuals perceive Yugoslavia as a burden; the Slovenes' 'nightmare [was] to be dragged down by feckless southern neighbours to a sort of third world status'.[14] Comparing their own republic to neighbouring Austria and northern Italy, feeling economically exploited by the poorer republics, resenting the influx of workers from 'the South' and resisting assimilation with the Yugoslav 'Balkans' and its policy of cooperation with the Third World, Slovenian writers began calling for Slovenia's adherence to the 'Central European space' and a loosening of ties with the rest of Yugoslavia.[15]

The Slovenian writers' first battle against pressures from the centre came in 1982, when a federal proposal for a Yugoslavia-wide 'common core curricula' for secondary schools was launched. This debate inaugurated the revival of the Slovenian national question in the 1980s, united critical intellectuals and the communist leadership and rendered the role of the Slovenian Writers' Society 'a classical example of the impact of an interest group upon political processes'.[16] The aim of the federal project was to revive a degree of cultural

---

pp. 33–7, and Drago Jančar, 'Srednja Evropa kao meteorološko pitanje', *Književnost*, XLII/6, June 1987, p. 880).

[13]Ibid., pp. 880–1 passim.

[14]Michael Scammell, 'Slovenia and its Poet', *New York Review of Books*, 24 Oct. 1991, p. 56.

[15]Zlobec, op. cit., p. 289. A public echo of the fear of being absorbed into the 'south' can be found in opinion polls of the time, which showed both an increase of those who claimed that the Slovenian language, culture and way of life were threatened and a less manifest interest in the development of close relations with other Yugoslavs. (Slovenian sociologist Silva Mežnarić interviewed in *NIN*, 9 Jan. 1983, p. 17)

[16]Adolf Bibič, 'The Emergence of Pluralism in Slovenia', *Communist and Post-Communist Studies*, XXVI/4, December 1993, p. 372.

Yugoslavism, by reducing republican control over secondary school teaching and separate 'national' school programmes. It promoted:

—the education of students in the spirit of brotherhood, unity, togetherness, equality and the freedom-loving traditions established by the national liberation struggle and the socialist revolution ...; [and]
—the development of Yugoslav socialist patriotism, the respect for the cultural legacy of the nations and nationalities of the SFRY and the readiness to defend the homeland.[17]

For Slovenian writers, who noted that 'the protection of the mother tongue and national culture' only came towards the end of the proposal, the main questions that arose were:

How will [the Slovenian secondary school student] achieve consciousness of who he is, if he does not for three years... hear or read a single Slovenian poem? After he crosses that twelve-year spiritual desert, can he be convinced that his nation has any spiritual, cultural, historical or social identity and that he himself has any specificity?[18]

In the course of the debate, Slovenian intellectuals voiced their fears of assimilation of the Slovenian nation within the greater Yugoslav whole. In September 1984 Josip Vidmar, the president of the Slovenian Academy of Sciences stated that the Slovenes were 'the most tragic people in Europe', while in 1985 Ciril Zlobec, the newly-elected president of the Yugoslav Writers' Union, worried that small nations tended to 'disappear' under pressure from larger neighbours and announced that this tendency had to be resisted in Slovenia.[19]

Zlobec, along with the writers Tone Partljič and Janez Menart, led the campaign to reject the 'common core curricula'. They managed to get support in the highest political circles, presenting the issue as an attack on Slovenian sovereignty and on the constitution, which placed education in the domain of the federal units.[20] In August 1983 the Slovenian Writers' Society organised a public conference on the issue, rejected the proposal as a '*diktat*' and called upon the Slovenian

[17]Quoted in Zlobec, op. cit., p. 59. See also Budding, 'Serb Intellectuals and the National Question', op. cit., pp. 294–8, for a thorough discussion of the proposal.
[18]Ibid., p. 62.
[19]See 'Open Letter to Josip Vidmar' in Predrag Matvejević, *Otvorena pisma*, Belgrade, 1985, p. 77, and Zlobec, op. cit., p. 212.
[20]Ibid., pp. 65–82.

League of Communists to do the same.[21] For Slovenian intellectuals the struggle against the 'common core curricula', as well as the impact of their lobbying upon the Slovenian leadership, represented a victory.[22] As they stated at a conference organised by the Writers' Society in January 1985 on 'The Slovenian Nation and Slovenian Culture', they would defend their nation's sovereignty at any price. The exceptionally high attendance indicated that they had much popular support for this stance.[23]

While Slovenian intellectuals were increasingly turning away from Yugoslavia, members of the Belgrade critical intelligentsia were hoping to establish a closer collaboration with them and gain their support for a reform of the common state. This Serbian attitude towards the Slovenes differed considerably from that towards Croatian dissidents, most of whom had been involved in the 1971 nationalist 'mass movement' and who continued to be perceived as anti-Serbian and anti-Yugoslav.[24] Slovenian critical intellectuals, on the other hand, appeared to their Belgrade counterparts as logical partners to build a core for a pan-Yugoslav opposition. In the various debates between the two groups of intellectuals beginning in the mid-1980s, many Serbs stressed the 'traditional friendship' between the two peoples, compounded by 'the sameness of our national destinies [during the Second World War] and our brotherhood in our suffering and struggle, which did not take place to the same extent with the other South Slav peoples'.[25] Slovenes and Serbs had no territorial quarrels or minority problems with each other, nor a history of antagonism. In the first Yugoslav state Slovenes generally did not contest the common state and, during the Second World War, they spontaneously developed a strong resistance movement to the occupier. The fact that many Slovenes escaped to Serbia to avoid deportation and Germanisation policies was also perceived as having cemented the relationship

[21]*NIN*, 27 Jan. 1985, p. 62.

[22]Zlobec, op. cit., p. 65.

[23]Approximately 2,000 people attended, necessitating a change of hall to accomodate them, and reacted to the presentations with great enthusiasm (*NIN*, 27 Jan. 1985). Ciril Zlobec characterised this meeting as a 'moment of unity' between the Slovenian people and the intellectuals and a 'significant' step towards 'the securing of Slovenian national and social consciousness' (Zlobec, op. cit., pp. 176, 182).

[24]See Chapter 1.

[25]Dobrica Ćosić, discussion between Serbian and Slovenian PEN clubs, 5–6 Oct. 1987, in *Književne novine*, 742, 15 Nov. 1987, p. 17. See also Borislav Mihajlović-Mihiz in ibid., 743, 1 Dec. 1987, p. 17.

between the two peoples. In addition to this 'historical friendship', the two republics were also the most liberal in Yugoslavia, allowing for more effective mobilisation and common actions.

In the early years of post-Titoism, a number of links were created between the Serbian and Slovenian critical intellectuals: petitions against 'verbal offence' which originated in Belgrade received support in Ljubljana, a united petition of university students protested against the persecution of Kosovo Albanians in 1981, Slovenian intellectuals joined in the defence of Gojko Djogo and staged Jovan Radulović's proscribed play *The Pigeon Pit*. The Slovenian alternative press published Serbian dissidents' articles and interviews, while the Belgrade committees for the defence of free speech defended Slovenes when they experienced persecution.[26] The highpoint of inter-republican cooperation was witnessed in the case of the 'Belgrade Six' in 1984, the last genuinely common cause. Several of the numerous petitions against the arrest of the Six gathered over 200 signatures from Belgrade, Zagreb and Ljubljana and both *Mladina* and Radio Študent provided a blow-by-blow account of the trial and the protests.

Nevertheless, when Dobrica Ćosić embarked on his project of creating an all-Yugoslav Committee for the Defence of Freedom of Thought and Expression in 1984, he was unable to get willing participants among his Slovenian and Croatian colleagues. Later it was argued that they refused because Belgrade intellectuals 'never defended the "freedom of thought and expression" of their Albanian fellow-citizens'.[27] However, this represented an *ex post facto* justification; Kosovo was only taken up by the Belgrade intellectual opposition a year after the creation of the Committee and was not mentioned in any of the accounts of the debates between Serbian and Slovenian intellectuals prior to its creation.[28] In addition, the Committee did in fact defend the Kosovo Albanians' right to freedom of speech and condemned the trials of Albanian 'irredentists', although not quite in the same spirit as those of other individuals persecuted in Yugoslavia.[29]

However, it is true that at least one of the solicited intellectuals—

[26]In 1986 and 1987 they defended the sociologist Tomaž Mastnak, the journal *Nova revija*, the 'Laibach' punk group the poet Tomaž Šalamun and the Slovenian Youth Alliance. They also backed the Slovenian intellectuals' calls to rehabilitate the victims of the 1947 'Dachau Trials' (see *Naša reč*, 1986–7, for all of these petitions).

[27]See, for example, Quintin Hoare's letter to the editor, *New York Review of Books*, 11 Oct. 1990, p. 59.

[28]See also Michael Scammell's reply in ibid., p. 60.

[29]See Chapter 3.

the Croatian writer Predrag Matvejević—had reservations concerning Ćosić's nationalism, though these were still unrelated to Kosovo. Matvejević, who had published in 1982 a collection of articles entitled *Jugoslavenstvo danas*, (Yugoslavism Today) saw himself as a 'Yugoslav', despite the negative connotation the term had acquired by its association with unitarism. To him 'Yugoslavism' was an internationalist worldview and he disapproved of all nationalist manifestations, including the Slovenian stand in the debate on the 'common core curricula'.[30] In regard to Ćosić he noted as early as 1980 that the novelist's 'Yugoslavism of the 1960s has been narrowed to Serbianism'.[31] In April 1984, at the time of the creation of the Committee for the Defence of Freedom of Thought and Expression, Matvejević addressed an open letter to Ćosić expressing his shock at witnessing the staging of the play *The Kolubara Battle*—an adaptation of the second volume of Ćosić's novel *A Time of Death*—at the Belgrade Drama Theatre.[32] Matvejević noted the audience's 'ecstatic' reactions and a certain nationalist fervour which reminded him of 1971 in Croatia. He considered such manifestations dangerous and called upon Ćosić to have the play removed from the theatre's repertoire.[33] Following an exchange of letters in which Ćosić defended the play and the audience reactions and rejected the comparison with the Croatian 'mass movement',[34] Matvejević concluded that the Serbian writer stood for a 'pure' form of Serbian nationalism—one that was not intolerant and full of hatred towards others, but that was nevertheless not conducive to the promotion of common Yugoslav interests.[35] When he was asked to join the Committee a few months after this exchange, he declined.

Most of those consulted to join the Committee did not yet appear to share Matvejević's reservations. For example, the Zagreb Praxist Predrag Vranicki, defended Ćosić against regime accusations as someone who was known throughout Yugoslavia for 'his humanism, love of liberty and socialist ideals'.[36] Furthermore, the initiative for the Committee was originally launched by Ćosić and his long-time friends, writer Taras Kermauner in Slovenia and Praxist Rudi Supek in Croatia.

[30]Predrag Matvejević, *Jugoslavenstvo danas*, Zagreb, 1982, pp. 64, 59 and 155.
[31]Letter of 5 Nov. 1980 in Matvejević, *Otvorena pisma*, op. cit., p. 57.
[32]On the novel and the play see Chapter 2.
[33]'Letter to Dobrica Ćosić' in Matvejević, *Otvorena pisma*, op. cit., pp. 58–60.
[34]See Ćosić's letter to Matvejević, 4 May 1984, in ibid., pp. 62–4.
[35]Reply to Ćosić, 22 May 1984, in ibid., p. 67.
[36]See, for example, the defence of Ćosić by Predrag Vranicki in 'Moguće još nije i stvarno', *Književnost*, LXXV/8–9, Aug.-Sept. 1983, pp. 1400–21.

The first letter sent out to potential participants was signed by all three,[37] and each of them was supposed to find volunteers in his own republic. Supek had no success at all in Zagreb, where the few intellectuals who were potentially interested in joining (all associated with *Praxis*) felt the repressive climate in Croatia was not conducive to such action.[38] Kermauner, who doubted from the start that he would get a positive response in Slovenia, soon informed Ćosić that Slovenian intellectuals supported the idea, but that they did not want to join the Committee. Instead they were planning to create a separate committee of their own and hoped they could organise some common actions.[39] The Slovenes' rejection of the initiative was seen as a great blow by Ćosić and the other Belgrade participants.[40]

Although the Committee for the Defence of Freedom of Thought and Expression was constituted with only Belgrade members in autumn 1984, contacts with the Slovenian critical intellectuals continued with a view to adopting a common opposition platform. On Taras Kermauner's initiative, a meeting between the Belgrade group, represented by Ćosić and Praxists Mihailo Marković and Ljubomir Tadić, and the *Nova revija* editorial board was organised in Ljubljana in November 1985. Both Ćosić and one of the Slovenian participants, Spomenka Hribar, later published their accounts of this meeting, which took place in a restaurant appropriately called 'Darkness' (*Mrak*). In the view of both, this encounter—whose aim was to discuss, in Hribar's words, 'the shape of some 'third Yugoslavia'[41]—ended all hope of cooperation between the two groups.

According to Ćosić, the Slovenian intellectuals were united in their rejection of Yugoslavia and their desire to 'rejoin' Europe. They argued not only that Yugoslavia was historically dead, but that it had deprived Slovenia of its logical development into a modern European state, and the only common state they were willing to accept was one based on total national autonomy.[42] Hribar's account corroborates Ćosić's, but, according to her, the *Nova revija* intellectuals were only fighting for 'genuine equality' for Slovenia, which was contained in 'the sovereignty of republics on the basis of the right to self-

[37]It is reproduced in Mihajlović-Mihiz, *Kazivanja i ukazivanja*, op. cit., pp. 194–6.
[38]According to Predrag Palavestra, one of the participants in the talks (author's interview, 12 Aug. 1997).
[39]Mihajlović-Mihiz, *Kazivanja i ukazivanja*, op. cit., p. 196.
[40]Palavestra, author's interview, op. cit.
[41]Spomenka Hribar, 'Sestanek pri Mraku', *Delo* (Ljubljana), 4 Dec. 1993.
[42]Dobrica Ćosić, 'Simpozion u Mraku', *Duga*, 482, 16–29 Aug. 1992, p. 91.

determination'. They were not anti-Yugoslav, but they could only accept a common state which would not interfere with Slovenian independence—in other words, a confederation.[43] The Serbs, on the other hand, advocated a 'third and genuinely federal Yugoslavia' from what was, in their own view, an 'anti-nationalist and pro-Yugoslav' perspective.[44] But to the Slovenes they were merely hiding their 'Serbianism' behind the facade of 'Yugoslavism' and spoke about Yugoslavia only from the point of view of the Serbian national interest. Hribar argued that their views were simply irreconcilable with Slovenian sovereignty:

> To us, their 'proposal' of some kind of 'cultural autonomy' within a centralised federal state seemed ridiculous. Their statement that all confederations sooner or later develop into federations ... told us enough about what they really wanted ... The Serbian colleagues did not agree to a confederation, let alone the sovereignty of republics or independence. That is why we split.[45]

Whereas the Belgrade intellectuals had come to achieve agreement on common political action, their Ljubljana counterparts were only willing to offer them the possibility to publish their ideas on the Serbian question in an issue of *Nova revija*.[46] According to Hribar, the Serbs had begun the meeting with a 'haughtiness', which melted away as 'they listened to us incredulously': when the discussion was finished, 'our Serbian colleagues were depressed, disappointed, as if they couldn't understand that we were self-confident and firm in our standpoints and that it wasn't possible to 'achieve agreement' on anything'.[47] Ćosić confirms his own and his partners' dejection following the meeting; they felt 'beaten black and blue and reduced to silence' for the whole journey back to Belgrade.[48] This final confirmation of the Slovenes'

[43]Hribar, loc. cit.

[44]Ćosić, 'Simpozion u Mraku', op. cit., p. 92.

[45]Hribar, loc. cit. This seems to have been a common stance among Slovenian intellectuals at the time. Ciril Zlobec also argued that multiculturalism was unacceptable because it constituted a danger for Slovenia of having its 'sovereignty' reduced to mere 'folklore'. The objective was a Slovenian state, not cultural autonomy (Zlobec, op. cit., p. 251).

[46]Hribar, op. cit. The Serbian intellectuals never took them up on this offer, but compared to their expectations of the meeting it seems unfair to judge this as an act of bad faith. (For a different view, see Peter Vodopivec, 'Seven Decades of Unconfronted Incongruities: The Slovenes and Yugoslavia' in *Independent Slovenia*, op. cit., p. 41.)

[47]Hribar, loc. cit.

[48]Ćosić, 'Simpozion u Mraku', op. cit., p. 92.

rejection of an alliance with the Serbian intellectual opposition was shattering.

While these meetings between the groups around Ćosić and the *Nova revija* took place in private, the first open conflict between Serbian and Slovenian intellectuals occurred during the Ninth Congress of the Yugoslav Writers' Union in Novi Sad in April 1985. Ironically, this Congress—the first of its kind in ten years—was hailed as both the intellectuals' official 'exit from the ivory tower' and as 'the congress of unity'.[49] The Declaration adopted by the participants of the Congress demanded the abolition of 'verbal offence' from the Yugoslav penal code and was perceived as a great breakthrough for the intellectuals' united struggle for democratic change.[50] This veneer of common purpose was overshadowed by gaping national divisions, however. Already in the preparatory meetings, the president of the Writers' Association of Serbia, Miodrag Bulatović, made it clear that he wanted the Congress to be a manifestation of the 'spirit of Yugoslavism' and criticised the Slovenian stance on the 'common core curricula'. Ciril Zlobec, a member of the presidency of the Slovenian Writers' Society, on the other hand, opposed the slogan 'the congress of unity', arguing that it infringed upon the 'one nation-one vote' principle embodied in the Yugoslav constitution. By the end of the meeting, Bulatović—a notorious jokester and provocateur—warned Zlobec that if he continued to defend 'Slovenian separatism', he would 'cut him into little pieces' at the congress. Zlobec retorted that the title of his speech would then be 'For Slovenian Sovereignty'.[51] The heated quarrel that erupted between the two writers announced an open confrontation for Novi Sad.

The duel began on the first day of the Congress. Bulatović gave a speech lamenting the 'disintegration of everything called Yugoslav in this community' fed by eight '*artificial* state creations' and criticised 'autocephalous writers' who refused the 'universal, cosmopolitan Yugoslav consciousness'.[52] Zlobec picked up the gauntlet by replying that he was indeed 'an autocephalous writer and a Slovene' and warned that Slovenes would only accept a policy based on respect of Slovenian sovereignty and 'reciprocity', and that any attempt to change the status

---

[49]See, for example, *Danas*, 23 June 1987, p. 37.
[50]For the declaration, see *IX Kongres Saveza književnika Jugoslavije—Dokumenta*, Novi Sad, 1985, pp. 1–2.
[51]Zlobec, op. cit., pp. 205–14 passim.
[52]*IX Kongres*, op. cit., pp. 93–9 passim (emphasis added).

quo would be 'tragic'.[53] Other Slovenian writers supported him, some of them making a point of speaking in Slovenian and not in Serbo-Croatian (at which point some Serbian writers left the conference hall in protest).[54] The president of the Writers' Society of Croatia, Marija Peakić-Mikuljan, joined the Slovenian side by chastising Bulatović for 'criticising other Yugoslav nations and nationalities from the position of a supra-Yugoslav owner'.[55] Although the Congress ended on a more positive note with the adoption of the common declaration and the quarreling was portrayed by *Književne novine* as a 'constructive debate held in the spirit of tolerance',[56] relations within the Writers' Union rapidly deteriorated. First the case of the Writers' Society of Kosovo poisoned relations between the republican associations,[57] only to be replaced soon afterwards by an open conflict over the election of the president of the Writers' Union, which pitted two coalitions headed by the Slovenian and the Serbian associations in a bitter and protracted struggle.

The Yugoslav Writers' Union functioned in the same way as other federal institutions: both its assembly and collective presidency were made up of delegates elected by the associations of the various federal units. In return the latter were supposed to represent all the writers of the 'nations and nationalities' of that republic. The sole exception was the Slovenian Writers' Society, which was given a linguistically-defined ethno-national character by being allowed to represent all Slovenian writers regardless of where they lived (in fact, the Slovenian writers' delegation to the Novi Sad Congress even included Italian and Austrian citizens who wrote in Slovenian).[58] Organised according to this 'national key', the leadership of the Union's collective presidency rotated annually in alphabetical order, with a routine election of the president acting as *primus inter pares*. Hence the Slovenian president

---

[53]Ibid., pp. 112–14 passim.

[54]Bulatović was also reproached for not having learned Slovenian despite having lived in Ljubljana and being married to a Slovene (ibid., p. 239). He was already a *persona non grata* among Slovenian intellectuals for being 'disrespectful' of the Slovenian language. In the first issue of *Nova revija* of May 1982, Taras Kermauner had written Bulatović an open letter chastising him for his attitude towards the Slovenes.

[55]Ibid., p. 144.

[56]*Književne novine*, 687, 1 May 1985, p. 2.

[57]See Chapter 3.

[58]Hence also the difference in the name: the Slovenian Writers' Society as opposed to the Writers' Association of Serbia, Writers' Society of Kosovo, Writers' Society of Croatia etc.

of the Union, Ciril Zlobec, who was elected following the Novi Sad Congress, was supposed to be replaced by a Serb when his term expired in the spring of 1986.

In February 1986 the Writers' Association of Serbia decided to nominate Miodrag Bulatović as its candidate for president of the Union. Initially Serbian writers were not unanimous concerning the nomination and it was the Slovenian response that closed their ranks behind their controversial candidate. The delegates most violently opposed to Bulatović were the liberal intellectuals Nikola Milošević and Svetlana Slapšak, both active in the Committee for the Defence of Freedom of Creation. They reproached him for participating in the witch-hunt against the poet Gojko Djogo in 1982 and for criticising the Association's activism in the defence of civil rights.[59] Many dissidents saw Bulatović as a regime intellectual and demanded that a second candidate be nominated. In the runoff, Bulatović managed to win by a comfortable—though not overwhelming—margin of 20 votes to 12, signaling continuing divisions within the Serbian organisation.[60]

The response from Slovenia to Bulatović's candidature was immediate and categorical. In an open letter entitled 'He will not preside over me', the writer Janez Menart accused Bulatović of being a 'Greater Serbian' nationalist, 'ideologically violent' towards smaller Yugoslav peoples and 'insulting towards the national feelings of the Slovenes'.[61] His battle-cry was answered by the Slovenian Writers' Society, with only the *Nova revija* intellectual Dimitrij Rupel dissenting, on the basis that a rejection of Bulatović would represent 'meddling in the internal affairs of a sovereign association' and would set a bad precedent—'tomorrow someone might use it to meddle in our internal affairs'.[62] The Slovenes' stance was also supported by the Croatian, Kosovo and Montenegrin associations,[63] which gathered the four votes necessary to block Bulatović's election. After some delay, the showdown came at the congress of the Writers' Union held in June 1986 in the Slovenian town of Maribor. A definite change

---

[59]See the acerbic exchange of letters between Milošević and Bulatović in *Književne novine*, 707, 709 and 710, Apr.-May 1985.

[60]*NIN*, 16 Feb. 1986. Ironically, parts of the press saw the nomination of the second candidate, the literary critic Zoran Gavrilović, as an anti-Montenegrin act, since Bulatović was a Montenegrin!

[61]*Start*, 5 Apr. 1986, p. 18.

[62]*Danas*, 7 July 1987, p. 37.

in mood was noted by the media at this time; whereas the Novi Sad Congress had been painted in a positive light, the Maribor meeting was characterised by a 'coldness and even the lack of normal cordiality'.[64] For the Serbian participants, that congress was a confirmation of Slovenian nationalism—the introductory speech held by Janko Kos divided Yugoslav literature into 'Central European' and 'Byzantine' and no translators were provided for the speeches made in Slovenian.[65] The vote on the incoming president of the Writers' Union ended in a stalemate, preventing the Serbian candidate from being elected. In response the Writers' Association of Serbia announced its refusal to have its candidate 'dictated' and maintained Bulatović's nomination in a spirit of defiance.[66]

By the summer of 1986 the media referred to the Bulatović affair as 'the most important election in Yugoslavia' and an ominous 'harbinger of a change of behaviour in important spheres of Yugoslav political life'.[67] The two-year stalemate in the Yugoslav Writers' Union that resulted from the dispute over Bulatović not only embittered and entrenched the nationalism of both camps, but it also marked the first step in the process of disintegration of Yugoslavia's supranational organisations.[68] In the aftermath of the Maribor Congress, the Writers' Association of Serbia elected a new presidency, which included not only the rejected Bulatović, but a whole range of writers known for both their critical stance vis-à-vis the regime and their uncompromising position on the Serbian national question.[69] The new presidency announced a more hardline stand for the future. According to Dobrica Ćosić, one of its elected members, Serbian intellectuals were 'fed up with this Yugoslav humiliation, and for once were not so nihilistic as to tolerate this "brotherly" ultimatum'. Ominously, Ćosić

---

[63]Ibid., loc. cit. The Montenegrin association rejected Bulatović, despite his being a Montenegrin, on the grounds that he did not accept a separate Montenegrin national identity and that he equated Montenegrins with Serbs. The president of the Writers' Association of Montenegro at the time, Jevrem Brković, was a well-known advocate of Montenegrin independence and a close collaborator of the Writers' Society of Croatia.

[64]*Politika*, 12 June 1986.

[65]*Književne novine*, 712, 15 June 1986, pp. 4–5.

[66]Until spring 1988, when it finally relented and proposed another candidate (see Chapter 5).

[67]*Start*, op. cit., p. 18 and *Književne novine*, 706, 15 March 1986, p. 2.

[68]The Yugoslav Writers' Union was the first common organisation to disintegrate (see Chapter 5).

[69]See Chapter 3, p. 144.

depicted the Bulatović case as 'a metastasis of the Yugoslav cancer', a manifestation of Slovenian 'national paranoia', backed by Croatian 'Serbophobia', Albanian 'chauvinism' and Montenegrin 'Stalinism'.[70]

Repositories of the new nationalism: the draft 'Memorandum' of the Serbian Academy and 'Contributions for a Slovenian National Programme'

The worsening relations between Slovenian and Serbian intellectuals, the crisis in the Writers' Union, the polemics over Kosovo and the accompanying revelations of radically different visions of the common state all contributed to an increasing polarisation between the two most active intellectual oppositions in the country. By mid-1986 the positions were drawn and the tone set for the debates on the future of Yugoslavia. Two documents that appeared within four months of each other—the draft 'Memorandum' of the Serbian Academy of Sciences and Arts, which was disclosed unauthorised in September 1986, and the January 1987 *Nova revija* issue devoted to 'Contributions for a Slovenian National Programme'—embodied these two clashing visions.

On 24 September 1986 a bombshell shook Serbia's cultural scene, as an article appeared in the daily *Večernje novosti* (Evening News) announcing that 'Serbian nationalism has received its most open programme' in the form of a Memorandum of the Serbian Academy of Sciences and Arts. Quoting excerpts from this unfinished document, the article criticised it as 'a renewed call for civil war and bloodletting' and 'an openly nationalist and anti-communist programme, which in new form but with old arguments calls for Serbs to "rally together"'.[71] The following day the author of the article, Aleksandar Djukanović, called for public denunciation of the Academy as a bastion of nationalist chauvinism.[72] Since its disclosure the Memorandum has become probably the most-cited text of contemporary Serbian nationalism, both in former Yugoslavia and abroad; it has been widely regarded as a 'blueprint for war', a programme for 'Greater Serbia', Milošević's *Mein Kampf* and even as an incitement to 'ethnic cleansing'.[73] On the

---

[70]'Letter to Taras Kermauner', 15 July 1986, in Ćosić, *Srpsko pitanje—demokratsko pitanje*, op. cit., pp. 82–3.

[71] *Večernje novosti*, 24 Sept. 1986.

[72]Ibid., 25 Sept. 1986.

[73]See, for example, George Soros, 'Bosnia and Beyond', *New York Review of Books*,

other hand, the Memorandum's authors and defenders have presented it as an essentially 'pro-Yugoslav' text, an enlightened analysis of the country's crisis and an expression of critical thought and democracy in Serbia.[74] These radically different assessments of the document and the many misconceptions that abound concerning its content, authors and implications calls for a more thorough analysis.[75]

In reality there was very little that was new in the Memorandum. The first half of the text was devoted to an assessment of the Yugoslav crisis, along the lines already espoused in critical intellectuals' articles and opposition fora.[76] It blamed the country's economic woes on excessive decentralisation and the rise of autarky between the federal units, poor investment strategies and the precedence of political considerations over economic rationale in decisionmaking, 'parasitism' and corruption, as well as on the reluctance of the authorities to acknowledge the depth of the crisis and implement genuine reforms. The Memorandum also argued that Yugoslavia's political system was moribund, caught in a quagmire of 'bureaucratism' and competing

---

7 Oct. 1993, p. 15; P. J. Cohen, 'The Complicity of Serbian Intellectuals in Genocide in the 1990s', op. cit., p. 39; and Pierre Milza and Serge Berstein, *Histoire terminale*, Paris, 1993, p. 330. The Serbian Academy even charged Milza and Berstein with libel for their definition of 'ethnic cleansing' as a 'theory launched by the members of the Serbian Academy of Sciences'.

[74]Vasilije Krestić, author's interview, 22 Apr. 1992, and 'Memorandum. Šta se piše a šta se čita u ozloglašenom dokumentu Srpske Akademije nauka i umetnosti', *Duga*, special issue, June 1989, p. 5. See also Milorad Vučelić's introductory article in ibid., pp. 9–11. For a comprehensive defence of their text, see Kosta Mihailović and Vasilije Krestić, *Memorandum of the Serbian Academy of Sciences and Arts: Answers to Criticisms*, Belgrade, 1995.

[75]Philip J. Cohen's article on 'The Complicity of Serbian Intellectuals', op. cit., provides a very good example. Among Cohen's many erroneous claims are: that the Memorandum advocates that Serbia's borders must be expanded so that all Serbs must live in one enlarged Serbia (p. 39), that one of the key figures behind the text was Vaso Čubrilović, the author of the '1937 official government memorandum' on the expulsion of the Albanians (pp. 39–40), that one of its principal authors was Dobrica Ćosić, who had—according to Cohen—proposed in 1968 'that Serbs rise to destroy the multinational Yugoslav state' to fulfill the goal of 'Greater Serbia' (p. 40), or that another co-author of the text was Svetozar Stojanović (p. 55), who was in fact not even a member of the Academy. (On Čubrilović's and Ćosić's speeches of 1937 and 1968, see Chapters 3 and 1 respectively.)

[76]An excellent analysis of the 'Memorandum' as a response to the Yugoslav crisis can be found in Audrey Helfant Budding, 'Systemic Crisis and National Mobilization: The Case of the "Memorandum of the Serbian Academy"' in *Cultures and Nations of Central and Eastern Europe: Essays in Honor of Roman Szporluk*, Harvard Ukrainian Studies special volume, XXII, 1998, pp. 49–69.

national particularisms inherent to the prevailing confederate arrangement. Finally, it also diagnosed Yugoslav society as experiencing a deep
'moral crisis' resulting from the travesty of the original goals of the
communist revolution and the loss of social conscience and values.[77]

Although this first part of the Memorandum criticised Yugoslavia's
insufficient political liberty and condemned continued persecution
of individuals for 'verbal crimes',[78] it was in some ways a more
conservative document than many concurrent demands of the
intellectual opposition. It praised Yugoslavia's development before the
decentralisation of the mid-1960s—marked by a planned economy
with few market mechanisms and greater Party control over society
and culture—as one of 'progress and democratisation' and it did not
reject Yugoslav communism's ideological foundations or revolutionary
legacy.[79] Rather, it advocated the building of 'democratic socialism'
and a type of nonparty pluralism along the lines earlier espoused by
the Praxists—'free elections and recall of all officials, public oversight
of their work, a separation of powers, and the absence of bureaucratic
privileges', but not the creation of a multiparty system.[80] In this sense
the Memorandum fell short of the concurrent proposal for the
establishment of the rule of law of the Committee for the Defence of
Freedom of Thought and Expression, which included the right to all
forms of free political organisation, including political parties.[81]

In its nationalist content the Memorandum represented a faithful
reflection of the radical discourse that was coming to predominate in
the revision of history and the defence of the Kosovo Serbs. It presented
'the status of Serbia and the Serbian nation' as one of inequality, resulting
from the 'Comintern legacy' and the historical depiction of Serbs as
'oppressors', 'unitarists', 'centralists' or 'policemen' of other Yugoslav
nations.[82] It argued that economically Serbia suffered lower per capita
investment, unfair terms of trade with the other republics and excessive
contributions to the Federal Fund for Underdeveloped Regions. It

---

[77]'Memorandum' in *Memorandum of the Serbian Academy of Sciences and Arts: Answers
to Criticisms*, op. cit., pp. 95–119 passim. This is the version authorised by the Academy's
presidency. It is practically identical to the 'unofficial' versions that were circulated
in *samizdat* and published in various Yugoslav and émigré journals.

[78]Ibid., pp. 108–10.

[79]Although it does acknowledge certain flaws in the original system, notably
the overemphasis on the role of violence and dictatorship (ibid., pp. 115–18).

[80]Ibid., p. 117.

[81]See Chapter 1.

[82]'Memorandum', op. cit., pp. 121–3 passim.

complained that politically Serbs, who represented a demographic plurality in Yugoslavia, were not given a representative number of posts in federal bodies.[83] Finally, for the Memorandum's authors the 'worst misfortune of all' was that the autonomous provinces in the Republic of Serbia prevented Serbs from having 'their own state, as do all the other nations'.[84] It was this lack of state protection that had allowed 'genocide' in Kosovo, where 'an open and total war [had been] declared on the Serbian people' by Albanian 'neofascists' and the Serbs had to mount a 'resolute defence of their nation and their territory'.[85] The Memorandum's conclusion echoed the idea of the Serbs as a victim nation, central to the new nationalist vision:

In less than fifty years, for two successive generations, the Serbs were twice subjected to physical annihilation, forced assimilation, conversion to a different religion, cultural genocide, ideological indoctrination, denigration and compulsion to renounce their own traditions because of an imposed guilt complex.[86]

At the same time, the Memorandum did add two significant new elements to public nationalist discourse. For the first time since 1971 it directly raised the question of the Serbs of Croatia, this time more forcefully and radically, by portraying them as victims of discrimination and 'a subtle but effective policy of assimilation' aimed at weakening the bonds between them and the Republic of Serbia.[87] By claiming that, 'except for the time under the Independent State of Croatia, the Serbs in Croatia have never before been as jeopardised as they are today',[88] it compared the present situation—not of the Kosovo Serbs, as was already being done, but of Croatia's Serbs—to the greatest Serbian trauma of this century. Second, the Memorandum for the first time explicitly designated who was responsible for this situation—a Slovene-Croat coalition, which held the strings of power in communist Yugoslavia and which was embodied by the tandem of Tito, the Croat, and Edvard Kardelj, the Slovene. Thanks to their domination, the Memorandum argued, the two most developed

[83]Ibid., pp. 119–20.
[84]Ibid., p. 139.
[85]Ibid., pp. 127–8.
[86]Ibid., p. 138.
[87]Ibid., p. 131.
[88]Ibid., p. 133.

republics had 'accomplished their nationalist agendas' and were now 'zealous defenders of the existing system'.[89] They supported the fragmentation of the Serbian nation, as well as the 'genocide' of the Serbs in Kosovo and plotted to maintain Serbia in a subordinated an unequal position.

In view of its radical portrayal of the Serbs' situation, the Memorandum's recommendations are remarkably sedate. It does not advocate the redrawing of borders or ethnic cleansing, as has so often been alleged. In fact, it can hardly be called a 'blueprint' or even a 'national programme', if this is understood to mean a set of objectives and coveted territories, a time frame or a series of instructions for action. One of its few recommendations is for Serbia to undertake 'the task of clearly assessing its own economic and national interests, lest it be taken unawares of events'.[90] While the Memorandum does defend the Serbs' 'historic and democratic right' to 'complete national and cultural integrity, regardless of which republic or province they might be living in',[91] it does not call for the creation of an independent 'Greater Serbian' state, but for a 'thorough reexamination of the [1974] Constitution' and the establishment of 'a democratic, integrating federalism' in Yugoslavia, in which 'the principle of autonomy of the parts is in harmony with that of the unity of the whole'.[92]

The importance of the Memorandum as a nationalist text lies rather in the extremist language it uses to depict the situation of the Serbs and in the conspiracy theory it relies on to explain it. Despite the document's 'democratic' and 'Yugoslav' veneer and the few and relatively moderate policy recommendations (create a national programme, reexamine the constitution, promote 'democratic integrative federalism'), its claims make it very difficult to envisage how a common state is possible with nations who are perpetrating 'genocide' or plotting to 'oppress' the Serbs. Second, the Memorandum is significant in that it represents a repository of all the various strands of the new Serbian nationalism—the historical vision of the Serbs as a victim nation, the 'destiny of genocide', the national claim to Kosovo and the deep sense of betrayal by other Yugoslavs—in one 40–page text. Finally, the fact that its authors drafted the text under the aus-

[89]Ibid., p. 107.
[90]Ibid., p. 140.
[91]Ibid., pp. 138–40 passim.
[92]Ibid., p. 106.

pices of Serbia's most important cultural institution—the Academy of Sciences and Arts—gave the contentious document a greater weight than it would otherwise have had.

The affair of the Memorandum, which shook the Serbian political and intellectual scene so thoroughly, remains shrouded in mystery. Who ordered the document to be stolen and made public and for what purpose? What exactly is the connection between this text and Slobodan Milošević, who took power in Serbia exactly one year after the affair? To what extent did the Academy as an institution endorse the ideas espoused by the Memorandum and did the text reflect a majority stance or express the opinion of a vocal minority? While there are no clear answers to any of these questions, it is worth exploring some of the possible explanations.

First of all, how did the unfinished draft of the Memorandum appear in *Večernje novosti* and who was behind the document's theft? What has been established is that one of the approximately twenty copies of the text was taken from academician Jovan Djordjević, by his son-in-law, journalist Aleksandar Djukanović, who then wrote the damning articles.[93] Djukanović himself never disclosed his motivations or possible accomplices or requisitioners.[94] Some have argued that the federal ministry of the interior, headed at the time by Slovenian hardliner Stane Dolanc, was behind the affair, possibly as a way of putting pressure on the Serbian leadership, deemed too 'soft' on the rising nationalism in its republic, or on the Serbian Academy, an institution of enormous moral authority.[95] Another theory that circulated was that the Serbian leadership was behind the 'disclosure' of the text, in an attempt to discredit the Academy. However, Ivan Stambolić, Serbia's president at the time, has denied any involvement in the affair.[96]

[93]Djordjević admitted that he was unwillingly implicated in the document's publication (*Politika ekspres*, 2 Nov. 1986).

[94]According to journalist Slavoljub Djukić, who investigated the case and talked to Djukanović (author's interview, 16 March 1994).

[95]Dobrica Ćosić, author's interview, 25 March 1994. According to Ćosić, a copy of the Memorandum acquired by writer Antonije Isaković from the police contained comments in the margins written in the Croatian idiom and Latin alphabet, which would indicate a possible involvement of the more dogmatic communists in the Croatian party. Some of the sharpest criticisms of the Memorandum and the Serbian leadership (for condoning nationalism) came from Croats in the federal and Vojvodinian political instances (see D. Jović, op. cit., p. 238).

[96]Stambolić, op. cit., p. 125.

According to Slavoljub Djukić, one of Serbia's best investigative journalists, the top three members of the Serbian leadership—Stambolić, Slobodan Milošević, president of Serbia's Central Committee, and Dragiša Pavlović, president of the Belgrade City Committee—first read extracts from the Memorandum in the *Večernje novosti* article.[97] Considering the continuous criticism from the other republics that the Serbian leadership was soft on nationalism, Djukić has plausibly argued that it made little sense for Stambolić to launch the affair. His own explanation is that there was no conspiracy behind the Memorandum's theft; rather, it was the action of an ambitious journalist who thought he could capitalise on disclosing nationalist activity in the prestigious institution.[98] Considering that at the moment of the Memorandum affair, Serbia's Central Committee had launched a new attack against the Belgrade intelligentsia, the hypothesis of the 'leak' resulting from the efforts of an overzealous journalist appears plausible.[99]

Milošević's ambiguous stance during the affair of the Memorandum has led to another argument concerning the circumstances of the document appearance. This theory portrays Milošević as the dark force behind the Memorandum and makes him responsible for the Memorandum's disclosure to the press, with a view of taking over the leadership of Serbia on this nationalist platform.[100] This explanation is based on two main arguments: first, it sees Milošević's muted criticism of the Memorandum at the time of the affair as proof of his collusion, and second, it equates his subsequent policies and statements with the ideas expressed in the text. While the observations on which the argument is based are essentially correct, this theory provides no evidence of Milošević's prior knowledge or implication in the affair and, secondly, it shows a faulty assessment of the Serbian situation.

If Milošević had wanted to plant the seeds of nationalism in the

---

[97]Djukić, author's interview, op. cit.

[98]Ibid. See also Djukić, *Kako se dogodio vodja*, op. cit., pp. 113–14.

[99]A day before the Memorandum's disclosure, a Serbian Central Committee plenum condemned the rising nationalism in the republic and called for greater vigilance (*Politika*, 23 Sept. 1986).

[100]This vision was espoused particularly in Croatia and in Croatian émigré circles after 1989. See for example, *Le nettoyage ethnique*, op. cit., p. 233. In accordance with this vision, the Memorandum has at times even been compared to Hitler's *Mein Kampf*.

Serbian public sphere he hardly needed the Memorandum, since the Belgrade intelligentsia, the Serbian Church and the Kosovo Serbs were already doing so very successfully. Secondly, Milošević did not come to power by popular mandate or on the basis of the 'general will', but through an internal Party struggle a whole year after the Memorandum became public.[101] Before the affair of the Memorandum there was no indication that Milošević had any nationalist propensities and there is nothing to indicate that the Memorandum's authors would have considered an alliance with him. He was at the forefront of most of the actions against the critical intelligentsia as head of the Belgrade City Committee and, even after he took over the leadership of the Serbian Central Committee in January 1986, he was a known Party conservative opposed to manifestations of Serbian nationalism. While remaining relatively silent on the Memorandum in public, Milošević did take part in the Serbian leadership's 'ideological offensives' against the intellectual opposition and expressed himself against the text in closed meetings.[102] As late as June 1987 he characterised the Memorandum as 'the darkest nationalism, which proposes the break-up of Yugoslavia and... the liquidation of the existing socialist arrangement of our country, after whose disintegration there is no survival for any Yugoslav people'.[103] His continuous references to maintaining Tito's legacy in the first period of his rule also appear at odds with the ideas of the Memorandum.[104]

So why then did Milošević not take a more public stand against the Memorandum? Slavoljub Djukić has argued that Serbia's future leader was probably already personally inclined towards some of the ideas espoused in the text, but knew that any deviation from the official line in the affair could cost him his political career.[105] Perhaps Milošević was coming to understand the potency of the nationalist card and was simply waiting to see how the situation would develop. From this vantage point, the Memorandum affair may have helped crystallise new possibilities for national policy.[106] However, Milošević

[101]See Chapter 5.

[102]See D. Jović, pp. 239–40.

[103]Milošević's speech at the Institute for Security in Belgrade, 4 June 1987, in *Vreme*, 16 Aug. 1993, p. 13.

[104]See Chapter 5.

[105]Djukić, *Kako se dogodio vodja*, op. cit., p. 120.

[106]According to Ivan Stambolić, his own relations with Milošević—who was until then his best friend and right-hand man—began to change with the affair of the Memorandum. After the document's appearance, 'there was a quiet tearing

himself never subsequently referred to the document as an inspiration or even acknowledged reading it. Another explanation is that Milošević simply did not believe in wasting time on futile debates with intellectuals, preferring direct action, practical solutions and the strengthening of the Party as the vector of 'positive' change.[107] Whatever the truth of the matter, unless Milošević decides to speak out there is little likelihood that the controversy about his behaviour during the Memorandum affair will be resolved.

Many misconceptions also abound concerning the authorship of the document. The drafting committee created in June 1985 included sixteen members nominated by their respective departments and was chaired by the vice-president of the Academy, Antonije Isaković. Contrary to some claims, the novelist Dobrica Ćosić was not part of the group, because, as a well-known 'dissident', his inclusion would have provoked the authorities.[108] He and his friend the Praxist Ljubomir Tadić, did participate in some of the discussions, however, and the affair broke at the moment they took the document to add their own remarks and criticisms.[109] Furthermore, not all the committee members actively took part in the drafting of the text. Its principal authors were Isaković, the economist Kosta Mihailović, the philosopher Mihailo Marković and the historian Vasilije Krestić, who has since admitted authorship of the 'historical' parts of the document.[110] Also, the Memorandum was not intended as an opposition platform to be presented to the public. Rather, its recipient was to be the Serbian government, which—according to the committee— needed a 'critical analysis of the current state of affairs in Yugoslavia and Serbia'.[111] Only the first part of the text, analysing the Yugoslav crisis, was in fact approved by the committee as a whole.

So how widespread were the visions espoused in the unfinished text among academicians? The answer to this question remains obfus-

---

apart in the League of Communists, an internal separation between those who did not publicly condemn the Memorandum and those of us who condemned it even more vehemently because of that' (Stambolić, op. cit., p. 131).

[107]D. Jović, op. cit., p. 240.

[108]*Vreme*, 16 Aug. 1993, p. 12.

[109]Dobrica Ćosić, author's interview, op. cit.

[110]Vasilije Krestić, author's interview, op. cit. This view concerning the Memorandum's authorship is shared by Budding, 'Systemic Crisis' op. cit., pp. 65–6, note 31.

[111]*Memorandum of the Serbian Academy of Sciences and Arts: Answers to Criticisms*, op. cit., p. 14.

cated by the official witchhunt that took place against the Academy. Almost every day for several months a new attack was launched in the media against the institution, with headlines ranging from the initial 'A Proposal for Hopelessness' (*Večernje novosti*) to 'Chauvinist pamphlet' (*Danas*), 'The Poisoners of Conscience' (*Politika ekspres*), 'Not a Case, but Premeditated Action' (*Borba*), 'The Memorandum of Destruction' (*Komunist*) or 'The Memorandum—Hatred as a Principle' (*Politika*). Partisan veteran's organisations and workers' councils were mobilised to denounce the text; Josip Vrhovec, Croatia's representative to the Federal Presidency, called it 'the expression of well-organised enemy work'; Ivan Stambolić saw it as 'a stab in the back of Yugoslavia, Serbia, socialism, self-management, equality, brotherhood and unity'; and regime intellectuals accused the Academy of being 'not a scholarly and artistic institution but ... a nest of chauvinism'.[112] The Serbian media harked for a 'settling of accounts' with the head of the Memorandum committee, Antonije Isaković, 'and all those like him'.[113] The Serbian leadership threatened to withdraw the Academy's funding, while pressure was applied on the institution to condemn the Memorandum and its authors.

When the Academy's presidency scheduled a special assembly on the issue in December 1986, the Serbian leadership believed it would reject the document, as the institution's communist *aktiv* had already done.[114] At the assembly the Serbian government representative Vukoje Bulatović made it very clear what was expected of the Academy: it had to take an unequivocal stand on the content of the document and present the Yugoslav public with 'convincing proof' that the Memorandum only represented the reflection of a small minority.[115] In fact only two academicians openly did so, as they had already done in their preceding interviews with the Belgrade press: the physicist and former Academy president Pavle Savić and the historian Vaso Čubrilović (author of the 1937 speech on 'The Expulsion of the Albanians').[116] The historian Sima Ćirković adopted a nuanced stance. He criticised the witch-hunt against the Academy and the Memorandum's authors, but also expressed scepticism about some of the document's positions,

---

[112]Quoted in *Večernje novosti*, 2 Nov. 1986 and *Politika*, 31 Oct., 1986.

[113]*Politika ekspres*, 18 Oct. 1986.

[114]*Politika*, 16 Oct. 1986. Ironically several members of the *aktiv* had been on the 'Memorandum' committee.

[115]*Književne novine*, 723–4, 1–15 Jan. 1987, p. 15.

[116]*Večernje novosti*, 19 Dec. 1986.

subjects and themes. He argued that the Academy had to remain faithful to its original mission to represent universal values of objectivity, moderation and criticism in a 'rational scholarly spirit', and not get bogged down in everyday politics.[117]

Several academicians who had worked on the Memorandum adopted a relatively conciliatory approach towards the authorities, showing their reluctance to be perceived as opponents of the regime. They reiterated in a more measured language the less contentious arguments about the dimensions of the crisis in Yugoslavia and the defects of the constitution and stated that 'we cannot deny that the Serbian question today is a real question', but concurrently stressed that nobody in the Academy wanted to create difficulties for the leadership.[118] One of the document's authors, the economist Kosta Mihailović, compared the Serbian Academy to its counterparts in Croatia and Slovenia, which were close to their leaderships, noting that if the Serbian leadership had cooperated with intellectuals the Memorandum might not have been necessary.[119]

Academicians who belonged to the intellectual opposition, particularly those who were members of the Committee for the Defence of Freedom of Thought and Expression, took a more defiant stand. The poet Matija Bećković read out a protest letter signed by eight academicians, affirming that the unacceptable disclosure of the unfinished text rendered the Memorandum nonexistent for the Academy.[120] The former Partisan general and memoirist Gojko Nikoliš compared the 'pogrom' against the Memorandum to Stalin's ultimatum of 1948.[121] Dobrica Ćosić denounced the Serbian leadership for its 'persistently disastrous policy' and claimed for the Academy 'the moral right to be concerned with the future of the nation'; in his view, the work on the Memorandum had been undertaken in the spirit of democracy and the Academy had to resist pressure to turn against its members on the basis of their 'moral and political suitability'.[122] He called upon his fellow academicians to defend the

---

[117]*Književne novine*, 723–4, op. cit., p. 14.

[118]Ivan Maksimović, in ibid., p. 15.

[119]Ibid., p. 18.

[120]*Naša reč*, 382, Feb. 1987, p. 10. The other signatories were Desanka Maksimović, Ivan Antić, Dragoslav Srejović, Milka Ivić, Olga Jevrić, Stevan Raičković and Irena Grickat-Radulović.

[121]*Književne novine*, 723–4, op. cit., p. 16.

[122]Ibid., p. 18.

'intellectual dignity and moral integrity' of their institution and assert their political independence. His appeal was reiterated by the artist Mića Popović, who stated that the Academy faced a choice between a vote of confidence to its Executive Committee or humiliation of the whole institution.[123] Of the Academy's 137 members present at the assembly 115 answered this call by giving the presidency their unequivocal support; even Antonije Isaković received 88 votes in favour.[124]

This vote of confidence thus represented an assertion of the Academy's independence vis-à-vis the regime, rather than an endorsement of the Memorandum and, although the media attacks continued for some time, it effectively meant that the Serbian political leadership had lost the battle. Short of liquidating the Academy or embarking on massive repression in the republic, there was little that it could do. On the other hand, the Academy's rejection of the regime's ultimatum prevented any discussion of the Memorandum's contentious and nationalist claims, making it impossible to know how much support they actually received in its ranks. Because of this the Memorandum effectively got the 'seal' of Serbia's most prestigious institution—at least in the public's perception—without ever actually having been debated.

In addition, the Memorandum affair sparked an inordinate interest in the document and allowed for the transmission of its main nationalist messages through the media, despite their being denounced. The Academy's stand in the face of pressure also received much attention: 'never in the history of the Academy had there been more journalists, photographers and television cameras than at its special assembly'.[125] The public reaction was predictable:

People start asking themselves what is in this text which has attracted such widespread political interest. Some beg individuals close to newspaper publishers or media circles to lend them the 'Memorandum' for a day or an hour, and when they get it, they rush to photocopy machines, not even asking how much it costs. In this way, the Memorandum becomes a *samizdat* and achieves a mind-boggling number of copies and the largest circulation of any of the contentious books.[126]

---

[123] *Naša reč*, 384, Apr. 1987, pp. 8–9.
[124] Srpska Akademija nauka i umetnosti, *Godišnjak za 1986*, Belgrade, 1987, p. 111.
[125] *Politikin svet*, 24 Dec. 1986.
[126] Milo Gligorijević, 'Koliko su dva i dva', *Književne novine*, 722, 15 Dec. 1986.

In a situation already burdened with uncertainty and fear for the future, the dissemination of this text—which was much shorter than the complicated histories or lengthy novels—hit fertile ground.

Within a few weeks of the Academy's special session on the Memorandum a new scandal involving intellectuals shook Yugoslavia: the publication in January 1987 of *Nova revija*'s 'Contributions for a Slovenian National Programme'. The Slovenian intellectuals had embarked on their project in 1985—at approximately the same time as the Serbian academicians on theirs[127]—and this issue of their journal was labelled in parts of the press as the 'Slovenian Memorandum'.[128] The issue was ready in the autumn of 1986, but the virulent reaction to the Serbian document persuaded the *Nova revija* editors to wait until the situation had calmed down.[129] When the 'Contributions for a Slovenian National Programme' were published, the editors mentioned the Memorandum in their introduction, noting that the national question in Yugoslavia was a 'hot and controversial theme'.[130] One of the contributors, the philosopher Ivan Urbančič, referred to the Memorandum as a legitimate endeavour, even a 'strong stimulating force' for the debate on Yugoslavia's problems, and criticised the way it had been attacked by the authorities and the press.[131] In return, the Belgrade intelligentsia's main journal, *Književne novine*, translated and published a number of the *Nova revija* articles, defending the Slovenian intellectuals' right to write on their national question.[132]

Indeed there are some striking similarities between the two documents, the most important being that they both represented repositories of all the various nationalist grievances against the common state, rather than coherent 'blueprints' for action. Like their Serbian counterparts, the *Nova revija* intellectuals argued that creating a national programme was vital for the Slovenes' 'survival' and that they were threatened with 'disappearance as a nation'.[133] They com-

[127]Hribar, 'Sestanek u "Mraku"', loc. cit. In this sense the claim that Slovenia's national revival and the *Nova revija* issue were merely a reaction to the Memorandum is inaccurate. (For such a view see, for example, Križan, op. cit., p. 134.)

[128]*Danas*, 3 March 1987.

[129]D. Jović, op. cit., pp. 291–2.

[130]'Prispevki za slovenski nacionalni program', *Nova revija*, VI/57, Jan. 1987, p. 1.

[131]Ivan Urbančič, 'Jugoslovanska 'nacionalistièna kriza' i Slovenci v perspektivi konca nacije' in ibid., p. 39.

[132]*Književne novine*, 728, 15 March 1987, pp. 4–9 and 729, 1 Apr. 1987, pp. 15–19.

[133]Spomenka Hribar, 'Avantgardno sovraštvo in sprava', *Nova revija*, op. cit., p. 100 and Urbančič, loc. cit.

plained of Slovenia's 'unequal' status in the federal state: the Slovenian language was 'second class' in Yugoslavia and Slovenia's economic development suffered from having to sustain the underdeveloped republics.[134] The fact that the Slovenian army was merged into the Yugoslav People's Army after the war (and had to use Serbo-Croatian as the 'language of command') was also seen as an infringement upon Slovenian sovereignty and a 'military-defensive castration', while the presence of the Yugoslav army in Slovenia was depicted as 'a military occupation by a nationally foreign army'.[135] The 'dangerously high' influx of immigrant workers from the 'southern' parts of Yugoslavia, combined with the low Slovenian fertility rate, raised 'the prospect of a national catastrophe' of Slovenia becoming a 'multinational republic', a 'time bomb' comparable to Kosovo.[136] One contributor also argued that 'we will remain half-formed, crushed and broken individuals if we cannot achieve at least the right to speak openly about our desires ... as Slovenes, members of the Slovenian nation'.[137]

Despite this underlying similarity, there were two significant differences between the two documents. Contrary to the Memorandum, the 'Contributions for a Slovenian National Programme' made no pretension of offering solutions for Yugoslavia. Indeed, as Jože Pučnik noted' 'How other nations and nationalities organise their relations is their problem and their decision; it is certainly not a Slovenian problem.'[138] Some authors did not even see Yugoslavia as their own state. According to the writer Drago Jančar, it did not matter whether the state to which the Slovenes belonged had been called 'Austria-Hungary, the Kingdom of Yugoslavia, Democratic Federal Yugoslavia, Federal People's Republic of Yugoslavia or Socialist Federal Republic of Yugoslavia' because none of these was ever 'a homeland. [None] was ever called Slovenia.'[139] Tine Hribar also noted that the Slovenes had 'only known foreign states until now' and argued that even the definition of Slovenia as the 'Republic of Slovenes and other nationalities of Slovenia' in the Yugoslav constitution raised the minorities to the same status as Slovenes, making Slovenia function 'above all as a Yugoslav territory and not as the

[134]Urbančič, op. cit., p. 54.
[135]Ibid., p. 56. See also S. Hribar, pp. 80–9.
[136]Ibid., loc. cit.
[137]T. Hribar, 'Slovenska državnost', in ibid., op. cit. p. 24.
[138]Jože Pučnik, 'Politični sistem civilne družbe', *Nova revija*, op. cit., p. 142.
[139]Drago Jančar, 'Slovenski eksil', *Nova revija*, op. cit., p. 225.

inalienable homeland of the Slovenes'.[140] Others argued that Yugoslavia was 'illegitimate', since the Slovenian people had never pronounced themselves on whether to adhere to the common state or
not.[141] Their reactions to the Memorandum illustrated this inherent
anti-Yugoslavism. What bothered the *Nova revija* intellectuals about
the Serbs' text the was its mixing of 'legitimate Serbian nationalism'
with 'unitarist Yugoslavism' and, while they could accept the first as
'normal', the second made them 'very uncomfortable'.[142] Their problem was with Yugoslavia, not with Serbia or the Serbs, and—in contrast to the Memorandum—they did not present a Serbian conspiracy
or the 'national masochism' of their own communists as the source
of Slovenia's problems. The main target of their critiques were the
'centralists' and 'dogmatists' in the Yugoslav army and the federal
leadership.[143]

Secondly, the authors of the 'Contributions for a Slovenian National
Programme' pointed to what they saw as the essential difference
between their project and the Memorandum. As Spomenka Hribar
and Jože Snoj, two of the *Nova revija* authors, told the Croatian
newsweekly *Danas*,

A false impression is being created that *Nova revija* laments and cries over
the fate of Slovenia and Slovenes in Yugoslavia, as does the Memorandum
over the fate of the Serbian people, insisting on questions of the past. In
fact, we wanted to do exactly the opposite—to give Slovenes self-confidence
and the desire to fight for their future by their own forces.[144]

Whereas the Memorandum was originally an 'internal' document
aimed at the Serbian leadership, the 'Contributions' were specifically
aimed at heightening popular awareness. They openly endorsed the
idea of 'civil society' as the vehicle of both democratic and national
transformation, rather than advocating a 'revolution from above'.
Slovenes themselves, spearheaded by their intellectuals, had to take
charge of their destiny and direct their energy towards political action.

[140]Tine Hribar, op. cit., p. 22.

[141]France Bučar, 'Pravna ureditev položaja Slovencev kot naroda', in ibid, p.
155.

[142]Urbančič, op. cit., p. 39. In fact, none of the articles specifically amalgamated
Yugoslavia with Serbia. Although references were sometimes made in other contexts
that Yugoslavia was dominated by Serbs, the 'Contributions to the Slovenian National
Programme' remained remarkably free of such claims.

[143]This is well argued by D. Jović, p. 300.

[144]*Danas*, 26 Jan. 1988, p. 13.

Exactly what the final outcome of that action should be remained, however, a matter of some disagreement, ranging from overt calls for secession to a more moderate position that the Slovenes were still better off within Yugoslavia, albeit only a substantively reformed, confederate Yugoslavia.[145] Ivan Urbančič thus argued that small, weak nations may at a particular time be forced to join larger federations to protect themselves, but that over time, they could grow stronger and 'become capable of seceding from the federal state'.[146] France Bučar argued that the world was moving away from the 19th-century nation-state construct and that Yugoslavia as a state was 'only possible' as a 'confederation'. However, he also warned, that 'as a people, we have the right to organise ourselves as an independent state, and that, as a state, we can forge stronger or weaker ties with others'.[147] Tine Hribar noted that 'among many Slovenes, the wish is awakening that— after having liberated ourselves from foreign nations—we finally gain our independence from kindred peoples'.[148] Peter Jambrek went so far as to specify the conditions that made Slovenia's secession from the federation possible.[149] It was Jože Pučnik, the opposition's presidential candidate in Slovenia's first multiparty elections in 1990, who best captured the position of the *Nova revija* intellectuals:

Whether at the end of this evolution Slovenia will exist in a confederation, become an independent state or achieve some other form, is of secondary and semantic importance, as long as our inalienable right to national sovereignty and statehood is respected and realised in practice.[150]

What mattered was the substance of Slovenia's independence, not necessarily the form. The 'Contributions for a Slovenian National Programme' and the Memorandum thus exposed to what extent the two nationalist platforms were irreconcilable. Although both were critical of Yugoslavia as it was,[151] the Memorandum still relied on reform and recentralisation of the federation to fulfill the Serbian national goal of 'all Serbs in one state'. The 'Contributions for a

---

[145]This was notably the position of Spomenka Hribar, op. cit., p. 100.

[146]Urbančič, op. cit., p. 44. He also noted the 'favourable fact' that Slovenia's ethnic and republican borders largely coincided.

[147]France Bučar, op. cit., p. 155.

[148]T. Hribar, op. cit., p. 26.

[149]Peter Jambrek, 'Pravica do samoodločbe slovenskega naroda' in ibid., pp. 165–70.

[150]Pučnik, op. cit., p. 142.

[151]See also Olivera Milosavljević, 'Jugoslavija kao zabluda', in *Srpska strana rata*, op. cit., pp. 60–88.

Slovenian National Programme', on the other hand, no longer saw Yugoslavia as the vehicle through which to fulfill Slovenian national interests and called for the loosening of ties between the republics.

A final difference concerned the reaction of the two republican leaderships towards these manifestations of nationalism: whereas the Serbian leadership under Ivan Stambolić was trying to promote change through internal channels and constitutional reform and attempted to coerce the Academy into rejecting the Memorandum and its authors, the Slovenian regime of Milan Kučan was markedly more conciliatory towards the *Nova revija*. In the rest of Yugoslavia, the appearance of the 'Contributions for the Slovenian National Programme' caused a considerable outcry. In particular, the Federal Presidency denounced *Nova revija* as anti-Yugoslav and anti-communist, and the federal prosecutor asked his Slovenian counterpart to take legal action against the journal.[152] Yet in Slovenia itself, the leadership's response was muted; although some members of the Slovenian political elite denounced the 'Contributions' as 'a nationalist provocation of the highest order', there was nevertheless 'total unity' concerning 'the measures that need to be undertaken'.[153] Instead of repression, the Slovenian leadership 'organised an open, useful and argumentative dialogue' in the context of the Socialist Alliance.[154] A number of Slovenian politicians went so far as to argue that *Nova revija* was merely asking—though in a politically unacceptable way—the same questions as others in the republic. Jože Smole, president of Slovenia's Socialist Alliance, rejected the comparison between the 'Memorandum' and the 'Contributions for the Slovenian National Programme', and the veteran communist Mitja Ribičič even saw the provocative nature of *Nova revija* as a positive occurrence in that it rang the 'alarm clock' for Slovenia and Yugoslavia.[155] Milan Kučan, president of the Slovenian Central Committee, rejected the accusation that the journal was promoting secessionism, arguing that it merely wanted the 'legal recognition' of the right to secession, and defended the refusal by the Slovenian prosecutor to undertake legal action against the journal.[156] Although *Nova revija*'s editors had to step down, the journal suffered no further consequences.

The same question that arose in the case of Milošević's ambivalent

---

[152]*Danas*, 26 Jan. 1988, pp. 14–15.
[153]See *Danas*, 7 Apr. 1987, p. 9, and *Borba*, 28 Feb.-1 March 1987.
[154]*Danas*, 3 March 1987, p. 18.
[155]Quoted in *NIN*, 1 March 1987, p. 31 and *Danas*, 7 Apr. 1987, p. 8 respectively.
[156]*Danas*, 26 May 1987, p. 9, and 26 Jan. 1988, p. 15.

response to the 'Memorandum' becomes even more valid in this instance: did Milan Kučan's leniency towards *Nova revija* express his fundamental agreement with the ideas of the intellectuals and his embracing of nationalism? According to one of the journal's editors, Dimitrij Rupel, 'Kučan skillfully manoeuvred between the hard-liners and the liberals within the Party, and slowly prepared for the break with Belgrade'.[157] Clearly the Slovenian League of Communists had been manifesting a certain sensitivity to cultural national issues since the early 1980s. The Slovenian Party's 1982 congress issued a declaration promoting the use of the Slovenian language and the republic's Socialist Alliance set up a 'language court', whose aim was to maintain the purity of Slovenian by having individuals report linguistic mistakes noticed in the public sphere.[158] Its endorsement of the intellectuals' rejection of the 'common core curricula' for secondary schools also showed to what extent the cultural and political elites saw eye to eye on certain issues. As Aleksa Djilas, a regular commentator on Yugoslavia's dissident activity, put it, 'Instead of being in direct conflict with the Communist Party, the dissidents often appear as a more radical version of the reformist groups in the Party.'[159]

On the other hand, in May 1985 Milan Kučan affirmed that there was no 'serious basis' for Slovenia's secession and that the Helsinki Conference had confirmed the inviolability of international borders,[160] and in 1987 and 1988 the Slovenian leadership endorsed the proposal to amend the federal constitution, despite the widespread con-demnation by the republic's intelligentsia.[161] Concurrently Kučan was promoting liberalisation in Slovenia to shore up support for his regime at a time of declining communist popularity.[162] Already the acceptance of the launching of *Nova revija* in 1982 had represented a marked departure from previous policy, as the journal's initiators remarked themselves.[163] In the mid-1980s Slovenian communists had begun to use the term 'civil society' in their discourse and argued that the new social movements were integral to the republic's public

---

[157]Rupel, 'Slovenia's Shift', op. cit., p. 186.

[158]*NIN*, 25 Apr. 1982, p. 9, and 9 Jan. 1983, p. 17.

[159]Aleksa Djilas, 'Dissent and the Future of Yugoslavia', *South Slav Journal*, XI/1, spring 1988, p. 33.

[160]*Danas*, 26 May 1987, p. 9.

[161]See below.

[162]This argument is convincingly made by D. Jović, op. cit., pp. 300–5.

[163]See the declaration by Taras Kermauner in *NIN*, 6 June 1982, p. 32.

sphere,[164] so that by 1988 Slovenia had no political prisoners and virtually free media.

In this sense it appears that, rather than following a defined secessionist 'plan' set out by the critical intellectuals, Kučan—like his Serbian counterpart Slobodan Milošević—was not thinking out all the consequences of his actions, but letting the situation develop before taking a clear stand.[165] Like Milošević, who has never made any reference to the Memorandum as the impetus for his subsequent policies, neither has Kučan acknowledged that the 'Contributions for a Slovenian National Programme' inspired his own approach. The fact that neither leader took a clear stand against the two texts bode badly for Yugoslavia's future, however. Although in 1987 it was too early to speak of an alliance between the nationalist intelligentsias and their republican leaderships, the foundation for elite convergence around irreconcilable national platforms had been lain.

The constitutional debate and the scramble for national programmes, 1987–8

In February 1987 the Presidency of the League of Communists of Yugoslavia presented the republics with a 'Proposal for Change of the SFRY Constitution' drafted by a working group of the Federal Parliament. The approximately 120 amendments to the 1974 Constitution were deemed by the supporters of the 'Proposal' to be the minimum necessary for the reform of the federation. They were finally passed after years of debate, partly in response to pressures by the International Monetary Fund to strengthen the federal administration in order to establish monetary discipline and repay the foreign debt.[166] At the same time, the 'Proposal' represented a compromise, aiming to satisfy both the 'defenders' and the 'reformers' of the 1974 order. The amendments aimed primarily to recreate a unified legal system, bring railroad, postal and telecommunications systems under a central authority and tighten the Yugoslav economy at the expense of the economic sovereignty of the individual federal units.[167] They also included changes that would allow the extension of Serbia's legal

---

[164]See *NIN* 5 Oct. 1986, p. 12.
[165]Woodward, op. cit., p. 94.
[166]Ibid., pp. 82–3.
[167]Ramet, *Nationalism and Federalism*, op. cit., p. 219. See also *Politika*, 30 Dec. 1987.

and police jurisdiction over the autonomous provinces.[168] The presentation of the 'Proposal' was, however, accompanied by reassurances for those opposed to recentralisation: it was 'specifically emphasised that there will be no changes in the key constitutional principles' and no encroachment upon the republics' sovereignty and decisionmaking by consensus in the federal centre.[169]

In Slovenia, the 'Proposal' was met by varying degrees of criticism. The most vehement opposition came from the republic's critical intellectuals. The Slovenian Writers' Society immediately organised a public debate, which opened to a full house in Cankar Hall (*Cankarjev Dom*) on 16 March 1987. In the five hours of heated discussion, which was attended by several Slovenian politicians, the predominating opinion was that the 'Proposal' was centralist and unitarist, an echo of the Serbian Academy's Memorandum, and that the Slovenian Parliament should reject it outright. The attempts by the party functionaries to explain the opposing view were met by boos and whistles. The writer Ciril Zlobec, along with several other participants, called for the creation of a Slovenian national programme, while *Nova revija* co-editor Dimitrij Rupel appealed to the Slovenian leadership not to turn against 'its people and its intelligentsia'.[170]

The Slovenian Parliament did not heed these appeals, however, and two days after the Cankar Hall rally it almost unanimously voted to accept the 'Proposal'. Although this decision was widely condemned not only by the intellectual opposition, but also by establishment intellectuals,[171] it did not actually represent an endorsement of the 'Proposal' by the Parliament—only its acceptance as the basis for a public debate on constitutional change. Milan Kučan himself noted that the 'Proposal for Constitutional Change' threatened to 'break our agreement that there will be no changes to the fundamental principles of our Constitution' and that it transferred an excessive number of questions from federal units to the centre.[172] Instead the Slovenian leadership submitted to the Federal Commission changes to thirty of the proposed constitutional amendments. In the course of the year the Slovenian Writers' Society relentlessly lobbied against the

[168]*NIN*, 17 Jan. 1988, p. 17.
[169]*Danas*, 17 Feb. 1987, pp. 10–11.
[170]*NIN*, 23 March 1987, p. 13 and *Danas*, 21 July 1987, pp. 39–40.
[171]See, for example, the critiques by the jurist Ivan Kristan, the rector of Ljubljana University, and Ciril Ribičič, a professor of constitutional law, in *Danas*, 24 Feb. 1987, p. 21, and 28 July, 1987, p. 12, respectively.
[172]*Danas*, 25 Aug. 1987, p. 23.

'Proposal'. In July 1987 it issued a declaration calling for transparency of the political debate on constitutional change and urged the Slovenian Parliament to hold a referendum on the question.[173] By October 1987 it demanded that the Slovenian Parliament ask of the Federal Parliament to withdraw the 'Proposal' because it threatened Slovenes' national rights.[174] Less than a month later the Slovenian Writers' Society announced that it had created its own commission to write an alternative Slovenian constitution.[175]

Belgrade critical intellectuals were much slower to react to the proposed constitutional changes. They finally did so in the winter of 1988, after a year in which the Slovenian rejection of the common state dominated the media, public fora and intellectual debates. Aside from the 'Contributions for a Slovenian National Programme' and the Slovenian Writers' Society's rejection of the proposed constitutional amendments, 1987 was marked by two events that focused attention on Serbian-Slovenian relations. The first of these was the publication by the Serbian press of a series of 'Letters to a Serbian Friend' by Slovenian writer Taras Kermauner and the second, the holding of two meetings on 'Serbs and Slovenes Today' by the republics' PEN societies. Both these events were crucial in exposing the depth of the chasm between the two critical intelligentsias.

Taras Kermauner's 'Letters to a Serbian Friend' provoked deep displeasure and disappointment in Serbia. As Dobrica Ćosić, Kermauner's long-time friend and the unnamed addressee of his missives, noted, 'there are few journalistic texts in Tito's Yugoslavia which had such a tremendous and disconcerting echo as Kermauner's "Letters to a Serbian Friend"'.[176] In his letters Kermauner reflected with some nostalgia on the period before 1981, when Slovenian intellectuals persecuted in their own republic had been taken in by Ćosić and the Praxists in Belgrade, forging a 'cohesive circle of a critical Yugoslav intellectuals'.[177] After 1981, Kermauner claimed, these ties were weakened when Slovenes became the scapegoats for

---

[173]*Danas*, 21 July 1987, p. 40.

[174]'Izjava Društva književnika Slovenije povodom Nacrta amandmana na ustav iz 1974' in *Književne novine*, 740, 15 Oct. 1987, p. 1.

[175]The Commission included writers Janez Menart, Tone Peršak, Tone Pavček, Veno Taufer and Milan Apih and jurists Matevz Krivič, France Bučar and Peter Jambrek. The last two also had articles in the 'Contributions for a Slovenian National Programme' (*Danas*, 10 Nov. 1987, p. 21).

[176]Ćosić, 'Simpozion u Mraku', op. cit., p. 92. See also Predrag Palavestra's interview with *Danas*, 5 July 1988, p. 37.

[177]*Borba*, 24 June 1987, p. 8.

the Serbs' 'blind rage' at the Albanian 'ethnic victory' and pressures to submit to 'the model of brotherhood-terror';[178] Serbs were now faced with a 'civilisational dilemma' of proving their 'Europeanness' by abandoning their 'blood and soil' ideology. Slovenes, in contrast, were in the process of 'reaching civil society', did not 'exploit anybody in Yugoslavia' and had no territorial demands vis-à-vis any other nation.[179] Serbs had to recognise that Slovenes were generally content with their leadership, which was backed 'almost consensually', and that all they wanted was to be left to 'live according to the lot that we have created for ourselves'.[180]

Kermauner expressed some of the anti-Yugoslav sentiments that had come to predominate among the Slovenian intelligentsia:

You will understand, friend, that we, Slovenes, have a hard time identifying with a pro-Asian or pro-African Yugoslavia, that we cannot equate ourselves with such a country as long as we have the spirit that we forged in our thousand-year history ... We were marked by the way of life that was being created in Central-Western Europe.[181]

Kermauner reiterated that Slovenia was facing an 'ethnic threat' from immigrant workers from the 'south', who were 'Yugoslavicising' Slovenia and making it 'non-Slovenian', and noted that Slovenes were beginning to feel like the Serbs of Kosovo.[182] All in all, Slovenes had embarked on the process of 'joining the developed world' and would not let their membership in Yugoslavia stop them. The only way Yugoslavia could be saved was if each nation pursued its own aims without interference; the Serbs therefore had to give up their 'centralism, plans for a united railroad, common core curricula in education, the 'Kosovoisation' of Yugoslavia, the desire for a single official language and a homogenous, unitary society'.[183]

Kermauner's letters, published in the daily *Borba* and newsweekly *NIN*, unleashed an overwhelming public response in Serbia, filled with resentment and recrimination. A letter by a 'Group of Real Serbs' expressed in a crude way the overarching emotional response:

Let us divorce as soon as possible and you can take your brothers of the same religion... with you, and we will be what we were before the 'rotten' and

---

[178]*Borba*, loc. cit.
[179]*NIN*, 26 July 1987, p. 23.
[180]Ibid., p. 22.
[181]Ibid., loc. cit.
[182]*NIN*, 9 Aug. 1987, p. 23.
[183]*NIN*, 26 July 1987, p. 23.

'overly ripe' Yugoslavia, and you can be what you want ... The Serbian people, due to their goodness and naïveté, were alone in believing in brotherhood and unity, and you and others like you have opened their eyes.[184]

In the many letters to the editor, Kermauner was compared to Nazis and neo-fascists, accused of 'Eurocretinism' and classified as a '*Lumpenintelligent*'.[185] The journalist Milorad Vučelić argued that— instead of hiding behind the unsubstantiated accusations against the Serbs—the Slovenes should just 'take full responsibility' and 'honestly and openly' state their separatist aims.[186] Kermauner's Serbian 'friends' remained silent throughout the affair; they did not write him or publicly respond to his missives.[187] In turn Kermauner himself professed his shock and disappointment at these reactions and decided to withdraw from all dialogue with Serbs. While he professed that his letters were an attempt at 'saving' Yugoslavia through open communication, to the Serbian public they were merely the confirmation of the Slovenes' secessionist aims.[188]

The last attempt to forge some sort of agreement between intellectuals came in the autumn of 1987, when the Serbian and Slovenian PEN Clubs organised two debates on 'Slovenes and Serbs Today'. Meeting first in Ljubljana and a month later in Belgrade, the two groups of writers agreed that they had 'never been at such a low point in the history of [their] relations' and vowed to try to overcome their 'misunderstandings'.[189] The Slovenian arguments ran along the lines that had been defined in earlier debates: Slovenes had joined Yugoslavia in order to preserve their separate 'nationhood', not give it up.[190] As Dimitrij Rupel argued, the Slovenian nation would remain a part of Yugoslavia only if it enabled them to realise their interests, provided them with a level of economic development comparable to Slovenia's western neighbours and guaranteed them 'equality' in the form of parity in decisionmaking and the right of veto.[191] For Rupel the fact that Slovenes and Serbs did not 'understand' each other

---

[184]*NIN*, 30 Aug. 1987, p. 6.

[185]Quoted in *NIN*, 16 Aug. 1987, pp. 4–5, and in *Danas*, 4 Aug. 1987, pp. 36–7, and 11 Aug. 1987, p. 32.

[186]*NIN*, 9 Aug. 1987, pp. 18–19.

[187]The sole exception was Praxist Mihailo Marković, who characterised Kermauner's statements as 'thoughtless and insulting' in an interview in *Danas*, 8 Sept. 1987, pp. 38–9.

[188]*Vreme*, 4 Nov. 1991, p. 20.

[189]*Književne novine,* 742, 15 Nov. 1987, p. 12.

[190]See Miloš Mikeln, France Bučar and Drago Jančar, in ibid., pp. 12, 15.

[191]Dimitrij Rupel in ibid., p. 14.

did not matter since 'understanding was only important within one community', whereas relations with other communities merely had to be based on the principle of non-interference in each other's affairs.[192] France Bučar seconded that vision by arguing that Yugoslavia should only be 'the lowest common denominator' of relations between its nations; cooperation was advisable only in areas in which it is absolutely necessary.[193]

The Serbian writer Slobodan Selenić expressed most coherently the way that Slovenia and its intellectuals were viewed from Belgrade. He argued that there was no fundamental disagreement between Slovenian desire for 'civil society' and the democratic strivings of the vast majority of the Belgrade intelligentsia. The problem lay rather in the Slovenes' tendency to portray civil society as something inherent to the Slovenian 'national essence', while casting Serbs in the role of authoritarians and centralists. According to Selenić, Slovenian nationalism had taken overtly racist overtones, depicting Serbs as primitive and uncivilised 'Balkans' and Slovenes as inherently democratic and superior 'Europeans'. Selenić acknowledged the claim of his Slovenian colleagues that Yugoslavia was frustrating Slovenia's economic development, but reminded them that this was a result of the system and that none of the Yugoslav nations had been able to develop in proportion to its capabilities. He told the Slovenian participants that they had to decide whether they wanted to be a part of Yugoslavia or not, but that if they did they would have to make compromises and align their own interests with those of the others.[194]

Most of the Serbian participants in the debate reflected, like their Slovenian counterparts, on the question of the common state, presenting the arguments that had come to prevail in their intelligentsias. Borislav Mihajlović-Mihiz argued that the two nations' different historical experiences shaped their attitudes towards Yugoslavia: since Slovenes had never had their own state and were ruled by foreign empires until 1918, they had an 'obstructionist and centrifugal' approach towards the common state, whereas Serbs—who had been the first Balkan people to liberate themselves and had invested a tremendous amount of human capital into the creation of Yugoslavia— were inevitably more committed to its survival.[195] Selenić argued that the communist federation was created essentially to suit the Croats

[192]Ibid., p. 15.
[193]France Bučar in *Književne novine*, 743, 1 Dec. 1987, p. 17.
[194]*Književne novine*, 742, 15 Nov. 1987, p. 14.
[195]Ibid., p. 13.

and Slovenes and only in the last order the Serbs, and that 'to speak after 1944 of Serbian hegemony and Belgrade centralism is truly cynical'—that even those who favoured this arrangement 'would have to admit that Yugoslavia would be arranged quite differently if Serbs had had greater influence on its constitution during the last forty years'.[196] In the present situation of total state disintegration and systemic collapse, however, the Serbs had to ask themselves whether this Yugoslavia was in their interest. If the Slovenes wanted a confederation they would have to get the other Yugoslav nations to agree on it.[197] The jurist Kosta Čavoški noted that 'Slovenes have a national state and Serbs do not' and that, in fact, there were more Serbs outside Serbia than there were Slovenes in Slovenia. He too argued, that the Belgrade intellectual opposition agreed with the Slovenian demands for democracy on the Western model, but that it could accept a confederation only if Yugoslavia's internal borders were renegotiated.[198] The debate finished predictably; in the words of Predrag Palavestra, 'we met, we said what we thought and we continued to roll on our parallel tracks'.[199] The Slovenian participants went back to Ljubljana to draft their announced Slovenian constitution, while their Serbian counterparts began to work on their own position on the proposed constitutional changes.

A third group of intellectuals from Zagreb, Ljubljana and Belgrade, who also opposed the regime's proposal for constitutional changes but believed that the present debate was not constructive, issued in autumn 1987 their own 'Call to the Yugoslav Public for Different Constitutional Amendments'. This text argued that the disagreements over the state structure (federation or confederation) were impeding the 'true democratisation' of Yugoslavia and that, instead, a consensus of democratic forces around the demands common to all sides (abolition of single party monopoly, the creation of an independent judiciary, human and civil rights) represented the necessary first step for further discussion on the future of Yugoslavia.[200] The open letter was published in *Mladina* in October 1987, followed

---

[196]Ibid., p. 14.
[197]Ibid., loc. cit.
[198]*Naša reč*, 389, Nov. 1987, p. 3.
[199]*Danas*, 5 July 1988, p. 37.
[200]*Danas*, 8 Dec. 1987. This proposal was initiated by the economist Branko Horvat and sociologist Žarko Puhovski from Zagreb, two eminently pro-Yugoslav intellectuals. The other co-authors were Peter Jambrek (one of the authors of the 'Contributions for a Slovenian National Programme'), Matevž Krivic from Ljubljana and Zoran Vidaković from Belgrade.

by 116 names from all parts of the country; within four months the list had grown to 6,000.[201] In Belgrade this letter was endorsed by a 'Call by a Group of Citizens', co-authored by well-known members of the intellectual opposition: Kosta Čavoški, Srdja Popović, Vojislav Koštunica and Nebojša Popov. It was signed by sixty-four intellectuals, including most of the prominent 'petitionists' and over half of the members of the Committee for the Defence of Freedom of Thought and Expression.[202] Judging by the signatures, the two proposals were acceptable to all intellectuals who had advocated party pluralism and the respect of civil rights. Nevertheless, this underlying agreement on the need for democracy could not stop the rising nationalist momentum. The Serbian and Slovenian intellectuals' scramble for their respective national programmes continued unabated.

The months that followed this initiative confirmed both the liberal and the nationalist orientation of the Belgrade intellectual opposition, as was indicated by two open letters by the Committee for the Defence of Thought and Expression. In November 1987 the Committee issued a 'Proposal for the Establishment of Political Democracy in the SFRY', which criticised the official constitutional amendments as 'futile and meaningless'—mere cosmetic changes to the system—and called for the introduction of free elections, the abolition of the Party's monopoly of power, public accountability of holders of political office, the elimination of all constitutional restrictions to basic freedoms, the respect of human and civil rights, freedom of the press, an independent judiciary and independent trade unions and the right to strike.[203] In February 1988 the Committee issued another critique of the proposed constitutional amendments—this one concerned with the federal arrangement of the state. Its 'Proposal to Establish Genuine Equality Among the Peoples of Yugoslavia' argued that the amendments did not go far enough and called for a new federal arrangement based on the 'full national, spiritual and cultural integrity' of each Yugoslav nation through links of each republic with 'parts of its people' in other republics.[204] In addition it demanded that national groups left in other republics be given their own political and cultural institutions

---

[201] *Danas*, 29 March, 1988, p. 19.

[202] Čavoški and Koštunica, along with Ivan Janković, Zagorka Golubović, Matija Bećković, Borislav Mihajlović—Mihiz, Mića Popović, Mladen Srbinović and Vesna Pešić. Neither Dobrica Ćosić nor the Praxists Mihailo Marković and Ljubomir Tadić were among the signatories, indicating the beginnings of disagreement within the Committee (in *Naša reč*, 392, Feb. 1988, pp. 5–6).

[203] In *South Slav Journal*, X/4, winter 1987–8, p. 51–4.

[204] In *South Slav Journal*, XI/1, spring 1988, p. 53.

and associations, normally a right reserved for national minorities ('nationalities') which did not have their own republics. Third, it proposed reviving the Federal Council of Citizens, elected according to the one citizen–one vote principle, which was bound to advantage the larger nations and temper the consociational nature of the Yugoslav state structure. Finally, the Committee judged that the existence of autonomous provinces had to be based on 'valid and universally acceptable reasons' and applied throughout the country.[205]

These two proposals formed the backbone of the new national programme—with specific guidelines for a new Yugoslav constitution on the basis of democratic principles, a mixed economy and a solution to the national question—which was endorsed in March 1988 by virtually the whole of Serbia's intellectual opposition.[206] The platform, entitled 'Contribution to the Public Debate on the Constitutional Changes', called, first of all, for the abolition of the single-party state and its ideological foundations, the respect of human and civil rights, free elections and democratic institutions. Second, it contained a number of provisions to establish a social-democratic model of market economy, combining pluralist forms of ownership with a well-defined social policy, the reintroduction of a Federal Council of Producers and extensive workers' rights. Finally, it advocated both a 'revival' of the federation to ensure 'the establishment of total national, spiritual and cultural integrity of each Yugoslav people, regardless of republic and province' and the constitution of the Republic of Serbia as a state with powers extending over its whole territory. The autonomous provinces were to lose the trappings of statehood, particularly their direct representation in the federal centre and their veto power in the republic.[207]

In many ways, the text was a compromise, as Dobrica Ćosić, who presented it to the assembly of the Writers' Association, noted himself. Some participants in the debates argued that it still had too strong a 'socialist' character, others that it went too far in its demands for systemic change. More radical nationalists saw it as insufficient and called instead for the abolition of the autonomous provinces (Vuk Drašković and Borislav Mihajlović-Mihiz) or a redrawing of internal Yugoslav borders (Vojislav Šešelj), whereas anti-nationalists disagreed with some

---

[205]Ibid., p. 56.

[206]It was voted on in the Writers' Association of Serbia and the republic's sociological and philosophical societies and backed in the debates on constitutional reform in the Serbian Academy.

[207]'Prilog javnoj raspravi o ustavu', *Književne novine*, 751, 1 Apr. 1988, pp. 1–4.

standpoints on the national question.[208] All in all, however, the text remained pro-Yugoslav and, as Vesna Pešić put it, 'exuded a clear demand for democratic change',[209] making it acceptable to the vast majority.[210]

In its resolution of the national question, this proposal was ridden with a fundamental contradiction: on the one hand, the Republic of Serbia was to become 'equal' to other republics in the federation by becoming a state while, on the other hand, the Serbs were to be guaranteed national unity in Yugoslavia regardless of republic boundaries. The first part of the equation implied a maintenance of Yugoslavia's 'confederate' structure, with its insistence on republican statehood and existing borders, whereas the second went against the grain of this arrangement by effectively ignoring both. This inherent contradiction, however, represented the only way by which Serbs could both claim the ethnically preponderantly Albanian province of Kosovo while concurrently promoting their own national unity, alternating between constitutional and ethno-national arguments according to need. Despite their many grievances against Yugoslavia, this platform reflected the fact that for Serbs, the common state still represented the best framework for the solution of their national question. Yet, its inherent contradiction was bound to be exposed if the country disintegrated. The Serbs would be faced with either the acceptance of the existing internal division of Yugoslavia, which left a over a third of their co-nationals outside its jurisdiction, or the option of calling for a change of borders on the basis of the principle of 'national self-determination', which would also legitimise the same claim by Serbia's own minority populations, particularly in Kosovo.

There was no such incoherence with the Slovenian national programme, which appeared within a month, in April 1988, when the Slovenian Writers' Society and the republic's sociological and philosophical societies adopted their own 'Proposal for a New Slovenian Constitution'. Like its Serbian counterpart, the Slovenian intellectual opposition overwhelmingly rallied behind this platform, playing—in the words of one sympathetic observer—'one of the most decisive constitutional roles in recent Slovenian history'.[211] And similarly this

---

[208]Ibid., pp. 4–12. For a more complete elaboration of Drašković's argument, see 'Šta menjati u ustavu', in Drašković, *Koekude Srbijo*, op. cit., pp. 75–6. On Šešelj's approach to the national question, see Chapter 1.

[209]Quoted in Ćetković, op. cit., p. 103.

[210]The final vote was over 300 in favour, 9 against and 3 abstentions.

[211]Bibič, op. cit., p. 372.

short text encompassed proposals for both democratic transformation and for a solution to Slovenia's national question. Yet the Slovenes' democratic concerns were narrowed only to their own republic and the reform of Yugoslavia was to occur only to allow greater republican independence. Slovenian intellectuals faced no significant internal minority problem in claiming that the Republic of Slovenia was 'the state of the Slovenian nation', since republican and ethnic boundaries largely coincided. Evoking Slovenia's 'historical right to self-determination, including the right to participation in a union of states or the secession from such a union of states, the right to free decisionmaking about internal political relations and about matters of defence', they insisted that only once this right had been put into practice should the republic enter negotiations to define its future relationship with the rest of Yugoslavia.[212]

By 1988 Slovenian and Serbian intellectuals had arrived at a dead end. Their uncompromising stand in the defence of their respective 'national interests' and their apparent incapability for any sort of empathy with the other side left no room for agreement on the common Yugoslav state. Their demands for 'equality' of their nations in Yugoslavia had essentially brought them to a zero-sum situation. For Slovenes, who represented a small nation even by Yugoslavia's standards, 'equality' implied total national sovereignty and the right to veto any decisions they disagreed with, regardless of the majority will in the federation. For Serbs, who were both the most dispersed people throughout Yugoslavia and the only ones whose republic had two autonomous provinces, 'equality' meant both statehood for Serbia and national unity in a reintegrated Yugoslavia. Yet the more they insisted on their nation's 'equality', the more the Slovenes felt that their own 'equality' was threatened. By mid-1988 the incompatibility of the Slovenian and Serbian national programmes indicated that Yugoslavia could not accommodate both, despite the lack of historical animosity or minority issues between the two nations. Although the two intellectual oppositions presumed that a solution to their respective national questions implied a change of the communist system, they were to be proven wrong. In mid-1988 the Slovenian and Serbian political leaderships adopted national policies that echoed those of their intellectual oppositions. When they did so, the death of Yugoslavia became a virtual certainty.

[212]'Predlog slovenačkih pisaca: republički Ustav', *Književne novine*, 755, 1 June 1988, p. 17.

5

THE VICTORY OF 'NATIONAL HOMOGENISATION', 1988–91

By early 1988 Serbia was in a pre-revolutionary situation. In the eyes of the population Yugoslavia's founding myths, its unique variant of socialism and the Partisan slogan of 'brotherhood and unity' had lost their legitimacy. Confidence in the League of Communists was fading, as neither the country's economic problems nor the thorny 'Kosovo question' were receiving any viable answers. Mobilisation of angry Kosovo Serbs had reached a highpoint, with protests and demonstrations taking place on a regular basis. In these circumstances, Serbia's critical intelligentsia became bolder in its demands and increasingly capable of presenting an alternative to the moribund Party and its unpopular apparatchiks. At this point, however, something unexpected happened: rather than seizing the momentum and channelling this social discontent towards a change of the system, dissident intellectuals mitigated their opposition to he regime and accepted Serbia's communist president, Slobodan Milošević, as the leader of the nation.

Milošević's policy to reintegrate Serbia and Yugoslavia, inaugurated in summer 1988, put the republic's intellectual opposition before a new dilemma. Until then it could unequivocally combine its struggle for democracy with that for the nation, since the regime it criticised was failing both. But now the new leader's defence of the Kosovo Serbs and his purge of the hated 'bureaucrats' held responsible for Serbia's divisions indicated that a qualitative change had occurred in the regime's national policy. Faced with the dilemma of whether to maintain their opposition or rally to the new leadership's call for national unity, many former dissidents opted for the latter. The same factors that influenced Milošević's appeal in the general population also affected intellectuals: a sense that something had to be done about Kosovo, increasing disillusionment with fellow—Yugoslavs who seemed set on fulfilling their own national agendas and a genuine belief—naive in retrospect, but no less potent at the time—that Milošević would steer Serbia towards greater stability and a more liberal regime. Finally they laboured under the illusion that democracy could be postponed until the difficult 'national question' had been resolved.

The intellectual opposition's fateful choice of nation over democracy and the resulting lull in its activism, which allowed Milošević to reinforce his rule in Serbia, became impossible to reverse after mid-1989, when former dissidents realised they had made a mistake and resumed their struggle for systemic change. As the situation in Yugoslavia became increasingly polarised in 1990 and 1991, the Belgrade intelligentsia remained caught in its own dilemma of how to combine democracy and the resolution of the Serbian question. With the advent of multipartism, the internal differences among its members, until now suppressed, re-emerged. Unable to formulate a common platform with which it could successfully challenge the regime's policy, the opposition also proved incapable of agreeing on a leader who could contest Milošević's by now tremendous popularity among Serbs.

Serbia's intellectual opposition and Slobodan Milošević, 1988–9

From mid-1988 to mid-1989 a remarkable convergence took place between the Belgrade intelligentsia and Serbia's communist leadership. As Slavoljub Djukić, one of the most astute analysts of the Milošević phenomenon, put it:

[Milošević] succeeded in something that no Serbian politician had managed: he was widely accepted by the intelligentsia ... It was difficult to recognise certain learned individuals who had courageously opposed Tito's regime now rallying with such fervour around the Serbian leader ... They opened the door of history for him, with a love that made the flower of the Serbian intelligentsia hardly recognisable.[1]

The intelligentsia's rapprochement with the regime is all the more perplexing considering that Milošević was initially perceived as a true 'Titoist', even receiving the tacit endorsement of the autonomist province leaderships when he seized power during the Eighth Session of Serbia's League of Communists.[2] He not only represented the

---

[1]Slavoljub Djukić, *Izmedju slave i anateme*, Belgrade, 1994, pp. 126–7.
[2]Vojvodina's and Kosovo's representatives abstained in the crucial vote cementing

system that dissident intellectuals opposed, but had personally orchestrated much of their persecution in the 1980s as head of the Belgrade communists and then as Serbia's Party chief. Furthermore, as the new regime took power it seized the republic's most important media and continued to resist he critical intelligentsia's demands for free political association and elections. The marriage between Milošević and members of the intelligentsia was thus not an obvious relationship between like-minded individuals; for the latter, entering into it meant an abdication of their role as opponents of the regime—a role that had defined their self-image as the moral conscience of their society and the true representatives of their nation.

This convergence between the Serbian regime and opposition intellectuals did not occur immediately with Milošević's rise to power. Although Milošević's famous words 'No one is allowed to beat you!', pronounced in Kosovo Polje in April 1987, gained him the allegiance of Kosovo Serb activists, they did not translate into any substantive change of policy towards the opposition in Belgrade nor did they immediately win him support in the intelligentsia.[3] Indeed, in the less quoted parts of that speech, Milošević sought to reaffirm the role of the Party against the intellectual opposition, which had championed the rights of Kosovo Serbs until then. He thus appealed to 'the Serbian people in Kosovo' to 'differentiate' between 'the forces of socialism, brotherhood, unity and progress and those of separatist nationalism and conservatism'.[4] At the same time dissident intellectuals continued to criticise the regime throughout 1987 and early 1988.[5] For them the new measures in the Serbian media and political sphere merely meant that 'yet again one of Serbia's leaders—in the manner of our

---

Milošević's power at the Eighth Session. On the Eighth Session, see in particular Djukić, ibid., pp. 49–93; Vujačić, *Communism and Nationalism*, op. cit., pp. 268–308; and D. Jović, op. cit., pp. 255–77.

[3]The one notable exception was the publication of a poem eulogising Milošević's Kosovo Polje speech on the first page of the main opposition journal, *Književne novine*. (731, 1 May, 1987, p. 1). It should be noted, however, that the poem was written by a Kosovo Serb poet and that its publication was not accompanied by any comment or article. Considering that *Književne novine* did not make any further favourable references to Milošević until much later, it seems reasonable to conclude that the publication of the poem set the tone for the future rather than marking definitive change in editorial policy.

[4]'Noć i zora u Kosovu Polju', in Slobodan Milošević, *Godine raspleta*, Belgrade, 1990, p. 145. For an analysis of Milošević's discourse of the time, see D. Jović, op. cit., pp. 241–50.

worst political tradition—has embarked on a quest for power and subordinated all the other pressing problems of the community to his career advancement'.[6] The writer Dobrica Ćosić, who was later much criticised for his endorsement of the Serbian regime, characterised Milošević's September 1987 coup as a victory in 'a conflict between an opportunist and a belligerent Titoism' using 'traditional communist and Titoist methods'.[7] For many intellectuals the significance of the Eighth Session lay primarily in the defeat of the powerful Stambolić family, which had exerted considerable influence in postwar Serbia.[8] The change in the Party leadership was not perceived as the advent of any significant transformation of the republic's politics.

The turning point in the tenuous relationship between the regime and the opposition came in the summer of 1988. Milošević took the initiative, as he outlined his new policy orientation in an interview in Serbia's main newsmagazine *NIN* in June 1988. In contrast to his earlier espousal of 'differentiation', he now appealed for *'sloga'*—or entente—of all national forces wishing to overcome the economic crisis, establish Serbia as a state and rejuvenate the Yugoslav federation—goals that, along with political pluralism, had formed the backbone of the opposition's demands. In a language that was reminiscent of the intelligentsia's nationalist discourse, he lamented the Serbs' traditional divisions and uncharacteristically referred to historical themes, so dear to intellectuals but so absent until then from his own image as a future-oriented politician. He criticised the characterisation of the

[5]See notably the Committee for the Defence of Freedom of Thought and Expression's November 1987 petition against the pressures on Serbian media and cultural institutions, its March 1988 'Proposal for the Establishment of Political Democracy in the SFRY' and its April 1988 protest against the attempts by the Serbian leadership to prevent the founding of independent political associations and to delay democratisation (in *Naša reč*, 391, Jan. 1988, pp. 7–8, and *South Slav Journal*, X/4, winter 1987–8, pp. 51–4, and XI/4, winter 1988–9, pp. 59–60 respectively. See also Chapters 1 and 4).

[6]Slobodan Selenić, 'Zar opet!', *Književne novine*, 15 June 1987, reproduced in *Iskorak u stvarnost*, Belgrade, 1995, pp. 14–15. See also the editorial comment on Milošević's ascendancy at the Eighth Session in *Književne novine*, 739, 1 Oct. 1987, p. 2.

[7]Quoted in Djukić, *Čovek u svom vremenu*, op. cit., p. 282.

[8]Author's interviews. These perceptions were mirrored in the educated public, as the 1987 New Year's poll of Serbia's most important newsweekly *NIN* showed : only 5% cited Milošević as the personality that most attracted their attention during the year and neither the Kosovo speech nor the Eighth Session were even mentioned among the most memorable events of 1987 (*NIN*, 10 Jan. 1988, p. 14).

Serbs as an 'oppressor nation' in the first Yugoslav state and argued that only the bourgeoisie can be an exploiter—'the Serbian, but also the Croatian and Slovenian'.[9] Like the intellectuals, he openly blamed the situation in Kosovo on the 'brutal' end to the post-war 'spirit of Yugoslavism and brotherhood' and acknowledged the 'apathy' in the rest of Yugoslavia towards the plight of the Kosovo Serbs and the lack of solidarity of 'some Serbian politicians in the past years with their own people'. He too noted that, if things did not change, 'the Serbs would probably be the only nation in the world who—without being forced to—accepted to live in three separate states'.[10] Extending an olive branch to the intelligentsia, he called it 'our great, inestimable treasure' and blamed the Party's formerly poor relations with it on 'certain insufficiently educated politicians' and 'spiritually and professionally inferior individuals' who had now been replaced.[11]

Words were accompanied by actions. Although the Serbian regime still issued the occasional ban,[12] its response to the July 1988 'Proposal for the Critical Re-Examination of the Historical Role of Josip Broz Tito' presented by the Committee for the Defence of Freedom of Thought and Expression reflected the change in attitude.[13] While the document met with outrage in the Federal Presidency, the Socialist Alliance and a variety of veteran, youth and other organisations, the new Serbian leadership—supposedly the principal defender of Tito's legacy—remained remarkably subdued.[14] From then on, Milošević allowed an unprecedented liberalisation of the Serbian cultural scene, leading many former oppositionists and even the staunchest anti-communists to hail his 'anti-bureaucratic revolution' as the advent of democratisation in Serbia. Former dissidents now found themselves

[9]*NIN*, June 1988, reproduced in Milošević, op. cit., pp. 220–1. In an echo of Dobrica Ćosić's famous pronouncement that Serbs were 'victors in war but losers in peace', Milošević argued that 'As we were once great in war, we must today be great in peace' (speech of 7 July 1988 in Milošević, op. cit., pp. 244–7 passim).

[10]Ibid., p. 234. The reference to 'three states' is for 'inner' Serbia and the two autonomous provinces. At this stage he made no references to the Serbs in Croatia and Bosnia-Hercegovina.

[11]Ibid., pp. 228–9.

[12]Notably of the July 1988 issue of *Književne novine*, which contained a contentious text on Goli Otok (Dragoslav Mihailović, 'Zločinci i žrtve', *Književne novine*, 757–8, 1–15 July, 1988, p. 3).

[13]In *South Slav Journal*, XI/2–3, summer-autumn 1988, pp. 68–72.

[14]This lack of reaction was particularly noted by the more orthodox communists in Croatia (see *Danas*, 16 Aug. 1988, p. 24).

solicited by the media and encouraged to express their ideas freely, publish their work and undertake projects prohibited only a few years earlier.[15]

This wooing of the intellectuals paid off. Dobrica Ćosić, who gained access to the mass media for the first time since 1968, praised Milošević for granting intellectual freedoms which we have not had until now',[16] while long-standing critics of the regime, like the poet Matija Bećković and the painter Mića Popović, accepted prizes from the regime and even Milošević personally in highly publicised events.[17] That the atmosphere had changed drastically became most obvious when Milovan Djilas, Yugoslavia's first and most persecuted dissident intellectual, was finally allowed out of isolation. In consequence, even he, a seasoned and principled critic of communism, had to admit: 'I have a soft spot for him—Milošević gave me the possibility to publish my books'.[18] For many critical intellectuals who had left the country, the negative attitude in the West towards the new Serbian regime was anathema; in a letter to the French daily *Libération*, the writer Milovan Danojlić noted how ironic it was that the Western media was talking of 'the fascisation of Serbia' at a time of liberalism unknown in the republic since the war.[19]

While the more tolerant atmosphere in the republic contributed to Milošević's acceptance by the intelligentsia, it was nonetheless most of all his uncompromising defence of Serbia's integrity as a republic that spurred the outburst of general enthusiasm for his regime. The dramatic events of the summer and autumn of 1988, known as the 'anti-bureaucratic revolution' and 'the happening of the people', swayed most Serbian intellectuals, like the rest of the population. Milošević's open endorsement of the genuinely popular Kosovo Serb cause represented a change in regime rhetoric and appeared to many as a signal hat the new Serbian leader was responsive to the demands of 'the people'. Like the intellectual opposition, he defined the emigration of Kosovo Serbs as 'the latest genocide of the 21st century' and

---

[15]Notably the publication of the collected works of Slobodan Jovanović (see Chapter 2).

[16]Quoted in Djukić, *Čovek u svom vremenu*, op. cit., p. 314.

[17]Matija Bećković received the 7th July Prize, the republic's highest cultural recognition, in July 1989. In the same month, Mića Popović received the *Politika* prize originally due to him in 1971 (*NIN*, 16 July 1989, p. 63).

[18]*NIN*, 24 May 1991, p. 17.

[19]Letter to *Libération* of 3 Nov. 1988 in *Naša reč*, 400, Dec. 1988, p. 2.

characterised their mobilisation as resulting from the 'incapability of existing institutions and individuals to stop the terror' against them.[20]

Furthermore, Milošević's defence of Serbia went hand-in-hand with his defence of Yugoslavia. In this sense, too, his programme was in line with that espoused by the intelligentsia.[21] As he put it in the November 1988 'Brotherhood and Unity Rally' in Belgrade, Tito's Yugoslavia had been achieved through 'a glorious revolution' and would not 'breathe its last breath at the conference table, as its enemies hope'.[22] Clearly seeing himself as Tito's successor, he called upon 'the people' to join forces to defend the country in a new great struggle.[23] In addition, Milošević saw the reintegration of Serbia as merely the first step towards the recentralisation of the federation as a whole; hence after the adoption of the amendments to the Serbian constitution in March 1989 he warned that Serbia's struggle to change the 'confederate' 1974 Constitution was still not finished.[24]

Milošević's objectives of reintegrating Serbia and Yugoslavia were not fundamentally different from those of his predecessor, Ivan Stambolić,[25] yet Stambolić had relied on gradualism, persuasion and the forging of intra-Party agreement, working within the existing political structures and rejecting the more radical discourse and demands of the Belgrade intelligentsia and the Kosovo Serbs. Milošević, on the other hand, embraced that discourse and populist, 'revolutionary' mobilisation to put into place new cadres loyal to him, who would toe the line in the debates on the future of Yugoslavia. It was therefore reasonable for Slovenes and Croats to see the involvement of the Serbian regime in the overthrow of the leaderships of Vojvodina, Montenegro and Kosovo as *de facto* coups d'état and to fear the export of Milošević's 'revolution' to their own republics. However, in Serbia the facts that the Kosovo Serbs' 'rallies of truth' were still partly spontaneous expressions of widespread discontent and that the toppled 'bureaucrats' in Vojvodina and Montenegro were genuinely unpopular meant that the changes they provoked were generally seen as a victory of 'democratic' popular pressure.[26] In 1988 there was not a single

---

[20]Speech of October 1988 in Milošević, op. cit., pp. 267–9 passim.

[21]See Chapter 4.

[22]'Jugoslavija je velikom borbom stvorena, velikom će se borbom i braniti', in Milošević, op. cit., p. 277.

[23]Ibid., loc. cit.

[24]This point is convincingly argued by D. Jović, op. cit, pp. 277–81. Quote p. 279.

[25]Stambolić himself acknowledged this, in *Put u bespuće*, op. cit. pp. 151 and 259.

[26]It is often assumed that the Serbian regime orchestrated all the 'rallies of

town in Serbia that did not hold its own 'rally of truth', attracting impressive numbers of people, and Milošević's authority with the demonstrators was tremendous.[27] Even those who did not participate in the rallies approved: a September 1988 poll in Serbia showed that 66% of respondents believed that the rallies expressed 'legitimate discontent' (compared to only 16%, who saw them as nationalist), and 55% thought that they should take place in other republics because they would contribute to a better understanding of the Kosovo Serbs' situation.[28] The Montenegrin and Vojvodinian leaderships' appeals to 'the institutions and law and order' and attempts—backed by the northern republics—to send in the police against the demonstrators were widely seen in Serbia as deeply undemocratic.

For Serbian opposition intellectuals, the Milošević revolution had a twofold impact: first of all, it presented them with an opportunity to 'rejoin' their nation, in a common quest for the resolution of the thorny national question. Milošević's overwhelming popularity meant that if they continued to criticise the regime they would set themselves against popular will and lose any support they had hitherto gained as the defenders of the nation. For former dissidents, who had come out of their social isolation and gained access to the media, it was difficult to return to a situation of marginality and public insignificance, especially when they were now being offered the possibility to present their opinion on all the burning social and national issues. Furthermore, many felt—like Borislav Mihajlović-Mihiz—that it was not the intelligentsia which had relinquished its ideas in order to gain favour

---

truth' of summer and autumn 1988, but this is not correct. Although the Serbian leadership did have links with the Kosovo Serb Committee and became progressively more involved in planning its actions, it was not behind the initial rally in July 1988 in Novi Sad, which sparked the series of 'anti-bureaucratic revolutions'; in fact, Milošević's envoy to Kosovo Polje unsuccessfully tried to dissuade Kosovo Serb leaders from staging it at that time. As Croatian journalist Darko Hudelist, who wrote a book on the subject, has argued: 'There was a link between Šolević and the other Kosovo Polje activists and the Serbian political leadership, but that link was not so simple ... Not only did Milošević not control the Kosovo Serbs, but he was in a sense commissioned by them.' (Hudelist's interview in *Danas*, 16 May 1989, p. 25)

[27] The numbers were blown up Milošević-controlled media, but they were still impressive. The largest, 'Brotherhood and Unity', rally in Belgrade on 19 November 1988, attracted over 1,000,000 people. Some of the participants were brought in by buses organised by the authorities, but this was not the whole story (see Djukić, *Izmedju slave i anateme*, op. cit., pp. 104–5).

[28] *NIN*, 11 Sept. 1988, p. 12.

with the regime, but 'the regime that has aligned itself with us', making the maintenance of opposition difficult to justify.[29]

Secondly, in those heady days of 1988 it was difficult not be seduced by the generalised euphoria that has been coined 'the happening of the people'; for the first time in over a decade a feeling of hope overshadowed the gloomy reality of the crisis, national pride eclipsed discontent and a sense of unity conquered the endemic social anomie. Although most intellectuals continued to be critical of the regime's reliance on docile apparatchiks and of its unabashed references to the Party as the sole vehicle of progress, they saw in Milošević a man of principle and were willing to give him a chance to make more radical changes.[30] Many believed that it was only a small step from responding to the 'people's voice' to actually giving a political content to that voice. Even those who did not, such as Vesna Pešić, a member of the Committee for the Defence of Freedom of Thought and Expression and a prominent anti-nationalist intellectual, have described how indeterminate the atmosphere in 1988 was, with 'both more nationalism and more freedom' existing side by side and how difficult it was still to judge which way things would go—towards genuine democratic change or greater intolerance and fear.[31]

This sense that anything was still possible and that their republic had embarked on a process whose end result was still open crystallised most clearly in debates with Slovenian and Croatian intellectuals, who unfavourably compared what was happening in Serbia with the concurrent 'national homogenisation' in Slovenia. Slovenian mass mobilisation found its catalyst in the trial of an army officer and three journalists from the opposition journal *Mladina* for allegedly disclosing military secrets.[32] Most Slovenes saw the acts of putting the accused before a military tribunal, not allowing them to defend themselves from liberty and, most of all, holding the trial in Serbo-Croatian rather than Slovenian as part of a policy orchestrated from Belgrade to reduce Slovenia's sovereignty.[33] Building on the already prevalent anti-military sentiment in Slovenia, the '*Mladina* affair'

[29]Interview in *Duga*, 6–20 Dec. 1990, p. 56. This point is also made by Aleksandar Pavković in 'Intellectual Dissidence', op. cit., p. 121.

[30]See, for example, Ćosić, in Djukić, *Čovek u svom vremenu*, op. cit., pp. 313–14.

[31]Ćetković, op. cit., pp. 102–4.

[32]For a detailed account of the affair, see James Gow, *Legitimacy and the Military*, London, 1992, pp. 78–88; D. Jović, op. cit., pp. 305–11, and Silber and Little, op. cit., pp. 48–57.

[33]Gow, op. cit., p. 85.

contributed to the unification of the youth alternative's battle against the Yugoslav army and the intellectuals' combat for the loosening of Slovenia's ties with Yugoslavia. The Committee for the Defence of Human Rights, set up by activist Igor Bavčar in protest against the trials, rallied together all the different tenets of the Slovenian alternative scene—the new social movements, youth groups and the intellectuals with their organisations. It came to include over 1,000 organisations and more than a hundred thousand individual members and—in contrast to its counterpart in Belgrade, the small and select Committee for the Defence of Freedom of Thought and Expression, which still limited its actions to petitions and protest letters—it represented the equivalent of a mass opposition party, organising rallies and political actions and engaging in a direct dialogue with the Slovenian regime.[34] Bavčar, the *de facto* leader of this opposition, was formally received by Slovenia's president Janez Stanovnik, while the republic's Party leader Milan Kučan publicly defended the rallies and even spoke at the first one held in June 1988.

The *Mladina* affair unified Slovenes in a way that no other organised action had done. The petition to free the defendants received half a million signatures—representing a quarter of Slovenia's population— and the rallies in front of the court drew thousands of protesters.[35] As members the Slovenian intelligentsia recognised, this 'national homogenisation' of the republican leadership, the intelligentsia and the masses represented a key step on the road to independence.[36] In Slovenia, as in Serbia, national unity was perceived as a positive phenomenon and a necessary reflex against outside pressures. Whereas for Serbs the hostile forces were the northern republics and the 'autonomist' province leaderships, which supported the division of Serbia and thwarted efforts to change the status quo, for Slovenes, the principal enemy was the federal army, believed to be allied with the Serbian leadership.[37]

In such circumstances, the Belgrade intelligentsia's response to

[34]Mastnak, 'Civil Society in Slovenia', op. cit., p. 59 For the contrast with the Belgrade committee, see the interview with Vojislav Koštunica, in *Duga*, 11–24 Nov. 1989, p. 36.

[35]See Thompson, op. cit., p. 45.

[36]See, for example, Rupel, 'Slovenia's Shift', op. cit., p. 188.

[37]Apparently this was a mistaken belief; Serbia had nothing to do with the military trial of the four Slovenes in 1988. The forging of the tenuous coalition between the Serbian leadership and the army only took place much later, in the course of 1991 (Gow, op. cit., p. 85).

the '*Mladina* affair' reflected a estrained solidarity, without nearly as much enthusiasm as previous civil rights actions. Although all the usual institutions protected the trial of the four Slovenes—the Writers' Association of Serbia and its Committee for the Defence of the Freedom of Creation, the Committee for the Defence of Freedom of Thought and Expression, the Solidarity Fund and the Serbian PEN— and a number of Belgrade intellectuals became members of the Bavčar Committee, there was little enthusiasm in Belgrade for Slovenian actions.[38] What irked Serbian intellectuals most was the way Slovenes like the sociologist Tomaž Mastnak contrasted their own 'democratic' national mobilisation with the Serbs' 'totalitarian' one:

> The platform of the homogenisation of the Slovenian nation is the struggle for political democracy, the respect of basic human rights, the rule of law. The source of Serbian homogenisation is *Blut und Boden* ...[39]

Whereas he denounced the Serbian 'anti-bureaucratic revolution' as 'mass raids of the chauvinist mob',[40] in his eyes the Slovenian national movement 'never took a stand against any other Yugoslav nationality'.[41] As a survey taken during a roundtable at the Zagreb Faculty of Political Sciences in October 1988 showed, such views also prevailed among intellectuals in Croatia: the characteristics most attributed to the Slovenian national movement were modernisation, democratisation and individualism (although ethnocentrism was also included), while those seen as most representative of the Serbian movement were ethnocentrism, populism, authoritarianism, anti-intellectualism and expansionism.[42]

Serbian intellectuals, on the other hand, denied that there was a substantial difference between the two processes. Some, such as jurist Vojin Dimitrijević, argued that both Bavčar's Committee for the Defence of Human Rights and the Kosovo Serbs' Committee for the Organisation of Protest Rallies were similar in that they addressed genuine human rights problems.[43] Others, like Praxists Svetozar

---

[38]Interestingly, those who joined included both anti-nationalists, like lawyer Srdja Popović and philologist Svetlana Slapšak, and nationalists, like writers Vuk Drašković and Gojko Djogo and sociologist Vojislav Šešelj.

[39]Quoted in *Danas*, 16 Aug. 1988, p. 27.

[40]Mastnak, 'Civil Society in Slovenia', op. cit., p. 104.

[41]Quoted in Magaš, op. cit., p. 148. See also Križan, op. cit., pp. 121–40.

[42]*Danas*, 18 Oct. 1988, p. 10.

[43]Interview in *Delo*, 10 Sept. 1988, in Nadežda Gaće, *Jugoslavija—Suočavanje sa sudbinom*, Belgrade, 1990, pp. 123–4.

Stojanović and Zagorka Golubović, emphasised the social, 'democratic', component of the 'rallies of truth'.[44] Even the non-nationalist members of the Belgrade intelligentsia, later staunchly opposed to Milošević, such as sociologist Vesna Pešić, noted the non-Yugoslav character of the Slovenian initiatives and the Slovenes' lack of desire to cooperate with other parts of the country.[45] Although they condemned the nationalism of the Serbian rallies, they reminded their colleagues in Croatia and Slovenia that it was inconsistent to condemn nationalism one case, but support it in another.[46] As sociologist Nebojša Popov put it, it had to be recognised that Serbian 'national homogenisation' was just the last link in a chain of nationalisms nurtured for decades in Yugoslavia through the existing constitutional order.[47] Zoran Djindjić, a well-known younger intellectual, was perhaps most explicit.[48] Facetiously wondering why Slovenian intellectuals were so fearful of Serbian national mobilisation, he argued:

> If it is true that [the Serbian mass protests] are leading towards ethnic homogenisation, with the aim of forging an ethnically based republic-national state, then we have here an exact repetition of the model of integration claimed for the last decade by none other than Slovenia.[49]

Djindjić elaborated his argument in a series of articles in the journal *Književne novine*. Asking 'Who is conservative in Yugoslavia?', he directly took issue with the commonly accepted differentiation, emanating from the northern republics and often taken up in the West, between the 'conservative South-East, with an oriental-Stalinist model of social integration' and 'the liberal-pluralist North-West, steadfast in its

---

[44]Stojanović in *NIN*, 13 Nov. 1988, p. 24, and Golubović in *Danas*, 15 Nov. 1988, pp. 29–30.

[45]*Danas*, 26 July, 1988, p. 16. See also the comments made by Zagorka Golubović or Slobodan Selenić in *Delo*, 3 June 1989 and *NIN*, 12 June 1988 respectively. This opinion was shared by Yugoslav-oriented intellectuals in Zagreb, such as Žarko Puhovski and Predrag Matvejević (see *Studentski list*, 9 March 1988 and *NIN*, 31 July 1988).

[46]Golubović in *Danas*, loc. cit.

[47]Interview in *South Slav Journal*, XII/1–2, spring–summer 1989, p. 79. See also Božidar Jakšić's interview in *Danas*, 20 Sept. 1988, p 27.

[48]As Djindjić rose to the leadership of the Democratic Party in 1993, he adopted a nationalist discourse, probably out of political expediency. However, in 1988 he was one of the few who openly criticised the project of 'regaining' Kosovo, arguing that it was unachievable without the revival of authoritarianism (Zoran Djindjić, 'Srbija i Kosovo', *Književne novine*, 15 June 1988, p. 3).

[49]*Književne novine*, 764, 15 Nov. 1988, p. 3.

affirmation of subjective rights of individuals, turned towards the West
... and ready to throw off its South-Eastern shadow at the appropriate
moment to join those to whom it belongs.'[50] In fact, Djindjić noted,
'it is none other than the North-West that has forced upon Yugoslavia
the ethnic understanding f the nation.'[51] It was Slovenia and Croatia
which interpreted the right to self-determination as the right, first of
all, to national autonomy and, only secondly, as the right to autonomy
of citizens/individuals. The Slovenian goal of civil society thus came
at the end of the strategy of reforming socialism, only once the ethno-
national unit had already been achieved. It was, therefore, cynical, in
his view, to proclaim Serbia's bandwagoning and belated use of such
'language of ethnicity' as 'an obstacle to communication'. Djindjić
argued that the only way the 'North-West' could consistently criticise
Serbia's national movement was if it stood for a different model of
reform—but this it clearly did not.

These Serbian intellectuals aptly exposed the double standards
regarding 'national homogenisation' prevailing in Yugoslavia's 'North-
West'.[52] Nevertheless, a fundamental difference remained between
the Serbian and Slovenian cases. Although both 'homogenisations' were
predominantly nationalist, the Slovenes' defence of their sovereignty
always went hand-in-hand with a clear commitment to the creation
of democratic political institutions in their republic.[53] Serbian national
mobilisation, on the other hand, was focused overwhelmingly on the
figure of Slobodan Milošević—hailed as an almost mythical figure
and compared to the most revered national heroes of the epic songs—
without any 'rational' reference to the creation of representative political
or state institutions, the introduction of 'checks and balances' to control
government actions.[54] The fact that Milošević alone had the power
to determine the means that would be used to resolve the 'Serbian
question' gave 'the happening of the people' a distinct authoritarian
tinge.[55]

[50]Zoran Dindjić, 'Ko je konzervativan u Jugoslaviji?', *Književne novine*, 770, 15
b. 1989, p. 3.

[51]Ibid., loc. cit.

[52]See also Milica Bakić-Hayden and Robert M. Hayden, 'Orientalist Variations
on the Theme "Balkans": Symbolic Geography in Recent Yugoslav Cultural Politics',
Slavic Review, LI/1, spring 1992, pp. 1–15.

[53]See Patrick Hyder Patterson, 'The East is Read: The End of Communism,
Slovenian Exceptionalism and the Independent Journalism of *Mladina*', *East European
Politics and Societies*, XIV/2, 2000, pp. 411–59.

[54]For the slogans brandished at the rallies, see Djukić, op. cit., pp. 103–24.

[55]See Nebojša Popov, *Srpski populizam*, *Vreme*, 24 May 1994 (special edn).

That Milošević's means were anything but democratic became evident at the latest by winter 1989, when his drive to have amendments to the Serbian constitution adopted by the autonomous provinces caused the first loss of life in what turned out to be the road to war. Setting the pattern for his future policies, Milošević maintained a surface legality to his actions by following the procedure stipulated in the 1974 Constitution (which necessitated the approval of both autonomous provinces for any changes to the Serbian constitution), but resorted to purges and repression in order to achieve his objectives. Following the successful 'anti-bureaucratic revolution' in Vojvodina in October 1988, the only obstacle that remained for the formal 'reunification' of Serbia was the approval of Kosovo's institutions. Kosovo was a tough nut to crack, however; not only did its leadership resist the reduction of the province's autonomy, but large demonstrations took place in November 1988 in protest against the impending changes. Milošević resorted to old-style demagoguery of labelling the Albanian resistance as 'counter-revolution' in order to force the replacement of the province leadership with 'loyal' Albanians. The purge of the Kosovo leadership, in turn, provoked the largest popular revolt in the province since 1981, spearheaded by the Albanian miners of the Trepča consortium, who went on a hunger strike and refused to leave their pits until the new Milošević-backed leadership in Kosovo resigned and a guarantee was issued that there would be no retreat from the fundamental principles of the 1974 Constitution.[56] As in 1981, the federal government proclaimed a state of emergency in the province, on the urging of Serbia's leadership.[57]

The handling of the Albanian revolt in Kosovo provided the Belgrade intellectual opposition with its first concrete test of its commitment to democracy. Whereas it was possible for Serbian intellectuals to defend the 'happening of the people' in Vojvodina and Montenegro, where it enjoyed a large degree of popular support and led to the fall of genuinely undemocratic leaderships, in Kosovo the Albanian majority was clearly opposed to a return to Serbian rule over the province and defended Kosovo's purged leaders. The declaration of a state of emergency in Kosovo and the fact that police repression of the Albanian demonstrations resulted in the deaths of at least twenty-four people in March 1989 should have provided the

[56]For a list of the demands see Magaš, op. cit., pp. 180–1, and *Intervju*, 3 March 1989, p. 13.
[57]Slovenia and Croatia accepted the imposition of martial law, as, paradoxically, did Kosovo's representatives in the federal institutions (see D. Jović, op. it., p. 316).

Belgrade intellectual opposition ample cause for protest and for the articulation of a principled stance against all constitutional changes not made in a peaceful and negotiated manner.[58] Instead, most Belgrade intellectuals hailed the 'reunification' of Serbia and the 'return' of Kosovo with an enthusiasm that was difficult to contain.

Milošević's most ardent supporters belonged to the group of academicians who had produced the 1986 draft Memorandum.[59] The Serbian regime's declared political orientation embodied the very aspects that their document had called for: the return of the provinces under Serbia's control and a resolute stand against Albanian 'separatism and terrorism', the reintegration of Yugoslavia, as well as a revival of socialism as a 'pure' ideology, free from the ballast of 'bureaucratic degeneration'. This similarity between the ideas espoused in the draft Memorandum and Milošević's political discourse sparked a revival of publicity around the 1986 text. This revival began in early 1989, when the Croatian Party leadership decided it was high time to oppose Milošević and embarked on a strategy of 'exposing and raising awareness of the threat of Serbian nationalism'. In this context the editorial board of *Naše teme* (Our Themes), the journal of the Centre for Ideological-Theoretical Work of the Central Committee of the League of Communists of Croatia, published for the first time in Yugoslavia the integral text of the Memorandum, reproducing the main official condemnations from the time of its appearance as well as the academicians' defence of their text.[60] While the journal's editorial board aimed to stimulate a public discussion of the text, by 1989 the situation in Yugoslavia had become so polarised that no dialogue actually took place. The Croatian media and intellectuals interpreted the 1986 Memorandum as the 'master plan' of Serbs' historical striving for hegemony, now embodied by Milošević's policy.[61] In Serbia,

---

[58]This was the official figure, but unofficial sources alleged over a hundred dead. For more on these events, see Mertus, op. cit., pp. 179–84.

[59]This point is also noted by Pavković, 'Intellectual Dissidence ...', op. cit., p. 123.

[60]See Dragutin Lalović's introduction to the issue on the 'Memorandum', *Naše teme*, 1–2, 1989, pp. 119–27.

[61]See for example *Vjesnik*, 3 May 1989 or *Danas*, 11 Apr. 1989, pp. 25–6. For the most complete portrayal of the text as the expression of the Serbs' historical striving for hegemony, see Miroslav Brandt, 'Antimemorandum' in Bože Čović (ed.), *Izvori velikosrpske agresije*, Zagreb, 1991, pp. 207–55. The continuity between the Memorandum and Milošević's policy is drawn by Zdravko Tomac, 'Oživotvorenje memorandumskih ciljeva', in ibid., pp. 301–23. The same kind of arguments became common in Slovenia at this time. See, for example, the opinion of Ciril Ribičič, the president of the Slovenia's Central Committee, in *Danas*, 21 March 1989, p. 12.

at the same time, the Memorandum became 'rehabilitated' as an enlightened and prescient analysis of Yugoslavia's woes, giving credence to the interpretations being voiced in the northern republics.

The publication of the Memorandum in *Duga*, one of Serbia's most popular magazines just before the celebration of the 600th anniversary of the Battle of Kosovo—Milošević's symbolic coronation as national leader—confirmed the change in the authorities' attitude to the text and its ideas.[62] Whereas previously the Memorandum had always been presented as 'the darkest nationalism', now the official media were arguing that 'time has shown that many of its claims and assessments have been both true and justified' and portrayed the document as an enlightened analysis of the Yugoslav crisis and an expression of the 'traditions of critical thought and democracy' in Serbia.[63] Although Antonije Isaković, the former chairman of the Memorandum committee, and the Memorandum's other authors were given plenty of opportunity to deny that their document represented any kind of programme, their wholehearted endorsement of the Serbian regime merely served to confirm the extent to which they saw Milošević's policy as the practical realisation of their ideas.[64] In the debate on constitutional change in the autumn of 1988, philosopher Mihailo Marković even boasted that the Serbian Academy had 'significantly aided' by its behaviour during the Memorandum affair the emergence of a strong and influential 'critical public opinion' in Serbia—which, in turn, had enabled the rise of its 'new type of political leadership'.[65] Such exaggerations of the text's 'merit' in helping Milošević come to power only further fanned the popular, though misleading, perceptions of the Academy as the brain behind Serbia's new national policy.[66]

These academicians represented only the peak of support for Serbia's

---

[62]*Duga*, Special Issue, June 1989, p. 5.

[63]Milorad Vučelić, 'Memorandum: šta piše a šta se čita u ozloglašenom dokumentu Srpske Akademije Nauka i Umetnosti?', in ibid., p. 9.

[64]See for example Isaković's interview with Miroslav Samardžić, in *Govori i razgovori*, op. cit., p. 369.

[65]In *Književne novine*, 762, 15 Oct. 1988, p. 5.

[66]Most analysts argue that the only real 'brains' behind Milošević's policies were his own and his wife's. All the academicians who rallied around the Serbian leadership in the late 1980s and early 1990s were progressively sidelined, frustrated that Milošević did not seem to be following a coherent—and genuinely nationalist—policy. See particularly Djukić, *On, ona i mi*, Belgrade, 1997, pp. 25–48, and Lenard Cohen, *Serpent in the Bosom: The Rise and Fall of Slobodan Milošević*, Boulder, CO, 2001, pp. 103–15 passim.

regime within the intelligentsia. At the time of the promulgation of the amendments to Serbia's constitution, Milošević was swamped with public declarations of love and allegiance, even from the most unlikely quarters. Writer Milovan Danojlić, one of the best known campaigners for freedom of expression in the 1980s, thus wrote an open letter to Milošević in which he stated that 'that which you have achieved for your people in the last two years deserves admiration ... You have resuscitated the Serbian soul'.[67] Although Danojlić later regretted this emotional outburst and participated in the organisation of the political opposition, his letter remains representative of the general euphoria that engulfed the Serbian intelligentsia at the time.[68] In symbolic terms, when faced with the choice between the nation and democracy, most members of the former critical intelligentsia put the nation first.

Several related factors played into this choice. The first of these was the generalised feeling that—despite using undemocratic means—Milošević had rectified a longstanding injustice and achieved 'equality' for Serbia in the federation.[69] As one of Milošević's most ardent supporters, philosopher Mihailo Marković, put it, 'to Serbs it seems that finally a leader has appeared who is not ashamed of his people and who appears to be set on rectifying some obvious injustices'.[70] Even intellectuals who were less enthralled than Marković with the way the reunification of Serbia was carried out viewed the use of what they knew were 'unsavoury political tactics' with a certain dose of pragmatism. After all, repression was hardly a novelty in communist Yugoslavia and most intellectuals adopted a position of 'tacit consent' with a policy that, despite not being one they would have advocated, had redressed a situation that they saw as 'illogical and unjust'.[71] There was no question in the minds of most Serbs that Kosovo was a Serbian land that had unlawfully been taken away and needed to be 'returned', regardless of whether its Albanian population agreed.[72]

Secondly, by this time national stereotyping of Albanians had gained such proportions that all their actions were seen as part of an orchestrated plot to achieve the secession of an 'ethnically cleansed' Kosovo. The way that *Književne novine*, the main journal of the critical

---

[67]For the letter, see *Književne novine*, 788–9, 15 Dec. 1989–1 Jan. 1990, p. 7.

[68]For other such expressions of support by Belgrade intellectuals, see Djukić, *Izmedju slave i anateme*, op. cit., pp. 128–9.

[69]No other republic had autonomous provinces (see Chapter 2).

[70]Quoted in Slavoljub Djukić, *Izmedju slave i anateme*, op. cit., p. 128.

[71]Dragoljub Mićunović's interview in *NIN*, 7 May 1989, p. 15.

[72]See Chapter 3.

intelligentsia, presented the Albanian demonstrations and the Trepča miners' hunger strike illustrates this perception. The editor-in-chief Miodrag Perišić sympathised with the plight of the miners, but saw it as 'a ritual sacrifice of workers for a narrow national goal' and as an attempt to cover up what was in fact a separatist political struggle by presenting Albanians as victims rather than the 'victimisers' that they were.[73] The editorialist Milorad Vučelić, who later gained key positions in the regime-controlled media, compared the miners hunger strike to the fanaticism of Islamic fundamentalists. Noting that the journal had never before approved of the application of extraordinary measures or state repression, he argued that in this case the actions of the state had to be seen as a 'rational policy in the interest of all those who are threatened [in Kosovo]'.[74] After years of listening to stories of Albanian 'terror' against Serbs in Kosovo, many members of the intelligentsia believed that some degree of state intervention was—as Vučelić put it—'a necessary act that any law-abiding and democratic state in the world would have done in similar or even far less threatening situations'.[75]

Finally, as the artist Mića Popović explained, this was not a time for divisions and criticism:

In order to survive in these times, Serbia has to achieve, above all, a great degree of homogenisation ... We must not forget that national belonging is older than political belonging and, therefore, it is necessary—before we look for political solutions—to find national solutions.[76]

A conference held at the Writers' Association of Serbia in January 1989 exposed to what extent the imperatives of 'national survival' had squeezed out the issue of systemic transformation. Gathered around a theme provocatively entitled 'Serbophobia', speaker after speaker referred to the Comintern and the Second World War Ustasha crimes against Serbs, to account for the present day 'hatred' of Serbs by other Yugoslav peoples.[77] Although two participants—sociologist Nebojša Popov and jurist Vojin Dimitrijević, both of whom later became prominent anti-nationalist activists—questioned the use of the term 'Serbophobia' and criticised the tendency towards national

---

[73] *Književne novine*, 771, 1 March 1989, p. 2.
[74] Ibid., p. 3.
[75] Ibid, 773, 1 Apr. 1989, p. 2.
[76] In *NIN*, 16 July 1989, p. 63.
[77] For these theories, see Chapter 2.

stereotyping, most argued that the Serbs were surrounded by enemies and that 'national homogenisation' represented the only defence against a renewed 'genocide'.[78]

The conviction of an anti-Serbian conspiracy in Yugoslavia reached its highpoint in February 1989, when the various associations of the Slovenian intelligentsia organised a mass rally in Ljubljana's Cankar Hall to protest against the impending changes of Kosovo's status and to gather financial assistance for the striking Albanian miners. Serbia's main television channel directly transmitted the event, showing Slovenian intellectuals and activists—wearing badges with the yellow Star of David and the slogan 'Kosovo, my homeland'—making impassioned speeches condemning Belgrade's 'nihilistic, cynical and barbarian' policy, proclaiming that 'the Kosovo tragedy is above all a tragedy of Albanians and not of Serbs and Montenegrins', lauding the Albanians' 'dignified' and 'Gandhi-like' stance and comparing the plight of the Albanians to that of the Jews in Hitler's Germany.[79] Even Slovenia's communist leadership joined in the protest and Party leader Milan Kučan made a speech lauding the Kosovo miners not only for defending their own equality, but also 'the equality of each— including the Slovenian—republic and nation within Yugoslavia'.[80] As the president of Serbia's PEN Association, Predrag Palavestra, noted in a 1989 interview: 'Some of my Slovenian friends do not want to believe it, but it is the truth—the greatest demonstrations in Belgrade in March were not provoked by unrest in Kosovo, but by the anti-Serbian rally in the Cankar Hall.'[81] Within a few hours of the television transmission of the Ljubljana manifestation, Belgrade was in uproar. The seething volcano of pent-up frustration, sense of injustice and bitterness blew its top, unleashing a veritable explosion of insults, denunciations and accusations against the Slovenes. Over the course

[78]See particularly the speeches by Milan Bulajić, Vojislav Lubarda, Slobodan Vitanović, Vladeta Jerotić, Petar Džadžić and Milo Gligorijević, in *Književne novine*, 768, 15 Jan. 1989, pp. 1–4, and 769, 1 Feb. 1989, pp. 6–7. For Popov and Dimitrijević, see ibid., 768, p. 4, and 769, p. 6 respectively. On the theme of 'genocide', see Chapter 2.

[79]For the speeches, see Dragan Belić and Djuro Bilbija (eds), *Srbija i Slovenija: Od Cankarevog Doma do 'Jugoalata' i Gazimestana. Dokumenti*, Belgrade, 1989, pp. 22–3. The badges, made by the Slovenian Youth Alliance, were modelled on those used in an earlier campaign to promote the Slovenes' allegiance to Slovenia, their own 'homeland'.

[80]In ibid., p. 28–31 passim.

[81]Interview in *Delo*, 5 Aug. 1989, in Palavestra, *Književnost i javna reč*, op. cit., p. 81.

of twenty-four hours a crowd of a million people gathered in front of the federal parliament, chanting 'Slovenia is lying' and 'Slovenia is a traitor' and calling upon the Serbian leadership to stand firm against the Albanians and their 'sponsors'.[82]

Serbia's critical intellectuals, who had tried in vain since the early 1980s to forge an alliance with their Slovenian colleagues, shared this acute sense of betrayal.[83] Poet Matija Bećković, the president of the Writers' Association of Serbia, dramatically captured the feelings of anger and disappointment experienced by many members of the intelligentsia:

> For years our hand, extended toward Slovenia, remained suspended in the air. We endured their indifference, suppressed our sensitivities, accepted the explanation that they simply lacked information. Our greatest efforts have met with the worst results. Our arguments are not accepted, we are spoken of with disdain, our truths are always presented with scorn. Indifferent to our desire for friendship and impervious to the pain they inflict on us, they are spreading fear of Serbs and mocking Serbian shrines and sufferings ... Instead they defend and aid false Jews.[84]

It was particularly the Jewish comparison that offended Serbian intellectuals, especially because they had claimed that parallel for their own nation—as victims of Ustasha mass extermination, as well as of present-day 'terror' in Kosovo.[85] The Society of Serbian-Jewish Friendship, set up by Belgrade intellectuals in May 1988, thus declared: 'If there is any comparison with the suffering of the Jewish people, then this can be made only in reference to Serbs, Montenegrins and progressive Albanians [in Kosovo], who are in many ways in a similar situation as Jews under Hitler.'[86] It also denounced the 'malicious attribution of the Star of David to those in Kosovo who are systematically carrying out persecution, violence and genocide against the whole non-Albanian population'.[87]

All the institutions of the Belgrade intelligentsia joined in the

---

[82]See *Srbija i Slovenija*, op. cit., p. 47.
[83]On these efforts, see Chapter 4.
[84]*Književne novine*, 772, 15 March 1989, pp. 1,4 passim.
[85]See Chapter 2.
[86]In *Srbija i Slovenija*, op. cit., p. 67. See also *NIN*, 5 March 1989. On the creation of the Society, see Chapter 2. As an expression of his disapproval against these blatant attempts to use Jews for political purposes, writer Filip David left the Society in the spring of 1989 (see *NIN*, 15 Oct. 1989, p. 31).
[87]Ibid., loc. cit.

general uproar against the Cankar Hall rally. The Serbian Academy of Sciences and Arts characterised it as 'the greatest insult to the Serbian people in its history'[88] and the Writers' Association of Serbia announced that it was breaking off relations with its Slovenian counterpart because of its role 'at the rally of hatred against the Serbian people'.[89] The editorial board of *Književne novine* published a declaration entitled 'Political, National and Cultural Disgrace', which stated that the masks had fallen and finally the Slovenes' 'false democratic jargon' had been revealed as being nothing more than support for Albanian separatism, as a first step towards ensuring their own secession.[90] In response to the Cankar Hall rally Serbian intellectuals staged a series of public manifestations in which Slovenes were likened to Nazis, denounced as racists and accused of wanting the 'decapitation of Milošević'.[91]

A recurring theme in all the speeches was that the Ljubljana rally had served to 'sober up' the traditionally pro-Yugoslav Serbs and had exposed to what extent Yugoslavia was 'a rotten creation'—a 'corpse' whose stench was already perceptible.[92] In such circumstances many argued that the elaboration of a new Serbian national programme had become a matter of the utmost urgency.[93] Yet although these intellectuals believed Tito's Yugoslavia was dead, it remained unclear how they imagined the contours and the nature of the state which would replace it. There was no general endorsement of Vuk Drašković's position that Serbia's western borders needed to be defined in such a way as to encompass all territories marked by Serbian 'pits and tombs' from the Ustasha massacres of the Second World War.[94] The reluctance of the vast majority of Belgrade intellectuals to envisage publicly a 'post-Yugoslav' scenario mirrored not only the ambivalence they felt towards the disintegration of the common state but also the enormity of disagreements within the intellectual opposition. These disagreements became both deeper and more open as Yugoslavia progressed towards disintegration and Serbia introduced multipartism.

---

[88]*Politika*, 2 March 1989.
[89]*NIN*, 5 March 1989, p. 32, and *Srbija i Slovenija*, op. cit., p. 67.
[90]*Književne novine*, 771, 1 March 1989, p. 1.
[91]In *Srbija i Slovenija*, op. cit., pp. 82–90 passim.
[92]Brana Crnčević, in *Književne novine*, 772, 15 March 1989, p. 5.
[93]See ibid., pp. 1–7 passim.
[94]Drašković in ibid., p. 7. The only generally accepted proposal was a reiteration of the 1988 position on a reformed Yugoslav federation (see ibid., p. 1. On the 1988 proposal, see Chapter 4).

Disintegration, multipartism and the end of the Belgrade critical intelligentsia, 1989–91

While most Serbian intellectuals rejoiced at their republic's 're-unification' and praised their communist leadership for what it had achieved, their counterparts in Slovenia and Croatia put themselves to the task of creating new political parties. In January 1989 the principal Slovenian interlocutors of the Belgrade intellectuals, the collaborators of the journal *Nova revija*, founded the Slovenian Democratic Alliance, the first independent political party in Yugoslavia.[95] Under the leadership of the sociologist Dimitrij Rupel, the Alliance promised to fight for the twin goals of democracy and independence.[96] In the course of the year a host of other parties followed, which joined with the Slovenian Democratic Alliance to form the Slovenian United Opposition—a coalition known as Demos. At the same time, in February 1989, Croatian intellectuals also began to create new political organisations, notably the centrist Croatian Social Liberal Alliance (later Party; HSLS) and the right-wing Croatian Democratic Union (HDZ).[97]

While these new parties organised their membership, drafted programmes, lobbied for free elections and mobilised support, all that emanated from the ranks of the Belgrade critical intelligentsia—which in the 1980s had represented a leading force for democracy in Yugoslavia—was a lukewarm reiteration of its earlier demands for multipartism and free elections, which came in the form of a document entitled 'Serbia and Democracy, yesterday, today and tomorrow' by the Writers' Association of Serbia. Arguing that the period of national homogenisation had borne its fruits and that Serbia had been 'shaken out of its lethargy, reunited and had found its voice', the authors of the text stated that it was time to proceed with party pluralism and the staging of democratic elections.[98] Yet, as a concurrent document

---

[95]See Bibič, op. cit., p. 378.

[96]The slogan of the Alliance was 'There is no sovereignty without democracy and there is no democracy without sovereignty' ('Programme Statement by the Slovenska Demokratična Zveza', *South Slav Journal*, XI/4, winter 1988–9, p. 61).

[97]On the creation of Croatian parties, see Hudelist, *Banket u Hrvatskoj*, op. cit., and Lino Veljak, 'The Collapse and Reconstruction of Legitimacy: An Introductory Remark', *Nationalities Papers*, XXV/3, Sept. 1997, pp. 449–52. It should be noted that the first political movement that sprang up in Croatia was the Association for a Yugoslav Democratic Initiative (UJDI), under the leadership of Professors Branko Horvat and Žarko Puhovski; it did not materialise into a party before the 1990 elections, however, leaving the 'Yugoslav' option largely in the sphere of the former Croatian League of Communists, renamed Party of Democratic Change.

[98]In *Književne novine*, 776, 15 May 1989, p. 1.

issued by the Committee for the Defence of Freedom of Thought and Expression showed, intellectuals were still reluctant to criticise Milošević—blaming only 'certain conservative officials' for Serbia's lag in creating independent political associations and calling on him to proceed with the necessary democratic changes.[99] Some, such as the literary critic and former president of the Writers' Association of Serbia, Aleksandar Petrov, even urged Milošević to allow free elections, because he—'the first President of the re-united and reborn Serbia'—deserved to be elected democratically.[100]

Finally, by the end of 1989, members of the intellectual opposition came to understand that they had lost precious time in their struggle for democracy in Serbia. Several factors contributed to this realisation. First, the accelerated pace of change in Slovenia and Croatia was contributing to their positive image in the West at a time when outside pressures and alliances were becoming more important, while Serbia was acquiring an increasingly negative image as 'bolshevik', hegemonic and bullying.[101] Although many Belgrade intellectuals were sneering at Slovenia's and Croatia's democratisation as merely an 'image, with which the local national and nationalist elites recommend themselves to the West', they also realised that Serbia was falling further and further behind.[102] Secondly, the democratic revolutions in East-Central Europe—despite the Serbian regime's attempts to minimise them[103]—added to the sense of urgency. As the Praxist Svetozar Stojanović noted:

There is no point in fooling ourselves that we have long made the changes that are now taking place in Eastern Europe and the Soviet Union and that we are still some sort of avant-garde, because it simply is not true. We are lagging behind in many areas, first of all in the institutionalisation of political pluralism.[104]

[99]In *South Slav Journal*, XI/4, winter 1988–9, pp. 59–60.
[100]Quoted in *Književne novine*, 774, 15 Apr. 1989, p. 3.
[101]The feeling of being misunderstood and portrayed unfairly in the West was a recurring theme in the manifestations of Serbian intellectuals and contributed to the siege mentality that characterised Serbian nationalism in the 1980s and 1990s. See, for example, the speeches at the 'Assembly of Serbian Cultural Workers' held in reaction to the Cankar Hall rally in February 1989, in *Književne novine*, 772, op. cit.
[102]Ljubomir Tadić's interview in *NIN*, 31 Dec. 1989, p. 15.
[103]Such as Milošević's declaration that 'there is no reason to equate the events in Yugoslavia with those of other socialist countries. They are now creating the world we created in 1948' (*Borba*, 2 Jan. 1990).
[104]*NIN*, 17 Nov. 1989, p. 19.

The old-style election of Milošević as President of Serbia, which was—as the Committee for the Defence of Freedom of Thought and Expression put it—'not free, nor democratic, nor an election', provided the catalyst that shook critical intellectuals out of their complacency.[105] Now they finally realised that they had been waiting in vain for Milošević to transform his 'anti-bureaucratic revolution' into a democratic one and they began asking themselves: 'What if Milošević once again cleverly postpones the end of communism and if tomorrow, after the elections in Eastern Europe, Serbs remain—along with the Albanians, Chinese and Cubans—the last communist fools mocked by the whole world?!'[106] The former opposition sprang back into action, but this time it did not stop at petitions and calls for democratisation.

The advent of multipartism in Serbia took place in the particularly difficult circumstances of Yugoslavia's national polarisation and the disintegration of common institutions, which exposed that the Serbian national question had been far from resolved. First of all, although the regime had brought the provinces under the republic's control, this move had merely further alienated Serbia's Albanian population and rendered Kosovo even more unstable. From 1989 the province was under permanent police and military supervision, while Albanian intellectuals—led by Ibrahim Rugova, the last president of the Kosovo Writers' Society—organised their resistance to Serbian rule. Secondly, Milošević's drive to recentralise Yugoslavia had contributed to the entrenchment of the Slovenian position and the awakening of Croatian nationalism, repressed since the 1971 'mass movement'. The chasm between Serbia and the two northern republics thus deepened rapidly, raising the spectre of state disintegration and the concomitant question of what would happen to the sizeable Serbian populations outside Serbia.

All these problems initially played themselves out in the cultural sphere and the first federal institution to collapse, more than six months before the League of Communists, was the Yugoslav Writers' Union—which had once been a stronghold of critical intellectuals and had held out the promise of bringing together an all-Yugoslav opposition to the regime.[107] Ironically, the year before that finally saw the resolution of the Serbian-Slovenian conflict over the election of the Union's

---

[105]Petition of 2 Nov. 1989, in *Književne novine*, 786, 15 Nov. 1989, p. 2.
[106]Gojko Djogo's interview in *Pogledi*, 15 June 1990, p. 58.
[107]See Chapter 1.

president, which had immobilised the institution since 1986.[108] In June 1988 the Writers' Association of Serbia had withdrawn the controversial candidacy of Miodrag Bulatović and proposed novelist and playwright Slobodan Selenić. Although Selenić was greeted as 'a president of European charm' even in Slovenia and Croatia,[109] his election was soon exposed as merely a temporary lull in the deepening quagmire of quarrels and mutual accusations between Yugoslav writers.

Already the Congress of the Writers' Union, held to formalise Selenić's election, showed that none of the underlying problems had been overcome and relations between writers' associations deteriorated rapidly. At the congress the Serbs and Montenegrins in the Writers' Society of Kosovo announced they had resigned from their organisation, complaining of constant 'majorisation' by the predominant Albanians. They were supported, as usual, by the Writers' Association of Serbia and now also by the new pro-Serbian leadership of the Writers' Association of Montenegro, which broke off relations with the Kosovo association. The Montenegrin organisation's former president, Jevrem Brković, who represented the 'Green' or Montenegrin-nationalist tradition, had, in turn, been accepted as an honorary member of the Writers' Society of Croatia, which pitted the Montenegrin and Croatian organisations against each other.[110] The president of the Writers' Association of Serbia, poet Matija Bećković—himself of Montenegrin origin—joined in the mayhem by publicly defending 'the right of Montenegrins to feel as Serbs'.[111] The Croatian and Slovenian associations now openly backed the Writers' Society of Kosovo, seeing 'no rational argument' for the Serbs' and Montenegrins' resignation and refusing to accept this instance of 'meddling in the internal affairs' of another association.[112] A few months later, following the Cankar Hall rally held in support of the Albanians' protest against the reduction of Kosovo's autonomy, the Writers' Association of Serbia broke off relations with the Slovenian Writers' Society; in turn, the Kosovan organisation broke off with the Serbian. Although Slobodan Selenić, as president of the Writers' Union, tried to mediate between Slovenian and Serbian writers in the spring of 1989, his efforts bore no fruit.[113]

---

[108]See Chapter 4.
[109]*Danas*, 11 Oct. 1988, pp. 38–9.
[110]*Danas*, 21 Feb. 1989, pp. 38–9, and 28 Feb. 1989, p. 48.
[111]*Književne novine*, 762, 15 Oct. 1988, p. 3.
[112]Rudi Šeligo quoted in *NIN*, 12 March 1989, p. 38.
[113]See *Danas*, 4 Apr. 1989, pp. 35–7.

The final meeting of the presidency of the Yugoslav Writers' Union was a complete fiasco: the writers' societies of Croatia and Kosovo did not even take part, while the delegates from Serbia, Montenegro and Slovenia argued for hours, unable even to produce a concluding statement. When the Slovenian representatives tried to force a vote on a number of controversial issues, the others simply refused to comply.[114] This time it was the Slovenes' turn to complain of 'majorisation' and to announce that they would no longer participate in an organisation where they had been victim to Serbian 'ultrahegemonic and destructive action'.[115] Soon a joint letter followed from the Slovenian and Croatian Societies announcing that 'because of the discontinuation of relations between several members of the Yugoslav Writers' Union, the Union no longer exists'.[116]

For most Serbs, the Slovenes' and Croats' exit from the Writers' Union was merely a 'rehearsal for something much more serious'.[117] As Slobodan Selenić noted, the Slovenes had never seen any problem with 'majorisation' when it went against the Serbs—as in the long obstruction of the election of the President of the Writers' Union or in the case of the Serbs in the Kosovo Society—but now that they had been outvoted for the first time, they no longer wanted to take part in the organisation. Selenić openly stated that he was having 'more and more trouble understanding how our Slovenian colleagues ... imagine democracy: voting is voting when others are outvoted, but voting is a deadly sin when Slovenes are outvoted'.[118] The Slovenes and Croats, on the other hand, refused to participate in an organisation which did not function according to a confederal model—giving them veto power over all decisions of importance—and they announced they would return to the common organisation only if its statutes were changed.[119] After several unsuccessful attempts to break this latest stalemate in the writers' organisation, at the end of the year Selenić finally threw in the towel. Asked by the media about the future of the Writers' Union, the president of the now defunct

[114]*Danas*, 11 Apr. 1989, pp. 35–6.

[115]*Danas*, 20 June 1989, p. 43.

[116]*Danas*, 27 June 1989, p. 38.

[117]Slobodan Selenić interviewed in *Osmica*, 12 Oct. 1989, in *Iskorak u stvarnost*, op. cit., p. 50. See also the reaction of Miodrag Perišić, the editor of *Književne novine* and the newly-elected President of the Serbian PEN Club, in *NIN*, 2 July 1989, p. 44.

[118]Ibid., p. 39.

[119]*Danas*, 27 June 1989, p. 38.

federal organisation merely replied: 'Tell me what the fate of Yugoslavia is and I will immediately tell you that of the Writers' Union.'[120]

The future of the common state looked increasingly grim. In May 1989 Demos—the recently created Slovenian United Opposition—issued a declaration on sovereignty, announcing its 'firm decision to prepare the ground for ... the possibility of a unilateral declaration of independence'.[121] In September the Slovenian parliament adopted a series of constitutional amendments paving the way for eventual secession. Two months later it legalised the creation of political parties and announced elections for the following spring. In December, the Slovenian regime banned a Kosovo Serb 'rally of truth' in Ljubljana, which was a thinly veiled attempt by the Serbian regime to 'export' its 'anti-bureaucratic revolution' and, possibly, provoke a state of emergency. In the meantime Milošević—emboldened by the success of his 'reunification' of Serbia and the 'anti-bureaucratic revolution' in Montenegro, which had gone off without any serious resistance in the federal centre—called for a boycott of Slovenian goods in Serbia. As nationalist passions in Serbia and Slovenia reached their highpoint and relations between the two republics broke down, Croatia too was witnessing its own problem of national polarisation, marked by the mobilisation of Serbs in the republic and the return of former 'mass movement' figures on to the political scene.

Differences between Serbs and Croats in Croatia reappeared, as in the 1960s, with a renewed 'language debate'.[122] In the mid-1980s Stipe Šuvar, Croatia's leading communist and the main proponent of the pro-Yugoslav faction in the republic's party, embarked on a quest to replace the official designation of 'Croatian literary language' as the national language of the republic with 'Croatian or Serbian' or some other variant which would give equal weight to the two names used by Croatia's two constitutive nations. Croatia's ten majority Serb municipalities, its Serbian Orthodox Church and most of its Serbian intellectuals declared themselves in favour of 'Croato-Serbian' as the name of the republic's language.[123] All of Croatia's cultural institutions rejected this proposal, however, and many prominent intellectuals openly criticised wha they saw as Šuvar's 'manipulations' with the

---

[120]Selenić interviewed in *NIN*, 17 Nov. 1989, p. 34.
[121]Quoted in 'Samostojna Slovenija', *Nova Revija*, IX/95, March 1990, p. 612.
[122]On the 1967 'language debate', see Chapter 1.
[123]*Danas*, 23 May 1989, p. 37.

'very essence of the Croatian nation'.[124] The Croatian parliament's decision in August 1989 to maintain the existing designation 'Croatian literary language' marked the first important victory for Croatian intellectuals. It also alienated many Serbian intellectuals in the republic, however, who felt that their objections had simply been ignored and who now called for the creation of their own national institutions.[125]

Initially the Serbian 'question' in Croatia remained limited to cultural concerns. In October 1986 Serbian intellectuals in the Yugoslav Academy of Sciences and Arts set up a Committee for the Coordination of the Study of History and Culture of the Serbs of Croatia and two years later they began to lobby for the resuscitation of Prosvjeta, their cultural organisation banned in 1971. As was shown in the debates surrounding the new Prosvjeta, deep divisions existed among Serbs in Croatia. In the discussions one group wanted closer links with the Serbian Academy of Sciences and Arts, where a Committee for the Study of Serbs of Croatia had been created by the historian Vasilije Krestić—author of the infamous article on the 'genesis of the genocide' of Serbs in the Independent State of Croatia and one of the authors of the 1986 Memorandum—whereas others, such as historian Drago Roksandić, argued against Prosvjeta becoming 'the official interpreter of Serbian cultural and national interests' and warned of the 'ghettoisation' of the republic's Serbs. In Roksandić's opinion, Prosvjeta's role was to promote inter-national dialogue and understanding.[126] It was this second, bridge-building option that eventually prevailed in Prosvjeta, but by this time cultural concerns had been overshadowed by the political mobilisation of Serbs in the former Military Frontier, the Krajina.

---

[124]The writer Petar Šegedin's 'Open Letter to Stipe Šuvar' quoted in *Danas*, 3 Nov. 1987, p. 37. Šegedin was a member of both the Writers' Society and the Yugoslav Academy of Sciences and Arts in Zagreb.

[125]See the interviews with Dušan Starević, a member of the Yugoslav Academy of Sciences and Arts, in *NIN*, 10 Sept. 1989, p. 21, and Stanko Korać, the former head of Prosvjeta, in *Danas*, 6 Sept. 1988, pp. 17–18.

[126]*NIN* and *Danas*, Sept. 1988, loc. cit. On Krestić, see Chapters 2 and 4. Roksandić, a former lecturer at the Belgrade University, had disagreed with Krestić, who was his PhD advisor, in his interpretation of 19th Century Croatian Illyrianism. Accused by Krestić of offering a 'hypercritical' interpretation of Serbian history and an 'idealised' presentation of Croatian history, in 1987 Roksandić was refused his PhD, which eventually cost him his lectureship. Roksandić at this point returned to Zagreb, where he was awarded it and given an academic post at the university. See *Danas*, 5 Dec. 1989, pp. 44–5. The documentation related to this case can be found in *Naše teme*, XXXIV/3–4, 1990, pp. 516–600.

The fateful 27 February 1989—the same day as the Albanian miners' strike in Kosovo, the Cankar Hall rally in Ljubljana and the anti-Slovenian demonstration in Belgrade—also marked the beginning of a new chapter in relations between Croats and Serbs in Croatia. Two events inaugurated this phase: the founding assembly of historian Franjo Tudjman's Croatian Democratic Union (HDZ) in the Writers' Society of Croatia and the first mass rally of the Serbs of Knin, organised to protest against Slovenian and Croatian support for the Kosovo Albanians.

The Croatian Democratic Union was one of several new political parties created by intellectuals and political figures associated with the 1971 'spring'.[127] Although they all shared a commitment to Croatian sovereignty—possibly as part of a Yugoslav confederation or preferably as a fully independent state—the Croatian Democratic Union soon profiled itself as one of the most nationalist and right-wing.[128] It insisted on Croatia's 1,000-year-old 'state right', glorified Croatian historical figures, placed considerable emphasis on Catholicism as a defining characteristic of Croatian identity, showed particular concern about the Croats' 'biological' decline and adopted conservative anti-abortion and anti-feminist positions.[129] In his pre-election campaign Tudjman—author of the controversial *Impasses of Historical Reality*, which minimised the Ustasha terror in the Second World War[130]—adopted an mbiguous stance towards the wartime Independent State of Croatia, referring to it as 'not only a fascist institution but also the expression of the Croatian people's centuries-old craving for an independent state'.[131] He also called for the 'self-determination

[127]Their return on the Croatian political scene and their rising popularity as leaders of the new political parties grew impressively over the course of 1989, provoking the Zagreb weekly *Danas* into heading one of its end-of-the-year articles 'Happy New 1971' (*Danas*, 12 Dec. 1989, p. 26).

[128]See Jill A. Irvine, 'Ultranationalist Ideology and State-Building in Croatia, 1990–1996', op. cit. It should be noted, however, that the HDZ was a heterogenous organisation containing more moderate and more radical factions.

[129]See the HDZ party programme in *Naše teme*, XXXIV/3–4, 1990, pp. 699–704, and its critique in *Danas*, 20 March 1990, pp. 12–13.

[130]See Chapter 2.

[131]*Danas*, 6 March 1990, p. 14. He had already made such claims in 1981, when he stated that the Independent State of Croatia meant 'the realisation of the goals held dear not only by the radical, separatist currents in Croatian political life but also by the majority of the Croatian people' (Franjo Tudjman, *Nationalism in Contemporary Europe*, 1981, excerpt in *So Speak Croatian Dissidents*, op. cit., p. 33).

of the whole Croatian nation within its natural and historical borders'[132] and made promises to create an independent Croatian army and 'rectify' the over-representation of Serbs in republican institutions—warning them not to forget 'who is the host and who the newcomer' in the republic.[133] The message to the Serbs of Croatia was clear: if the Croatian Democratic Union won the election and Tudjman became president, the best they could hope for was the status of second-class citizens.

Serbian political mobilisation in Croatia partly represented a reaction to these new trends on the Croatian political scene. As the Zagreb weekly *Danas* noted in March 1989:

Many Serbs are afraid that the present political thaw could give rise to a revival of Croatian nationalism and, as proof of such fears, they cite the possible political resuscitation of the so-called 'mass movement leaders' ... These fears, along with the Kosovo events, which have struck an emotional chord of national solidarity, and certain statements of the Croatian leadership, have provoked the public unrest of Serbs in Croatia.[134]

At the same time, however, the Krajina Serbs were clearly also under the spell of Milošević's 'happening of the people' in Serbia reflecting the same discourse, the same declarations of love and support for the 'national leader' and the same slogans and insignia.[135] During their celebration of the 600th anniversary of the Battle of Kosovo in July 1989, their leaders warned that Serbs in Croatia were in danger of

[132]*Danas*, 16 Jan. 1990, pp. 8–9. In 1981 he wrote that 'the majority of the [Bosnian] Muslims is in its ethnic character and speech incontrovertibly of Croatian origin' and that the creation of a separate republic of Bosnia-Hercegovina had made 'the territorial and geographical position of Croatia extremely unnatural in the economic sense and, therefore, in the broadest national-political sense' (see Tudjman, *Nationalism in Contemporary Europe*, in ibid., pp. 36–7).

[133]Tudjman's speech in Dubrovnik, 18 Apr. 1990, quoted in Jovan Mirić, 'Hrvatska demokracija i srpsko pitanje', *Novi list* (Rijeka), June–July 1994, reprinted in *Republika*, VI/101, 1–15 Oct. 1994, p. 19. Serbs made up around 12.2% of the population of Croatia according to the 1991 census (not including those who declared themselves as 'Yugoslavs'). According to a 1986 study, they held a disproportionate number of administrative positions: 21.4% on the municipal level, 13.8% at the regional level and 24.8% at the republican level, as well as 17.7% of all positions of political leadership in the republic. This overrepresentation hardly gave them the capability to control the republic or hold its Croatian majority 'hostage', as Croatian nationalists claimed (*Danas*, 12 Sept. 1989, p. 19, and 12 June 1990, pp. 8–9).

[134]*Danas*, 7 March 1989, p. 20.

[135]Ibid., loc. cit., and Radulović, op. cit., pp. 11–12.

being completely assimilated, demanded that 'the centralist–Comintern cadres in Croatia' be replaced and called upon 'the Croatian people' to rise up against its own 'bureaucracy'.[136] The arrest of Jovan Opačić, one of the leaders of the new Knin-based Serbian Democratic Party, provoked the facetious remark by the Belgrade weekly *NIN* that he was in trouble because he had propagated the standpoints of *Književne novine* in the Krajina.[137]

Opačić's arrest caused a tremendous uproar in the Belgrade intelligentsia. The various intellectuals' committees immediately protested, issuing statements alleging that Opačić's indictment represented 'an attack on the historical, moral and cultural being of the whole Serbian people in Croatia' and a denial of rights it historically enjoyed even under the Austro-Hungarian Empire.[138] As before, the Writers' Association of Serbia organised a series of massively attended protest evenings, at which speaker after speaker accused the Croatian communists of continuing a 'historical' policy of 'eliminating' the Serbs of Croatia and drew parallels with the Ustasha persecution.[139] The President of the Writers' Association, Matija Bećković, pronounced the Serbs of Croatia 'the remnants of a slaughtered people', while novelist Dobrica Ćosić wondered whether the Serbs' destiny in Croatia was 'genocide in war and discrimination and assimilation in the socialist peace'.[140] Several intellectuals raised the issue of Croatia's 'undemocratic' borders which, in the words of the poet Milan Komnenić, had been drawn 'with slaughtered Serbs'.[141] Finally, most speakers pointedly asked why Croatian intellectuals, who had been so quick to defend Kosovo Albanians and 'anti-Serbian' Montenegrin writers, did not raise their voices against persecution of Serbs in their own republic.[142]

---

[136]*Start*, 22 July 1989 quoted in D. Jović, op. cit., p. 320.

[137]*NIN*, 17 Sept. 1989, p. 18. On Opačić's speech and its consequences see *Danas*, 11 July 1989, pp. 19–20.

[138]See the protest letters of the Committee for the Defence of Human Rights, the presidency of the Writers' Association of Serbia, PEN Club and the Committee for the Defence of Freedom of Thought and Expression (in *Književne novine*, 781, 1 Sept. 1989, p. 2 and 782, 15 Sept. 1989, p. 2 and *Naša reč*, 408, Sept.–Oct. 1989, pp. 21–2).

[139]See notably the speeeches by Vasilije Krestić, Vladimir Dedijer, Antonije Isaković, Gojko Djogo and Jovan Deretić (*Književne novine*, 782, op. cit., pp. 3–4 and 783, 1 Oct. 1989, pp. 4–5, as well as *Danas*, 12 Sept. 1989, p. 20 and 19 Sept. 1989, p. 11).

[140]Quoted in *Književne novine*, 782, op. cit., pp. 3 and 1 respectively.

[141]*Književne novine*, 783, op. cit., pp. 4–5.

[142]The Writers' Society of Croatia retaliated by organising its own special assembly on the theme 'Attacks by the Socialist Republic of Serbia on the State

Support for Croatia's Serbs did not stop at declarations and protests. A number of Belgrade intellectuals played a role in their political organisation and none more so than novelist Dobrica Ćosić. In his first public speech held in the Montenegrin town of Budva in June 1989 Ćosić openly admitted: 'For a long time I have not been convinced that a priori Yugoslavism is in the Serbs' interest and even less that this Yugoslavism is democratic and socialist.'[143] Although he did not directly criticise Milošević's drive to reintegrate the federation, he stated that he did not believe that 'all those who are defending Yugoslavia with traditional patriotism and the ideology of the League of Communists' could save the common state. Instead, he argued, Serbs had to seek 'new political answers for the ethnic preservation of their diaspora'.[144] As he later explained, he believed that at a time when Yugoslavia was falling part and Tudjman's Croatian Democratic Union was emerging as the leading political force in the republic, Serbs had no choice but to mobilise; the alternative was 'acceptance of subordination, discrimination and silent expulsion'.[145] The influential and well-connected writer thus helped organise the Serbian Democratic Parties in Croatia and Bosnia-Hercegovina and even personally handpicked their leaders—his long time friends, psychiatrists Jovan Rašković and Radovan Karadžić.[146] As he told Borisav Jović, at the time Serbia's representative in the federal presidency and Milošević's closest collaborator, he also guaranteed the 'reliability' of their leaderships and promised to help coordinate their policies with those of the Serbian regime.[147]

The defence of Jovan Opačić proved to be the last common action of the Belgrade critical intelligentsia, which also began to break up into political parties in the autumn of 1989. While it was not realistic to expect large cultural institutions, such as the Writers' Association or the Academy of Sciences, to produce parties, eyes were turned

---

and Territorial Integrity of the Socialist Republic of Croatia' (See *Danas*, 26 Sept. 1989, p. 37).

[143]Dobrica Ćosić, 'Uspostavljanje istorijskog uma', *Književne novine*, 779–80, 1–15 July 1989, p. 3, also carried in *Borba*, 12 and 13 June 1989.

[144]Ibid, loc. cit. Borisav Jović, Milošević's right-hand man at the time, notes this disagreement between Ćosić and the Serbian leadership (B. Jović, *Poslednji dani SFRJ*, Belgrade, 1995, pp. 28, 125).

[145]Djukić, *Lovljenje vetra*, op. cit., p. 169.

[146]Ibid., loc. cit. and Djukić, *Lovljenje vetra*, op. cit., p. 168. This is confirmed by Rašković, interview in *Duga*, 23 Nov.-7 Dec. 1991, p. 92.

[147]B. Jović, op. cit., p. 193.

towards the most prominent and most active grouping of critical intellectuals and their unofficial leader—the Committee for the Defence of Freedom of Thought and Expression and Dobrica Ćosić. There were major ideological and political differences that prevented this relatively small (twenty-person) organisation to crystallise into a party, however. Although the committee had acted in unison when it came to protecting individuals persecuted for the 'verbal offence' and standing up for democratic transformation of the system, in the end the divergence between its members on both the national question and the Serbian regime eventually prevailed. As the committee disintegrated, some of its members withdrew from political activism.[148] The others split into several groups.

The first group consisted of anti-nationalist intellectuals—the lawyer Ivan Janković, the sociologist Vesna Pešić, the former Partisan general and memoirist Gojko Nikoliš and the Praxist Zagorka Golubović— and they became more vocal and more assertive in opposing the continued repression in Kosovo and the shrill nationalist discourse in their republic. They joined the budding Yugoslav-oriented groupings that began to spring up in early 1989, the most important of which was the Association for a Yugoslav Democratic Initiative. The other members of the Committee for the Defence of Freedom of Thought and Expression placed greater emphasis on the resolution of the Serbian 'national question', but differed in their assessment of Milošević and his policy. Within the group that supported the Serbian regime, the Praxist Mihailo Marković was the most open and the most committed, becoming in 1990 one of the two vice-presidents of Milošević's Socialist Party of Serbia.[149]

It is unlikely that Marković joined the regime for opportunistic reasons; he was a well-known philosopher, who enjoyed an impeccable reputation as a dissident intellectual and was a frequent guest lecturer abroad since his ouster from Belgrade University in 1975. It was also not only Milošević's uncompromising and belligerent defence of the nation that attracted him. Marković, like other former opposition intellectuals who joined the regime, belonged to the 'Partisan' generation, which had once fought for national and social liberation,

[148]These were archaeologist Dragoslav Srejović, artist Mladen Srbinović and sociologist Neca Jovanov.

[149]The other vice-president was writer Antonije Isaković, who had played an important role in the disclosures about the Goli Otok prison camps in the early 1980s and had been the director of the 'Memorandum' committee in the Serbian Academy.

and Milošević appealed to them precisely because he was inviting them to shape what they believed was a new revolution. As Marković put it, becoming part of Milošević's team had given him the opportunity to 'show theoretically and practically that, with the destruction of bureaucratic regimes, circumstances were right for the creation of a society which combined the idea of freedom with the idea of social justice'.[150] Although he had earlier endorsed petitions for party pluralism, he now became the most vocal advocate of 'non-party pluralism' as a political 'third way'.[151]

The remaining members of the committee were neither anti-nationalist nor wholeheartedly pro-regime and thus sought forms of activism that would continue their struggle for both the democratic transformation of society and the resolution of the national question. The new political formation that best embodied this orientation was the resuscitated Democratic Party. As was put by the jurist Vojislav Koštunica who, with his colleague Kosta Čavoški, was co-author of the 1983 liberal critique of the Yugoslav communist system, *Party Pluralism or Monism* and created the party: 'It was to be expected that among the founders of the Democratic Party would be many of those who for years participated in the series of democratic initiatives and activities in the defence of freedom of thought and expression.'[152] Yet the two intellectuals did not manage to rally much support within the committee: most of their co-activists either wanted to maintain their 'independent' role and were unwilling to get involved in party politics, or they used a host of personal reasons to refuse—they were too old, too ill or too committed to their work as writers or academics. Finally, some believed that creating a political opposition would break the national unity necessary for the successful resolution of the Serbian question.[153] In the end only the Praxist Ljubomir Tadić and literary theorist Nikola Milošević joined the new party. The literary critic Borislav Mihajlović-Mihiz and artist Mića Popović initially participated in the meetings, but when their proposals to adopt a more overtly nationalist orientation and call the party 'Serbian Democratic Party' were rejected, they withdrew from the project.[154]

---

[150]Interview in *NIN*, 13 July 1990, p. 15.

[151]Ibid, loc. cit. The promise of an economic 'third way' had already lured the three economists of the 'Memorandum' committee—Kosta Mihailović, Ivan Maksimović and Miloš Macura—in April 1988.

[152]In *Demokratija*, 10 Feb. 1991, p. 5.

[153]Ibid., loc. cit.

[154]See Nenad Stefanović, *Pokrštavanje petokrake*, Belgrade, 1994, pp. 95–6.

In 1990 Dobrica Ćosić was probably the only intellectual with enough authority to keep the critical intelligentsia together and present a political alternative capable of defeating Milošević at the polls, yet he repeatedly refused to get involved with party politics or run for president of Serbia.[155] Publicly he argued that 'a writer who has written books with the content and ideas which I have written ... cannot fit into any political party' and that he was most useful to his nation if he maintained an independent stance.[156] Ćosić's commitment to independence was relative, however. In March 1990 he met Milošević for the first time and, according to Milošević's right-hand man Borisav Jović, 'Ćosić wholeheartedly supported our policy, particularly the battle for the constitutional changes in Serbia'.[157] The rapprochement between Serbia's president and the leading figure of the intellectual opposition was reinforced when in spring 1990 Milošević came round to Ćosić's point of view that Yugoslavia could not be saved and that Serbs had to create a new state for their nation. Differences between the two continued to persist, both regarding the means to be used for the dissolution of the federation and the territories claimed for the new Serbian state. Ćosić favoured a peaceful process based on 'democratic' national referenda and remained generally loyal to the ethnic principle, thus advocating the relinquishing of most of Kosovo, whereas Milošević's strategy—divulged in private only to his closest collaborators—revolved around 'expelling' the Slovenes and Croats from the common state and 'cutting off' parts of Croatia, while keeping the Republic of Serbia intact with its autonomous provinces.[158] Nevertheless, as Ćosić told Borisav Jović in an extensive discussion in September 1990, he believed Serbia's main task was not 'party politics and the struggle for power', but the resolution of the national question, and he clearly saw Milošević as the man for the job.[159] Assuming that he could exercise influence behind the scenes, he thus preferred to wager on the existing Serbian leadership.[160] On 1 July 1990 Ćosić

---

[155]Djukić, *Lovljenje vetra*, op. cit., p. 160.

[156]In *NIN*, 6 July 1990, p. 38.

[157]B. Jović, op. cit., p. 130.

[158]For Ćosić, see his *Srpsko pitanje—demokratsko pitanje*, op. cit., p. 227 and Djukić, *Lovljenje vetra*, op. cit., p.169. For his 'ethnic map', see B. Jović, op. cit., pp. 193–4. For Milošević's policy, also see B. Jović, op. cit., p. 160. Of course, Ćosić never publicly stated how he imagined peaceful separation between populations that were so intermingled.

[159]B. Jović, op. cit., pp. 193–4.

[160]On Ćosić's belief that he could influence Milošević, see Djukić, *Lovljenje vetra*, op. cit., pp. 162–3.

dealt a devastating blow to the opposition by publicly siding with Milošević on the necessity of adopting a new Serbian constitution before organising multiparty elections. In a statement carried by both *Politika* and *Politika ekspres*, Serbia's two main dailies, he noted that 'in Yugoslavia, since its creation until today, no constitution was ever brought on the basis of total democratic principles' and directly called in question the legitimacy of opposition party leaders.[161] In the first multiparty elections in December 1990 it was an unofficial secret that Ćosić had voted 'the right way—for Milošević and the Socialists'.[162]

In the end, three main opposition political formations arose in Serbia from the former critical intelligentsia: the centrist Democratic Party, the right-wing Serbian Renewal Movement and the left-wing Association for a Yugoslav Democratic Initiative and Alliance of Reform Forces.[163] Despite the non-participation of some of Serbia's most prestigious intellectuals from the Committee for the Defence of Freedom of Thought and Expression, the Democratic Party nevertheless regrouped many individuals whose intellectual prestige was matched by their 'national' credentials and it initially held tremendous promise.[164] The founding assembly of the Democratic Party, held on 3 February 1990, was an impressively attended event, gathering the cream of Serbia's intellectual opposition. Visitors included not only all the prestigious members of the Committee for the Defence of Freedom of Thought and Expression who had earlier refused to join the party—Matija Bećković, Dobrica Ćosić, Borislav Mihajlović-Mihiz, Mića Popović and Predrag Palavestra—but also Yugoslavia's first and best-known dissident, Milovan Djilas. Speakers at the assembly guaranteed that the party's only guiding force would be reason,

---

[161]*Politika*, 1 July 1990. Ćosić later explained that Milošević had tricked him into supporting the regime during the referendum (in Djukić, *Lovljenje vetra*, op. cit., p. 163).

[162]Miodrag Bulatović quoted in Dušan Radulović and Nebojša Spaić, *U Potrazi za demokratijom*, Belgrade, 1991, p. 110. Ćosić later admitted as much himself (in Djukić, *Lovljenje vetra*, op. cit., p. 164).

[163]On the creation of these parties see Robert Thomas, *Serbia under Milošević*, London, 1997.

[164]Aside from four former members of the Committee for the Defence of Freedom of Thought and Expression, the party included the writers Milovan Danojlić, Borislav Pekić and Gojko Djogo, the Praxist Dragoljub Mićunović, the political scientist Slobodan Inić and philosopher Zoran Djindjić, the editor of *Književne novine* Miodrag Perišić, the theatre director Vida Ognjenović, the film director Aleksandar Petrović, and several important figures from the democratic emigration, notably Desimir Tošić, the editor of the British-based monthly journal *Naša reč*, which had relentlessly published all the petitions of the intellectual opposition since the 1970s.

democratic means and the promotion of rational dialogue.[165] The Praxist Dragoljub Mićunović, who was elected party president, read out a Special Declaration on Kosovo which blamed the difficult situation in Kosovo on the Communist Party (not, as was usual, on Albanian 'chauvinists and terrorists') and called on all sides to refrain from using violence, proposing instead the organisation of a round table needing to work out a peaceful solution.[166]

The Democratic Party essentially took over the 'programme' of the Belgrade critical intelligentsia, as it was voted by the Writers' Association of Serbia, the Philosophical and Sociological Societies and endorsed by the Committee for the Defence of Freedom of Thought and Expression and the Serbian Academy of Sciences and Arts during the 1988 debate on constitutional change.[167] Its guiding lines were: the defence of human and civil rights, the demand for parliamentary democracy and a market economy, and the advocacy of 'democratic federalism' based on a new 'historical agreement' between the Yugoslav nations. It proposed the creation of two houses of parliament—representing the federal units and Yugoslavia's citizens—and the universalisation of the principle of territorial autonomy to areas of either a different ethnic make-up or cultural-historical identity. It also called for cultural rights to be granted to all nations and minorities in Yugoslavia, including official use of their own languages and 'spiritual and cultural' links with the rest of their nation.[168]

The second important party to emerge from the Belgrade critical intelligentsia was the right-wing Serbian Renewal Movement, representing the ideological and political equivalent of Franjo Tudjman's Croatian Democratic Union in the neighbouring republic. As the Zagreb weekly *Danas* noted in early 1990, the two parties were 'antipodes which have a lot in common': like the Croatian Democratic Union, the Renewal Movement rejected any form of 'Yugoslavism', aiming instead at the creation of a Serbian state in its 'historical and ethnic borders', possibly as part of a Yugoslav confederation.[169] It welcomed the secession of the two northern republics, but conditioned it on their 'paying back their debts to Yugoslavia (including war repa-

[165]Quoted in *Naša reč*, 413, March 1990, pp. 2–3.

[166]Ibid., p. 3.

[167]See Chapter 4.

[168]'Declaration on the Founding of the Democratic Party' of 11 Dec. 1989 in *Naša reč*, 411, Jan. 1990, p. 2.

[169]*Danas*, 16 Jan. 1990, pp. 10–11.

rations from Croatia to the Serbian nation)' and the redrawing of inter-republican borders. As the Movement's leader Vuk Drašković had made clear in the debates within the Writers' Association of Serbia, 'no span of land soaked with Serbian blood and marked by Serbian churches and tombs' would be allowed to secede or become 'confederalised'; the new Serbian state would contain not only all the territories that had been part of the Kingdom of Serbia in 1918, but also all regions in which Serbs had been the ethnic majority in 1941, before the Ustasha genocide.[170]

Like Tudjman regarding the Serbs of Croatia, Drašković affirmed that Kosovo Albanians would be granted full minority rights, as 'in the most democratic states of Europe and the world', but they would get 'no more than that' and certainly no political autonomy.[171] Drašković too reminded Albanians of who were 'the autochthons' of Kosovo, but even went a step further than his Croatian counterpart (who promised only to 'redress' the ethnic balance in Croatia by purging Serbs from their state employment and promoting Croatian demographic growth); he threatened to expel all 'immigrants' from Albania and proposed a special fund to finance the re-population of Kosovo by Serbs. Like Tudjman, Drašković saw Bosnian Muslims as merely converted members of his own nation and laid claims to Bosnia-Hercegovina.[172] Finally, Drašković also proposed the rehabilitation of historical figures (notably the anti-communist general Draža Mihailović) and a typically right-wing programme including the encouragement of the nation's demographic growth, mandatory religious education, return of the monarchy and public support for the peasantry as 'the economic and biological foundation of he state'.[173]

The final challenge to the regime came from the anti-nationalist moderate left, embodied by the Association for a Yugoslav Democratic Initiative (UJDI) and the Alliance of Reform Forces of Yugoslavia. Created in Zagreb in January 1989, the UJDI only belatedly became a political party.[174] Its most successful activities lay in the domain of creating an alternative press; in March 1989 the bi-monthly

---

[170]SPO declaration reproduced in Stefanović, op. cit., p. 233.
[171]Ibid., loc. cit.
[172]Quoted in *Danas*, 9 Jan. 1990, p. 26.
[173]See Vujačič, *Communism and Nationalism*, op. cit., pp. 421–6.
[174]In the words of Branko Horvat, one of the founders of UJDI, its members 'are not interested in power', but in 'the creation of conditions which will enable [democratic] change' ('Uvodna riječ', *Republika*, I/1, March 1989, p. 1).

journal *Republika* began to appear and in the autumn of 1990 one of the organisation's leaders, the lawyer Srdja Popović, initiated the independent Belgrade weekly *Vreme* (Time). In the first half of 1990 the UJDI also tried to establish a constructive Albanian-Serbian dialogue and sponsored several round tables on Kosovo.[175] The Alliance of Reform Forces, created in July 1990 by the Federal Prime Minister Ante Marković, emphasised the necessity of economic reform as the basis for democracy and a new, rationally-based Yugoslav union; Marković himself was an able economic manager of 'respectable' communist background and a strong Yugoslav orientation who— although he was a Croat—could hardly be accused of separatism or nationalism on the Croatian-Slovenian pattern.[176]

Whereas the Democratic Party, the Association for a Yugoslav Democratic Initiative and the Alliance of Reform Forces challenged Milošević's support in urban centres and among the educated, the Serbian Renewal Movement attracted anti-communists and right-wing nationalists; the 'parliamentary' threat to Serbia's president represented by the first three was thus compounded by the Renewal Movement's 'street' challenge. More charismatic and a better orator than Serbia's communist leader and just as much of a populist, Vuk Drašković soon achieved a mass following in the republic. As one journalist pointed out, while other political parties held their assemblies in half-empty halls of provincial cultural centres and cinemas, the Renewal Movement rallies were huge events, forced by the sheer number of participants to take place in town squares, football stadiums and other large public spaces.[177]

Subjected to these pressures from different sides of the political spectrum, Milošević appeared by the summer of 1990, to be in serious trouble. With the defeat of the former communist parties in both Slovenia and Croatia in the April 1990 elections, many believed that the Serbian communists' bell had tolled as well; the Belgrade intelligentsia's transition to party pluralism seemed to be following the by now usual East-Central European pattern of success. On 13 June 1990 the first mass rally of the Serbian opposition took place in Belgrade, attracting some fifty thousand demonstrators against the

---

[175]It also set up an independent commission to investigate some of the main Serbian claims regarding emigration from Kosovo, whose results were published as *Kosovski čvor—drešiti ili seći?* (see Chapter 3 and *Republika*, II/3–4, April 1990, pp. 5–6).

[176]Ibid., p. 409.

[177]Stefanović, op. cit., pp. 234–5.

regime; it demanded the setting of a date for multi-party elections and the immediate institutionalisation of round table negotiations according to the Polish model to secure the transition, draft laws on political association and ensure equal access to media.[178] In addition, the Serbian Orthodox Church also progressively turned against Milošević; its press increasingly attacked him as a communist and by the time of the December 1990 elections it openly called upon its followers not to vote for his party.[179] Despite Milošević's still great popularity, which made him the most likely victor in the presidential contest, most analysts predicted that his party, the Socialist Party of Serbia, would surely lose. They expected instead a repetition of the Slovenian outcome: the election of the former communist leader as President (as a reward for services rendered to the nation) with an opposition-dominated Parliament.[180]

Milošević's ability to turn this situation around in the following six months and to ensure, not only his own, but his party's electoral victory—setting the pattern of Serbia's future political evolution—was the result of three interconnected factors: first, the Yugoslav context, defined by a radicalisation of the spiral of nationalism and disintegration; second, the Socialist Party's control over all instruments of state power and the media; and third, the weakness and lack of unity of the Serbian opposition in presenting an alternative to the regime.

The first problem opposition intellectuals faced was the fact that until this point they had themselves argued that the resolution of the national question needed to take precedence over democracy. With the victory of the separatist forces in the first multi-party elections in Slovenia and Croatia in April 1990—represented by Slovenia's opposition coalition Demos and the Croatian Democratic Union—it was difficult to argue that now the Serbian question was anywhere near resolution. Less than a month before the election, in March 1990, Demos' leading figures announced in an issue of *Nova revija* that they would seek independent statehood within a year, possibly accompanied by loose confederate ties with the rest of the Yugoslavia.[181]

---

[178]Petition of the united opposition reproduced in Radulović and Spaić, op. cit., p. 17.

[179]The Church favoured Drašković's Renewal Movement (see Radić, op. cit., pp. 285–6).

[180]Even Ćosić gave the Socialist Party no more than 30% in a democratic election (in B. Jović, op. cit., p. 194).

[181]'Samostojna Slovenija', *Nova revija*, IX/95, March 1990.

The newly-constituted republican Parliament immediately passed a 'Declaration on Slovenian Sovereignty' and in December of that year held a referendum on independence, receiving overwhelming public support.[182] In Croatia Tudjman's new government immediately proposed a draft for a new constitution, which defined Croatia as 'the national state of the Croatian nation' and relegated the Serbs in the republic from being a 'constitutive nation' to a national minority, like the far fewer Hungarians, Czechs, Slovenes, Italians and Muslims.[183] This move was accompanied by a 'Croatisation' of all aspects of the public life, from the renaming of streets and cultural institutions to the rehabilitation of old Croatian symbols, such as the checkerboard flag, which had also been used under the wartime Independent State of Croatia.[184] Whereas Serbian nationalism was partly responsible for Tudjman's victory, this in turn fed the radicalisation of the Serbs in the republic. At first Jovan Rašković's Serbian Democratic Party attracted little support, even in the rural areas: it won only five seats in the Croatian Parliament, while most Serbs voted for the only non-national party, the former communists, renamed Party of Democratic Change.[185] Yet the more the Tudjman government pushed for the parallel objectives of 'Croatising' his republic and promoting its 'independence' from Yugoslavia, the more the Krajina Serbs pursued their own goal of creating their own *corpus separatum*, ready to take it out of the republic if Croatia seceded from Yugoslavia.[186]

Finally, the untenable and ever-deteriorating situation in Kosovo

[182]Turnout at the referendum was 88% of the population, of whom 93% voted for independence. (Bibič, op. cit., p. 380) A poll held in Slovenia in January 1990 already showed that 55.4% of the population wanted secession from Yugoslavia (see *Danas*, 20 Feb. 1990, pp. 18–19).

[183]The Preamble of the new Croatian Constitution, adopted in December 1990, began by emphasising 'the millenial national sovereignty of the Croatian nation and the continuity of its statehood confirmed by the course of its entire historical experience' and defined Croatia as 'the national state of the Croatian nation and the state of the members of its nations and minorities, who are its citizens' (*Ustav Republike Hrvatske*, Zagreb, 1991, pp. 3–5 passim; see also Robert M. Hayden, *Blueprints for a House Divided*, Ann Arbor, 2000, pp. 69–71).

[184]This included Croatia's the two main cultural institutions; in the spring of 1990, the Writers' Society of Croatia became the Society of Croatian Writers and the Yugoslav Academy of Sciences and Arts the Croatian Academy of Sciences and Arts.

[185]Immediately following the elections, however, the Party of Democratic Change supported many of the new government's actions, notably in regard to the new constitution, alienating both its Serbian voters and its left wing, which quit the party.

[186]See Silber and Little, op. cit., pp. 98–103, and Srdjan Radulović, *Sudbina Krajine*, Belgrade, 1996, pp. 20–3.

represented Milošević's trump card and helped him win the first round of the public contest against the opposition in July 1990. This test of strength came in a referendum on what Serbia needed to do first— hold democratic elections or promulgate a new Serbian constitution. Milošević gave priority to the new constitution, arguing that it was necessary to forestall Albanian separatism in Kosovo and formally establish Serbia as a state at a time when Slovenia and Croatia were themselves consolidating their own statehood and their negotiating positions for the debate over the future of Yugoslavia. The Serbian opposition—although it did not call for a boycott of the referendum—denounced this as a ploy to delay elections and expressed serious reservation about the proposed draft of the constitution. As Serbia was preparing for the referendum, Kosovo once again flared up as its parliament adopted a 'Constitutional Declaration' designating Kosovo as a republic and the Albanians as a nation, with the right to self-determination including secession.[187] Milošević's appeal for Serbian unity in the face of external threat and his presentation of the opposition's demand for multiparty elections as divisive and inopportune now appeared convincing, with the referendum showing an overwhelming 96.8% of the population giving priority to the new constitution.

The second main problem of the opposition was that it was facing— not a weakened communist party like those of other East European countries—but one that had effectively overcome its legitimacy crisis. Homogenisation, which had been supported or at least tolerated by the vast majority of the critical intelligentsia at the end of the 1980s, could not be simply switched off. As opposition party leader Dragoljub Mićunović aptly put it,

Our Prague happened in Gazimestan [in Kosovo Polje, where the celebration of the six hundredth anniversary of the battle took place], our Berlin at the Confluence [in Belgrade, where the massive November 1988 rally—the 'happening of the people'—took place] ... At the end of communism, Milošević used nationalism to homogenise the masses, pre-empting a wave of anti-communism as a collective ideology and energy.[188]

Furthermore, Milošević's party managed to pool all the republic's key financial and institutional resources, whilst maintaining control over

---

[187]'Constitutional Declaration Adopted by the Kosovo Assembly, July 2, 1990' in Philip E. Auerswald and David P. Auerswald (eds), *The Kosovo Conflict: A Diplomatic History Through Documents*, Cambridge/The Hague, 2000, pp. 43–5.

[188]Quoted in Stefanović, op. cit., p. 117.

the media, the courts, police and army and keep complete legislative, financial and political power in Serbia.[189] It resorted to a variety of undemocratic means to ensure its electoral victory in December 1990: the promulgation of laws governing political association and elections that disadvantaged the opposition, along with delays on and only partial fulfilment of promises made to it; the unauthorised appropriation of federal funds to pay pensions and salaries in crisis-ridden Serbia before the election; monopoly over the state media serving as a *de facto* propaganda machine for the Socialist Party; the creation of 'satellite parties' to divide the vote of the opposition and drown the voice of real political adversaries; and, finally, even the use of police brutality against the opposition, as during the first opposition rally in June 1990, when several prominent opposition figures were beaten up.[190]

Furthermore, Milošević's appropriation of most of the elements of the intellectual opposition's platform for reorganising the federal state made it very difficult for opposition parties to create alternative national programmes. Milošević's proposal for a 'democratic federation' was a mirror image of that advocated by the Democrats and the Reform Forces: it called for a dual Federal Parliament, made up of a House of Citizens and a House of Republics, with more decisionmaking by qualified majority. The federation would be in charge of national defence and state security, foreign relations, economic policy and legislation.[191] However, Milošević specified at the same time that if some republics considered this proposal unacceptable, then Serbia would 'take into account another possible option: Serbia as an independent state'; naturally, in this case, 'the question of the borders of Serbia would become an open political question'.[192] In this way Milošević maintained his role as spokesman for both the 'Yugoslavist' and 'Serbian' alternatives.

By maintaining a 'Yugoslavist' discourse in favour of 'democratic federalism' in the talks with his Slovenian and Croatian counterparts in 1990 and 1991, Serbia's president could also play the card of 'moderation' and let his media relentlessly accuse his most dangerous

---

[189]On Milošević's ability to hold on to power in the 1990s, see particularly Eric Gordy, *The Culture of Power in Serbia*, University Park, PA 1999.

[190]See Radulović and Spaić, op. cit.

[191]'A Concept for the Constitutional System of Yugoslavia on a Federal Basis' in *Yugoslav Survey*, XXXI/4, 1990, pp. 13–25.

[192]Quoted in *NIN*, 29 June 1990, p. 13.

rival Vuk Drašković, of sponsoring 'dark forces that were pushing Serbia into chaos'.[193] While Milošević himself was unassailable as Serbia's 'real' national leader, who had united the republic and helped the Serbs outside Serbia regain their 'consciousness' and their 'voice', the Socialists' main pre-election slogan was 'With us, there is no uncertainty'—promising peace, security and social benefits.[194] As elections approached, Drašković moderated his discourse, either because he genuinely realised where nationalism was leading the country following the first skirmishes between the Krajina Serbs and the Croatian authorities in Summer 1990, or because he believed that his radical rhetoric, especially as it was denounced by the Milošević media, would not win him the presidency.[195] Ultimately Drašković's new tone only served to alienate the hard-line nationalists who had supported him, without managing to convince his critics. Meanwhile, as Dobrica Ćosić had promised, the leaderships of the Serbian Democratic Parties in Croatia and Bosnia-Hercegovina openly backed the regime—thus showing who the 'remnants of a slaughtered people' considered to be their true protector.[196]

Milošević's 'moderation' in the contest with Drašković was balanced by his 'patriotism' vis-à-vis the 'pro-Yugoslav' parts of the opposition, which were widely and relentlessly accused of being traitors to the Serbian nation. By September 1990, therefore, even the Democratic Party moved closer to the position of the Socialists and the Renewal Movement concerning the idea of 'all Serbs in one state'. Its revised party programme stated that—although it still favoured the maintenance of the Yugoslav federation—if other republics insisted on leaving, 'the national policy of the Serbian state would, exactly as other national states, aim towards the incorporation of all territories predominantly inhabited by Serbs into one state'.[197] As Praxist Ljubomir Tadić noted in an interview, by December 1990 it was clear that 'all opposition parties in Serbia, except UJDI [and the Reform Forces], agree that the Serbian nation should live in one state'.[198]

[193]Quoted in Djukić, *Izmedju slave i anateme*, op. cit., p. 160.
[194]In ibid., loc. cit.
[195]In October 1990, Drašković thus stated that his party was in favour of maintaining the Yugoslav federation and that it would favour internal border changes only if the 'confederal' option won out (in Radulović and Spaić, op. cit., pp. 68–9).
[196]See *NIN*, 6 Dec. 1990.
[197]*Program Demokratske stranke*, Belgrade, 1990, p. 7.
[198]*Duga*, 20 Dec. 1990–5 Jan. 1991, p. 12.

Aside from the fact that an anti-nationalist party had little chance of success in a context of generalised nationalist mobilisation, three main problems made the Alliance of Reform Forces particularly vulnerable to criticism: first, the party was only created in summer 1990, after the elections in Slovenia and Croatia, allowing the regime to present it as a tactical move, meant to break Serbian unity; second, it had in its ranks many former communists who had belonged to the unpopular Stambolić party faction defeated in the Eighth Session and who had already been branded as representatives of the policy of 'weak Serbia, strong Yugoslavia'; and, finally, it looked for support to national minorities, including the Kosovo Albanians, without managing to persuade them to participate in the elections (and thus losing a large base of support) while opening itself up to the accusation of trying to create an anti-Serbian bloc to govern Serbia.[199] Remaining loyal to its 'Yugoslavist' position and arguing that the key issue for Serbs—as for everyone else—was to live in a democratic state (or states) rather than a national one, the Alliance also did not present any real solution on how to manage the federation's disintegration, which by December 1990 appeared inevitable.[200]

Without a clear alternative to Milošević's national programme, faced with a context of worsening inter-ethnic relations and a polarisation of ever-more entrenched positions of the republican leaderships, as well as with a powerful political adversary unwilling to play by the rules of a real democratic contest, the Serbian opposition lost its last real means by which it could hope to defeat the ruling party—unity. In the words of journalist Slavoljub Djukić:

What Tito had never managed to do, Milošević achieved: he broke the once united intellectual opposition. Former friends became determined adversaries. Former political allies, united in their opposition to the communist leadership,

---

[199]For these critiques, see *NIN*, 3 Aug. 1990, pp. 10–13, and Radulović and Spaić, op. cit., pp. 86–7.

[200]In March 1991, UJDI and the Reform Forces issued their 'New Programme of Reform', in which they acknowledged that some republics wanted to leave the federation. They argued that changing borders would inevitably lead to war and, in their eyes, Serbia's 'national interest' was democracy rather than a state of all Serbs (in *Republika*, III/16, 16 March 1991, pp. 6–8). Paradoxically a similar stance was taken by some of the best known Serbian 'nationalists'; artist Mića Popović and literary critic Borislav Mihajlović-Mihiz both argued that Serbia needed to become an independent state, even at the cost of maintaining its existing borders. (See the interviews with Popović interview in *Delo*, 30 Sept. 1989, in Gaće, op. cit., pp. 201–2, and Mihajlović-Mihiz in *Intervju*, 26 Oct. 1990, p. 13.)

now declared themselves as socialists, monarchists, Chetniks, democrats, greater Serbian nationalists and advocates of Yugoslav civil society. Ideologically disunited, unstable and susceptible, with competitive leadership ambitions, the opposition was an easy chunk to swallow for Milošević.[201]

The problem of factionalisation and splintering, which was to plague the Serbian opposition for the whole of the Milošević era, affected all three political formations—the right, the left and the centre.[202] The Serbian Renewal Movement lost most of its initial founders when Drašković transformed himself into a 'peace-promoter' and was accused of 'selling out' the Serbs outside Serbia. The most important split took place in June 1990, when former dissident Vojislav Šešelj, who stayed true to his extreme right-wing nationalism, broke away from his earstwhile friend and created the Chetnik Movement (which transformed itself to the Serbian Radical Party in February 1991).[203] The left was divided from the start between several smaller parties, the most important of which was the Alliance of Reform Forces. The most prone to splintering was the centrist and ideologically heterogenous Democratic Party, which lost members on both its left and right wings over questions of national policy and membership in wider opposition coalitions.[204]

In the run-up to Serbia's first multi-party election in December 1990, the main dilemma for the opposition was whether to go forward and participate in what promised to be anything but a real democratic contest, or to boycott it, thus preventing the stamp of legitimacy from gracing Milošević's rule. Although the opposition parties managed to muster up enough unity to stage a rally in September, demanding genuinely democratic conditions for the election campaign and threatening a boycott if Milošević did not comply within ten days, by the time their ultimatum expired, they had lost their resolve and

---

[201]Djukić, *Izmedju slave i anateme*, op. cit., p. 161.

[202]For the splits in the opposition parties see Stefanović, op. cit., and Thomas, op. cit.

[203]For a collection of Šešelj's opinions and ideas, see his *Razaranja srpskog nacionalnog bića*, Belgrade, 1992.

[204]These were the defection of a group of its left-wing intellectuals in autumn 1990, who then created the short-lived Democratic Forum, followed by two important splits led by its founders Kosta Čavoški and Nikola Milošević in 1991 and Vojislav Koštunica in 1992 to create the Serbian Liberal Party and the Democratic Party of Serbia respectively. At the end of 1993 the party splintered again, when Zoran Djindjić became its new leader and former party president Dragoljub Mićunović left to found the Democratic Centre (see Thomas, op. cit., pp. 59–62).

become disunited among public quarrelling and mutual accusations of collaboration with the regime. A further attempt at presenting a united front after losing the first round of the elections was as short-lived as it was ineffective.[205]

The events following the opposition rally of 9 March 1991 presented a last glimmer of hope before Yugoslavia's final breakdown. The Serbian leadership's crackdown on the demonstration and the concurrent arrest of its leader Vuk Drašković—in an unsuccessful attempt to provoke a state of emergency and a military coup in Yugoslavia[206]—sparked mass public resistance in Serbia's capital, as students joined the political opposition in demanding Drašković's release, freedom of the press and the resignation of the chief editors of the government-controlled media and the Serbian Minister of the Interior. A number of Serbia's foremost intellectuals who had refrained from joining the opposition so far—such as Matija Bećković, Borislav Mihajlović-Mihiz, Dragoslav Mihailović, Pavle Ivić, Predrag Palavestra and Slobodan Selenić—and representatives of the Serbian Orthodox Church joined the protest. As the crowd chanted 'Sloba-Saddam' and 'Sloba-Stalin' and called for Milošević's resignation, it seemed once again that the regime's time was up.[207]

And again, Milošević's weakness appeared to be an illusion. Although Belgrade had returned to its former role as the 'hotbed of opposition', provincial Serbia, intoxicated by the official media, remained loyal to the regime, as did most of the workers and the older and less educated social strata. Until well into the wars of the Yugoslav succession, Milošević also received support from the leaders of the Serbs in Croatia and Bosnia-Hercegovina.[208] Finally, Milošević, the

---

[205]The final election results were: 44.1% for Milošević's Socialist party (SPS), 15.8% for Drašković's Renewal Movement (SPO) and only 7.4% for Mićunović's Democratic Party (DS). Thanks to the majoritarian electoral law, the SPS captured 194 of the 250 seats in the Parliament, the SPO 19 and the DS 7. Milošević won the Presidency with 65.3% of the vote; Vuk Drašković, his most serious contender, received only 16.4%. For a complete analysis, see Vladimir Goati (ed.), *Elections to the Federal and Republican Parliaments of Yugoslavia {Serbia and Montenegro} 1990–1996. Analyses, Documents and Data*, Berlin, 1998.

[206]See Silber and Little, op. cit., pp. 119–28, and B. Jović, *Poslednji dani SFRJ*, op. cit., pp. 283–94.

[207]In *Borba*, 19 March 1991. 'Sloba' was Slobodan Milošević's nickname in Serbia.

[208]During the events of 9–11 March 1991 Radovan Karadžić, president of the Serbian Democratic Party of Bosnia-Hercegovina, openly declared his 'full support' for Milošević and the Serbian government 'in their efforts to ensure the safety of

master-tactician, managed to maintain his hold on power by granting just enough concessions to stop the opposition's mobilisation from spreading but never enough to really threaten him. In March 1991 he thus gave in to the opposition's demands to release Drašković, call back the tanks and replace some of his *apparatchiks* in the Serbian government and media, without making any substantive changes to the way the republic or its media were run.[209] When, in June 1991, the 'United Serbian Democratic Opposition' acknowledged that Milošević had not fundamentally met any of its demands, the energy of the Belgrade uprising had already been spent and the political opposition was disunited once again.

With this final defeat of the opposition in the streets, following its loss at the polls, Milošević's power was now firmly embedded in Serbia. The 'revolutionary' period was over, but it had not produced either of the former critical intelligentsia's goals—democracy or national unity. The Yugoslav wars of succession that were just beginning would take the Serbs further and further away from both.

Serbia's citizens and the Serbian nation as a whole' (quoted in *Borba*, 19 March 1991, p. 7). Babić, the leader of the SDS in Croatia, also condemned the opposition (*NIN*, 22 March 1991, pp. 17–18).

[209]The individuals who resigned from their media directors' and government positions were simply replaced by other cadres loyal to Milošević and the initial appearance of greater media freedom soon dissipated.

CONCLUSION

In the autumn of 2000, twelve years after Milošević's 'happening of the people', Serbia's opposition achieved what many thought was never going to happen: it defeated Milošević first in the polls and then in the street. Over the course of the 1990s war, deprivation, corruption and international isolation, culminating in the NATO bombing of Serbia in 1999, had eroded Milošević's popularity and forced the regime to resort to increasing repression and more open authoritarianism. In a situation marked by uncertainty and extremely low living standards, Milošević's increasingly autistic rhetoric about resisting the dangers of America's imperialist 'New World Order' signalled the perpetuation of Serbia's poverty and isolation. For the first time Serbs saw change as both imperative and less risky than the maintenance of the *status quo*.[1] The opposition finally put aside its quarrels and petty leadership ambitions and united behind a candidate who had not discredited himself in the past by engaging in the rampant corruption or entering into unsavoury deals with the regime, and who promised to take Serbia out of its dismal situation without compromising its national interests.[2]

For the country's new leaders Vojislav Koštunica, President of

---

[1] This point was made by Susan Woodward in her lecture on 'Stages of the Revolution in Federal Republic of Yugoslavia', School of Slavonic and European Studies, University College London, 31 Oct. 2000. On the evolution of the Milošević regime, see Cohen, *Serpent in the Bosom*, op. cit.

[2] On Serbia's democratic revolution, see Ivana Spasić and Milan Subotić (eds), *Revolucija i poredak. O dinamici promena u Srbiji*, Belgrade, 2001, and Dragan Bujošević and Ivan Radovanović, *5. Oktobar. Dvadeset četiri sata prevrata*, (3rd edn) Belgrade, 2001.

Yugoslavia, and Zoran Djindjić, Prime Minister of Serbia, the revolution of October 2000 marked the end of more than twenty years in opposition, first as members of the Belgrade critical intelligentsia and then as opposition party leaders. They now need to tackle the formidable task of reversing the economic, political and social catastrophe produced by Milošević's misguided and reckless policies, compounded by decades of communist mismanagement. They also face the still unresolved national question, which—as this book has argued—was not 'invented' or 'imagined' either by intellectuals or by Milošević in the 1980s, but is the structural legacy of the region's historical development and the Yugoslav communists' federal division of the country's territory. Although the Yugoslav wars of succession have altered this structural reality to some degree, drastically reducing the proportion both of Serbs outside and of non-Serbs inside Serbia, there are still several outstanding issues that new government will have to resolve: the future of the post-1992 Yugoslav federation made up of Serbia and Montenegro; Serbia's relations with the Serbian 'entity' in Bosnia-Herzegovina; and the final status of Kosovo, which is still *de jure* if not *de facto* a part of Yugoslavia. Considering its failure in the 1980s, what is the likelihood that the former opposition will now find a genuinely democratic solution to the national question? I would argue that the same factors that determined the trajectory of the Belgrade critical intelligentsia in the 1980s remain relevant today.

The analysis presented in this book indicates, first of all, that the vocabulary, choice of themes and underlying premises which inform the worldview articulated by intellectuals (as well as by the media and political elites) are just as important, if not more so, than their putative commitment to democratic practices. In the 1980s the intellectual opposition's solutions to the national question mostly remained moderate and pro-Yugoslav, though full of contradictions over the shape of its envisioned 'third' Yugoslavia. At no point during this period did the intelligentsia's programme appeal to 'Greater Serbian hegemony', a sense of racial superiority or the desire for territorial conquest; nor did it contain a 'blueprint' for war or a call for 'ethnic cleansing', as has so often been claimed. Nevertheless, the discourse that emerged and became predominant in the intellectual opposition—with its focus on the Serbs' 'history of victimisation' and conspiracy theories of a 'stab in the back' and continuous 'genocide' by other Yugoslav nations—was profoundly anti-Yugoslav and inherently at odds with the pursuit of negotiation and compromise, which would have formed the basis of any democratic solution to the national question. Indeed, it made the use of force in defence of 'the nation under threat' both more logical and more acceptable.

In addition to the importance of discourse in shaping political processes, this book has sought to show that the rise of extreme nationalism is context-specific and relational, rather than historically immutable and isolated. In the Serbian case it grew out of the particular conditions of the post-Tito decade, marked by a deep and all-encompassing crisis and apparent failure of communist Yugoslavia as a state. Three related ways in which Yugoslavia's crisis manifested itself were especially important in the elaboration and spread of the nationalist discourse of victimisation within the intellectual opposition. First, there was the problem of the 'unsurmounted past', combined with the presence of traumatic historical memory. The restrictions and ideological myths that the communist regime had imposed on both research and discussion of the distintegration of the first Yugoslav state, the internal national differences that had plagued not only the 'bourgeois' political parties but also the illegal communist movement, and—what was most important for Serbs—the scale and causes of Serbian mass extermination in the wartime Independent State of Croatia provided the ideological space for the articulation of interpretations that were woven together into the historical narrative of national victimisation.

Secondly, Yugoslavia's regime—despite its 'Western' trappings and greater tolerance of dissent—was an essentially illiberal regime, in which breaches of human and civil rights were endemic. For Serbs in the 1980s this problem concerned primarily the allegations of mistreatment and forced Serbian emigration from Kosovo. Without publicly controlled institutions to investigate such grievances and enforce respect for human rights, exaggeration and hearsay became widespread and were easily integrated into the emerging vision of national victimisation. The regime's precedent of substituting territorial autonomy and 'statehood' for genuine democratisation in the 1970s also contributed to turning the issue of human rights into a call for collective entitlements and national control over territory: for the Serbian intellectual opposition, as for the Albanian, protection of human rights was indistinguishable from the demand for statehood. Finally, without supranational state institutions specifically devoted to the defence of human rights, it was easy for those who opposed the constitutional changes that Serbs were demanding to deny the existence of any human rights problem in the first place—which in turn fuelled the stories of nationalist collusion against Serbia.

Thirdly, the trajectory of the Belgrade critical intelligentsia shows that nationalisms do not develop in isolation, but interact with each other to produce a spiral of radicalisation. Since 1918 such a 'dialectical' relationship existed primarily between Serbian and Croatian nationalism, reappearing in the Tito era with the 'language debate' of 1967. The repression in Croatia after 1971 pushed Croatian nationalism underground and essentially 'froze' this relationship until the late 1980s, when it resumed in more radical form. A similar interaction existed between Serbian and Albanian nationalism, fueled on both sides by a history of conflict, marked by periods of national oppression of one side by the other. In addition to these two longer standing relationships, in the 1980s, it was particularly the rise of Slovenian nationalism that fanned the feelings of betrayal and injustice which underlay Serbian nationalist discourse—precisely because the Serbs considered Slovenes as traditional allies in Yugoslavia, with whom they had never had any territorial disputes or minority problems.

The new Yugoslav government brought to power in 2000 has, up till the time of going to press, succeeded in avoiding the extreme nationalism of the previous fifteen years, in terms of both discursive practices and policy: neither Vojislav Koštunica nor Zoran Djindjić, the two political leaders of post-Milošević Serbia, have resorted to the rhetoric of victimisation and conspiracy theories that were so characteristic of the 1980s and Milošević's rule. In August 2000 Koštunica summed up the main message of the Democratic Opposition's electoral campaign:

There is no great emphasis on the state, on national interests or Serbism. Our problem simply consists in whether we are going to live in a normal state like the rest of the world or not ... I call for things that do not exist in our public life: normal dialogue, tolerance, the exclusion of revanchism, verbal abuse and hate speech.[3]

Both Djindjić and Koštunica have adopted some questionable gestures in the past, such as Djindjić's visit to the Bosnian Serb leadership when NATO issued its ultimatum for the withdrawal of artillery around Sarajevo and Koštunica's photograph brandishing an automatic gun at the onset of conflict in Kosovo. Since coming to power, however, their approach to the national question has been moderate and rational.

While Djindjić tends to concentrate on economic issues and makes

[3]Interview in *Vreme*, 12 Aug. 2000, p. 7.

few declarations concerning matters of nation and state, it is Koštunica who, as President of Yugoslavia, focuses on the national question. Koštunica has admitted that he is a nationalist—'obsessed' with the fact that the Serbs are entering the new millennium without a state— yet he is adamant that this state can only be 'democratic and legal'.[4] He has declared respect for Montenegro's 'strong state tradition' and is flexible on the internal arrangement that should regulate relations between the two republics.[5] Although he has been critical of the Montenegrin government's desire for independence, he has repeatedly affirmed that if a referendum decided against union with Serbia, its choice would be respected. Regarding Kosovo and the Albanian question, he advocates a policy based on 'realism' and cooperation with Europe and the United States, despite his bitterness about the NATO intervention of 1999. When in 2001 the Yugoslav government used force to put down the Albanian rebellion in southern Serbia, it acted with restraint, under the supervision of the international community, and continued with its efforts to find a negotiated political solution. Although Koštunica insists on the fact that, under Resolution 1244 of the United Nations Security Council, Kosovo is still formally a part of the Federal Republic of Yugoslavia, he recognises that 'Kosovo is not under our sovereignty, but under that of the international community.'[6] His government's priority has been to ensure the safe return of the Serbs expelled after June 1999, and its encouragement of Kosovo Serbs to vote in the province's November 2001 legislative elections was a sign that it considers the safety and human rights of Serbs as more important than Yugoslavia's 'state right' to Kosovo. As for Bosnia, Koštunica has never hidden the fact that he hopes for a loose union of all Serbian states in the future and will seek close relations with the Republika Srpska. Nevertheless, the Yugoslav government has formally recognised Bosnia-Herzegovina as an independent state and has vowed to respect the Dayton Agreement, along with all the international obligations entered into by Milošević.

In the end, however, Serbia's ability to shed permanently the extreme nationalism that produced Milošević's belligerent and aggressive policy will hinge on the same three contextual factors that influenced its initial rise in the 1980s: the process of 'coming to terms with the past', the building of institutions and mechanisms to deal with questions

[4]Interview in *Vreme*, 14 Dec. 2000, pp. 19–20.
[5]Ibid., p. 21.
[6]Interview in *Danas*, 16–17 Sept. 2000.

of human rights, and the successful concurrent de-radicalisation of all regional nationalisms. The process of 'coming to terms with the past' is inevitably a long-term one, but the experience of communist Yugoslavia shows that the sooner it is begun the less space there will be for the perpetuation of national myths, conspiracy theories and exaggeration. For this process to be constructive, it is imperative that it treat no subject as taboo, be analytical rather than ideological or simply polemical, and be undertaken in the form of an intra-regional dialogue. In this respect, internationally sponsored efforts at reestablishing scholarly debate across state borders are a positive step,[7] as is the setting up in Serbia of a 'Truth and Reconciliation Commission'—although it remains to be seen whether this body manages to escape from simply becoming a tool of 'decommunisation' or 'intra-national reconciliation'.

The severe violations of human rights that characterised the wars of Yugoslav succession have made it all the more imperative to create institutions and mechanisms that will instill a sense of personal security and confidence. While the enforcement of human rights is no panacea for the region's more complex questions of political representation, statehood and the nature of intra-national links across state borders, it is the *sine qua non* of any successful discussion of these issues. At the very least it will enable the de-coupling of debates on (individual) human rights and (collective) minority and national rights. In this regard, Serbian nationalism will be influenced particularly by the treatment of Serbs remaining in Kosovo, Bosnia and Croatia. Considering that both Bosnia and Kosovo are going to be international protectorates for the foreseeable future, it is the international community that will have to act as the guarantor of the Serbs' human rights—a task it has not hitherto mastered with much success.

Finally, the 'de-radicalisation' of nationalism in the region will clearly take time, but recent trends in Serbia and Croatia have been promising. Like its Serbian counterpart, the post-Tudjman Croatian government has shed the extreme nationalist discourse predominant since the late 1980s and is beginning to engage in its own process of 'coming to terms with the past' and making Croatia a 'normal' democratic state.

---

[7]The most important project of this kind has been the 'Croatian-Serbian Historians' Dialogue' sponsored by the Friedrich Naumann Stiftung, which has taken place regularly since November 1998. The results of these meetings have been published in Hans-Georg Fleck and Igor Graovac (eds), *Dijalog povjesničara-istoričara*, (vols I–IV), Zagreb 2000–1.

Serbs and Croats are establishing new links on all levels and, while they are unlikely to ever achieve consensus on the causes of their conflicts in the 20th century, they may at least find ways of articulating their experiences in a more tolerant and less volatile manner. The Hungarian intellectual István Bibó noted in 1946 at the end of another bloody war that destroyed the region:

Being a democrat means, primarily, not being afraid; not being afraid of those who have differing opinions, speak different languages, or belong to other races; not being afraid of revolutions, conspiracies, the unknown malicious intent of enemies, hostile propaganda, being demeaned, or any of those imaginary dangers that become truly dangerous *because we are afraid of them.*[8]

If Serbs and Croats succeed in laying their fears to rest, they will finally have set a positive precedent in the search for a democratic solution to the region's lingering national question.

---

[8]István Bibó, 'The Distress of the East European Small States' in Károly Nagy (ed.), *István Bibó. Democracy, Revolution, Self-Determination. Selected Writings*, Boulder, CO, 1991, p. 42 (Bibó's emphasis).

BIBLIOGRAPHY

INTERVIEWS

ANDJUS, Radoslav, biologist, Serbian Academy of Sciences and Arts (SANU) member; Belgrade, 21 Apr. 1992.

BATAKOVIĆ, Dušan, historian; Paris, 20 June 1992.

BEĆKOVIĆ, Matija, poet, SANU member; London, 1 Dec. 1997.

ČAVOŠKI, Kosta, jurist; Belgrade, 24 Apr. 1992.

ĆIRKOVIĆ, Sima, historian, SANU member; Belgrade, 17 Apr. 2000.

ČOLOVIĆ, Ivan, ethnologist; Belgrade, 22 March 1994.

ĆOSIĆ, Dobrica, writer, SANU member; Belgrade, 25 March 1994 and 20 Apr. 2000.

DANOJLIĆ, Milovan, writer; Paris 17 Apr. 1992.

DJILAS, Milovan, writer; Belgrade, 16 March 1994.

DJUKIĆ, Slavoljub, journalist; Belgrade, 16 March 1994.

DJURIĆ, Ivan, historian; Paris, 17 Jan., 30 Jan. and 18 March 1992.

KRESTIĆ, Vasilije, historian, SANU member; Belgrade, 22 Apr. 1992.

LADJEVIĆ, Petar, sociologist; London, 22 Feb. 1998.

MIHAILOVIĆ, Kosta, economist, SANU member; Belgrade, 24 Apr. 1992.

MITROVIĆ, Andrej, historian, SANU member; Belgrade, 17 Apr. 2000.

PALAVESTRA, Predrag, literary historian, SANU member; London, 12 Aug.1997.

PERIŠIĆ, Miodrag, writer, editor-in-chief of *Književne Novine* (1983–93); Belgrade, 22 and 23 Apr. 1992.

PETRANOVIĆ, Branko, historian; Belgrade, 22 Apr. 1992.

POPOV, Nebojša, sociologist; Belgrade, 19 Apr. 2000.

SELENIĆ, Slobodan, writer, SANU member; Belgrade, 24 Apr. 1992.

SIMIĆ, Mirko, immunologist, SANU member; Belgrade, 22 Apr. 1992.

SLAPŠAK, Svetlana, philologist; Paris, 17 Dec. 1993.

STOJANOVIĆ, Lazar, cinematographer; London, 28 Feb. 1998.

STOJANOVIĆ, Svetozar, philosopher; by e-mail, 21–23 August. 1999.

262 *Bibliography*

TADIĆ, Ljubomir, philosopher, SANU member; Belgrade, 24 Apr. 1992.
TRGOVČEVIĆ, Ljubinka, historian; Belgrade, 19 Apr. 2000.
VEJVODA, Ivan, political scientist; Belgrade, 22 Apr. 1992.

DOCUMENTS, COLLECTIONS OF DOCUMENTS

Amnesty International. *Yugoslavia: Prisoners of Conscience*. London: Amnesty
International Publications, 1985.
BELIĆ, Dragan and Djuro BILBIJA (eds), *Srbija i Slovenija. Od Cankarevog
Doma do 'Jugoalata' i Gazimestana*. Belgrade: Tera, 1989.
*Četrnaesta sednica CK SK Srbije: Savez Komunista u borbi za nacionalnu
ravnopravnost, maj 1968*. Belgrade: NIP 'Komunist', 1968.
'A Concept for the Constitutional System of Yugoslavia on a Federal Basis',
Yugoslav Survey, XXXI/4, 1990, pp. 13–25.
Constitution of the Federal People's Republic of Yugoslavia, 31 January 1946
(excerpts) in TRIFUNOVSKA, Snežana (ed.), *Yugoslavia Through
Documents. From its Creation to its Dissolution*. Dordrecht: Nijhoff, 1994,
pp. 212–24.
The Constitution of the Republic of Serbia. Belgrade: Secretariat for Information
of the Republic of Serbia, 1990.
*The Constitution of the Socialist Federal Republic of Yugoslavia: Constitutional
Amendments*. Belgrade: Prosveta, 1969.
*The Constitution of the Socialist Federal Republic of Yugoslavia, Promulgated on 21
February 1974*. Belgrade: Secretariat of the Federal Assembly Information
Service, 1974.
'Constitutional declaration Adopted by the Kosovo Assembly, 2 July 1990'
in AUERSWALD, Philip E. and David P. (eds), *The Kosovo Conflict: A
Diplomatic History Through Documents*. Cambridge, MA/The Hague:
Kluwer Law International, 2000.
'Deklaracija o nazivu i položaju hrvatskog književnog jezika', *Hrvatska revija*,
XVII/1–2, 1967, pp. 15–18.
Demokratska Stranka, 'Program i Statut'. Belgrade: Demokratska stranka,
1990.
———, 'O osnovnim pitanjima nacionalnog i ekonomskog programa'.
Belgrade: Demokratska stranka, 15 Sept. 1990.
Demokratski forum, 'Tri Deklaracije'. Belgrade: Inicijativni odbor Demokrat-
skog foruma, 1990.
———, 'Načela demokratskog ustava. Ustavna deklaracija Demokratskog
Foruma'. Belgrade: Demokratski Forum, 19 June 1990.
'Dissent Since Tito: A Collection of Documents': *Review of the Study Centre
for Jugoslav Affairs*, II/5: pp. 409–96.
DJILAS, Aleksa and Vane IVANOVIĆ (eds), *Zbornik o ljudskim pravima*. London:
Naša reč, 1983.
Godišnjak Srpske Akademije nauka i umetnosti. XCII for 1985 and XCIII for
1986, Belgrade: SANU, 1986 and 1987.

Hrvatska demokratska zajednica, 'Programska deklaracija', *Naše teme*, XXXIV/ 3–4, pp. 699–704.

Hrvatska socijalno liberalna stranka, 'Programska načela', *Naše teme*, XXXIV/ 3–4, pp. 716–17.

JOSIĆ VIŠNJIĆ, Miroslav (ed.), *Saopštenja, zapisnici i pisma Odbora za zaštitu umetničke slobode pri beogradskoj sekciji pisaca u Udruženju književnika Srbije*. Belgrade: author's edition, 1984.

'Memorandum of the Serbian Academy of Sciences and Arts' in Kosta Mihajlović and Vasilije Krestić (eds), *Memorandum of the Serbian Academy of Sciences and Arts: Answers to Criticisms*. Belgrade, SANU, 1995, pp. 93–140.

'Motion for the Adoption of a New Constitution of the SFRY' and 'Proposal of the Presidency of SR Slovenia Concerning the Federation and Federal System', *Yugoslav Survey*, 1/1990, pp. 3–24.

Odbor za odbranu slobode misli i izražavanja. Dokumenti i saopštenja 1984–1986. Belgrade: authors' edition, 1986.

O nekim idejnim i političkim tendencijama u umjetničkom stvaralaštvu, književnoj, kazališnoj i filmskoj kritici, te o javnim istupima jednog broja kulturnih stvaralaca u kojima su sadržane politički neprihvatljive poruke. Zagreb: Centar CK SKH za informiranje i propagandu, 21 March 1984, reprinted in *Intervju*, (special edn no. 11), 10 May 1989.

'Predlog slovenačkih pisaca: republički ustav'. *Književne novine*, 755, 1 June 1988, p. 17.

'Prilog javnoj raspravi o ustavu'. *Književne novine*, 751, 1 Apr. 1988, pp. 1–4.

'Prispevki za slovenski nacionalni program'. *Nova revija*, VI/57, 1987.

'Proposal for Consideration', in SPALATIN, Christopher, 'Serbo-Croatian or Serbian and Croatian? Considerations on the Croatian Declaration and the Serbian Proposal of March 1967', *Journal of Croatian Studies*, VII–VIII, 1966–7, pp. 10–11.

'Samostojna Slovenija', *Nova revija*, IX/95, March 1990.

Slovenska demokratična zveza, 'Programme statement'. *South Slav Journal*, XI/4, winter 1988–9, p. 61.

SPASOJEVIĆ, Svetislav (ed.), *Slučaj Martinović*. Belgrade: Partizanska knjiga, 1986.

Srpska demokratska stranka, 'Programski ciljevi'. *Naše teme*, XXXIV/3–4: pp. 774–81.

Srpsko pitanje danas. Kongresni materijal, Second Congress of Serbian Intellectuals, Belgrade, 22–23 Apr. 1994. Belgrade: Srpski sabor, Matica Srba i iseljenika Srbije, Udruženje univerzitetskih profesora i naučnika Srbije, Odbor SANU za nacionalno pitanje, Udruženje Srba iz RS Krajine i Hrvatske, Crnogorski sabor srpske sloge, Udruženje Srba iz BiH u Srbiji, 1994.

The Truth on Kosova. Tirana: Academy of Sciences of the Republic of Albania, 1993.

Udruženje za jugoslavensku demokratsku inicijativu, 'Manifest za jugoslavensku demokratsku inicijativu', *Naše teme*, XXXIV/3–4; pp. 787–8.

Ustav Republike Hrvatske, Zagreb: Narodne novine, 1991.

'1938 Convention Regulating the Emigration of the Turkish Population From the Region in Southern Serbia in Yugoslavia', in Robert ELSIE (ed.), *Kosovo in the Heart of the Powder Keg*, Boulder, CO: East European Monographs, 1997, pp. 425–34.

IX Kongres Saveza Književnika Jugoslavije. Dokumenta. Novi Sad, 18–20 april 1985. Novi Sad: Kniževna zajednica, 1985.

PRESS AND PERIODICALS

Anali Pravnog Fakulteta u Beogradu
Borba
Časovnik, I/1, autumn 1979: (only issue of banned *samizdat* literary journal)
Corriere della Sera
Danas (Belgrade)
Danas (Zagreb)
Delo
Demokratija
Demokratija danas
Dialogue (France)
Duga
The Economist Intelligence Unit
Hrvatska revija (Argentina)
Intervju
Journal of Croatian Studies (US)
Književna reč
Književne novine
Književnost
Književna kritika
Komunist
Le Monde
Naša borba
Naša reč (UK)
Naše teme
Nedeljne informativne novine (NIN)
Neue Zürcher Zeitung
New York Times
Nova Hrvatska (Germany)
Nova revija
Oko
Oslobodjenje
Osmica
Pogledi
Politika
Politika ekspres

Politika International Weekly
Pravoslavlje
Radio Free Europe / Radio Liberty Research Report
Report on Eastern Europe
Republika
Review of the Study Centre for Jugoslav Affairs (UK)
South Slav Journal (UK)
Der Spiegel
Srpska reč
Start
Stav
Theoria
The Times
Večernji list
Večernje novosti
Vjesnik
Vreme

UNPUBLISHED DISSERTATIONS AND PAPERS

BEHSCHNITT, Wolfgang, 'Nationalismus bei Serben und Kroaten 1830–1914. Analyse und Typologie der nationalen Ideologie'. PhD, Faculty of Philosophy, University of Cologne, 1976.

BUDDING, Audrey Helfant. 'Serb Intellectuals and the National Question'. PhD, Department of History, Harvard University, 1998.

———. 'End of Dialogue: Serbs, Slovenes and the Collapse of the League of Writers of Yugoslavia'. Unpublished paper.

DJOKIĆ, Dejan. 'The Second World War II: Reconciliation among Serbs and Croats and Irreconciliation of Yugoslavia'. Unpublished paper.

JOVIĆ, Dejan. 'The Breakdown of Elite Ideological Consensus: The Prelude to the Disintegration of Yugoslavia'. PhD, Department of Government, London School of Economics and Political Science, 2000.

VUJAČIĆ, Veljko Marko. 'Communism and Nationalism in Russia and Serbia'. PhD, Department of Sociology, University of California at Berkeley, 1995.

BOOKS

ALEXANDER, Stella. *Church and State in Yugoslavia since 1945*. Cambridge University Press, 1979.

ALLCOCK, John. *Explaining Yugoslavia*. London: Hurst, 2000.

ALTER, Peter. *Nationalism*. London: Edward Arnold, 1989.

ANDERSON, Benedict. *Imagined Communities. Reflections on the Origin and Spread of Nationalism*. London/New York: Verso, 1991.

ANŽULOVIĆ, Branimir. *Heavenly Serbia*. London: Hurst, 1999.

266 Bibliography

ARSIĆ, Mirko and Dragan R. MARKOVIĆ. '68. Studentski bunt i društvo. Belgrade: Istraživačko-izdavački centar SSO Srbije, 1988.

BANAC, Ivo. The National Question in Yugoslavia: Origins, History, Politics. Ithaca, NY: Cornell University Press, 1984.

————. With Stalin against Tito. Ithaca, NY: Cornell University Press, 1988.

————, John G. ACKERMAN and Roman SZPORLUK (eds), Nation and Ideology: Essays in Honor of Wayne S. Vucinich. Boulder, CO: East European Monographs, 1981.

BATAKOVIĆ, Dušan. The Kosovo Chronicles. Belgrade: Plato, 1992.

BAUMAN, Zygmunt. Legislators and interpreters: on modernity, post-modernity, and intellectuals. Cambridge: Polity, 1987.

BELOFF, Nora. Tito's Flawed Legacy. Yugoslavia and the West, 1939–1984. London: Gollancz, 1985.

BENDA, Julien. La trahison des clercs. (1927) Paris: Grasset, 1975.

BENDERLY, Jill, and Evan KRAFT (eds), Independent Slovenia: Origins, Movements, Prospects. London: Macmillan, 1994.

BLAGOJEVIĆ, Marina and Ruža PETROVIĆ, Seobe Srba i Crnogoraca sa Kosova i Metohije. Belgrade: SANU, 1989.

BLAGOJEVIĆ, Slobodan. Tri čiste obične pameti. Belgrade: Radio B92, 1996.

BOBAN, Ljubo. Sporazum Cvetković-Maček. Belgrade: Institut društvenih nauka, 1965.

————. Kontroverze iz povijesti Jugoslavije. Dokumentima i polemikom o temama iz novije povijesti Jugoslavije (vols I–II). Zagreb: Školska knjiga, 1987, 1989.

BODIN, Louis. Les intellectuels. Paris: Presses Universitaires de France, 1962.

BOGAVAC, Dušan. Kako iz beznadja. Belgrade: Multiprint, 1991.

BOGDANOVIĆ, Dimitrije. Knjiga o Kosovu. (1985) Belgrade: Književne novine, 1990.

BOKOVOY, Melissa, Jill A. IRVINE and Carol S. LILLY (eds), State-Society Relations in Yugoslavia. Basingstoke: Macmillan, 1997.

BOŽIĆ, Ivan, Sima ĆIRKOVIĆ, Vladimir DEDIJER, Milorad EKMEČIĆ. Istorija Jugoslavije. Belgrade: Prosveta, 1972.

BOZOKI, Andras (ed.). Intellectuals and Politics in Central Europe. Budapest: Central European University Press, 1999.

BUJOŠEVIĆ, Dragan and Ivan RADOVANOVIĆ. 5 Oktobar. Davadeset četiri sata prevrata. Belgrade: Medija Centar, 2001.

BULAJIĆ, Milan. Ustaški zločin genocida. (vols I–IV). Belgrade: Narodna knjiga, 1989.

BUNJAC, Vladimir. Jeretički Branko Ćopić. Belgrade, Narodna knjiga, 1984.

BURG, Steven L. Conflict and Cohesion in Socialist Yugoslavia. Princeton University Press, 1983.

ČALIĆ, Marie-Janine. Der Krieg in Bosnien-Hercegovina. Ursachen, Konflikt-strukturen, Internationale Lösungsversuche. Frankfurt: Suhrkamp, 1995.

ČAVOŠKI, Kosta. Tito: tehnologija vlasti. Belgrade: Dosije, 1990.

————. Na rubovima srpstva. Srpsko pitanje danas. Belgrade: Tersit, 1995.

———— and Vojislav KOŠTUNICA, *Stranački pluralizam ili monizam. Društveni pokreti i politički sistem u Jugoslaviji 1944–1949*. Belgrade: Institute for Social Sciences, 1983.

CEMOVIĆ, Momčilo. *Djilasovi odgovori*. Belgrade: Svetlostkomerc, 1997.

ĆETKOVIĆ, Nadežda. *Možeš ti to, Vesna, možeš*. Belgrade: Medijska knjižara Krug, 2000.

CHARLE, Christophe. *Naissance des 'intellectuels' 1880–1900*. Paris: Les éditions de Minuit, 1990.

ĆIMIĆ, Esad. *Politika kao sudbina*. Belgrade: Slobodan Mašić, 1982.

COHEN, Lenard J. *The Socialist Pyramid: Elites and Power in Yugoslavia*. Oakville/London: Mosaic Press, 1989.

————. *Broken Bonds. The Disintegration of Yugoslavia*. Boulder, CO: Westview, 1993.

————. *Serpent in the Bosom: The Rise and Fall of Slobodan Milošević*. Boulder, CO: Westview, 2001.

COHEN, Robert S. and Mihailo MARKOVIĆ, *Yugoslavia: The Rise and Fall of Socialist Humanism*. Nottingham: Spokesman, 1975.

ČOVIĆ, Bože (ed.). *Izvori velikosrpske agresije*. Zagreb: August Cesarec/Školska knjiga, 1991.

CLISSOLD, Stephen. *Djilas: The Progress of a Revolutionary*. Hounslow: Maurice Temple Smith, 1983.

ĆOSIĆ, Dobrica. *Vreme smrti* (vols I–IV). Belgrade: Prosveta, 1972, 1975, 1979.

————. *Stvarno i moguće*. (1982) Ljubljana/Zagreb: Cankarjeva založba, 1988.

————. *Grešnik*. Belgrade: BIGZ, 1985.

————. *Otpadnik*. Belgrade: BIGZ, 1986.

————. *Vernik* (vols I–II). Belgrade: BIGZ, 1990.

————. *Srpsko pitanje—demokratsko pitanje*. Belgrade: Politika, 1992.

————. *Promene*. Novi Sad, Dnevnik: 1992.

————. *Piščevi zapisi*, (vols I, 1951–68 and II, 1969–1980). Belgrade: Filip Višnjić, 2000 and 2001.

CRNČEVIĆ, Brana. *Srpska posla*. Belgrade: Litera, 1990.

CROCKER, David A. *Praxis and Democratic Socialism. The Critical Social Theory of Marković and Stojanović*. Atlantic Highlands, NJ: Humanities Press, 1983.

ČUBRILOVIĆ, Vasa. *Istorija političke misli u Srbiji XIX. veka*. Belgrade: Prosveta, 1958.

ČULIĆ, Marinko. *Tudjman. Anatomija neprosvijećenog apsolutizma*. Split: Feral Tribune, 1999.

CURRY, Jane Leftwich (ed.) *Dissent in Eastern Europe*. New York: Praeger, 1983.

CUSHMAN, Thomas and Stjepan G. MEŠTROVIĆ (eds). *This Time We Knew. Western Responses to Genocide in Bosnia*. New York University Press, 1996.

268   Bibliography

DANILOVIĆ, Rajko. *Upotreba neprijatelja. Politička sudjenja 1945–1991 u Jugoslaviji.* Valjevo: Anecija Valjevac, 1993.

DEDIJER, Vladimir. *Novi prilozi za biografiju Josipa Broza Tita* (vol. II). Rijeka: Liburnija, 1981.

———. *Veliki buntovnik Milovan Djilas.* Belgrade: Prosveta, 1991.

DELETANT, Dennis and Harry HANAK (eds). *Historians as Nation-Builders.* London, Macmillan, 1988.

DELLANOI, Gilles and Paul André TAGUIEFF (eds). *Théories du nationalisme.* Paris: Kimé, 1991.

DENITCH, Bogdan. *Limits and Possibilities: The Crisis of Yugoslav Socialism and State Socialist Systems.* Minneapolis: University of Minnesota Press, 1990.

DERETIĆ, Jovan. *Kratka istorija srpske književnosti.* Belgrade: BIGZ, 1990.

DIAMOND, Larry and Marc F. PLATTNER (eds). *Nationalism, Ethnic Conflict and Democracy.* Baltimore: Johns Hopkins University Press, 1994.

DJAKOVIĆ, Spasoje. *Sukobi na Kosovu.* Belgrade: Narodna knjiga, 1984.

DJILAS, Aleksa. *The Contested Country: Yugoslav Unity and Communist Revolution, 1919–1953.* Cambridge, MA: Harvard University Press, 1991.

——— (ed.). *Srpsko pitanje.* Belgrade: Politika, 1991.

DJILAS, Milovan. *The New Class.* New York: Praeger, 1957.

———. *Land Without Justice.* New York: Harcourt, Brace, 1958.

———. *Anatomy of a Moral.* New York: Praeger, 1959.

———. *Conversations With Stalin.* New York: Harcourt, Brace & World, 1962.

———. *The Unperfect Society.* New York, Harcourt Brace & World, 1969.

———. *Memoir of a Revolutionary.* New York: Harcourt Brace Jovanovich, 1973.

———. *Wartime.* New York: Harcourt Brace Jovanovich, 1977.

———. *Tito: mon ami, mon ennemi.* Paris: Fayard, 1980.

———. *Rise and Fall.* New York: Harcourt Brace Jovanovich, 1985.

DJINDJIĆ, Zoran. *Jugoslavija kao nedovršena država.* Novi Sad: Književna zajednica Novog Sada, 1988.

DJOGO, Gojko. *Vunena vremena.* (1981) Belgrade: Srpska književna zadruga/ BIGZ, 1992.

DJORGOVIĆ, Momčilo. *Djilas: vernik i jeretik.* Belgrade: Akvarijus, 1989.

DJUKIĆ, Slavoljub. *Čovek u svom vremenu. Razgovori sa Dobricom Ćosićem.* Belgrade: Filip Višnjić, 1989.

———. *Slom srpskih liberala. Tehnologija politickih obraćuna Josipa Broza.* Belgrade: Filip Višnjić, 1990.

———. *Kako se dogodio vodja. Borbe za vlast u Srbiji posle Josipa Broza.* Belgrade: Filip Višnjić, 1992.

———. *Izmedju slave i anateme. Politička biografija Slobodana Miloševića.* Belgrade: Filip Višnjić, 1994.

———. *On, Ona i Mi.* Belgrade: Radio B92, 1997.

———. *Kraj srpske bajke.* Belgrade: Samizdat B92, 1999.

———. *Lovljenje vetra. Politička ispovest Dobrice Ćosića.* Belgrade: Samizdat B92, 2001.

DJURETIĆ, Veselin, *Saveznici i jugoslovenska ratna drama* (vols I–II). Belgrade: Politika, 1985.

DJURIĆ, Ivan. *Istorija—pribežište ili putokaz?* Sarajevo: Svjetlost, 1990.

DODER, Duško. *The Yugoslavs.* New York: Random House, 1979.

DRAŠKOVIĆ, Vuk. *Sudija.* (1981) Belgrade: Nova Evropa, 1990.

―――. *Nož.* (1982) Belgrade: Nova Evropa, 1990.

―――. *Koekude Srbijo.* (1989) Belgrade: Nova Evropa, 1990.

Druga Srbija. Belgrade: Plato/Beogradski Krug/Borba, 1992.

DUIJZINGS, Ger, Dušan JANJIĆ and Shkelzen MALIQI (eds). *Kosovo-Kosova Confrontation or Coexistence.* Nijmegen: Peace Research Centre, 1997.

DYKER, David A. and Ivan VEJVODA (eds). *Yugoslavia and After: A Study in Fragmentation, Despair and Rebirth.* London: Longman, 1996.

DŽADŽIĆ, Petar. *Nova ustaška država? Od Starčevića do Pavelića i Tudjmana.* Belgrade: Politika, 1991.

EKMEČIĆ, Milorad. *Stvaranje Jugoslavije 1790–1918* (vols I–II). Belgrade: Prosveta, 1989.

―――. *Srbija izmedju srednje Evrope i Evrope.* Belgrade: Politika, 1992.

ELSIE, Robert (ed.). *Kosovo in the Heart of the Power Keg.* Boulder, CO: Westview, 1997.

EMMERT, Thomas A. *Serbian Golgotha: Kosovo 1389.* Boulder, CO: European Monographs, 1989.

FEJTÖ, François. *Histoire des démocraties populaires* (vols I–II). Paris: Seuil, 1952, 1979.

FINK-HAFNER, Danica and John R. ROBBINS (eds). *Making a New Nation: The Formation of Slovenia.* Aldershot: Dartmouth Publishing Co., 1997.

FLECK, Hans-Georg and Igor GRAOVAC (eds). *Dijalog povjesničara—istoričara* (vols I–IV). Zagreb: Friedrich Naumann Stiftung, 2000, 2001.

GAĆE, Nadežda. *Suočavanje sa sudbinom.* Belgrade: Dušan Mrdjenović and Nadežda Gace, 1990.

GARTON ASH, Timothy (ed.). *Freedom for Publishing: Publishing for Freedom: the Central and East European Publishing Project.* Budapest: Central European Press, 1995.

GELLA, Alexander (ed.). *The Intelligentsia and the Intellectuals: Theory, Method and Case Study,* Beverly Hills: Sage, 1976.

GELLNER, Ernest. *Nations and Nationalism.* Oxford: Blackwell, 1983.

GJIDARA, Marc, Mirko GRMEK and Neven SIMAC (eds). *Le nettoyage ethnique. Documents historiques sur une idéologie serbe.* Paris: Fayard, 1993.

GLENNY, Misha. *The Fall of Yugoslavia: The Third Balkan War.* London: Penguin, 1992.

GLIGORIJEVIĆ, Milo. *Odgovor Miće Popovića.* Belgrade: Slobodan Mašić, 1984.

―――. *Slučajna istorija.* Belgrade: BIGZ, 1988.

GLUŠČEVIĆ, Zoran. *Kosovo i nikad kraja ...* Belgrade: Marica Josimčević and Zoran Gluščević, 1989.

GOATI, Vladimir (ed.). *Elections to the Federal and Republican Parliaments of Yugoslavia (Serbia and Montenegro) 1990–1996: Analyses, Documents and Data.* Berlin: Sigma, 1998.

GOLUBOVIĆ, Zagorka (ed.). *Društveni karakter i društvene promene u svetlu nacionalnih sukoba.* Belgrade: Institut za filozofiju i društvenu teoriju/ Filip Višnjić, 1995.

GORDY, Eric. *The Culture of Power in Serbia: Nationalism and the Destruction of Alternatives.* University Park: Pennsylvania State University Press, 1999.

GOULDING, Daniel J. *Liberated Cinema: The Yugoslav Experience.* Bloomington, Indiana University Press, 1985.

GOW, James. *Legitimacy and the Military: The Yugoslav Crisis.* London: Pinter, 1992.

GRAFENAUER, Niko (ed.). *The Case of Slovenia.* Ljubljana: Nova revija, July 1991.

GRIFFITH, William E., (ed.). *Central and Eastern Europe: the Opening Curtain?* Boulder, CO: Westview Press, 1989.

GRUENWALD, Oskar. *The Yugoslav Search for Man: Marxist Humanism in Contemporary Yugoslavia.* South Hadley, MA: J.F. Bergin Publishers, 1983.

────── and Karen ROSENBLUM-CALE (eds). *Human Rights in Yugoslavia.* New York: Irvington Publishers, 1986.

HAWKESWORTH, Celia (ed.). *Literature and Politics in Eastern Europe.* New York: St. Martin's Press, 1992.

HAYDEN, Robert M. *Blueprints for a House Divided: The Constitutional Logic of the Yugoslav Conflicts.* Ann Arbor: Michigan University Press, 2000.

HELD, David. *Models of Democracy.* Cambridge: Polity Press, 1996.

HOBSBAWM, E.J. *Nations and Nationalism since 1780: Programme, Myth, Reality.* Cambridge University Press, 1990.

HOFMAN, Branko. *Noć do jutra.* (1981) Zagreb: Znanje, 1982.

HOLMES, Leslie, *Politics in the Communist World,* Oxford: Clarendon Press, 1986.

HORVAT, Branko. *Kosovsko pitanje.* Zagreb: Globus, 1989.

HROCH, Miroslav. *Social Preconditions of National Revival in Europe.* Cambridge University Press, 1985.

HUDELIST, Darko. *Banket u Hrvatskoj. Prilozi povijesti hrvatskog višestranačja 1989–1990.* Zagreb: Centar za informacije i publicitet, 1991.

IRVINE, Jill A. *The Croat Question: Partisan Politics in the Formation of the Yugoslav State.* Boulder, Westview, 1993.

ISAKOVIĆ, Antonije. *Tren 2.* (1981) Belgrade: Dečje novine, 1988.

──────. *Listovi o Kosovu.* Belgrade: Prosveta, 1990.

──────. *Govori i razgovori.* Gornji Milanovac: Dečje novine, 1990.

IVANOVIĆ, Ivan. *Crveni kralj.* (1969) Belgrade: BIGZ, 1984.

IVIĆ, Pavle. *Srpski narod i njegov jezik.* Belgrade: Srpska književna zadruga, 1986.

JAKŠIĆ, Božidar. *Balkanski paradoksi.* Belgrade: Beogradski krug, 2000.

JANIĆIJEVIĆ, Milosav. *Stvaralačka inteligencija medjuratne Jugoslavije.* Belgrade: Prosveta, 1984.

JANKOVIĆ, Vladeta and Milan (eds). *Drugi - o Mihizu.* Belgrade: Stubovi kulture, 1998.

JELAVICH, Barbara. *History of the Balkans* (vol. II). Cambridge University Press, 1983.

JELAVICH, Charles. *South Slav Nationalisms. Textbooks and Yugoslav Union Before 1914.* Columbus: Ohio State University Press, 1990.

JELIĆ-BUTIĆ, Fikreta. *Ustaše i NDH.* Zagreb: Sveučilišna naklada Liber, 1977.

JENNINGS, Jeremy and Anthony KEMP-WELCH (eds). *Intellectuals in Politics: From the Dreyfus Affair to Salman Rushdie.* London: Routledge, 1997.

JEVTIĆ Miloš. *Živa reč Milorada Ekmečića.* Gornji Milanovac: Dečje novine, 1990.

———. *Istoričari.* Belgrade: Dečje novine, 1992.

JOVANOVIĆ, Slobodan. *Sabrana dela Slobodana Jovanovića* (vols I–XII). Belgrade: BIGZ, 1991.

JOVIĆ, Borisav. *Poslednji dani SFRJ. Izvodi iz dnevnika.* Belgrade: Politika, 1995.

JOVIČIĆ, Miodrag (ed.), *'Jako srpstvo - jaka Jugoslavija'. Izbor članaka iz 'Srpskog glasa', organa Srpskog kulturnog kluba, 1939–1940.* Belgrade: Naučna knjiga, 1991.

JUDAH, Tim. *The Serbs. History, Myth and the Destruction of Yugoslavia.* New Haven and London, Yale University Press, 1997.

JUDT, Tony. *Past Imperfect. French Intellectuals 1944–1956.* Berkeley: University of California Press, 1992.

KAMENKA, Eugene (ed.). *Nationalism. The Nature and Evolution of an Idea.* London: Edward Arnold, 1976.

KAPPELER, Andreas (ed.). *The Formation of National Elites.* New York University Press, 1992.

KARDELJ, Edvard. *The Nations and Socialism.* Belgrade: STP, 1981.

KATICH, Boris (ed.). *So Speak Croatian Dissidents.* Toronto: Zirval, 1983.

KEKEZI, Harillaq and Rexhep HIDA (eds). *What the Kosovars Say and Demand.* Tirana: '8 Nëntori', 1990.

KIŠ, Danilo. *Čas anatomije.* (1977) Belgrade: BIGZ, 1995.

KNEŽEVIĆ, Miloš. *Tvorci i tumači.* Belgrade: Dom kulture 'Studentski grad', 1994.

KOČOVIĆ, Bogoljub. *Žrtve Drugog svetskog rata u Jugoslaviji.* London: Naša reč, 1985.

———. *Nauka, nacionalizam i propaganda. Izmedju gubitaka i žrtava Drugog svetskog rata u Jugoslaviji.* Paris: Editions du Titre, 1999.

KOŁAKOWSKI, Leszek. *Modernity on Endless Trial.* University of Chicago Press, 1990.

272 Bibliography

KOMNENIĆ, Milan. *Izgon*. Belgrade: BIGZ, 1987.

KONRAD, Gyorgy. *L'Antipolitique*. Paris: La Découverte, 1987.

―――. and Ivan SZELENYI. *La marche au pouvoir des intellectuels. Le cas des pays de l'Est*. Paris: Seuil, 1979.

KONSTANTINOVIĆ, Radomir. *Filosofija palanke*. Belgrade: Nolit, 1981.

Le Kosovo-Metohija dans l'histoire serbe. Lausanne: L'Age d'Homme, 1990.

KRESTIĆ, Vasilije Dj., *Srpsko-hrvatski odnosi i jugoslovenska ideja (1860–1873)*. Belgrade: Narodna knjiga, 1983.

―――. *Un peuple en hôtage. Les Serbes de Croatie face à l'Etat croate*. Lausanne: L'Age d'Homme, 1992.

KRLEŽA, Miroslav. *Eseji* (vol. VI). Zagreb: Zora, 1967.

KUPCHAN, Charles (ed.). *Nationalism and Nationalities in the New Europe*. Ithaca, NY: Cornell University Press, 1995.

KUZMANIČ, Tonci and Slavko GABER (eds). *Kosovo-Srbija-Jugoslavija*. Ljubljana, Univerzitetna konferenca ZSMZ, May 1989.

LAMPE, John. *Yugoslavia as History. Twice there Was a Country*. Cambridge University Press, 1996.

LAQUEUR, Walter and George L. MOSSE (eds). *Historians in Politics*. London: Sage, 1974.

LEKIĆ, Jasmina. *Otvoreni prelom*. Belgrade: Vreme knjige, 1996.

LEVINSOHN, Florence Hamlish. *Belgrade: Among the Serbs*. Chicago: Ivan R. Dee, 1994.

Liberalizam i socijalizam. (Liberalne i socijalističke ideje i pokreti na tlu Jugoslavije). Belgrade: Centar za filozofiju i društvenu teoriju, 1984.

LJUŠIĆ, Radoš. *Knjiga o Načertaniju. Nacionalni i državni program Kneževine Srbije, 1844*. Belgrade,―BIGZ, 1993.

LUBARDA, Vojislav. *Anatema*. (1982) Belgrade: Dečje novine, 1990.

LUKIĆ, Sveta. *Contemporary Yugoslav Literature: A Sociopolitical Approach*. Urbana, IL: University of Illinois Press, 1972.

LUSTIG, Michael M. *Trotsky and Djilas: Critics of Communist Bureaucracy*. New York: Greenwood Press, 1989.

LYDALL, Harold. *Yugoslavia in Crisis*. Oxford: Clarendon Press, 1989.

MACFARLANE, Bruce. *Yugoslavia—Politics, Economics, and Society*. London: Pinter, 1988.

MACLEAN, Ian, Alan MONTEFIORE and Peter WINCH (eds). *The Political Responsibility of Intellectuals*. Cambridge University Press, 1990.

MAGAŠ, Branka. *The Destruction of Yugoslavia: Tracing the Break-Up 1980–92*. London: Verso, 1993.

MALCOLM, Noel. *Kosovo: A Short History*. London: Macmillan, 1998.

MANNHEIM, Karl. *Essays on the Sociology of Culture*. London: Routledge & Kegan Paul, 1956.

MANOJLOVIĆ, Ljubiša. *Čitajte izmedju redova. Optuženi za nacionalizam, unitarizam, nihilizam, liberalizam, birokratizam, etatizam, itd., itd ... (sve odjedanput)*. *Dosije*. Kragujevac: Nova Svetlost, 1991.

MARÈS, Antoine (ed.). *Histoire et pouvoir en Europe médiane*. Paris: L'Harmattan, 1996.

MARKOVIĆ, Milivoje. *Preispitivanja. Informbiro i Goli Otok u jugoslovenskom romanu*. Belgrade: Narodna knjiga, 1986.

MARKOVIĆ, Predrag J. *Beograd izmedju Istoka i Zapada 1948–1965*, Belgrade: Službeni list SRJ, 1996.

MATVEJEVIĆ, Predrag. *Otvorena pisma*. Belgrade: Slobodan Mašić, 1985.

———. *Jugoslavenstvo danas. Pitanja kulture*. Zagreb: Globus, 1982.

MEDAKOVIĆ, Dejan. *Efemeris* (vols I–V). Belgrade: BIGZ, 1990–5.

MERTUS, Julie A. *Kosovo. How Myths and Truths Started a War*. Berkeley: University of California Press, 1999.

MIHAILOVIĆ, Dragoslav. *Kad su cvetale tikve*. (1968) Belgrade: Prosveta, 1992.

———. *Goli Otok* (vols I–III). Belgrade: Politika, 1990, 1995.

MIHAJLOVIĆ-MIHIZ, Borislav. *Kolubarska bitka*. Belgrade, Jugoslovensko dramsko pozoriste 'ARS Dramatica', no. 27, Dec. 1983.

———. *Portreti*. Belgrade: Nolit, 1988.

———. *Autobiografija - o drugima* (vols I–II). Belgrade: BIGZ, 1992, 1994.

———. *Kazivanja i ukazivanja*. Belgrade: BIGZ, 1994.

MILARDOVIĆ, Andjelko. *Srbijanski masovni pokret i Hrvatsko pitanje*. Zagreb: Globus, 1991.

MILETIĆ, Antun. *Koncentracioni logor Jasenovac* (vols I–III). Belgrade/Jasenovac: Narodna knjiga, 1986, 1987.

MILIĆ, Miodrag. *Radjanje Titove despotije. Prilog fenomenologiji jugoslovenske revolucije*. Harrow: Naša reč, 1985.

MILLER, Robert F. (ed.). *The Development of Civil Society in Communist Systems*. Sydney: Allen & Unwin, 1992.

MILOJKOVIĆ-DJURIĆ, Jelena. *Tradition and Avant-Garde: Literature and Art in Serbian Culture, 1900–1918*. Boulder, CO: East European Monographs, 1988.

MILOŠEVIĆ, Slobodan. *Godine Raspleta*. Belgrade: BIGZ, 1990.

MIŁOSZ, Czesław. *The Captive Mind*. London: Penguin Books, 1981.

Milovan Djilas (1911–1996). Zbornik radova. Belgrade: GIP Kultura, 1996.

MIRIĆ, Jovan. *Sistem i kriza. Prilog kritičkoj analizi ustavnog i političkog sistema Jugoslavije*. Zagreb: Cekade, 1985.

MITROVIĆ, Andrej. *Raspravljanja sa Klio. O istoriji, istorijskoj svesti i istoriografiji*. Sarajevo: Svjetlost, 1991.

NAGY, Károly (ed.). *István Bibó. Democracy, Revolution, Self-Determination: Selected Writings*. New York: Columbia University Press, 1991.

NENADOVIĆ, Aleksandar. *Razgovori s Kočom*. Zagreb: Globus, 1989.

———. *Mirko Tepavac—Sećanja i komentari*. Belgrade: Radio B92, 1998.

NIKOLIĆ, Milan. *Šta je stvarno rekao Dobrica Ćosić*. Belgrade: Draganić, 1995.

NOVAK, Viktor. *Magnum Crimen*. (1948) Belgrade: Narodna knjiga, 1986.

274   Bibliography

PALAVESTRA, Predrag (ed.). *Novija srpska književnost i kritika ideologije.* Belgrade: SANU, 1989.
———. *Književnost i javna reč.* Požarevac: Centar za Kulturu/Edicija Braničevo, 1994.
PAVIĆ, Milorad. *Dictionary of the Khazars.* (1984) Trans. by Christina Pribičević-Zorić, New York: Vintage international, 1989.
PAVKOVIĆ, Aleksandar. *Slobodan Jovanović: An Unsentimental Approach to Politics.* Boulder, CO: Westview, 1993.
———. *The Fragmentation of Yugoslavia: Nationalism in a Multinational State.* London: Macmillan, 1997.
———. Halyna KOSCHARSKY and Adam CZARNOTA (eds). *Nationalism and Postcommunism: a Collection of Essays.* Aldershot: Dartmouth, 1995.
PAVLOVIĆ, Dragiša. *Olako obećana brzina.* Zagreb: Globus, 1988.
PAVLOVIĆ, Živojin. *Ispljuvak pun krvi* (1984), Belgrade: Grafički atelje 'DERETA', 1991.
PAVLOWITCH, Stevan K. *The Improbable Survivor: Yugoslavia and its Problems, 1918–1988.* London: Hurst, 1988.
———. *Tito: Yugoslavia's Great Dictator: A Reassessment.* London: Hurst, 1992.
———. *History of the Balkans, 1804–1945.* London: Longman, 1999.
PEKIĆ, Borislav. *Odmor od istorije.* Belgrade: BIGZ, 1993.
———. *Vreme reči.* Belgrade: BIGZ, 1993.
PEKOVIĆ, Ratko. *Ni rat ni mir: panorama književnih polemika 1945–1965.* Belgrade: Filip Višnjić, 1986.
PEROVIĆ, Latinka. *Zatvaranje kruga - ishod rascepa 1971–1972.* Sarajevo: Svjetlost, 1991.
———. *Ljudi, dogadjaji i knjige.* Belgrade: Helsinški odbor za ljudska prava u Srbiji, 2000.
PEŠIĆ, Desanka. *Jugoslovenski komunisti i nacionalno pitanje (1919–1935).* Belgrade: Rad, 1983.
PETRANOVIĆ, Branko and Momčilo ZEČEVIĆ. *Agonija dve Jugoslavije.* Belgrade: Svedočanstva, 1991.
PETROVICH, Michael Boro. *A History of Modern Serbia 1804–1918* (vols I–II). New York: Harcourt Brace Jovanovich, 1976.
PETROVIĆ, Momčilo. *Pitao sam Albance šta žele a oni su rekli: republiku ... ako može.* Belgrade: Radio B92, 1996.
POPOV, Nebojša. *Društveni sukobi—izazov sociologiji.* Belgrade: Institut za filozofiju i društvenu teoriju, 1983.
———. *Contra Fatum. Slučaj grupe profesora Filozofskog fakulteta 1968–1988.* Belgrade: Mladost, 1989.
———. *Jugoslavija pod naponom promena. Dvanaest ogleda (1968–1990).* Belgrade: Geca Kon, 1990.
——— (ed.). *Srpska strana rata. Trauma i katarza u istorijskom pamćenju.* Belgrade: BIGZ, 1996.
POPOVIĆ, Danko. *Knjiga o Milutinu.* (1985) Belgrade: Književne novine, 1986.

————. *Vreme laži.* Belgrade: Književne novine, 1990.
POPOVIĆ, Miroslav. *Udri Bandu.* Belgrade: Filip Višnjić, 1988.
POPOVIĆ, Srdja, Dejan JANČA and Tanja PETOVAR (eds). *Kosovski čvor: drešiti ili seći?* Belgrade: Chronos, 1990.
PROTIĆ, Miodrag B. *Nojeva barka. Pogled s kraja veka* (vol. II: *1965–95*). Belgrade: Srpska knjivevna zadruga, 1996.
QOSJA, Rexhep. *Nezaštićena sudbina.* Zagreb: Hrvatska socijalno liberalna stranka, 1990.
RABIA, Ali and LIFCHULTZ, Lawrence (eds). *Why Bosnia?* Stony Creek: Pamphleteer's Press, 1993.
RADONJIĆ, Lila. *Nač slučaj* (vols I–II). Belgrade: Stubovi kulture, 1996.
RADULOVIĆ, Dušan and Nebojša SPAIĆ. *U Potrazi za demokratijom.* Belgrade: Dosije, 1991.
RADULOVIĆ, Jovan. *Drame: Golubnjača (1982), Učitelj Dositej (1990).* Belgrade: BIGZ, 1993.
RADULOVIĆ, Srdjan. *Sudbina Krajine.* Belgrade: Dan Graf, 1996.
RAIČKOVIĆ, Stevan. *Suvišna pesma. Devet fragmenata o genocidu i predgovorom i komentarima.* Belgrade: Srpska književna zadruga, 1991.
RAMET, Pedro (ed.). *Yugoslavia in the 1980s.* Boulder, CO: Westview, 1985.
RAMET, Sabrina P. *Nationalism and Federalism in Yugoslavia 1962–1991.* Bloomington: Indiana University Press, 1992.
————. *Balkan Babel. The Disintegration of Yugoslavia from the Death of Tito to Ethnic War.* Boulder, CO: Westview, 1996.
RANČIĆ, Dragoslav. *Dobrica Ćosić ili predsednik bez vlasti.* Belgrade: Art studio 'Crno na belo', 1994.
RAŠKOVIĆ, Jovan. *Luda zemlja.* Belgrade: Akvarijus, 1990.
Raspad Jugoslavije: produžetak ili kraj agonije (zbornik). Belgrade: Institut za evropske studije, 1991.
RUPNIK, Jacques. *L'Autre Europe.* Paris: Odile Jacob, 1990.
————. (ed.). *Le Déchirement des nations.* Paris: Seuil, 1995.
RUSINOW, Dennison. *The Yugoslav Experiment, 1948–1974.* London: Hurst, 1977.
————. (ed.). *Yugoslavia, a Fractured Federalism.* Washington, DC: Wilson Center Press, 1988.
SCHNAPPER, Dominique. *La communaute des citoyens. Sur l'idée moderne de nation.* Paris: Gallimard, 1994.
SCHÖPFLIN, George. *Politics in Eastern Europe, 1945–1992.* Oxford: Blackwell, 1993.
SEKELJ, Laslo. *Yugoslavia: The Process of Disintegration.* Boulder, CO: Social Science Monographs, 1993.
SEKULIĆ, Tomislav. *Seobe kao sudbina.* Priština: Novi svet, 1994.
SELENIĆ, Slobodan. *Memoari Pere Bogalja.* (1968) Belgrade: Prosveta, 1991.
————. *Prijatelji.* Novi Sad: Matica srpska, 1980.
————. *Pismo/Glava.* (1982) Belgrade: IP 'Beograd', 1992.
————. *Očevi i oci.* (1985) Belgrade: BIGZ, 1990.

————. *Timor Mortis.* (1987) Sarajevo: Svjetlost, 1990.

————. *Iskorak u stvarnost.* Belgrade: Prosveta, 1995.

SEROKA, James and Vukašin PAVLOVIĆ (eds). *The Tragedy of Yugoslavia: The Failure of Democratic Transformation.* Armonk, NY: M.E. Sharpe, 1992.

ŠEŠELJ, Vojislav. *Horvatove ustaške fantazmagorije.* Belgrade: ABC Glas, 1992.

————. *Razaranja srpskog nacionalnog bića.* Belgrade: ABC Glas, 1993.

SHER, Gerson S. *Praxis: Marxist Criticism and Dissent in Socialist Yugoslavia.* Bloomington: Indiana University Press, 1977.

SHOUP, Paul. *Communism and the Yugoslav National Question.* New York: Columbia University Press, 1968.

SILBER, Laura and Allan LITTLE. *The Death of Yugoslavia.* London: Penguin, 1995.

SIMOVIĆ, Ljubomir. *Istočnice. Kniževne novine* (supplement), Apr. 1983.

————. *Galop na puževima.* Belgrade: Stubovi kulture, 1997.

SKILLING, H. Gordon. *Samizdat and Independent Society in Central and Eastern Europe.* Basingstoke: Macmillan, 1989.

SLAPŠAK, Svetlana. *Ogledi o bezbrižnosti. Srpski intelektualci, nacionalizam i jugoslovenski rat.* Belgrade: Radio B92, 1994.

SMITH, Anthony D. *The Ethnic Revival.* Cambridge University Press, 1981.

————. *Theories of Nationalism.* London: Duckworth, 1983.

————. *National Identity.* London: Penguin, 1991.

SPASIĆ, Ivana and Milan SUBOTIĆ (eds). *Revolucija i poredak. O dinamici promena u Srbiji.* Belgrade, Institut za filozofiju i društvenu teoriju, 2001.

STAMBOLIĆ, Ivan. *Put u bespuće.* Belgrade: Radio B92, 1995.

STANKOVIĆ, Djordje Dj. *Nikola Pašić i jugoslovensko pitanje* (vols I–II). Belgrade: BIGZ, 1985.

STANKOVIĆ, Slobodan. *The End of the Tito Era: Yugoslavia's Dilemmas.* Stanford, CA: Hoover Institution Press, 1981.

STANOJEVIĆ, Branimir B. *Alojzije Stepinac: zločinac ili svetac?* Belgrade: Nova knjiga, 1986.

STEFANOVIĆ, Nenad. *Pokrštavanje petokrake. Tajni život srpske opozicije, 17 novembar 1989—1 februar 1994.* Belgrade: BIGZ, 1994.

STOJANOVIĆ, Svetozar, *Propast komunizma i razbijanje Jugoslavije.* Belgrade: Filip Višnjić, 1995.

SUBOTIĆ, Dragan. *Srpski Socijalisti i nacionalno pitanje.* Belgrade: Istraživačko-izdavački centar SSO Srbije, 1990.

SUGAR, Peter and Ivo LEDERER (eds). *Nationalism in Eastern Europe.* Seattle: University of Washington Press, 1971.

Sukob ili dijalog. Srpsko-albanski odnosi i integracija Balkana. Zbornik radova. Subotica: Otvoreni Univerzitet/Evropski gradjanski centar za rešavanje konflikata, 1994.

SUNIĆ, Tomislav. *Titoism and Dissidence.* Frankfurt: Peter Lang, 1995.

SUNY, Ronald Grigor and Michael D. KENNEDY (eds). *Intellectuals and the Articulation of the Nation.* Ann Arbor: Michigan University Press, 1999.

SUSSEX, Roland and J.C. EADE (eds). *Culture and Nationalism in Nineteenth-Century Eastern Europe.* Columbus: Slavica Publishers, 1985.

TADIĆ, Ljubomir. *Da li je nacionalizam nasa sudbina? I druge rasprave i polemike o naciji, socijalizmu i federaciji.* Belgrade: Multiprint, 1986.

———. *O 'Velikosrpskom hegemonizmu'.* Belgrade: Politika, 1992.

TERZIĆ, Velimir. *Slom Kraljevine Jugoslavije 1941: uzroci i posledice poraza* (vols I–II). Belgrade: Narodna knjiga, 1982, 1983.

THOMAS, Robert. *Serbia under Milošević.* London: Hurst, 1997.

THOMPSON, Mark. *A Paper House: The Ending of Yugoslavia.* London: Vintage, 1992.

———. *Forging War: The Media in Serbia, Croatia and Bosnia-Hercegovina.* London: Article 19/International Centre against Censorship, May 1994.

TÖKES, Rudolf (ed.). *Opposition in Eastern Europe.* Baltimore: Johns Hopkins University Press, 1979.

TOMASEVICH, Jozo. *The Chetniks.* Stanford University Press, 1975.

TOŠIĆ, Desimir. *Srpski nacionalni problemi.* Paris: Oslobodjenje, 1952.

———. *Stvarnost protiv zabluda. Srpsko nacionalno pitanje.* Belgrade: Slobodan Mašić, 1997.

TRGOVČEVIĆ, Ljubinka. *Naučnici Srbije i stvaranje jugoslovenske države 1914–1920.* Belgrade: Narodna knjiga/Srpska književna zadruga, 1986.

———. *Istorija Srpske književne zadruge.* Belgrade: Srpska književna zadruga, 1992.

TRIPALO, Miko. *Hrvatsko proljeće.* Zagreb: Globus, 1990.

TUDJMAN, Franjo. *Bespuća povijesne zbiljnosti. Rasprava o povijesti i filozofiji zlosilja.* Zagreb: Hrvatska sveučilišna naklada, 1994.

UDOVIČKI, Jasminka and James RIDGEWAY (eds). *Yugoslavia's Ethnic Nightmare. The Inside Story of Europe's Unfolding Ordeal.* New York: Lawrence Hill Books, 1995.

VILIĆ, Dušan and Milan ATEJEVIĆ. *Specijalni rat.* Belgrade, 1983.

VUČELIĆ, Milorad. *Conversations with the Epoch.* Belgrade: Ministry of Information of the Republic of Serbia, 1991.

WACHTEL, Andrew Baruch. *Making a Nation. Breaking a Nation. Literature and Cultural Politics in Yugoslavia.* Stanford University Press, 1998.

WATSON, Rubie S. (ed.). *Memory and Opposition Under State Socialism.* Santa Fe: School of American Research, 1993.

WILSON, Duncan. *The Life and Times of Vuk Stefanović Karadžić, 1781–1864: Literacy, Literature and National Independence in Serbia.* Ann Arbor: University of Michigan/Michigan Slavic Publications, 1986.

WOODWARD, Susan. *Socialist Unemployment: The Political Economy of Yugoslavia.* Princeton University Press, 1995.

———. *Balkan Tragedy: Chaos and Dissolution after the Cold War.* Washington, DC: Brookings Institution Press, 1995.

Yugoslavia: The Failure of 'Democratic' Communism. New York: Freedom House, 1987.

278   *Bibliography*

ŽERJAVIĆ, Vladimir. *Gubici stanovništva Jugoslavije u Drugom svjetskom ratu.* Zagreb: Jugoslavensko viktimološko društvo, 1989.

——. *Opsesije i megalomanije oko Jasenovca i Bleiburga.* Zagreb: Globus, 1992.

ZLOBEC, Ciril. *Slovenska samobitnost i pisac.* (1986) Zagreb: Globus, 1987.

ZUPAN, Vitomil. *Menuet za gitaru.* (1979) Ljubljana: Društvo slovenskih pisateljev, 1988.

——. *Levitan. Roman koji to nije.* Zagreb: Globus, 1983.

ARTICLES AND SPECIAL ISSUES OF PERIODICALS

ALLCOCK, John. 'In Praise of Chauvinism: Rhetorics of Nationalism in Yugoslavia'. *Third World Quarterly,* 11, 1989; pp. 208–22.

ANDELMAN, David A. 'Trois ans après Tito'. *Politique étrangère,* 2, 1983; pp. 1–12.

ARMSTRONG, John. 'Toward a Framework for Considering Nationalism in East Europe'. *Wilson Center Occasional Papers,* no. 8, April 1987.

BAKIĆ-HAYDEN, Milica and Robert HAYDEN. 'Orientalist Variations on the Theme 'Balkans': Symbolic Geography in Recent Yugoslav Cultural Politics'. *Slavic Review,* LI/1, spring 1992; pp. 1–15.

BANAC, Ivo. 'Political Change and National Diversity'. *Daedalus,* CXIX/1, winter 1990; pp. 141–59.

——. 'The Fearful Asymmetry of War: The Causes and Consequences of Yugoslavia's Demise'. *Daedalus,* CXXI/2, spring 1992; pp. 141–74.

——. 'Historiography of the Countries of Eastern Europe: Yugoslavia'. *American Historical Review,* XCVII/4, October 1992; pp. 1084–1104.

——. 'Misreading the Balkans'. *Foreign Policy,* 93, winter 1993–4; pp. 173–82.

BASKIN, Mark. 'Crisis in Kosovo'. *Problems of Communism,* March-Apr. 1983; pp. 61–74.

BAUMAN, Zygmunt. 'Intellectuals in East-Central Europe: Continuity and Change'. *East European Politics and Societies,* I/2, spring 1987; pp. 162–86.

BELOFF, Nora. 'Progress of a Revolutionary'. *New York Review of Books,* 11 Apr. 1985; pp. 12–14.

——. 'La Yougoslavie. Le ventre mou de l'Europe'. *Politique étrangère,* 3, autumn 1985; pp. 735–50.

BERLIN, Isaiah. 'The Bent Twig: A Note on Nationalism'. *Foreign Affairs,* LI/1, 1972; pp. 11–30.

BERTSCH, Gary. 'The Revival of Nationalisms'. *Problems of Communism,* XXII/6, Nov.-Dec.1973; pp. 1–15.

BIBERAJ, Elez. 'Kosovë: The Struggle for Recognition'. *Journal of Conflict Studies,* 137/138, 1982; pp. 23–43.

BIBIČ, Adolf. 'The Emergence of Pluralism in Slovenia'. *Communist and Post-Communist Studies,* XXVI/4, Dec. 1993; pp. 367–86.

BOBAN, Ljubo. 'Jasenovac and the Manipulation of History'. *East European Politics and Societies,* IV/3, fall 1990; pp. 580–92.

BRACEWELL, Wendy. 'Rape in Kosovo: Masculinity and Serbian Nationalism'. *Nations and Nationalism*, VI/4, 2000; pp. 563–90.

BUDDING, Audrey Helfant. 'Yugoslavs into Serbs: Serbian National Identity, 1961–1971'. *Nationalities Papers*, XXV/3, 1997; pp. 407–26.

———. 'Systemic Crisis and Nationalist Mobilization: The Case of the Memorandum of the Serbian Academy'. *Cultures and Nations of Central and Eastern Europe: Essays in Honor of Roman Szporluk*. *Harvard Ukrainian Studies*, special vol. XXII, 1998; pp. 49–69.

BUGAJSKI, Janusz and Maxine POLLACK. 'East European Dissent: Impasses and Opportunities'. *Problems of Communism*, XXXVII/2, March-Apr. 1988; pp. 59–67.

BURG, Steven L. 'Elite Conflict in Post-Tito Yugoslavia'. *Soviet Studies*, XXXVIII/2, Apr. 1986; pp. 170–93.

———. 'Nationalism and Democratization in Yugoslavia'. *Washington Quarterly*, XIV/4, Autumn 1991; pp. 5–19.

———. and Michael L. BERBAUM. 'Community, Integration and Stability in Multinational Yugoslavia'. *American Political Science Review*, LXXXIII/2, June 1989; pp. 535–54.

CARPENTER, John. 'Animals and Angels: The Literature of Destruction'. *Cross Currents Yearbook*, V/5, 1986; pp. 79–97.

ĆIRKOVIĆ, Sima. 'Historiography in Isolation. Serbian Historiography Today'. *Helsinki Monitor*, special issue, 1994; pp. 35–40.

CLISSOLD, Stephen. 'Croat Separatism: Nationalism, Dissidence and Terrorism'. *Conflict Studies*, 103, Jan. 1979.

CONNOR, Walter D. 'Dissent in Eastern Europe: A New Coalition?' *Problems of Communism*, XXIX/1, Jan.-Feb. 1980; pp. 1–17.

COSTA, Nicholas J. 'Kosovo: a Tragedy in the Making'. *East European Quarterly*, XXI/1, March 1987; pp. 87–97.

ČUBRILOVIĆ, Vaso. 'The Expulsion of the Albanians' (1937) in ELSIE, Robert (ed.), *Kosovo in the Heart of the Powder Keg*. Boulder, CO: East European Monographs, 1997; pp. 400–24.

CVIIC, Christopher. 'Religion and Nationalism in Eastern Europe: The Case of Yugoslavia'. *Millennium*, XIV/2, summer 1985; pp. 195–206.

———. 'Das Ende Jugoslawiens'. *Europa Archiv*, XLVI/14, 1991; pp. 409–15.

———. 'Croatia's Violent Birth'. *Current History*, CIII/577, Nov. 1993; pp. 370–75.

DEAK, Istvan. 'Uncovering Eastern Europe's Dark History'. *Orbis*, winter 1990; pp. 51–65.

DENICH, Bette. 'Dismembering Yugoslavia: Nationalist Ideologies and the Symbolic Revival of Genocide'. *American Ethnologist*, XXI/2, 1994; pp. 367–90.

The Disintegration of Yugoslavia: Inevitable or Avoidable? Nationalities Papers, XXV/3, Sept. 1997; pp. 377–610.

DJILAS, Aleksa. 'The Myth of Tito. Patriot or Despot?' *New Leader*, July 14, 1980; pp. 8–11.

———. 'Dissent and Human Rights in Post-Tito Yugoslavia'. *Review of the Study Centre for Yugoslav Affairs*, II/5, 1980; pp. 497–512.

———. 'Jugoslavia since the Death of Tito'. *Political Quarterly*, LII/2, Apr.–June 1981; pp. 214–24.

———. 'A Profile of Slobodan Milošević'. *Foreign Affairs*, LXXII/3, summer 1993; pp. 81–96.

DJORDJEVIĆ, Jovan. 'Le Parti et les intellectuels'. *Questions actuelles du socialisme*, XXXIV/6, June 1984; pp. 82–9.

DRAGNICH, Alex N. 'The Rise and Fall of Yugoslavia: the Omen of the Upsurge of Serbian Nationalism'. *East European Quarterly*, XXIII/2, June 1989; pp. 183–98.

DRAKULIĆ, Slavenka. 'Intellectuals as Bad Guys'. *East European Politics and Societies*, XIII/2, 1999; pp. 271–7.

DŽADŽIĆ, Petar. 'Strele, jezuiti, simetrije'. *Stvarnost* (Banja Luka), I/1, 1997; pp. 4–7.

L'Ecrivain et le pouvoir. *L'Autre Europe*, nos. 17–18–19, Lausanne: L'Age d'Homme, 1988.

FEHER, Ferenc and Agnes HELLER. 'Gauche de l'Est—Gauche de l'Ouest' in MLYNAŘ, Žděněk (ed.), *Les crises des systèmes de type soviétique*, 1985.

GARTON ASH, Timothy. 'Does Central Europe Exist?' *New York Review of Books*, 9 Oct.1986; pp. 45–52.

———. 'The Opposition'. *New York Review of Books*, Oct.13 1988; pp. 3–6.

———. 'Eastern Europe: Après le Déluge, Nous'. *New York Review of Books*, Aug.16 1990; pp. 51–7.

GELLA, Alexander. 'The Life and Death of the Old Polish Intelligentsia'. *Slavic Review*, XXX/1, March 1971; pp. 1–27.

GELLNER, Ernest. 'Ethnicity and Faith in Eastern Europe'. *Daedalus*, CXIX/1, winter 1990; pp. 279–94.

GOW, James. 'Serbian Nationalism and the Hissssing Ssssnake in the International Order: Whose Sovereignty? Which Nation?'. *South East European Review*, LXXII/3, July 1994; pp. 456–82.

———. 'After the Flood: Literature on the Context, Causes and Course of the Yugoslav War'. *Slavonic and East European Review*, LXXV/3, July 1997; pp. 446–84.

GOLDSTEIN, Ivo. 'The Use of History. Croatian Historiography and Politics'. *Helsinki Monitor*, special issue 1994; pp. 85–97.

GRUENWALD, Oskar. 'The *Praxis* School: Marxism as a Critique of Socialism?' *East European Quarterly*, XV/2, June 1981; pp. 227–50.

———. 'Yugoslav Literature of Disclosure'. *Survey*, XXVIII/3 (122), autumn 1984; pp. 58–63.

———. 'Yugoslav Camp Literature: Rediscovering the Ghost of a Nation's Past-Present-Future'. *Slavic Review*. XLVI/3–4, winter 1987; pp. 513–28.

HAYDEN, Robert M. 'Constitutional Nationalism in the Formerly Yugoslav Republics'. *Slavic Review*, LI/4, winter 1992; pp. 654–73.

————. 'Balancing Discussion of Jasenovac and the Manipulation of History'. *East European Politics and Societies*, VI/2, spring 1992; pp. 207–17.

HELD, David. 'Democracy: From City-States to a Cosmopolitan Order?' *Political Studies*, XL, special issue, 1992; pp.10–39.

HOBSBAWM, E.J. 'Ethnicity and nationalism in Europe Today'. *Anthropology Today*, VIII/1, Feb. 1992; pp. 3–8.

HÖPKEN, Wolfgang. 'War, Memory and Education in a Fragmented Society: The Case of Yugoslavia'. *East European Politics and Societies*, XIII/1, winter 1999; pp. 190–227.

IGNATIEFF, Michael. 'The Balkan Tragedy'. *New York Review of Books*, 13 May 1993; pp. 3–5.

'Intellectuals and Change'. *Daedalus*, CI/3, summer 1972.

'Intellectuals and Tradition'. *Daedalus*, CI/2, spring 1972.

IRVINE, Jill A. 'Ultranationalist Ideology and State-Building in Croatia, 1990–1996'. *Problems of Post-Communism*, July-Aug. 1997; pp. 30–43.

IZETBEGOVIĆ, Alija. 'La Declaration islamique'. (1970) *Dialogue*, I/2–3, 1992; pp. 35–54.

JELAVICH, Charles. 'The Issue of Serbian Textbooks in the Origins of World War I'. *Slavic Review*, XLI/2, summer 1989; pp. 214–33.

JUDT, Tony. 'The Dilemmas of Dissidence'. *East European Politics and Society*, II/2, 1988; pp. 185–240.

————. 'The Rediscovery of Central Europe'. *Daedalus*, CXIX/1, winter 1990; pp. 23–54.

————. 'The New Old Nationalism'. *New York Review of Books*, 26 May 1994; pp. 44–51.

KARATNYCKY, Adrian. 'Slovenia's 'Mladina' Affair: Setback for Yugoslavia's Liberalism'. *The New Leader*, 31, Oct. 1988; pp. 9–10.

KARGER, Adolf. 'Die serbischen Siedlungsräume in Kroatien'. *Osteuropa*. XLII/2, 1992, pp. 141–6.

KLEIN, George. 'The Role of Ethnic Politics in the Czechoslovak Crisis of 1968 and the Yugoslav Crisis of 1971'. *Studies in Comparative Communism*, VIII/4, winter 1975; pp. 339–69.

KOVAČ, Miha. 'The Slovene Spring'. *New Left Review*, 171, 1988; pp. 113–28.

KRAFT, Ekkehart. 'Kirche und Politik in Jugoslawien seit dem Ende der 80er Jahre: Die Serbische Orthodoxe Kirche'. *Südosteuropa*, 1, 1992; pp. 48–62.

KRIŽAN, Mojmir. 'Nationalismen in Jugoslawien. Von postkommunistischer nationaler Emanzipation zum Krieg'. *Osteuropa*, XLII/2, 1992; pp. 121–40.

————. 'New Serbian Nationalism and the Third Balkan War'. *Studies in East European Thought*, XLVI/1–2, June 1994; pp. 47–68.

KRULIC, Joseph. 'La crise du système politique dans la Yougoslavie des années 1980'. *L'Autre Europe*, 3, 1987; pp. 245–60.

KUNDERA, Milan. 'The Tragedy of Central Europe'. *New York Review of Books*, 26 Apr. 1984; pp. 33–7.

LAZITCH, Branko. 'Espaces de liberté en Yougoslavie'. *Est & Ouest*, 41, Apr. 1987; pp. 7–10.

——. 'Belgrade: une défaite politique du pouvoir'. *Est & Ouest*, 54, May 1988; pp. 10–12.

LENDVAI, Paul. 'Yugoslavia without Yugoslavs: the roots of the crisis'. *International Affairs*, LXVII/2, 1991; pp. 251–61.

LEWIS, Flora. 'Reassembling Yugoslavia'. *Foreign Policy*, 98, spring 1995; pp. 132–44.

LIEBICH, André. 'Nations, States, Minorities: Why is East Europe Different?' *Dissent*, Summer 1995; pp. 313–17.

LUTARD, Catherine. 'Le conflit national en Yougoslavie'. *Vingtième siècle*, 33, Jan.-March 1992; pp. 65–76.

MACKENZIE, David. 'Serbia as Piedmont and the Yugoslav Idea, 1804–1914'. *East European Quarterly*, XXVIII/ 2, June 1994; pp. 153–82.

MARJANOVIĆ, Vladislav. 'Die kulturellen Ströhmungen in Jugoslawien nach dem Zweiten Weltkrieg (1945 bis 1984)'. *Der Donauraum*, 27, 1987; pp. 83–99.

MEIER, Viktor. 'Yugoslavia's National Question'. *Problems of Communism*, March-Apr. 1983; pp. 47–60.

MELCHIOR, Jean-Philippe. 'Du nationalisme serbe'. *Les Temps Modernes*, 560, March 1993; pp. 42–62.

MIHAILOVICH, Vasa D. 'Aspects of Nationalism in Dobrica Ćosić's Novel *A Time of Death*: Chauvinism or Sincere Patriotism?' *World Literature Today*, LX/3, summer 1986; pp. 413–16.

MILLER, Nicholas J., 'Searching for a Serbian Havel'. *Problems of Post-Communism*, XLIV/4, July-Aug. 1997; pp. 3–11.

——. 'The Nonconformists: Dobrica Ćosić and Mića Popović Envision Serbia'. *Slavic Review*, LVIII/3, 1999; pp. 515–36.

——. 'The Children of Cain: Dobrica Ćosić's Serbia'. *East European Politics and Societies*, XIV/2, 2000; pp. 268–87.

MILOJKOVIĆ-DJURIĆ, Jelena. 'The Influence of the Medieval Legacy on the Poetry of Dejan Medaković'. *East European Quarterly*, XXI/3, Sept. 1987; pp. 385–391.

——. 'Approaches to National Identities: Ćosić's and Pirjevec's Debate on Ideological and Literary Issues'. *East European Quarterly*, XXX/1, 1996; pp. 63–73.

MILUTINOVIĆ, Zoran. 'Mimezis u socijalizmu'. *Letopis Matice srpske*. XXV/ 1, 1996; pp. 445–54.

MIRIĆ, Jovan. 'Hrvatska demokracija i srpsko pitanje'. *Republika*, VI/101, 1–15 Oct. 1994; pp. 15–31.

MURAVCHIK, Joshua. 'The Intellectual Odyssey of Milovan Djilas'. *World Affairs*, CXLV/4, spring 1983; pp. 322–46.

NAKARADA, Radmila. 'The Mystery of Nationalism: The Paramount Case of Yugoslavia'. *Millennium*, XX/3, 1991; pp. 369–82.

PATTERSON, Patrick Hyder. 'The East is Read: The End of Communism, Slovenian Exceptionalism, and the Independent Journalism of *Mladina*'. *East European Politics and Societies*, XIV/2, 2000; pp. 411–59.

PAVLOWITCH, Stevan K. 'Kosovo: An Analysis of Yugoslavia's Albanian Problem'. *Journal of Conflict Studies*, 137/138, 1982; pp. 7–21.

———. Review of Ivo Banac, *The National Question in Yugoslavia*. *English Historical Review*, C/398, Jan. 1986, pp. 193–5.

———. 'L'Etat et les nationalités en Yougoslavie'. *L'Autre Europe*, 10, 1986; pp. 29–40.

———. 'Orientation bibliographique: Guerre et révolution en Yougoslavie—les nouveaux courants historiographiques'. *Bulletin de l'Institut d'Histoire du Temps Présent*, 27, March 1987; pp. 19–30.

———. 'L'histoire en Yougoslavie depuis 1945'. *Vingtième siècle*, XVII, 1988; pp. 83–91.

———. 'London-Moscow through the Fog of Yugoslavia's Wartime Drama'. *Storia delle Relazioni Internazionali*, 1988, III/4; pp. 369–94 and IV/1; pp. 195–213.

———. 'Who is "Balkanizing" Whom? The Misunderstandings between the Debris of Yugoslavia and an Unprepared West'. *Daedalus*, CXXIII/2, spring 1994; pp. 203–23.

PAVKOVIĆ, Aleksandar. 'Slobodan Jovanović and the Question of Human Rights'. *Slavic Review*, LI/1, spring 1992; pp. 131–6.

———. 'Intellectuals into Politicians: Serbia 1990–1992'. *Meanjin*, LII/1, 1993; pp. 107–17.

———. 'The Serb National Idea: A Revival, 1986–92'. *Slavonic and East European Review*, LXXII/3, July 1994; pp. 440–55.

———. 'From Yugoslavism to Serbism: the Serb National Idea, 1986–1996'. *Nations and Nationalism*, IV/4, 1998; pp. 511–28.

PEARTON, Maurice. 'Clio and the Nation'. Inaugural Lecture in the Senior Lecturer Series of Richmond College. American International College of London, Richmond, Surrey, 12 November 1984.

PETROVICH, Michael B. 'Continuing Nationalism in Yugoslav Historiography'. *Nationalities Papers*, VI/2, 1978; pp. 161–77.

PIPES, Richard. ''Intelligentsia' from the German 'Intelligenz'? A Note'. *Slavic Review*, XXX/3, Sept. 1971; pp. 615–18.

POPOV, Nebojša. *Srpski populizam. Od marginalne do dominantne pojave*, Vreme, special edn, 24 May 1993.

RACINE, Nicole and Michel TREBITSCH (eds). *Sociabilités intellectuelles. Lieux, milieux, réseaux*. Cahiers de l'Institut d'Histoire du Temps Présent, 20, March 1992.

RAMET, Pedro, 'Problems of Albanian Nationalism in Yugoslavia'. *Orbis*, XXV/2, summer 1981; pp. 369–88.

REINHARTZ, Dennis. 'Dissent in Yugoslavia'. *Problems of Communism*, July-Aug. 1980; pp. 80–3.

————. 'The Nationalism of Milovan Djilas'. *Modern Age*, XXIX/3, summer 1985; pp. 233–41.

REMINGTON, Robin Alison. 'Nation versus Class in Yugoslavia'. *Current History*, LXXXVI/523, Nov. 1987; pp. 365–89.

————. 'The Federal Dilemma in Yugoslavia'. *Current History*, LXXXIX/ 551, Dec. 1990; pp. 405–31.

RUPNIK, Jacques. 'La "deuxième bataille" du Kosovo'. *L'Autre Europe*, 10, 1986; pp. 41–6.

SCAMMELL, Michael. 'Yugoslavia: the Awakening'. *New York Review of Books*, June 28, 1990; pp. 42–7.

————. 'The New Yugoslavia'. *New York Review of Books*, July 19, 1990; pp. 37–42.

————. 'Slovenia and its Poet'. *New York Review of Books*, 24 Oct. 1991; p. 56.

SEROKA, Jim. 'The Political Future of Yugoslavia: Nationalism and the Critical Years, 1989–1991'. *Canadian Review of Studies in Nationalism*, XIX/1–2, 1992; pp. 151–60.

SETON WATSON, Hugh. 'Intelligentsia und Nationalismus in Osteuropa 1848–1918'. *Historische Zeitschrift*, XCCV; pp. 331–45.

SHARLET, Robert. 'Dissent and the Contra-System in Eastern Europe'. *Current History*, LXXXIV/505, Nov. 1985; pp. 353–88.

SHOUP, Paul. 'The National Question in Yugoslavia'. *Problems of Communism*, XXI/1, Jan.-Feb. 1972; pp. 18–29.

SINGLETON, Fred. 'Yugoslavia: Economic Grievances and Cultural Nationalism'. *The World Today*, XXXIX/7–8, July-Aug.1983; pp. 284–90.

SIRINELLI, Jean-François. 'Le hasard ou la nécessité? Une histoire en chantier: l'histoire des intellectuels'. *Vingtième siècle*, 9, Jan.-Mar. 1986; pp. 97–108.

————. (ed.). 'Générations intellectuelles. Effets d'âge et phénomènes de génération dans le milieu intellectuel français'. *Cahiers de l'Institut d'Histoire du Temps Présent*, no. 6, Nov. 1987.

SOROS, George. 'Bosnia and Beyond'. *New York Review of Books*, 7 Oct. 1993; pp. 15–17.

SPALATIN, Christopher. 'Serbo-Croatian or Serbian and Croatian? Considerations on the Croatian Declaration and the Serbian Proposal of 1967'. *Journal of Croatian Studies*, VII–VIII, 1966–7; pp. 3–13.

————. 'Language and Politics in Yugoslavia in the light of the events which happened from March 17, 1967 to March 14, 1969'. *Journal of Croatian Studies*. XI–XII, 1970–1; pp. 83–104.

————. 'Language Situation in Croatia Today'. *Journal of Croatian Studies*. XIV-XV, 1973–4; pp. 3–12.

STANKOVIĆ, Slobodan. 'La Yougoslavie de l'après-Tito'. *Est et Ouest*, 13, Dec. 1984, pp. 16–18.

STERBLING, Anton. 'Überlegungen zur Schlüsselbedeutung der Intelligenz in Südosteuropa'. *Südosteuropa*, XLII/1, 1993; pp. 42–58.

STOIANOVICH, Traian. 'The Pattern of Serbian Intellectual Evolution,

1830–1880'. *Comparative Studies in Society and History*, I, 1958–59; pp. 242–72.

STOKES, Gale, John LAMPE and Dennison RUSINOW, with Julie MOSTOV. 'Instant History: Understanding the Wars of Yugoslav Succession'. *Slavic Review*, LV/1, spring 1996, pp.136–60.

TISMEANU, Vladimir. 'Limits of Critical Marxism'. *Problems of Communism*, XXXV/1, Jan.-Feb. 1986; pp. 67–76.

VELJAK, Lino. 'The Collapse and Reconstruction of Legitimacy: An Introductory Remark'. *Nationalities Papers*, XXV/3, Sept. 1997; pp. 449–52.

'Voices From the Slovene Nation 1990–1992'. *Nationalities Papers*, XXI/1, 1993.

VUJAČIĆ, Veljko. 'Serbian Nationalism, Slobodan Milosevic and the Origins of the Yugoslav War'. *Harriman Review*, 12, Dec. 1995, pp. 25–34.

———. 'Institutional Origins of Contemporary Serbian Nationalism'. *East European Constitutional Review*, V/4, fall 1996; pp. 51–61.

———. 'Historical Legacies, Nationalist Mobilization and Political Outcomes in Russia and Serbia: A Weberian View'. *Theory and Society*, XXV, 1996; pp. 763–801.

'Yougoslavie: Penser la crise'. *Lignes*, 20, Sept. 1993.

'Yugoslavia: Tito and After'. *Survey*, XXVIII/3 (122), autumn 1984.

ZANINOVICH, M. George. 'A Prognosis for Yugoslavia'. *Current History*, LXXXVIII/541, Nov. 1989; pp. 393–405.

ŽARKOVIĆ-BOOKMAN, Milica. 'The Economic Basis of Regional Autarchy in Yugoslavia'. *Soviet Studies*, XLII/1, Jan. 1990; pp. 93–109.

INDEX

Serbo-Croatian letters are listed as follows: Č and Ć after C; Dž and Dj after D; Nj after N; Š after S; and Ž after Z.

Alliance of Reform Forces of Yugoslavia, 241, 243–4, 248–51 *passim*
Anali pravnog fakulteta (Annals of the Law Faculty), 47
Antić, Ivan, 187n
Apih, Milan, 197n
Association for a Yugoslav Democratic Initiative (UJDI), 227n, 238, 241, 243–4, 249, 250n
Avdić-Vllasi, Nadira, 146–7
Avramović, Zoran, 156–7

Bakarić, Vladimir, 114
Banac, Ivo, 6, 83
Barović, Jovan, 21n
Basta, Danilo, 45, 49n
Bavčar, Igor, 215, 216
Bećković, Matija, 20, 34n, 35n, 58n, 60, 61n, 101, 108n, 144, 187, 202n, 211, 225, 230, 236, 241, 252
Behschnitt, Wolfgang, 7
Belgrade: 11, 24, 31, 43, 48, 50, 53, 61–2, 66, 88, 103, 123, 135, 143, 147, 148, 169, 172, 200, 201, 244–5, 252; trial of 'Belgrade Six', 57–9, 84n
Belgrade University: 25, 27–8, 48–9, 50, 111, 123, 238; student demonstrations, 27, 47, 252; 1971 Law Faculty debate, 42–6, 47, 49, 84

Benda, Julien, 2
Bilandžić, Dušan, 76
'Black Wave', 22–5, 47, 48, 60
'Blue Book', 67
Bogavac, Dušan, 63
Bogdanović, Dimitrije: 41n, 60, 127–31, 148–9; *Knjiga o Kosovu* (Book about Kosovo), 127–31, 145
Bosnia-Hercegovina: 14, 57, 59, 73, 85, 235n, 237, 249, 255, 258; Serbs, 2, 54n, 85, 104–8, 114, 252, 257–9 *passim*; Serbian Democratic Party (SDS), 249; Muslims, 73, 85, 105, 106–9 *passim*, 235n, 243, 246; *see also* nationalism-Muslim
Brković, Jevrem, 150, 176n, 230
Bučar, France, 192, 197n, 200
Budding, Audrey Helfant, 8
Bulajić, Milan, 113
Bulatović, Kosta, 135, 141, 143
Bulatović, Miodrag, 136, 144, 145, 173, 175–7, 230
Bulatović, Vukoje, 186
Bulović, Irinej, 125

Cankar Endowment/Hall, 148–9, 196, 224, 226, 230, 234
Cesar, Ivan, 76
Cominformists, 13n, 20, 23–4, 81–3; *see also* Goli Otok

Comintern, 80, 86–8, 89, 94, 130, 179, 223, 236
Committee for the Defence of Freedom of Thought and Expression, 58n, 59–60, 103, 120, 127, 135, 140, 144, 162, 169–73, 179, 187, 202, 209n, 210, 214–16 *passim*, 228, 229, 238, 241, 242
Committee for the Defence of Human Rights (Slovenia), 215–16
Committee to Aid Democratic Dissidents in Yugoslavia (CADDY), 22
Communism: 5, 22, 27, 36, 70–1, 228; 'Titoism', 13–14, 17, 25, 29, 49, 206, 209; critiques of, 18–19, 21, 23, 25–7, 50–1, 59, 80–1, 96–7, 178–9
Communist Party (later League of Communists) of Yugoslavia: 13, 15, 17, 21, 26–8, 29–31, 35, 38–41, 48–9, 51, 53, 59, 64, 69–70, 71, 107, 143, 183–4, 193–5, 195–6, 206, 229, 237, 256; critiques of, 18–19, 21, 44, 46, 67–70, 78–88, 93–9, 113–14, 121–4, 242
Constitutions and constitutional amendments: Yugoslavia: 1963, 30, 130; 1967, 31; 1968, 39, 40; 1974, 66, 69, 84, 130, 152, 181, 212, 219; Serbia: 1989, 12, 212, 219; 1990, 247; Slovenia 1989, 232; Croatia 1990, 246; Kosovo 1990, 247; debates, 12, 42–6, 47, 68, 171–2, 195–205, 248, 256
Crnčević, Brana, 34n, 35n, 133
Croatia: 14, 29–31, 66, 69, 80, 85, 95, 98, 99, 109–10 *passim*, 114, 145–7, 186, 217–18, 220, 227–8, 230, 246–50 *passim*; dissent in, 11, 52, 54, 58–9, 62; 'mass movement' or 'Croatian spring', 14, 31, 42, 46–7, 69, 104, 109, 155, 168. 170, 232, 234–5 *passim*; Serbs, 2, 33–4, 42, 85, 104–6, 113, 180, 232–7, 246, 252, 259; Writers' Society, 150, 174, 175, 230–2, 234, 236n, 246n; Yugoslav (later Croatian) Academy of Sciences and Arts, 187, 233, 246n; League of Communists of Croatia (later Party of Democratic Change), 32, 34, 47, 61–2, 80, 220, 232, 236, 246; Croatian Democratic Union (HDZ), 227, 234, 237, 242–

3, 245–6; Croatian Social Liberal Alliance (later Party; HSLS), 227; Serbian Democratic Party (SDS), 236, 237, 246, 249; *see also* nationalism-Croatian, Independent State of Croatia
Časovnik (The Clock), 51
Čavoški, Kosta: 45, 49n, 58n, 60, 201, 202, 239, 251n; *Stranački pluralizam ili monizam* (Party Pluralism or Monism), 83–4, 239
Chetniks (Četniks), 36, 79, 100–2 *passim*, 110, 251
Ćubrilović, Vaso, 128–9, 178n, 186
Ćirković, Sima, 49n, 72, 74, 75, 77, 186
Ćosić, Dobrica: 8, 36, 37–42, 47, 50, 51, 52, 58n, 59, 60, 61, 89–96, 97, 108n, 122–3, 126, 135, 141–2, 144, 145, 169–73, 176–7, 178n, 182n, 185, 187, 197, 202n, 209, 211, 236–41 *passim*, 249; *Vreme smrti* (A Time of Death), 89–92, 94, 170; *Stvarno i moguće* (The Real and the Possible), 92–3; *Grešnik* (The Sinner), 93–6, 97

Danilović, Rajko, 16
Danojlić, Milovan, 55n, 132n, 211, 222, 241n
'Declaration Concerning the Name and Position of the Croatian Literary Language', 31–4
Dedijer, Vladimir: 78–80, 111, 114; *Novi prilozi za biografiju Josipa Broza Tita* (New Contributions for the Biography of Josip Broz Tito), 78–80
Dimitrijević, Vojin, 46, 216, 223
Dissent: 4–5, 13–14, 17n, 49–52; regional disparities, 14–15, 52, 57; inter-republican cooperation, 21–2, 51–2, 58–9, 62–3, 123, 162, 169, 170–1; 'flying university', 17, 20, 50–1, 53, 54, 57; petitions and 'petitionism': 17, 49–50, 53, 59, 63, 169, 202–3, 210, 215, 216, 241n; Djogo trial, 56; trial of 'Belgrade Six', 58–9, 169; Kosovo, 125–6, 134, 135, 137–40, 143; *see also* 'hostile propaganda'
Dogo, Marco, 72, 128
Dolanc, Stane, 58, 182

Drašković, Vuk: 106–8, 142, 203, 216n, 226, 243, 244, 249–53 *passim*; *Nož* (The Knife), 106–8
Dreyfus Affair, 56, 134
Džadžić, Petar, 35n
Djilas, Aleksa, 13, 194
Djilas, Milovan: 17–21, 48, 51, 57, 123, 124, 125n, 211, 241; *Anatomy of a Moral*, 18; *The New Class*, 18–19; *Conversations with Stalin*, 19
Djindjić, Zoran, 217–18, 241n, 251n, 255, 257–8
Djogo, Gojko, 54–6, 169, 175, 216n, 241n; *Vunena vremena* (Woollen Times), 54
Djordjević, Jovan, 182
Djordjević, Stevan, 45
Djukanović, Aleksandar, 177, 182
Djukić, Slavoljub, 53, 64, 183, 184, 207, 250
Djurić, Mihailo, 41n, 44–5, 47, 50
Djurić, Vojislav, 41n
Djuretić, Veselin, 101–3; *Saveznici i jugoslovenska ratna drama* (The Allies and the Yugoslav Wartime Drama), 101–3

Encyclopedia of Yugoslavia, 71, 72–7, 127
'Ethnic cleansing', 6, 130, 146, 222, 255

Gams, Andrija, 43, 49n, 60, 108n
Gavrilović, Zoran, 58n
Gellner, Ernest, 3, 4
Gluščević, Zoran, 35n, 132, 134, 152
Gojković, Drinka, 139n
Goli Otok, 24, 81–3 *passim*, 104, 210n, 238n
Golubović, Zagorka, 25, 48, 58n, 60, 139n, 202n, 216–17, 238
Gotovac, Vlado, 54n
Grafenauer, Bogo, 71n
Grickat-Radulović, Irena, 187n
Grol, Milan, 83

'Happening of the people', 1, 157, 211, 214, 218, 219, 235, 247, 254
Hayden, Robert, 109
Helsinki Committee, 62n
Höpken, Wolfgang, 86

Horvat, Branko, 154–8, 201n, 227n
'Hostile propaganda' or 'verbal offence' (Article 133 of Yugoslav penal code): 16, 19, 21 58, 115, 164, 238; petitions against, 50, 59, 140, 143, 169, 173, 178; *see also* 'dissent'
Hribar, Spomenka, 164, 171–2, 191
Hribar, Tine, 190, 192

Ignjatović, Dragoljub, 20n, 51
Imširović, Pavluško, 47n, 57, 58n
Independent State of Croatia, 11, 32, 36, 42, 85, 99, 102, 103, 108–10, 126, 180, 234, 246, 256; *see also* Ustasha movement
Indjić, Trivo, 48, 50n
Inić, Slobodan, 241n
Isaković, Antonije: 35, 36, 58n, 81–2, 144, 182n, 185, 186, 188, 221, 238n; *Tren 2* (Instant 2), 81–3
Ivić, Milka, 187n
Ivić, Pavle, 33, 35n, 41n, 108n, 252
Ivin, Danijel, 21n
Izetbegović, Alija, 59

Jakšić, Božidar, 47n
Jambrek, Peter, 192, 197n, 201n
Janča, Dejan, 121
Jančar, Drago, 166, 190
Janković, Ivan, 60, 120, 139n, 202n, 238
Jasenovac, 109–11 *passim*; 113–14, 133
Javnost (The Public), 51
Jevrić, Olga, 187n
Jevtić, Atanasije, 125, 126, 132
Jevtović, Milenko, 137
Jojić, Branislava, 46, 49n
Josif, Enriko, 60
Jovanov, Neca, 60n, 238n
Jovanović, Batrić, 132
Jovanović, Biljana, 55n, 139n
Jovanović, Gordan, 57, 58n
Jovanović, Slobodan, 88, 94–5, 97–8
Jović, Borisav, 237, 240

Kandić, Nataša, 121
Kapor, Momo, 35n
Karadžić, Radovan, 237, 252n
Karadžić, Vuk, 6
Kardelj, Edvard, 30, 61, 99, 180

Kermauner, Taras, 153, 170–1, 174n, 197–9
Kljajić, Jelka, 47n
Klopčič, France, 146–7
Književna reč (Literary Word), 80, 82
Književne novine (Literary Gazette), 34–5, 56, 80, 87, 100, 111–12 *passim*, 131, 140, 143–4, 150, 154, 156–7, 174, 189, 208n, 217, 222–3, 226, 236
Kočović, Bogoljub, 108–9
Komnenić, Milan, 133, 144, 160, 236
Kos, Janko, 176
Kosovo: 1–2, 9, 38–9, 54, 67–8, 74–5, 115–61, 190, 204, 207n, 212–13, 217n, 219–20, 222, 224–5, 229, 234, 238, 242, 244–7 *passim*, 255–8 *passim*; 'question', 11, 38–40, 115–32 *passim*, 151, 154–6 *passim*, 206; Battle of, 107, 124, 221, 235, 247; League of Communists, 72, 117, 119, 1132, 137, 146; Albanians, 9, 39, 85, 115–17, 126, 155, 219, 223–5 *passim*, 243, 250, 256, 258; Serbs, 11, 39, 115, 117–21, 126, 130, 133, 135, 137, 141, 143–4, 146, 154–6, 179–81, 198, 206–12 *passim*, 216, 224–5, 232, 256–9 *passim*; historiography, 72–3, 127–8, 131; Writers' Society, 136–7, 149–50, 159–61, 174, 175, 229–32; Academy of Sciences and Arts, 116n, 148–9
Koštunica, Vojislav: 49n, 60, 83–4, 202, 239, 251n, 255, 257–8; *Stranački pluralizam ili monizam* (Party Pluralism or Monism), 83–4
Krestić, Vasilije, 111–12, 185, 233
Krivić, Matevz, 197n, 201n
Krleža, Miroslav, 71
Kundera, Milan, 165
Kučan, Milan, 69, 193–4, 196, 215, 224

Lazić, Radmila, 139n
Liberalism and 'liberals': in League of Communists, 25–6, 30–1, 40n, 46, 47–8, 53, 62, 194; in opposition, 4–5, 21–2, 28, 35, 45–6, 48, 49, 50, 55, 56, 63, 83, 139, 158; in culture and media, 12, 15, 17, 22–3, 28, 62, 70–1, 72, 78, 163, 207, 210–11
Livada, Raša, 55n

Lubarda, Vojislav: 104–5, 106; *Anatema* (Anathema), 104

Macedonia, 43, 73, 84–5, 98–9, 127; *see also* nationalism-Macedonian
Macura, Miloš, 239n
Makavejev, Dušan: 24–5, 139n; *WR: Mysteries of the Organism*, 24–5
Maksimović, Desanka, 55n, 187n
Maksimović, Ivan, 239n
Malja, Agim, 160
Mandić, Igor, 62
Marjanović, Jovan, 40
Marjanović, Vladislav, 79
Marković, Ante, 244
Marković, Mihailo, 25, 37n, 41n, 48, 58n, 60, 61n, 108n, 171, 185, 199n, 202n, 221, 222, 238
Marković, Predrag, 15
Martinović, Djordje, 132–5 *passim*, 141, 144, 147–8
Martinović, Zarija, 132
Mašić, Slobodan, 21n
Mastnak, Tomaž, 216
Matić, Dušan, 33n, 34
Matvejević, Predrag, 170, 217n
Mekulli, Hassan, 135, 149
Menart, Janez, 167, 175, 197n
Mićunović, Dragoljub, 25, 48, 241n, 242, 247, 251n
Mihailović, Dragoslav, 23, 24, 55, 58n, 60, 61n, 83, 108n, 144, 252; *Kad su cvetale tikve* (When Pumpkins Blossomed), 23, 24, 55, 83
Mihailović, Draža, 243
Mihailović, Kosta, 41n, 185, 187, 239n
Mihajlov, Mihajlo, 21–2, 51, 123
Mihajlović-Mihiz, Borislav: 14, 19, 34, 35, 37, 41n, 55n, 58n, 60, 93, 108n, 134, 200, 202n, 203, 213, 239, 241, 250n, 252; *Kolubarska bitka* (The Battle of Kolubara), 93, 170
Mijanović, Vladimir, 47n, 57, 58n
Mijović, Pavle, 74
Milčinski, Janez, 147–8
Milić, Miodrag, 57, 58n
Miller, Nicholas, 8
Milošević, Nikola, 60, 61n, 170, 239, 251n

Milošević, Slobodan, 1, 2, 5, 9, 10, 12, 53, 88, 89, 135, 143, 157, 177, 182, 183–5 *passim*, 193, 195, 206–14, 218–22, 226–9 *passim*, 232, 235–40 *passim*, 244–58 *passim*
Mirić, Jovan, 77, 84; *Sistem i kriza* (The System and Crisis), 77, 84
Mladenović, Tanasije, 35, 60
Mladina (Youth): 163, 164n, 169, 201; 'Mladina Affair', 214–16
Montenegro: 2, 20, 43, 73, 85, 212–13, 219, 232, 237, 258; Writers' Association, 150, 175, 230; see also nationalism-Montenegro
'Moral-political suitability' criterion, 48, 50, 52, 187

Naša reč (Our Word), 120, 241n
Naše teme (Our Themes), 220
Nationalism and 'nationalists': 4–5, 22, 23, 35, 44–6, 50, 55, 59, 60, 65, 71–2, 77, 88, 114; theories of, 2–3; 'national homogenisation', 12, 47, 206, 215–18, 223; economic, 29–30; Albanian, 40, 72–3, 149, 159, 177, 257; Croatian, 7, 11, 14, 29–30, 31–4, 42, 47, 49n, 52, 109–11, 177, 229, 234–5, 257; Macedonian, 73n; Montenegrin, 73–4, 76; Muslim, 73; Serbian, 4–12, 33–5, 40–2, 43–5, 50, 55, 56, 76–7, 89, 93, 103, 109, 111, 114, 149, 155, 163, 170, 184, 191, 216–18, 246, 256–9 *passim*; Slovenian, 7, 11–12, 29–30, 76, 150–2, 163, 176–7, 200, 216–18, 257
New Left, 4–5, 22–3, 50, 55, 63, 139; *see also Praxis* and Praxists
Nikolić, Milan, 47n, 57, 58n
Nikoliš, Gojko, 58n, 60, 187, 238
Nogo, Rajko Petrov, 144
Nova revija (New Journal): 163, 165, 171–3 passim, 174n, 175, 193–4, 196, 227, 245; 'Contributions for a Slovenian National Programme', 163, 165, 177, 189–93, 195
Njegoš, Petar Petrović, 73n

Ognjenović, Vida, 139n, 241n
Olujić, Dragomir, 57, 58n

Opačić, Jovan, 236–7

Palavestra, Predrag, 20n, 55n, 61n, 73n, 108n, 162, 201, 224, 241, 252
Paraga, Dobroslav, 54n
Pašić, Nikola, 89
Patrljič, Tone, 167
Pavček, Tone, 197n
Pavić, Milorad, 35n, 41n
Pavković, Aleksandar, 7
Pavlović, Dragiša, 183
Pavlowitch, Stevan, 79
Peakić-Mikuljan, Marija, 150, 174
Pekić, Borislav, 241n
PEN Club, 60, 140, 162, 197, 199–201, 216
Perišić, Miodrag, 112, 223, 241n
Peršak, Tone, 197n
Pešić, Vesna, 60, 120, 202n, 204
Petovar, Tanja, 121
Petranović, Branko, 157, 158
Petrov, Aleksandar, 35n, 144
Petrović, Aleksandar, 241n
Petrović, Dragoljub, 140
Petrović, Milutin, 56
Philosophical Society of Serbia, 49, 86, 242
Pirjevec, Dušan, 38
Pleterski, Ranko, 76, 77
Popov, Nebojša, 27, 48, 139n, 202, 217, 223
Popović, Danko: 98–9; *Knjiga o Milutinu* (The Book about Milutin), 98–9
Popović, Mića, 8, 19, 34, 35, 37, 55n, 58n, 60, 133–4, 188, 202n, 211, 223, 239, 241, 250n
Popović, Srdja, 50, 120, 202, 216n, 244
Pravoslavlje (Orthodoxy), 126
Praxis and Praxists, 25–8, 37n, 44, 47, 48–9, 50, 56, 60, 170, 171, 179, 197
'Proposal for Consideration', 33
'Prosvjeta', 42, 233
Pučnik, Jože, 190, 192
Puhovski, Žarko, 201n, 217n, 227n

Qosja, Rexhep, 118, 136

Radović, Amfilohije, 125
Radović, Dušan, 34n

Radulović, Jovan: 104–6; *Golubnjača*
  (The Pigeon Pit), 105–6, 169
Raičković, Stevan, 35n, 55n, 133, 187n
Rakitić, Slobodan, 41n, 144
Ranković, Aleksandar, 30–1, 39, 40, 159,
  160
Rašković, Jovan, 237, 246
Republika (Republic), 244
Ribičič, Ciril, 76, 220n
Ribičič, Mitja, 193
Ristić, Pavle, 43
Roksandić, Drago, 233
Rugova, Ibrahim, 160–1, 229
Rupel, Dimitrij, 150–2, 165, 175, 194,
  196, 199, 227
Rusinow, Dennison, 114

Samardžić, Radovan, 60, 102
Savić, Pavle, 186
Selenić, Slobodan: 23, 41n, 96–8, 108n,
  123, 200, 230–2, 252; *Memoari Pere
  hagalja* (Memoirs of Pera the Cripple), 23, 96; *Prijatelji* (Friends), 123;
  Očevi i oci (Fathers and Forefathers),
  96–8
Selić, Momčilo, 20n, 51
Serbia: Kingdom, 39, 90–1, 160; Socialist
  Republic, 8, 21–2, 36, 43–5, 52–3,
  65, 66–8, 74–5, 77, 78, 116, 180,
  203–5, 211, 219–20, 222, 227, 232,
  240, 247, 251; 'national question', 7–
  9, 33–4, 36–7, 41–2, 46, 84, 205, 207,
  218, 229, 238, 245, 255; League of
  Communists, 30–1, 33–4, 35, 38, 47–
  8, 53, 61–2, 67–70, 79, 88, 103, 107,
  119, 121–2, 124–5, 130–1, 142–3,
  183–8 *passim*, 193–5, 207–9, 247;
  Socialist Party of Serbia (SPS), 238,
  245, 247–9 *passim*; Democratic Party
  (DS), 83, 217n, 239, 241–2, 244, 248–
  51 passim, 252n; Serbian Renewal
  Movement (SPO), 241–4 *passim*, 249,
  252n; Serbian Radical Party (SRS),
  58n, 251
Serbian Academy of Sciences and Arts:
  6, 36, 60–1, 81, 92, 102, 111, 113,
  120, 127, 131, 133, 138, 139, 177–
  89 *passim*, 221, 226, 233, 237, 242;

'Memorandum', 6, 61, 103, 111, 144,
  154n, 163, 177–89, 196, 220–1, 233,
  238n, 239n
Serbian Cultural Club, 94, 97, 128, 129
Serbian Literary Cooperative, 41, 47, 60
Serbian Orthodox Church, 107–8, 125–
  6, 184, 232, 245, 252
'Simina 9a group', 35–7, 44
Simović, Ljubomir: 35n, 41n, 56n, 100,
  108n, 144, 152; *Istočnice* (East Stars),
  100–101
Slapšak, Svetlana, 120, 175
Slovenia: 9, 29–30, 53, 62, 66, 67, 76, 84–
  5, 98, 106, 118, 145–6, 171–2, 193,
  196–200, 214–18, 224–5, 227–8, 230,
  232, 245, 247, 250; dissent in, 11–12,
  52, 53, 58–9, 62, 162, 163–5, 194–5,
  204–5; Writers' Society, 153, 149, 153,
  165–8, 173–6 *passim*, 196–7, 204,
  230–2; Academy of Sciences and Arts,
  167, 187; League of Communists,
  29–30, 69–70, 146–7, 167, 193–5,
  196–7, 215–16, 224; Slovenian Democratic Alliance (SDZ), 227; Slovenian United Opposition (Demos),
  227, 232, 245; *see also* nationalism-
  Slovenian
Smith, Anthony, 3
Smole, Jože, 193
Snoj, Jože, 191
Society of Serbian-Jewish Friendship,
  108, 225
Solidarity Fund, 63, 216
Srbinović, Mladen, 21n, 60, 238n
Srejović, Dragoslav, 60n, 187n, 238n
Stambolić, Ivan, 53, 68–9, 121–2, 131,
  143, 182, 183, 184n, 186, 193, 209,
  212, 250
Stanković, Djordje, 89, 102
Stanovnik, Janez, 215
Stojanović, Lazar, 48, 49
Stojanović, Svetozar, 25, 48, 178n, 216–
  17, 228
Stojković, Živorad, 19
Strossmayer, Josip Juraj, 111
Student, 28, 47
Supek, Rudi, 170–1
Surroi, Veton, 158

Šeligo, Rudi, 165
Šešelj, Vojislav, 57–9, 63, 158, 203, 216n, 251
Šolević, Miroslav, 135, 213n
Šuvar, Stipe, 232

Tadić, Ljubomir, 25, 48, 51, 60, 61n, 86–8, 108n, 150–2, 171, 185, 202n, 239, 249
Taufer, Veno, 197n
Terzić, Velimir, 111
Theoria, 86
Tito, Josip Broz, 17, 24, 27, 28, 31, 38, 45, 46, 48, 53, 54, 61, 64, 67, 78, 99, 102, 164, 180, 184, 210, 212
Tošić, Desimir, 241n
Trgovčević, Ljubinka, 7
Tudjman, Franjo: 54, 59, 110, 234, 237, 242–3, 246; *Bespuća povijesne zbiljnosti* (Impasses of Historical Reality), 110, 234

Urbančič, Ivan, 189, 192
Ustasha (Ustaša) movement, 32, 85, 86, 104–14 *passim*, 126, 223–6 *passim*, 234, 236, 243

Vasić, Dragiša, 94–5
Veselica, Marko, 54n
Vidaković, Zoran, 201n
Vidici (Perspectives), 28
Vidmar, Josip, 167
Vllasi, Adem, 137, 146
Vojislav of Zeta, 74
Vojvodina, 9, 43, 67–8, 74–5, 76, 85, 106, 130, 207n, 212–13, 219
Vračar, Stevan, 45, 49n
Vranicki, Predrag, 170
Vreme (Time), 244
Vrhovec, Josip, 186
Vučelić, Milorad, 89, 143–4, 156–8 *passim*, 199, 223
Vujačić, Veljko, 7

Wachtel, Andrew, 7, 8
World War I, 87, 89–92, 93–5 *passim*, 98, 112, 126

World War II, 11, 23, 36, 44, 70, 78–80, 85, 96, 100–14, 124, 134, 164, 168, 226, 234
'White Book', 61–2
Writers' Association of Serbia: 28, 33–4, 70, 53, 55–6, 125n, 131–2, 134, 138, 144, 146, 149–50, 159–61, 173–6, 216, 226, 227, 230–2, 236, 237, 242; protest evenings, 53, 56, 140–2, 144–5, 152. 236–7; Committee for the Defence of Freedom of Creation, 55, 56, 120–1, 132n, 144, 175, 216

Yugoslav Forum for Human Rights, 62n
Yugoslavia: Kingdom, 32, 87, 92, 95–8, 128, 190; Federative Peoples' (later Socialist Federal) Republic, 29, 129–30, 190, 212, 226, 232, 253; Federal Republic (Serbia and Montenegro), 255, 258; internal borders, 8–9, 41, 44–5, 84–6, 96, 203, 235, 236, 243, 248, 250n; decentralisation/'confederalisation', 8–9, 14, 29–31, 39, 43, 46, 66, 150–2; post-Tito crisis, 10–11, 53, 65–78, 214, 256; disintegration, 3–4, 10, 176, 237, 245, 250; historiography, 70–7, 86, 90, 100
Yugoslav People's Army, 25, 163, 190, 191, 214–15
Yugoslav Writers' Union: 149–50, 152–3, 167, 173–6 *passim*, 229–32; Novi Sad Congress, 136, 173–4, 176
Yugoslavism, 4, 7, 8, 28–9, 32, 36–7, 38, 41, 45, 95–6, 111, 170, 172, 191, 242, 248–9

Zenko, Franjo, 21n
Zirojević, Olga, 139n
Zlobec, Ciril, 149, 150, 165, 167, 172n, 173, 175, 196
Zukin, Sharon, 13–14
Žerjavić, Vladimir, 108–9
Žilnik, Želimir, 28
Životić, Miladin, 25, 48